Jungian Psychology
and the
Passions of the Soul

JUNGIAN PSYCHOLOGY SERIES

SUFISM AND JUNGIAN PSYCHOLOGY
Edited by J. M. Spiegelman, Ph.D. and Pir Vilayat Inayat Khan

JUNGIAN ANALYSTS: *Their Visions & Vulnerabilities*
Edited by J. M. Spiegelman, Ph.D.

JUNGIAN PSYCHOLOGY AND THE PASSIONS OF THE SOUL
By J. M. Spiegelman, Ph.D.

CATHOLICISM AND JUNGIAN·PSYCHOLOGY
Edited by J. M. Spiegelman, Ph.D.

BUDDHISM AND JUNGIAN PSYCHOLOGY
By J. M. Spiegelman, Ph.D. and Mokusen Miyuki, Ph.D.

HINDUISM AND JUNGIAN PSYCHOLOGY
By J. M. Spiegelman, Ph.D. and
Dr. Litt. Arwind U. Vasavada

JUDAISM AND JUNGIAN PSYCHOLOGY
Edited by J. M. Spiegelman, Ph.D. and Abraham Jacobson Ph.D.

JUNGIAN PSYCHOLOGY AND THE TREE OF LIFE
By J. M. Spiegelman, Ph.D.

THE QUEST
By J. M. Spiegelman, Ph.D.

THE NYMPHOMANIAC
By J. M. Spiegelman, Ph.D.

For a free catalog of all Falcon titles contact:
FALCON PRESS
1209 South Casino Center, Suite 147 • Las Vegas, NV 89104
U.S.A. 702-385-5749

Jungian Psychology and the Passions of the Soul

by

J. Marvin Spiegelman, Ph.D.

FALCON PRESS
LAS VEGAS

International Standard Book Number: 0-941404-71-4
Library of Congress Catalog Card Number: 88-081439

First edition – 1989
Published by Falcon Press

Book Design and Typography by
Royal Type
27 West 20th Street • Room 1005
New York, NY 10011

Cover Painting by Tom Schurr
Cover Design by Studio 31

FALCON PRESS
1209 South Casino Center, Suite 147
Las Vegas, Nevada 89104
1-702-385-5749

Manufactured in the United States of America

Contents

Introduction

Who has not struggled with the passions of the soul? It seems to be our human condition to be endlessly tossed about on the seas of desire, guarding our little crafts of free will with restraint lest we tumble and drown, losing our feeble lights of consciousness. Self-help books of all kinds instruct us in ways to tame our anger, guide our fantasies toward achieving those sought-after, sometimes unattainable, objects and ideals which we hope will satisfy us. Even if we are fairly calm in ourselves, our venturing on the freeways of life exposes us to violence and disregard, to other people's passions, which can also toss us into that sea, either by emotional contagion or by impact.

Yet even without the toxic thrust of crowded, modern city life, we are confronted from within. Images and fantasies arise; they also move us out of our calm or out of our routine condition and propel us into questionable action or more fantasy. We unconsciously dialogue with ourselves and try to control these passions in some meaningful way.

But our passions are not only dark and disruptive. They are joyful and ecstatic, pleasurable and fulfilling, sometimes with "objects"—as psychoanalese puts it—sometimes just with the emotions themselves. We are surely seekers after pleasure, as Freud understood, but we are also more than that. We are also driven by the urge to power, as Adler comprehended, but above all, as Jung recognized, we are creatures who require meaning in our lives. Without meaning and purpose, without connection to a higher principle which gives us direction and significance, we also drown, this time in a sea of meaninglessness and chaos.

Nor are our passions so clear-cut and distinctive. We all seek happiness, to be sure, but it is not so easily defined. Among the happiest periods of my life was during the latter half of the 1950s when my wife and I lived in Zurich, Switzerland. At long last, I had the chance to study at the C.G. Jung Institute, to undergo analysis again, and to train, along with fellow seekers from all over the world, in the profession I had chosen. My analytic work was far from smooth; it was filled, as it should be, with passions of all kinds. Yet, despite the depressions, despite the frustrations, I was happy as I could be. Why? I could focus on the soul and my life was filled with meaning. I felt that I was at the Omphallos, as the Greeks put, the Navel of the World. When one is focussed on the Self, the central core of one's being, one is centered not only at one's own navel, so to speak, but truly at the Navel of the World, allied with the deepest aspects of the souls of us all. To be immersed both in my inner world and in the outer world of European tradition and culture was to be at once rooted and searching. To share this search and longing with Egyptians, Swedes, Frenchmen, Germans, British, Americans, etc. was to sense, at last, the great Self of us all. That was the gift of Jung to so many of us, and that was the special boon that some of us could suffer/enjoy in those last years when his spirit and that of his immediate followers could find a valued place in the scheme of things.

Jung's psychology was not popular then. It was a period, prior to the storm of the '60s, when life—in America, at least—was relatively safe, conventional, ordered, and rather materialistic. It was wonderful to find, at the Institute, like-minded people from everywhere, east and west, who felt engaged in a similar spiritual search. Our present day is even more materialistic—and now this view prevails in much of the world—so we are once again in need of that Paradise where inner meaning and outer structure are in some harmony. Whenever that condition prevails, fragmentation is overcome and we experience happiness and fulfillment.

But most of us experience these periods of happiness and fulfillment in a limited way: sometimes for months or years, sometimes for moments only, sometimes never. Heaven is often on earth, but certainly not more often than Hell. Indeed, most of us experience the various stages of Purgatory much of the time. And this purgatory is the condition of our struggle with our passions.

The shorter Oxford English Dictionary informs us that the word, "passion," from the original Latin, *passionem*, means "suffering." It further gives three senses in which "passion" can be understood: (1) the suffering of pain, as with some bodily affliction, or the Passion of Jesus Christ (spelled with a capital P); (2) being passive, or affected by outside forces; (3) an affection of the mind: any vehement, commanding, or overpowering emotion; in psychology and art, any mode in which the mind is affected or acted upon, as ambition, avarice, desire, hope, fear, love, hatred, joy, grief, anger, revenge. The latter two uses also arise from the Greek, *pathos*, which also means emotion or deep feeling. And, from these comes our word "patient," one who bears pain, enduring and long-suffering.

So, from these definitions it is surely right for a psychotherapist and Jungian analyst to write about the "passions of the soul," since that is our daily bread, so to speak, that which we chew upon and digest, together with our patients. We hope to transform and be transformed by the passions which arise in the work, coming from within and from without, afflict the soul and make our lives different from animals.

It is there, perhaps, where we need to begin: animals do not suffer the passions as we do. They are God's loyal creatures, doing exactly what they are supposed to do, following the instinctive paths laid down for them. They are not required to suffer the crucifixion of opposites such as morality versus desire, lust versus love, ambition versus kindness. And that is why the juxtapositions of the above definitions of passion, active and passive, is strange from a definitional point of view, but so true psychologically.

But I must correct what I just said—as one must so often in psychological discussion—about animals. As I wrote this I was reminded of a dream I once had in which I saw several little animals of great warmth and beauty, nuzzling each other and in good spirits. These animals were suddenly confronted with some unknown threat, whereupon they suddenly displayed wings, and flew flutteringly up into the sky. I was overawed with this event and realized that these little dog-like animals were angels!

When I reflected on the dream, I understood that angels, spirit creatures, also exist at the instinctual level, as Jung said. At bottom, spirit and instinct are one. There are only moments, however, when we fully realize that the struggle between instinct and spirit, our animal nature and spiritual nature, is really the battle of the opposites with one common base. In fairness, then, our fellow animals are surely not just the mechanical creatures that Descartes thought. There has been an evolution, however, which makes *homo sapiens* different from them in some ways.

Ever since the development of the neo-cortex among our ancestors or, alternately, the decision of Adam and Eve to disobey divine rules, there has been conflict between the instinctive motions of the soul (e.g. desire) and the cultural and psychological strictures against their enactment or fulfillment (spirit). Indeed, the interplay of spirit and instinct is experienced *in* the soul or psyche, and this is the stuff of our lives. Passion leads us to the word emotion, which means "to be moved out of," and emotion is what moves us out of our ordinary routine. It is also the psychophysiological link between our bodily instincts and our mental constructions, realized in images.

Depth psychology, in particular, has focussed upon these passions of the mind. Indeed, the very attention to these passions is what lead to the discovery of the unconscious by Freud, and his recognition of the mechanism of repression, that trick we play upon ourselves to avoid experiencing those very painful passions which have harmed us in the past. As he went deeper, Freud found that a myth was at the core of the passions of love and lust, the Oedipus complex. Fixed as he was upon that one myth, the ground of his own psychology, he was unable to see that the entire basis of the psyche—and its ordering of the passions—rested in myths. It was Jung who discovered that the patterns of the psyche and, therefore, of behavior, gathered themselves in the stories of myth and that these were beautifully represented in the religions of humankind. Hence, it is not so surprising, after all, that our word for passion should be capitalized and used as the name for the chief myth of western culture, the passion of its outstanding divine representative.

Jung also demonstrated to us that the cultural stories, in myth and fairy tale and religion, reveal the workings of the soul. We need a key, however, a way to approach these stories so that we can better grasp their significance. With such a key, we can mitigate our passions, soften our suffering. This is usually accomplished through ritual: behavior is the healing way to gain access to the stories, without the need to understand them. (Hats off, here, to Behaviorists!) When ritual no longer suffices, when the meanings are no longer contained in the action, we then need a way into the background of it. The way is the symbol, as depth psychology has shown us, and the mode is interpretation. We retranslate the stories, so to speak, into the language of metaphor and symbol.

The "thirst" of the alcoholic, for example, was seen by Jung—when he helped give the idea to the founders of Alcoholics Anonymous—as a longing for the "spirit." The concretization of the symbol of "spirit" in "spirits," leading to addiction, was due to a lack of higher principle to connect with (the sense of deity). Fulfilling group life and ritual were also missing. So, it is not by chance that this insight helped to bring about one of the most effective antidotes to the modern scourge of alcoholism, Alcoholics Anonymous and its "twelve steps." Jung knew that an equivalent power of "spirit" was necessary.

It is probably not by chance that our day, which has witnessed a falling away from the effective impact of the "stories" of the religions, has also seen a concomitant rise in the addictions. The disintegration of our myths brings about both a return to fundamentalism (the longing for order and certainty) as well as the chaos of possession by passion (e.g. addictions).

One answer to this condition, particularly for a Jungianly-oriented psychotherapist, is to investigate the individual soul, to help each person in the discovery of and connection with his or her own myth. This search can also become a passion. The deeper we go with each person, the more we find that his/her myth is, in truth, also connected with the myths of humankind. The stories of the soul have a profound commonality, it turns out, not so unexpectedly, since we are, at bottom, much alike. Paradoxically, such efforts also reveal equally profound individuality. Commonality is balanced by difference, as examination of the world's religions might also have revealed to us.

So, individual leads to collective, which leads to the individual, and back again. This process is probably what the divine had in mind for us in the first place, according to the great Sufi mystic of Islam, Ibn Arabi. He saw that each of us carries a secret Name of the Divine, waiting to realize itself in our own unique, individual existence. None of us, not even the various religions, get the whole picture, but the sum of the Names constitute the Name of God. There is God in general (Allah) and our particular Name or Lord (Rabb); our task is to serve both. This is mightily like what people in long-term work with their own souls often find, too. They profit from looking at the parallels to their own dreams and fantasies in the religions and belief systems.

Because of this commonality, it is possible to read and write books which address the concerns of us all. So we come to the particular way that this book addresses the passions of the soul. I shall describe how it came about and then provide an outline, a guide whereby the reader can make this material of greater value to herself/himself.

Jung discovered a way to deal with the passions, which he called "Active Imagination." He describes this method in his essay on "The Transcendent Function" in Volume 7 of the Collected Works. Barbara Hannah has written a good book about this technique, *Encounters with the Soul*, and I have two essays on it in my little book, *The Nymphomaniac*. Jung's method was to have a dialogue with the unconscious, to engage his ego with whatever came up in dream or fantasy which was of a moving or troubling nature, such as passions. For example, if I am troubled by a rage reaction arising in response to someone blocking me on the freeway, I can turn and look at my rage, rather than engage in a dangerous competitive battle with the other chap or give him the hand-sign so dearly beloved these days. I allow the emotion to fill my being, but rather than express it out-wardly, I enquire as to how it looks, what it intends, etc. As I do this, I see a fire swirling. This fire is both hot and cold. I wonder at this fact, and recognize that my rage is, indeed, both hot and consuming, but also cold and ruthless. In my fantasy, I put my hand in this flame, and discover that I am not burned. It feels like—dare I say it?—a divine fire. Excited, I realize that my rage at my auto-opponent arose as a result of the sense of my Self being trampled on, not my silly ego. And this Self need not engage in such a trivial pursuit as vengeance on that hapless creature. Now I remember a poem of

Walter Savage Landor:

> *I strove with none, for none was worth my strife*
> *I warmed both hands before the fire of life*
> *It sinks, and I am ready to depart.*

The realization that I am only too ready to "strive" and that this is futile, now calms my rage and I am reconnected with this fire in my own soul, ready to employ it in better ways, such as right here.

Jung's method has proven to be very valuable for those who are looking for an ongoing relationship to their own passions and psyche generally. And so did I, for many years. After about sixteen years of this kind of work with myself, I found that the figures of my own active imagination now wanted to tell stories about their own quests and experiences, desiring my cooperation in this venture. As a result, I wrote two books of a kind of psycho-fiction. *The Tree: Tales in Psycho-mythology* had ten stories of individuation, pursued by people of different religious background and character; all of them had some passion to deal with. *The Quest*, the sequel to *The Tree*, also had stories related to myths, but these were accomplished in pairs. When these two books were completed, another figure appeared, calling himself "The Grandson of the Knight," a third-generation hero of this spiritual path. The book which emerged, however, was no longer fiction. Rather, it was an encounter with various images and myths having to do with the passions, particularly those of lust and love. That provided the basis of the present book.

The narrator of Part I, then, is the Grandson of the Knight, who discovers, in his own active imagination, a Magician. This remarkable being is able to connect with and relive figures of history and myth, as well as literature. The Knight's painful struggle with his passions is thereby aided at a deeper level. His particular conflict between the two passions of lust and love unfolds into larger issues such as monogamy and polygamy, monotheism and polytheism, the One and the Many. At every level, his passion is engaged.

With the help of the Magician, the Knight first interacts with the notorious figure of Don Juan, who embodies the "maniness" of love and lust. An interlude during this engagement with this dark side of lust and power comes in an examination of the tale of Bluebeard. Reliving these dark events of history and myth brings him, unexpectedly, to the Muses, who help him truly apprehend these abysses of the soul.

Following his immersion in the dark side of the passions, he undertakes an opposite path, that of Jesus and the Stations of the

Cross. This Passion carries him deeper into Love's meaning, but it does not end there. The Magician carries him onward to the story of the Goddess of Love, Aphrodite, and the Knight, through her "stations," can apprehend feminine aspects of love, left-out in the masculine grasp of this passion. Finally, the figure of Eros is engaged and the Knight comes to a resolution of his issue of One and Many, love and lust, light and dark.

Part II of the book is now taken up with the work of the Daughter of Guinevere, a kind of alchemical sister to the Knight. She deals with the problem of "pairs," of opposites in relationships, in her struggle for individuation. To this end, she suffers the conflict of "sisters" (Belly and Heart), and takes up many of the pair-stories in Greek mythology and religion, such as Father and Son, Father and Daughter (Zeus and Athena), Hecate, Husband and Wife (Zeus and Hera). She also immerses herself in the story of Mother and Son in a Christian context. She explores the mysteries of the Virgin Mary and her Rosary in detail. Finally, Mother and Daughter become resolved.

Volume Two continues the presentation, which now becomes increasingly clear as an attempt to build up an East-West Tree of Life, a kind of western psychological Kabbalah, in which the Greek myths, like those of the Hindu pantheon, find their place. Indeed, one of the most surprising discoveries of the work is the degree to which the Greek stories and gods, including their "stations," fit so well into an organization of western *chakras* (centers) and psychological functions. The psyche of the West has its own hidden order, much like that more explicitly described in the East.

Part III takes up the theme of the Group (after the One of the Knight and the Pair of Daughter of Guinevere). Now the two heroes combine forces, as alchemical brother and sister, in a mutual quest for wholeness. Maya the Yogini, from the East, comes to assist them as they undertake to connect with and interpret the tales of Dionysos, of Apollo, and of Hera.

Part IV, with the heading of "Union," carries the work onward by engaging the myths of Gaia and Kronos, Rhea and Zeus, Kronos and Zeus. The knowledge gained by such encounters requires a profound confrontation among the archetypes of Witch and Devil, Judge and Soul. Following this, they undergo a voyage among all the centers-chakras in both an eastern and western way, healing themselves thereby.

Part V, the culmination of the work, presents a schema of all the centers, along with the relevant Gods, psychological functions, types of consciousness and love, along with the animals and elements appropriate to each. "Hymns" to the various Gods are included. If this presentation is seen as comparable to certain Kabbalistic Trees of Life, or magical ones such as given by Dion Fortune in her book on the Magical Qabbalah, the author is pleased, for his intent is to continue that tradition, but with the significant admixture of the psychological information gained during the last century of depth-psychological work.

What began as a work with the passions became a passionate work. What started as a story emerged as a theoretical/practical schema, one meant to be inclusive. The task undertaken some twenty years ago, in the stories of the Knight and his friends, found their conclusion in the non-fictional efforts of the Grandson of the Knight and his friends. The product of four years of labor was received with lack of understanding then, but recent years have seen changes in consciousness.

The reader's attitude might best be that of the second meaning of passion, namely, "receiving." He/she need only accompany these two heroes and respond as they do to the Gods and figures from literature and myth who come to life here as a result of the work of the Magician. If one has read The Tree and The Quest, so much the better, but it is not necessary. Bring only one's own struggle with the passions and listen to how the alchemical brother and sister engage them.

If the readers find that their own myths are stimulated by these accounts and interpretations, so much the better. They might then make use of the hints given herein and embark upon their own voyage, perhaps using the final schema as a possible compass. It is enough, however, to absorb and react—in a "passionate" way!

A word must be added about the possible startle-effect of having a volume treating the sacred images of religions such as Christianity, Judaism, Buddhism and Hinduism on an apparent par with the ancient Greek religion and literary sources. I wish to affirm most forcefully that I mean no disrespect to any of these traditions; on the contrary, I am myself deeply immersed in them and am a "believer." Since my work as a Jungian analyst involves a religious attitude toward the psyche and its products, I can in no way discount or be disrespectful of the ground of the soul of us all, since it is made manifest in these self-same great religions. If a kind of "relativization" emerges, it does not mean that "anything is as good as everything" or that these stories are of equal value. The comparative approach puts the psyche at its center and respects it above all. If the reader, like me, is of the opinion that the psyche is created by the divine principle and finds its representation in its images, then he or she will know that respect for all does not involve reduction of value for any. Each person, each religion, must find his/her/its own truth. The true purpose of psychological work in this area, it seems to me, is to enable us to emerge from this with a deepened appreciation of differences and similarities. Indeed, the very task undertaken by the pair of Knight and Guinevere is an ecumenical one, culminating in a "world myth," so to speak, without loss of difference and individuality. If religious feelings are hurt, I beg pardon at once, and hope that any such person so offended will permit me to present my own symbol without asserting that anyone need follow it. God speaks to us all in his/her own way. That, indeed, is the very theme of the book! I think it is not too utopian, however, to intuit that our globe is painfully inching toward such a world-story, honoring and treasuring, one hopes, all the varieties of our individuality and religious traditions.

J. Marvin Spiegelman
Studio City, California
Spring 1989

VOLUME ONE

PART I

The One and the Many

Grandson of the Knight

I, Grandson of the Knight, wish to tell my tale, a story of passions. My Grandfather struggled with God and Chosenness; Father wrestled with the problem of finding himself, becoming a man, and a God-man. I have grappled with love. In a way, I am much like my father and grandfather. The Knight was a ladies' man, before he was called away by an Angel of God. My father, the Son of the Knight, was surely a lover as well, with his four Schizophrenia ladies. But I . . . My life and task have been different. Knights #1 and #2 found love only as a consequence of their path, their quest. For me, the problems of love have been central—not God, not God-man, but the passions of the soul.

In my early youth, from the days that I became aware of the voracious hunger of sexuality which burned inside me, I was obsessed with desire. Days, I would dreamily look at girls and women, thirsting to get my hands on them, but fearing that any advance on my part would meet with rebuff. Nights, I would fantasy and dream, these being even more intense than my day fantasies. I early on discovered the joys of making love to oneself, and once the initial fears that I might do damage to myself were alleviated (from hearing the talk of other boys my age), I indulged my heart's desire. Often I was troubled with guilt and worry, but this concern only served to increase my fantasy and made me reflect about desire itself. I was relieved to find that other boys were also preoccupied, but I saw, too, that not everyone was so one-sided, or fired up—so mad, perhaps. It was just the brighter ones, or the more gifted ones, or the more emotionally disturbed ones, I think (in retrospect), who were so obsessed. All the same, most of the boys were so involved, in one way or another. The girls were, too I suppose, although I never got close enough or had conversations enough to find out. In short, I lived in a fantasy world of relationships and love-making until I was more than half-way through my adolescence. I had a few experiences with girls—some fondling and lots of talk, but the former was almost always surreptitious (and done by both parties as if it were not really happening), and the latter was almost always in groups—as if we could not really be alone together out of fear and inadequacy.

There was one girl, however, with whom I established something more than a fantasy relationship. We played at love a little, though we did not really care very much about each other. We were practicing, I suppose. The sexual release, the living in reality of some of the wild and dark fantasies were gratifying, but I knew that I did not love.

One day, at seventeen, I met a girl who made me know what love was. She was no older than I, but she seemed as worldly as an "older woman," wise as the ancients, yet lovely as a passionate-eyed female can be. I trembled whenever I saw her, no matter how I tried to be cool and sophisticated. I longed to be with her, but her life was such that she visited where I lived only occasionally and we saw each other rarely. So again I lived in fantasy; I dared not even write to this creature who shook me so.

While waiting for the arrival of the One, I met another. This one did not stir me very much but she was willing, as they say, and I finally experienced sexual intercourse. I penetrated her again and again, but I did not call this making love to her. There was love and there was sex, and I now knew the difference.

In the midst of my concerns about women and sex and love, about the romantic and expectant love of a One, and the profane and earthy love of another, war came into my life—as it repeatedly does for most young men at most times in history and in most places.

This was not so terrible for me, since it allowed me to leave my home and travel far, see new places and people. Best of all, I could freely encounter many women. I became a sailor and traveled over the world. I was young and eager and wished to experience all races and nations. I fed my hunger, for now, unlike in my earlier youth, it was easy to find girls and women who were just as eager to lie with me. There were prostitutes, of course, from Egypt and Haiti, from France and Ceylon. And there were free-loving beauties besides, from Sweden and Australia, from England and Cuba. There was ample, there was much. There was beauty of body and ugliness of body; there was beauty of soul and ugliness thereof. I tasted, I devoured. Sometimes I had as many as three women in a day, and I was proud—for, of course, there was as much a need for conquest, for the display of power, as there was for release of tensions. Of love there was little, and only for moments. The need for union was with the romantic One of my native place, so far away.

So I savored and consumed, sought and captured. Sometimes I was so surfeited with sexuality that I was nauseous, vomited, and had to acknowledge the sailor's saying that one could be "whipped by the vagina."

Once, on leave I came back to my home. I brought star sapphires from India and took my beloved to a high hill where I worshipped her—as lovers do—under the night sky. Our desire was great and mixed therein was the longing for total union—a new emotion for me. I was so overpowered by this longing and the beauty of the time, the place, the girl, that I could not contain. It is the "young man's disease," of course, and I had been successful enough to know that upon repeated occasions things would be better. Within minutes, I was ready once again. But my Love froze over; she could not, would not. I accepted this sad failure, thought it would be different next time. But back to the wars I must go, just as had my fathers before me. I resumed my adventures—new women, new experiences, new life.

The wars over, I returned home and found that the One had changed. She made me jealous with my closest friend, she treated me cavalierly, she hurt me. I did not understand. Nor do I understand now. I only know that I wanted to marry her and that she married another, though she wept when she told me. I, too, wept, but I was young, I would love again.

And I did—or a form of it. I did not realize it then, but many girls and women paid for this rebuff. I seduced many, tried to make them fall in love with me, and then rejected them. A few years of this was sufficient, and I then met an older woman who I thought would guide me into matters of spirit and soul. She, however, wanted flesh, and I obliged. By then I felt split and problematic, so I sought the help of a wise man. With him I explored my history, my soul and my life. I acquired soul, I suppose, where before there had been only spirit and flesh. Now I was kinder to women, now I was more involved, now I saw pains and hurts I had not seen before. But now, too, I felt desire for union as well as passion. Relationships—for now they carried this meaning—were fewer now, but longer and deeper. And still, I had always more than one or two at any given time.

I was more and more despairing of ever meeting one whom I would love the way that I had loved One. Each relationship ended unhappily and I thought that I might never wed. At last, when I had given up hope altogether, I met another One. She was deeper and prettier, warmer and wiser than the other One. We loved, but we waited and put off love-making, for it felt right to do so. We wed, and loved. Only the passage of years have shown me how rare a love it was, how full, how uniting, how warm and peaceful, how gentle and tender, how passionate, too.

And so, I was happy, and at one with myself . . . for a time. Some years went by. We were happy. I sometimes was attracted to other women, but never felt right about pursuing this attraction until, one day, as people know, as life shows, as my own life can demonstrate, it is always "one day." I kissed another and was shaken. I ran away from this, felt threatened by it, determined to not have it hurt my beloved. But my dreams said that unless I went with this new experience, dark forces within me would make my dear wife suffer even more. And so I did, with pain, with horror, with clumsiness, with little joy. The facts of our lives determined that this relationship should be brief and we parted in pain, in lack of fulfillment. Where I could have been healed, I was broken; where I could have brought joy, I brought grief; where I could have learned and profited, I became stupid, clumsy and learned nothing.

The violation of vows, the break in my union, was somewhat healed. Children came and a new harmony resulted, but now that the monogamous fusion was broken, it could never be totally as it was at the beginning. From then on the problem of the One and the Many, the need to be true to the One and to love the Many, would never leave me. I struggled, spiritualized, transformed, violated. Relationship on a spiritual level provoked the need for concrete fulfillment. Concrete fulfillment by itself seemed paltry and miserable without spiritual union. Conflict raged. Years went by. Attempts at transformation were only partial, or illusory.

And so, after trial and error, search and frustration, fulfillment and disaster, I decided that I did not understand love nor myself. No, that is not a fully true statement. I understood myself: I was a man who loved the One, and the Many, but could not live with these opposite tendencies of his soul. When he loved the One, he was drawn to the Many. When he loved the Many, he hurt the One. What was such a man to do?

My dilemma and sadness were great. I decided that I should call upon the spirits of my Father and my Grandfather. Though my Grandfather was long since dead (he was essentially timeless, anyway), and my Father lived far from me physically and spiritually, I felt that I needed their knightly help and guidance, their audacious courage and devotion, if I wanted to come to some answer for myself. Though far from a hero, like Knight #1 or Knight #2, I was flesh of their flesh and from their loins sprung. I, therefore, felt free in summoning up their spirits in my need.

One link I had with the Knights, my Fathers, one link: I listened to my dreams. No hero I, but a listener to dreams. I thought: I will sleep, and in the depths of my sleep they will come and guide me.

That night, then, I prayed for a dream, one from God or—if that were not possible—one giving the guidance from the spirits, living and dead, of my Fathers.

I dreamt, all right, but not what I expected, nor from whom. Let me tell my dream and you shall see how and why I was startled at the unexpected.

In this dream, I was seated upon a small carpet, about the size of a Moslem prayer rug. The rug was several feet off the ground, but I was comfortable upon it. I was either in prayer or meditating upon this small rug. Suddenly, I saw next to me another rug, slightly larger than my own, and slightly higher, but of a magnificent color which made my black and red rug look pale and grey by comparison. What was even more startling, however, was that I saw a large man sitting upon this rug. He was dark and intense, like myself, but with Persian facial features. He wore a large pearl at his forehead and a turban. There was bright color all around this man, this potentate-appearing prince.

As I looked at him, in astonishment, he reached out his arms toward me. Thinking that he was going to box me or do battle, I made as if to defend myself. But he did not strike me. Instead, he embraced me. I am a warm and demonstrative person by nature, free to show affection verbally and physically as well, so that I can easily embrace another person, child, woman, or man. I was not used, however, to being embraced, being the one encompassed, so to speak, particularly by a man. On the contrary. I had been chagrined to find, in life, that men tended to stab me or ignore me, rather than embrace me. So this was startling already. What is more, however, is that the embrace of this man sent electric chills through me. It reminded me of Michelangelo's painting of God touching Adam's hand and thereby bringing life. And also—and this, I think, because I had been so hurt and hence suspicious of men—of Giotto's painting of Judas embracing and kissing Christ, the kiss of betrayal. But this embrace was no betrayal. Rather, I felt a warmth, a life force, a power from this figure, and benevolent. He was a Magician, it is true, and one greater and more vital than I. I awakened startled and impressed by this dream.

What did it mean? Was this the answer to my prayerful request of my Father and Grandfather? But a Persian came! Not of our people! What did that portend? That I was on a small magic carpet—somewhat ordinary, I understood well enough. I had, it is true, been able to experience my own power to some extent in my life. Not that I could be literally off the ground, but my love and my spirit had often helped me soar and I could even have substantial effect upon others. That could seem a bit magical, at least in a poetic sense. But this man? This prince—for such must he be with his pearl and his power—he seemed so much greater.

Why did such a figure appear to me when I had petitioned either God or my ancestors? This Persian potentate was surely neither, yet here he was to embrace me, to affect me with his vital powers. How could I avail myself of his magic?

I mulled the question of how to contact this Magician for many days, but each time that I tried to reach this strange being of my dreams, whether in fantasy or in some occult realm that I knew nothing about, I was frustrated. I would either become paralyzed in energyless passivity, or fall into a sleep which was neither satisfying nor refreshing. At other times, my mind would wander to other things, and I would think of all of my duties and responsibilities, desires and needs, angers and frustrations. There seemed to be no way that I could reach this Magician.

Then, one day, there came, unbidden, a glimpse of this Magician seated in a room beneath me, a subterranean place which was neither cave nor grotto, but a windowless library with many books in shelf after shelf. Unlike a dusty library, however, there was much color in this room. Each book had a different colored cover and there was an atmosphere of bright and variegated light.

As I focused upon this image, it vanished. As I turned away from it, to consider other things, it came again. I could only attend to it out of the corner of one eye. When I did this, I could see the Magician sitting at a chair in this room, diligently writing. Soon I could devote a whole eye to observing him.

The Magician then looked up and, to my astonishment, spoke to me. But he seemed also to be speaking to someone else besides me, making a statement. He said: "I write because I have to. It gives me joy and pleasure as well. I do not write because of power or prestige or money. These are available in other ways. I write for love. I write about love!"

His first remarks about writing, money and power seemed irrelevant to me, but when he spoke about love, I gave full attention, both eyes! At that point, I felt compelled to answer this Magician, not knowing whether he would hear me in the strange spaceless realm from which he addressed me.

"You write, Magician," I said, "but I am tired; even despairing. Besides, unlike you, I want such things in life as recognition, prestige. More than anything else, I want to understand about love. I want to come to some acceptance of the pain of love in my life. . . . But, even as I talk, I lose touch with you."

"Submit!" said the Magician.

Not knowing what else to do, nor even what I was submitting to, I submitted. Collapsed, perhaps, would be a more adequate word for what I was feeling and sensing. I collapsed and fell in upon myself. My head fell forward to my chest, my mouth popped open, and I found myself descending into the room where the Magician dwelt.

I now looked at him more closely, and I saw that his countenance changed. His face and features gradually transformed into a totally different being. He became a handsome gentleman of an earlier century. Intuitively I knew who he was. The figure before me was Don Juan, the infamous lover, the man of whom it was said that he captured many women and truly loved none.

In the same instant in which I knew that I was confronted with the figure of Don Juan, I also knew that it was the Magician who had performed this remarkable feat. I also knew that this was the magic which the Magician possessed: he could become a vehicle, within himself, for any figure of history or literature or art, he could incarnate within himself the Gods even. How this remarkable Magician could be so mercurial and magical I did not understand. I did not know whether he flew into Heaven, Hell, or Purgatory, or into occult realms of being of which I knew nothing. I did not know, even, if this were sheer fantasy, though I doubted it. I doubted it because I had spent much of my life with dreams and fantasy, and this experience was different from what I had known. But I could not be sure. I knew only that I could trust the movements of this Magician, and that I could—indeed, not only could, but had to—follow him wherever he led, into history and myth. Were I to submit willingly, I felt, I stood a good chance of solving my dilemmas of love and life. I needed only to "submit," he said.

I therefore watched this transformed figure of Don Juan, did not even question how it was that he arrived here. I looked only at what he was writing in his little book. As I watched his writing, the letters began to change and I found that I, myself, was writing his words! It was a great shock to me, for it seemed that I was losing my identity and becoming Don Juan himself. That is not quite accurate; I was becoming the medium by which Don Juan could express himself. And then I realized: I was becoming like the Magician himself. I could be a vehicle for the transformation of figures from history and art; I, too, could be a medium. But I was a small medium for a large medium!

I laughed, for this was a living experience of what my dream had suggested to me: I, on my small magic carpet, with its red and black, could transmit what was given to me by this great Magician, with his vast panoply of words and colors, his vast store of information and experience of people past and present, even fictional ones. Thus would I be this medium for a Medium! It was laughable, but pleasurable. More important, perhaps, was my chance to solve the riddle of my struggle with love. Was I not, after all, following in the tradition of my father and grandfather, the Knight and Son of the Knight? Knights One and Two were wanderers in many realms, too, were they not?

And, even if they were more heroic and knightly than I, one might suppose that a little of their magic flowed in my veins, too. Did not my dream say so? So did I convince myself.

Thus began my adventure into the magical realm, and so also began my adventure into the meaning of love. Now hear what I learned from this adventure, and hear, too, what I experienced.

The story begins with Don Juan, that strange figure of Spain of the 14th Century. I knew, as everyone does, that he seduced hundreds of women in Italy and Germany, in Turkey and France, to say nothing of Spain. I knew, too, that many had written about Don Juan, but that the facts of his life were meager. He was said to have come to a bitter end, being killed by Franciscan monks after the rake had seduced the daughter of the commandant of Ulloa and killed the father. Now I was confronted with his reality, and here is how he spoke to me.

Don Juan

"The life of a man who seeks love is not a happy one," began Don Juan. "Most men seek power, prestige, fame or money. They may or may not be happy in their quest, or in the finding of their goal. Other men seek meaning in life. They will be successful and happy because they care more for meaning than for success and happiness in the goods of this world. Success and happiness come to those who do not seek them. I think, moreover, that meaning is as much created as discovered, so that the man who pursues meaning will be successful. He will find his meaning by creating it.

"But I? . . . My life has not been one of pursuit of power, nor wealth, nor prestige. Neither has it been a pursuit of meaning, although I have also been a reflective man. No. What I have sought has been love. Do not laugh at me, nor mock me! I know what the stories have said of me. I know what the gossips have gossiped, the moralists moralized, the critics criticized. My very name is anathema. It is supposed to mean lovelessness, power-hunger and seduction, not love. I know.

"In a sense, the gossips and moralizers and critics are right. I was loveless. But I continued to seek love always, rarely finding it. Was the fault in myself or others? Was the lack one of constitution or upbringing? Experience or structure? Was it remediable? Or was it all a mere error of understanding? An ignorance of mind rather than a disease of heart? Such were my thoughts always, as I pursued woman after woman in town after town, country after country.

"Nor is it as simple as the documents and biographers liked to claim: that I seduced and took, giving nothing. It is not true. I gave of myself: of my flattery, of my attentions. I gave, too, of my caresses and my semen. Now these are not as nothing, I think. Why else, then, would so many have desired these things from me, panted after them, abandoning even husband and children for them? Even if only for a night, a week. That so many women wanted these things from me must signify that they had some value, does it not?

"Therefore, I have had something to give—if not love, then the close verisimilitude of it! But . . . and here's the rub, of course . . . I have been left hollow and sit here in the pale world, trying to understand, trying to redress—in mind and memory, if not in fact—

those whom I have hurt, offended and exploited. I also try to grasp what it is that I have not satisfied in myself about love: What is it? Do I have it? Have I given it? And, even in the questioning, confessing that I do not know."

"Oh, Don Juan," I, Grandson of the Knight, responded to this poor reflective man, "I, too, have posed such questions for myself, though my life has been different, almost opposite from yours. I have loved much, I know, staying true to my loves when they preferred me, not gone on in search of new ones. But I, too, have wondered about what love is, how to live it, how also to repair hurt and pain in the maniness of my love. I have loved the One and the Many simultaneously. You have loved them, I would guess, sequentially. You sound like a man who loves after all!"

"You speak like one who claims to know, Grandson of the Knight! If so, then tell me what is love. Tell me how you know it, and feel it."

"I know love in two ways, Don Juan, in two ways, at least. I know love as a caring, a seeking and desiring. Most deeply it is a passion to seek and find the soul of another. To understand and unite with the other soul in the subtleties of its feeling and thinking, in the vagaries of its being and becoming. 'Connect,' a wise writer wrote, 'only connect'—and that is what love is: a fiery appetite to know and unite with the soul of another. That is one way of love.

"The other way of love is adoration, Don Juan. Connection is the first, but Adoration is the second. To see and worship the God-Goddess of another; to praise and appreciate this being for the God-thing that it is. Thus to care, but not for the union of oneself with the other, nor even for the other alone, for its sake. Adoration-love is not one of union, nor of the asymmetry of the parent-child, teacher-pupil, healer-sick. Adoration-love is one of the worship of the God-Goddess in man.

"These are the two kinds of love, Connection and Adoration. I see, now, that I have also mentioned a third kind of love, one that is neither Connection nor Adoration, but a kind of Caring. That is what is involved in the selfless love of the parent, of the teacher, of the healer, is it not? So, I have learned something myself while I have tried to teach you about love! Thus, the teacher learns as he teaches. That, too, have I believed.

"And yet, there is a fourth kind of love; not only three, but four. This fourth love is the highest and best perhaps, for it is a love of equals, of brother and sister, of God with God, of Goddess with Goddess. And, it is also the love of lovers, the love of God with Goddess. That is the highest and best of all. Of that union, of that intermingling of souls which is of Self with Self, of totality with totality, of essence with essence, that love includes Connection, Adoration, Caring, but it is greater because it is co-equal. There is symmetry rather than asymmetry, mutual connection rather than one-sided understanding and acceptance, mutual adoration rather than simple praise of the other. That is, in short, the highest love of all, the love destined for the ages to come. Such love can be everywhere, in marriage, in friendship, in romance and, even with parent and child, teacher and pupil, doctor and patient. For, does not the child give care to the parent? Pupil teach the teacher? Patient heal the doctor? Yes, it is so, sometimes, and then it approaches this fourth love . . . what shall I call it? Mutuality.

"That is what I know of love, Don Juan; Connection, Adoration, Caring, Mutuality. Ultimately union, union of souls, that is what love is all about."

"Grandson of the Knight, you astonish me! You know much about love!"

"I suppose I do, Don Juan."

"You know much, Grandson of the Knight," continued Don Juan, "but you know nothing!" Now Don Juan's face turned red and angry and sneering. He looked brutal. For an instant, I thought I understood those who said of Don Juan that he was uncaring and power-driven, wanted only conquest, had lust only for his appetites. But Don Juan spoke further:

"You know nothing, Grandson of the Knight, for you speak of soul, you speak of Caring, of Connection, even of Adoration, to say nothing of equality or Mutuality. Those are very high loves indeed. But you know nothing! For love is a passion, a driving urge to penetrate, to possess, to squeeze the flesh of another in one's fingers, to sense and feel all nuances of the flesh of this being, to devour it, and be devoured in return. Love is jealousy and possession, desire and domination, sense and flesh. The love of souls is for priests and nuns!"

This outburst silenced me, momentarily, and I felt like a dainty little girl as a consequence of it. I remembered my life experience after a moment, however, and I nodded. "I know what you mean, Don Juan, for I have lusted and desired after the flesh as well. Indeed, that longing after the flesh of the Many is exactly what has disturbed my love of the One. That lust after possession, that darkness of jealousy, the wish to dominate the many, is just what has caused my grief, my pain, and just what has caused my bringing pain to others. I acknowledge you are right in that. But that, too, is in the loves I have mentioned, is it not? Is not the flesh present among the loves of Connection, of Adoration, of Caring, and of Mutuality? At least in some degree. But not lust, I suppose, that is true; lust must give way to soul when there is love."

Thus spoke I, in truth, but I sounded priggish to myself all the same. Don Juan simply looked at me with a half-sneer and went back to his own writing. I knew, now, that I had to wait. I had to overcome my priggishness and my girlish daintiness before I could once more address myself to this man. I also realized that I now had more respect for this man, this Don Juan, than I had initially. I was faced with an independent, reflective and passionate man, and I would find this no easy experience.

Some days went by, and I got up the courage to reapproach Don Juan. Once again I felt sleepy and sluggish as I tried to make contact, but this time I made connection with a love of mine first—as if I needed to make a contact outside before I could contact inside. After I did so, I found that I could easily go down once again into the basement room where I had first seen the Magician many days before. But this time there was a trap-door and a staircase which led easily down into the subterranean place. I was surprised to find this easier access. Was it because I made the effort to connect outside first and, therefore, overcame the resistance to connect inside? Or was it because I had already made one attempt at contacting the Magician, in his form of Don Juan?

As I reached the bottom step, I saw Don Juan sitting at the desk writing. My first gesture toward him was to gently touch his shoulder. He looked up, pleasantly enough, forgetting, perhaps that he was rude, angry, and sneering at me the last time I saw him. I overlooked this change in behavior without comment, but asked him about the trap-door and the staircase. How was it that there was this easier access this time?

Once again, Don Juan looked at me with disdain. He was as if long-suffering and sickened by my question. Of course there was now a staircase to him, of course there now was easier access! And why? Because I was making a genuine effort to connect to him, I was seeking him out, I was really inquiring of him, and not only passively expecting help and communication. Besides, was I not now openly showing my need and passivity outside, rather than pretending that I was always the strong one, the reliable one?

Having heard Don Juan's characterization of me, I was chagrined. I was accustomed to thinking of myself, over the past several years, as more actively sensitive in relationships than most men and many women. I was not used to having a man look at my capacity for love in a condescending way. And yet, this might be a most useful thing, after all! Had I not sought to find a man who could love as much or more than I? And it might just be possible that Don Juan was just such a one!

"Of course," said Don Juan. He had been listening to my silent thoughts, I suppose, though it may have been the Magician who transmitted my thoughts to him, rather than Don Juan, himself. No matter, however, since he seemed to know what I had been thinking without my having told him. "Of course!" he repeated. "I know more about women and about love because I have seen so much more of it than you. I have known hundreds of women, thousands even. I know more because I have invested time and energy and talent and love in the study of these women. You have invested only love, attention, adoration. All of that matters, of course, and your rewards have been to get their love, attention and adoration in return. But knowledge? Well, I wonder how much actual knowledge you have."

I acknowledged that I knew rather little about women as such, except to know how they felt from times that I had felt the same way. I also said that I was not sure if I trusted the superiority of his knowledge either. Having had intercourse with several thousand women proved only his capacity for conquest, or having much semen, not love necessarily.

Once again, Don Juan shrugged and turned away from me. He was not going to talk further to me until I acknowledged his superior capacity for love, it seemed. I could not do that in good conscience, yet I understood his need to be recognized for what he felt to be his greatest asset and capacity. Did not I have just such a need and resentment so often? Of course I had. I, however, had been unable to simply turn away from others who failed to recognize me; Don Juan, on the other hand, seemed to have this capacity. Perhaps I could learn from him at least that: how to know so strongly that one is right in one's spirit and, at the same time, not to be dependent on others to recognize it. I also wanted to learn once again how to be independent, how not to need approval. I had once felt like that, long ago, as a youth—an inheritance from my father and grandfather— but my long devotion to women, to love, to the feminine, seemed to take that away. So, I turned once again to Don Juan and said:

"Don Juan, I do not know whether I can bow to your superior capacity to love, since I am in great doubt about it, but I do bow to your capacity to be true to your own spirit and not be dependent upon other people's approval or their respect for your spirit. That I would learn from you, if I could."

"Well, then, Grandson of the Knight! Well then! You came to redeem us, perhaps, we poor ghosts of the nether realm. You with your superior capacity for love came like Jesus Christ into the occult realms to free us from our poor benighted state! And now you find

that perhaps you can learn something from us. That is not too bad, I
suppose, for a rank beginner like yourself. One small step forward, I
would suppose.

"If you can see your way clear to submitting yourself to me as a guru
for a little, I may indeed be able to teach you something about women,
about the feminine. What do you say to that?

I reflected a little: I had rather enough of gurus during the previous
years. I had enough of discovering the gurus to be less than I thought,
or betraying, or not recognizing my spirit. I had resolved long ago to
reject having any gurus at all. I was willing, of course—and even
eager—to go on joint voyages of discovery, to share as equals in a
relationship, but to submit to a guru? Well. I thought, too, of what
the Magician had demanded of me in the beginning: "Submit" he said.
A curious thing, Magician and Don Juan were requiring my submission. I did not know of any worldly gurus to whom I would submit,
but perhaps here, in the nether region, here I could submit. With
these thoughts, I responded to Don Juan that I would try to submit
and learn from him, although I had undergone bad experiences with
gurus before.

"Of course you have, foolish Grandson of the Knight! One always
outgrows one's guru and it is a rare master, indeed, that can take
kindly to this growth and really embrace his fledgling as a co-equal.
It is like a father for a son; does not the father always feel either a
certain protective feeling toward his son, or a secret and painful envy
or jealousy at the son's youth, vitality, or greater powers of mind or
heart? It is so; a darkness which has existed. We both know it. I will
tell you, some time, my own experience along this line. It happened
at the end of my life, with the commandant of Ulloa (the stories are
all wrong about it) and those bloody Franciscans. But that tale can
wait. For that story has to do with the love of man, not women, and
you, of course, know all about that!"

"Don Juan spoke his last sentence very sneeringly. I shook my head.
Why did he so often have to look down his nose at me? I had not
claimed so very much. I had not looked down my nose at him, beyond
the understandable susceptibility to the gossip that I had known from
generally accepted historical and literary sources. I had not hurt him.
So I asked him:

"Don Juan, why do you sneer at me and look down your nose at
me? I have not hurt you, I think. Nor does my attitude merit such
contempt."

Rather than answer me, Don Juan looked away and made a gesture
with his hands just as if he were a magician bringing some miraculous
event into being. I now felt even more strongly that Magician and

Don Juan were one person, but the implications of this identity were too much for me to consider at that moment. Instead, I fixed my eyes upon the scene which Don Juan had conjured up all too realistically. I was afraid to test the concrete reality of what I was seeing, but I allowed myself to enjoy what I saw.

There before me, in every way as real as anything one perceives in the sensations of daily life, were a man and woman in the act of making love. The heads of both were masked, but their bodies otherwise naked. They were lithe and graceful; she smooth and voluptuous, he athletic and strong. He grasped her firmly and passionately; she responded with equal force of desire. It was as if he were trying to contain her totally, to take her in and cover her; it was as if she were trying totally to contain him, take him in, be covered by him. It was exciting, arousing. These two masked ones brought to my mind many images and memories.

As their lust mounted in intensity and fury, the heat and energy which they radiated came across to me in waves. I felt engulfed in the warmth of it. I no longer knew if I was experiencing this heat and fire as coming from within myself—as my own passion—or coming from this outer mirage-actuality. But then their climax came and though I did not have orgasm myself, I felt as if I had climbed the top of a mountain and was gently and quietly descending the other side. The lovers rested exhausted.

A few moments later they sat up, as if aware of a lurking danger in the background. They huddled as if to protect their genitals or their total selves from view. At that instant a small man broke into the room in which they were lying. He brandished a pistol and was about to shoot. Was this the husband? A cuckolded and furious spouse? A jealous lover? The law? Then the scene faded, as if it were indeed a mere fantasy.

Hardly had the image vanished when Don Juan waved his hand once again, this time producing a different sort of scene. Two new figures appeared, again naked and masked, but now the man was seated upon a throne-like chair. The woman was seated opposite him, similarly. He summoned her and she came to him. She bent down on her knees, kissed his penis and then made love to him with her mouth. Both their eyes were closed in ecstasy. After a time, their roles were reversed: the woman sat in her throne-like chair, legs apart and uplifted, while the man made love to her genitals with his mouth. Once again, they reached their climax, but were robbed of their rest and relaxation, because into the room flew two young children, a boy and a girl, wide-eyed at what they saw. Were the children their own? Were they of one or the other? Was there hurt, shock, damage? This scene also faded before one could guess the answer.

Don Juan waited barely a moment before conjuring up the next scene with a small gesture of his finger. Now there were three people, rather than two: the same well-built male and female, naked and masked, with slits for their eyes as before, but now a young girl in her late teens was with them. She seemed to have been a daughter of the woman, but all three were in bed. The woman and man were both showing the young girl how to make love, the mother by showing her how to grasp his penis, how to put it to her lips and in her mouth, how to lick and go around his body actively, playfully, but also how to be receptive to his penis in her vagina, how to roll and move with his motion, as well as listen to her own. The man, in turn, awakened the girl's desire by fondling her, caressing her, kissing her and, finally, entering her. At last, all three were loving one another when, once again, the door flew open and a finger-pointing man with stern eyes rushed in and froze them in their places. Who was this man? Again, no time for questions or response; only a fading image, soon to be followed by another wave of Don Juan's hand.

Don Juan produced another pair of handsomely built people, masked as before. This time the man fondled and stroked the passively receptive woman, but she responded with sounds and trembling of flesh as he did so. He touched every part of her body, gently and passionately. He looked deeply into her eyes and followed every slight moist movement of them. He stroked and kneaded her flesh, finally settling one hand in the vaginal area, holding her gently, while stroking her pubis and buttocks. Finally he began to massage her clitoris, while making love to her with his other fingers, meanwhile holding first breasts and then buttocks firmly. She soon gasped in a frenzy of spent ecstasy. Again the roles were reversed, and the woman sought out all the tender, excitable places of the man, his belly and back, his anus and testicles. She stroked and caressed, she rubbed and kneaded. She, too, looked deeply into eyes, and, finally, rubbed his penis until his ejaculated semen shot across the room in a hot fountain of passion.

Hardly could they rest, however, when into the room came a sad-eyed woman, who, in turn, made the lovers sad. Who was she? Spouse? Sib? No answer.

Following this colorful display of sex and loving, Don Juan spoke.

"There is an answer for you, Grandson of the Knight, and there is a bit of instruction in the truths of love. I do not sneer at you, I have no contempt. I merely indicate other sides of what you have been pleased to call the various kinds of loving.

"Take the first scene: two people making intense and fulfilling, passionate love. That, I think, is your love of Mutuality, of co-equality. That totality of mutual in-taking, of covering and being covered, is rare enough as it is, but when it occurs, is the reeling with rapture not broken into by fear, by violence, by the codes of morality, by taboos? You know that is true. And, even more, if one follows such spontaneous loves, which are always brought about by the Goddess, then are not some other people often hurt? Spouses, for example, children? And does not jealousy and possessiveness break into such relationships in any case, whether in the form of another person, or in the form of parts of the people themselves, the relationship itself? Does not romance end in pain, frustration, agony? Thus my observation and experience. And thus, Grandson of the Knight, have I sought the sequential, the Many, and not remained with the One. For the vaunted Mutuality and Co-equality in love which you hold highest, is as doomed to pain and suffering and frustration as anything else in life. Perhaps more.

"Take the second scene," Don Juan continued. "Adoration was another kind of love of which you spoke, and there, in the flesh, is the concrete representation of what that is. Very satisfactory, very enjoyable, of course, but does not the child always break in? Does not the childish, the infantile, the demanding, the selfish, break in whenever we wish to adore another? When we adore God, aren't we also secretly asking for something? When we adore a love, are we not secretly waiting to be adored in return? And, even in those moments which are not so secretly self-seeking, is not the needy child in us hurt by adoration of another? Is not our own self-centeredness and self-lovingness merely put aside in this adoration? Is it not true that one is not so easily adored in return? Or by the wrong people?

"Take the third scene," Don Juan continued. "There is your asymmetrical love, the love of Caring. Here it is a caring in teaching a girl to love. Is there anything higher or more worthy of being taught? Of course not! But is not such a teaching hemmed in by taboo, by laws, by customs? Is not every form of free and spontaneous new learning bound to have to be restrained, held back, dampened by some old spirit of rigid law, of gossip, or moralizing? Are not other forms of Caring, such as parent for child, teacher for pupil, healer for sick, always under a thwarting and watchful eye of negative judgment: "bad" parent, "wicked" child, "incompetent" teacher, "dull" pupil, "quack" healer, "dissembling" sick. All these judgments and epithets are hurled whenever there is a new way to heal, a new ailment to repair. The conventional finger of judgment always comes in to return things to the past. Rare is the Caring which escapes the pain and rigidity of such a conservative force.

"And the fourth scene," said Don Juan, "is the same as the rest. For there is your love of Connection. 'Only connect' said your wise man, 'only connect.' But look at it: he connects totally, carefully, deeply, and involvedly with her. He brings her exquisite pleasure and joyful release. And she does no less for him. But who enters? Is it only a sad woman, a spouse or another love as in the case of the first, Mutual love? No. It is the feminine, the Goddess Herself. She is sad because the very purpose of Connection is lost in the connection. He connects with her, she connects with him, but in that totality of connection with the other, one is not connected with. One is alone with oneself. And it must be so to really connect with another; connection with another precludes mutual connection. A kind of paradox, but true. And, when one has the highest, as you say, Mutual connection, then all the pain and grief of loss of it, of pain of it, of hurt and violence and anger, of possessiveness, occur. So, we are then back to the first scene. And we begin again the round of the kinds of love, and the impossibility of them. For all seek union, just as you said, and all fail of it. Mutuality, Adoration, Caring, Connection, all seek, all find, but all fail.

"Thus am I sad, Grandson of the Knight, and thus am I sneering and contemptuous. Not of you, and not of your categorizing of love. I am sneering only because of my own pain, and my recognition that all unions end, all ecstasies are followed by agonies, all loves are less than perfect. Thus do I teach you, Grandson of the Knight."

I was so astonished and overcome by this vivid display of the knowledge of Don Juan that I stood open-mouthed and, I am sure, foolish-looking. Having finished his instruction, Don Juan sat back down at his desk and let his head fall into his arms, hands and fingers curling over his hair. I sensed that he was weeping. Mighty Don Juan, conqueror of women, disdainer of men, violator of codes of morality, breaker of laws, braggart of his powers, Don Juan was weeping. And he was weeping because of the pain of love. He was weeping because love always brings in its train frustration, hurt, pain, conflict, either to oneself or to another. He was weeping because in spite of his Maniness, in spite of his sequential love and lack of commitment to an already achieved union, he, too, experienced the pains and agonies that I had known in my commitment to the continuing love, the devotion to the person, the maintenance of the connection. Don Juan was as wounded as I. Nay, he was even more wounded, it seemed, for he wept. Here he sat in the strange Purgatory of history of the soul, accompanied by no one, not even the famous servant that Mozart had known with him. Here he was alone. His commitment to love rather than to people had brought him all the knowledge and experience, but had also brought him the same hurt, frustration and pain that one has when one is committed to people, to the personal, rather than to an ideal, even the ideal of love. And, his reward was to be here alone, with no one. What a striking "reward"! What a punishment of a man who sought love in the many, in the impersonal: to experience all the pains and hurts and to end up totally alone!

I, too, was sneering in a way, not at Don Juan, but at the paradoxes and bitterness of life. One has an ideal, one pursues a quest, one is both successful and thwarted and one ends up in a purgatory of pain, for one has forgotten the other half, the absent part. And God seems to demand that we know everything, experience everything, become everything, become whole, I suppose. For which we must require many lifetimes after all. . . .

In my reflections I was forgetting Don Juan, now a poor and wretched figure. I was becoming just as impersonal and unfeeling as the ages had wrongly reputed him to be. I reached over and put my hand on his shoulder. I gently raised him up and embraced him. He was larger than I, but I could reach around his arms and shoulders and hug him. He melted in my arms as if he were a child, and I was moved, for I was reminded of my own son who could also do this—as he grew to be a man, as large or larger than his father, to submit and be embraced by one smaller than himself. I knew this, and felt this: the love of father for son, of teacher for pupil, of healer for patient, can and should become the love of son for father, pupil for teacher, patient for healer. We had already know that. Don Juan and I, when we had both spoken of the love of Caring. But something more was here, something more.

"It is the love of men, Grandson of the Knight," said Don Juan, as he divined my thoughts, "It is the love of men. You and I have struggled in our ways to live and understand the love of women. We have striven with the kinds of love which belong to women, to the Goddess of Love, really. I, in my devotion to Love itself, impersonal, many and sequential; you, in your devotion to the love of the particular person, personal, few and continuing; both of us have served a Goddess of Love. In so doing, we have learned little of the love between men. Indeed, we have both been betrayed by men and hurt more deeply there than by women! It is not so"?

I had to acknowledge that this was true. I had believed that I had served a male god of love as well as a female one, if one permitted Don Juan's metaphors, an Eros as well as an Aphrodite, but I was forced to conclude that Don Juan was right. I had known little of male love except disappointment, frustration, rejection, injustice. But all these came at the hands of men who had known less of love than myself, were human and frail like myself, and my bitterness was growing less and less. I needed only to have myself and was ready to let the old hurts go. What about Don Juan? What about his hurts, I asked.

"Grandson of the Knight, my hurts and pains at the hands of men, of institutions, were many. Of these I need not speak. Let me speak only of the pains at the end of my life. Let me tell you of my experience with the Commandant of Ulloa and of those deceiving Franciscans who betrayed me."

"Tell me, then, Don Juan," I said, for I was interested in the problems of being a man among men, of deception and hurt and betrayal of man to man. Don Juan continued his story.

"The daughter of the Commandant of Ulloa was a very beautiful young woman. In contrast to how the Commandant and gossips had it, this young lady sought me out one day. The story she told me was not a pretty one, I can assure you. She told me a somewhat sordid tale about her father, the Commandant. This figure of social righteousness, upholding the common virtue of monogamous and faithful living, careful religious obedience to the established church, this military man of good reputation, had whored a good deal, only half secretly. Now this was not the source of sordidness, for such practice was not uncommon in those days—as it is not uncommon in most days of the Western world. (Indeed, there is even some sense in the continuing establishment of such places for people like youth and the Commandant, who are unable to find the pleasures of love in other ways.) In such situations, prudence and a certain modesty are called for, it seems to me, and the men who so act should be rather modest about being upholders of morality. The Commandant erred here in being righteous, rather than imprudent.

"The true sin of the Commandant, in my opinion, was in his treatment of his wife. And it was in this regard that the Daughter came for help. The Wife did not know of the Commandant's whoring, but this was her own fault, because she could easily have known so were she half tuned to and connected with her husband's being, or even with the real social situation. It was not the whoring, then, that was troubling her. Rather, the woman was depressed because she felt no love, felt incapable of love. Her husband continually assured her of his love, of his caring, and so on, but the woman felt nothing of this, and concluded that it was her own incapacity which made it seem so. In fact, it was the Commandant who felt no love, he only dissembled it. He acted as if she were the villain of the piece, loveless, impossible to live with. His sin was that he put his lovelessness upon her, rather than face it in himself. The daughter was able to see through this charade, but her loyalty and dogged half-love for her father was such that she did not want to hurt him, nor humiliate him publicly nor privately. She wanted only that her mother come to realize her own true loving capacity, which the daughter knew to be very great. The daughter thought that I, perhaps, could help the mother in this way. I, but I, I asked? Was she not mad? Did not everyone know that I was merely a rake, a seeker after power over women? No, she said. Only those like her father, who sought more after power themselves, would so think. Many people, and women especially, would know differently. Would I do this thing for her?

"I thought long and diligently about this matter. I was very attracted by what this young girl said, for I was not often recognized as a man capable of love and feeling, care even. I was seduced by the possibility of awakening a woman of some repute, of older years, but awakening her into her own capacity for love. This latter was a very great seduction for me, indeed. The idea that I could conquer without conquering, love in secret and produce love—that was most attractive, indeed. What chagrin, what foolishness; not in the goal and the achievement, those were great. The foolishness was in underestimating the power of power, the hurt to a bruised ego. As you know, the stories accuse me of having seduced the daughter. In truth, it was the daughter who seduced me, and not into having sex with her, but in making love to her mother! Well, you can imagine now, how the truth of things would look to a pompous and aggrieved father. Surely easier to ascribe to me seduction of his daughter, rather than the awakening of his wife! And so it was. But I go ahead of my story.

"I assured the daughter that I would do what I could to help her mother come to her own capacity to love and that the matter could be safely left in my hands. Not that I was so certain that I could make every woman in the world fall in love with me; despite what you have heard, I have never been as arrogant as all that. No. I knew that I could connect with many women, could tune into where they were, what they felt; I could actively feel into, and intuit what their minds and souls and feelings were about, and it is this which is seductive to many women. It is this capacity of mine, by both nature and nurture, by inheritance and dint of having known many women and struggled with them that I am enabled to actively connect with them. Many, many women are starved for this; many, many women are so hungry for this from a man that they will leave home and family, career and possessions, for only a little of this. Not all women need this, of course. Some have it already from an occasional man, others are not even aware of this need in themselves. So many are lacking this, needing this, that it is possible to see such a one as I as a Pied Piper of women, as a ladies' man who can seduce whomever he wishes. The need for connection is the seduction, of course, no other. I do this, and any man can do this ultimately by being aware of his own feelings, by coming to grips with the feminine being in his own soul, by worshiping the Goddess, after all, in his own soul and in the being of the women with whom he comes in contact, with whom he becomes involved. For that, of course, is what the Goddess insists upon—involvement.

"And you, poor Grandson of the Knight, you have fallen altogether for the Goddess. You have accepted involvement far beyond what men normally accept, far beyond their general capacity, far beyond what even the Goddess expects. The multiplicity of my way is the more masculine position, after all. I have accepted the Goddess, as have you, but I have kept my masculine spirit by going also with the many. The Goddess respects this in me, since I accept life, but she does not support me, she leaves me to the opprobrium and judgment of all the men of power, all the jealous ones, who cannot love at all! . . . But, I go away from my story again, and lose the thread of what I wanted to tell you. I continue in my bitterness, I regret to say, and this impedes me, this keeps me here in Purgatory. Let me finally have my say, speak my piece, and then, perhaps, I too will be freed from my 'resentiments' as the French put it, and can be free.

"I visited the wife of the Commandant of Ulloa and plied my charms. My charms, as I have told you, are merely to be open with myself, with my feelings, and to be very open to where the woman is, what she feels. I told her of the love from her daughter, what the daughter thought of the mother and her entrapment, of the father—all that I have already related to you. I also told her of the daughter's desire that I awaken the mother's love. I honestly added that I was not at all sure that I could do so, but that I was at her service if she so desired.

"The poor woman wept and wept. When she could finally speak, she told me that she was mostly overwhelmed with her daughter's love and care, and with that selfless devotion to the mother's well-being. She, the mother, had always known the truth of what the daughter had said, but, in her own devotion, had kept this to herself, to somehow spare the daughter and, also, to cause the husband no pain. It was true, however, that the mother had known only maternal love—for her own daughter, for her husband; she had never known the passionate love of woman. She did not even know if she had the capacity. She would like to try. She would like to know such love before she died, but she did not know if she could, nor if this would damage her husband. She hoped not, but now that she was aware of her daughter's feelings, this was far less of a problem. She had been chiefly concerned about her daughter—she was willing to risk the loss of her husband.

"With such an auspicious beginning, I welcomed the chance to bring this good woman an experience of love. Love, of course, was what I was always after. I squashed a small foreboding and promptly began my campaign of awakening romantic and passionate love in this woman.

"The wife of the Commandant was willing enough. Her initial scruples and moral guilts at the apparent betrayal of her husband were assuaged by the awareness that she needed to find out, at last, if she could love, and by the knowledge that her husband was no virtuous paragon but was, in truth, something of a hypocrite.

"At first we played at love. I, of course, was a highly experienced man in such matters and knew all the technical ways of making a woman happy. The main truth that I had discovered over the years was that the technique of love-making is of little importance: what counts, as I have said, is the connection with the movements of desire in one's soul, and the freedom to go where the impulse and the wish lead. Sensitivity to one's own need and awareness of the need of the other are paramount in this. One fails because one does not trust one's impulse, or the connection between the two people is impeded in some way.

"As I say, at first we played at love. Despite having given birth to a child, despite having been married many years, this woman knew little of lovemaking. Though she was inexperienced and unawakened, I was surprised to find she was remarkably open and responsive. She felt a natural connection with her body and the movements of her soul, only needing someone who would permit her to experience these things. I was continually amazed at how quickly and naturally she knew and experienced the secrets of love-making. Day after day, we would enjoy new delights. Strange to say, I truly fell in love with this woman. Her innocent purity, her delightful abandon, the quick and joyful, spontaneous and free movements of her body and soul captured me in ways that were new to me. I began seriously to consider abandoning my life-long restless movement. I found myself wondering how it would be to relinquish the many, and to rest comfortably and fully with this one woman. As I thought these thoughts, I began also to speak to my new lady-love. I found the reaches of her mind, her openness to new ideas, the byways of her sensitivity to art and human nature, to thought, reflection and intuition, all of these to be as delightful and fulfilling as the pleasures of her body.

"Had I found the One, I wondered? Was this woman meant to be the final love, the last of my Many? Strangely, I dared not share these thoughts with her, despite the other truth that I was unusually open with her. Weeks and months went by, and our love grew deeper. You, Grandson of the Knight, no doubt smile when I use these words: 'our love grew deeper,' for you have been committed to the depth of love. You will also laugh when I speak of weeks and months; for you, I know, have been committed for years, for decades, for lifetimes. But you must believe me when I say that I was discovering new things late in my life; I was seriously tempted to abandon a life-long position of maniness, of multiplicity, for oneness, a single-paired union of love.

"In the meantime, our love was increasing. We grew more and more to delight in the flow of our thought, as well as that of our bodies. I startled and entertained her as I told her of the many loves of my life, of my experiences in all the known countries of the world. I took joy in her totally open-mouthed wonder at all of that, and at her lack of a judgmental attitude. She said, 'You have had so much to give to women and to love!' That statement, made by no one else in my life, reached the core of me. It was an expression, a putting into words, that which I had always wordlessly felt, yet was too modest and immodest to state. Too modest, for how can one proclaim that one had much to give to women and love? And too immodest, for any woman can say these words and feel them to be true and still not be arrogant. It is only arrogant for a man to claim, with pride, that which is natural and non-arrogant for a woman, is that not so?

"So, then, as I say, this great woman, this charming and wonderful wife of the Commandant of Ulloa gradually grew into my heart. I found myself changing. For the first time in my life, I began to grow jealous. I, the great Don Juan, conqueror of women, envied and reviled by men, was growing jealous of the husband of this woman who was desired by none, sought after by none, not even her husband! Can you imagine it? I found it remarkable. I found that I began to hate him, to wish that he were gone, done away with. I found ever new reasons to question his honesty and integrity—already, and with good reason, very doubtful in any objective sense—and to judge him as one of the lowest of the low.

"It furthermore came to pass that the Commandant and I were thrown together now and again. We passed only the most formal conversation and we kept a smiling benevolence between us, but I, for one, was aware of his deception of himself and others, and despised him for it. On his part, he sneered at me, almost openly, for was I not the one with bad reputation? Was I not the rake, the seducer and betrayer, was I not the heartless one, aiming only at my own pleasure and power? Everyone knew that, of course!

"After many months went by, it was more and more difficult for the

Wife of the Commandant and I to keep the secret of our love. She was becoming more and more impatient to leave her husband and pursue a life with me, or on her own. She became self-reviling—not because of her love for me or mine for her, but because she continued to live with a man whom she did not love. Nay, she became aware that she never had loved him. The truth was that she did not realize her capacity to love with him since it had never been awakened. Now, out of her guilt and need to establish something more with this man with whom she had lived for so many years, she tried very hard to really reach him, to find a place where love could occur. But it was impossible. He did not seem to wish it. He seemed to wish only that he maintain and improve his social position, his bearing and prestige as a Commandant, as Defender of the Church, as Upholder of Morals, etc. His claims of his love for her left her with ashes and anger in her mouth. I tried very hard to assure her that he loved her in his fashion, to the extent that he was capable, but this only made her more despairing.

"Finally the Commandant found out about our liaison. The 'facts' subsequent to this are fairly well known, I think. It is common knowledge that I killed the Commandant, that I was enticed into the convent of Franciscans on a ruse, and that they, in turn, killed me, telling the people that it was the statue of the Commandant who came to life and did the killing. Besides that, it was a blessing to destroy such a one as myself. Yes, these 'facts' are known. They are known just as the other 'fact' is known that I 'seduced' the daughter of the Commandant. You now know, of course, that I did not seduce the daughter at all. Are you prepared to hear the rest? . . . You hesitate, Grandson of the Knight. Do you not trust me?"

"The truth is, Don Juan," I replied, "that I do not know what to trust. I have listened to you with interest. You seem to be telling the story as you really experience it. I do not believe that you are deceiving me in principle. But I also wonder if your truth is not only your truth, that perhaps the others might see it differently. Is it not so that almost every great event in life is capable of many interpretations, capable of many different perceptions even, and that the 'truth' is hard, indeed, to know? Is it not also true that you feel very deceived and misunderstood by both your contemporaries and history? That you feel that you were a great lover in a real sense, and not in the sense of opprobrium that history gives? Is not such discrepancy a reality of life and history? I am afraid so, for I have suffered just such discrepancy to my great pain and chagrin. In short, Don Juan, I do not know what to believe."

"Well said, Grandson of the Knight! You, indeed, do tell the truth.

For you speak the truth of your feelings and thoughts, you speak the truth of your own uncertainty, and you speak with an openness which is an attitude that one can envy. And yet, your voice is not just one of presumed reason, which ends up in a distorted, cold, and unfeeling pseudo-objectivity. You are a real man in this, for you try, indeed, to understand me. I appreciate this. Perhaps you must speak to the others, to the Commandant, to the Franciscans, to Wife, even, and the Daughter, to find a whole and total truth. But we all deceive ourselves, do we not? And it is hard to find the total truth. Know only how I saw a part of this. Hear me in my grief and pain, and know how I suffered, and how I did what I did.

"The Commandant found out about my relationship with his wife, as I have said. He then came to me and upbraided me with so many words of raw judgment as I have never heard. The gist of his remarks were that I was a contemptible scoundrel, incapable of the least moral sense. With a final sneer, he said that I was weak, of no value. He said that he would like to kill me, but that I—and the results that might occur to him if he did so—were not worth this act of violence. He was a soldier and true, and would kill only in a worthy cause.

"I was left weak and impotent by this verbal attack. I could not move and felt strangely impotent. I was not even able to administer a counter-attack in telling this man what a deceptive, unloving person he was. In truth, I was afraid, and cowardly. In further truth, I had to acknowledge that there was much justice in his castigation of me, but the justice had nothing to do with the present even, or very little. I had been a scoundrel very often, had indeed gone against morality, was often weak and contemptible. These dark epithets were partly true, but, paradoxically, they were least true of my relationship with the Commandant's wife! He was correct in pointing his finger at many of my past errors and guilts, and even correct in judging me as one who robbed him of his wife, but he missed all my virtues, and also missed that I could not rob him of something that he, in truth, had never had—his wife's love. He had not even tried to find and value this love!

"But I say no more! Let the condemners and the accusers speak for themselves!"

Don Juan II

After Don Juan made his statement, he seemed to melt away, and I was once again confronted with the figure of the Magician, seated at his table, quietly writing. I did not know if Don Juan were leaving me forever, but did not have long to wait. The Magician kept on writing with his long quill pen. I looked at the paper upon which he wrote and saw, not lines of words and sentences, but a sketch. As the Magician scribbled, the face of a man emerged. I knew, of course, that this must be the Commandant, and that Don Juan was being true to what he said and was allowing the others to emerge from this strange Purgatorial-like place that he was in. I felt honored by this as if, perhaps, that I, too, was being asked to judge and participate, and through this involvement on my part, I would be freed from my own purgatory of guilt and uncertainty.

I watched the figure of the Commandant emerge. Here was a face which was hard and angry at moments. Then it would change to being soft and warm, almost boyish. In its hard and lined character, I felt as if in the presence of a Torquemada, a cruel and cutting judge. In its soft and round character, I could not tell if this were a boyish man, in need of love and understanding, or a kindly cherub. The mercurial changeover was, itself, surprising.

The figure began to speak from this sketch. That is, the lips began to move and form words, but there was no sound. Finally a guttural sound came out of the lips, as if this were an ancient ghost, a sepulchral emanation. But the sound was formless, only a sound, as if from a throat with the capacity to express itself without a mouth. The lips took one kind of shape, but the sound was separate, independent. I marveled at this. I sensed a certain horror and pain in this creature. I leaned forward, almost taking the pen out of the hands of the Magician, in my eagerness to help. But the Magician snapped it away and shouted at me.

"Fool!" he said, "Don't you see what is happening? The creature is undergoing the agony of the awareness of his separation! His sounds and words do not match! His feelings and ideas do not match! His views and behavior do not match! His role and his being do not match! His old man and boy do not match! He suffers this, at last! Do you not see it, Grandson of the Knight? Do you not see it?"

I did not like being called a fool, and felt that the Magician was being, in a way, just as judgmental and negative as both Don Juan and the Commandant had been. But, aside from a momentary pique at being called a name, I could see that I was foolish in being slow to comprehend what I was seeing, what the Magician was presenting before my eyes. Now I saw it in a flash of awareness of what the "truth" was! The Commandant had been, indeed, split and not aware of his being broken into opposites, one side not knowing the other. He had been utterly convinced that he was only good, honest, righteous, and did not know how much he was, in truth, their opposites. Now, he was suffering this conflict, this agony of knowing both sides and being unable to reconcile them. Now he could not longer put his own darkness on others. But my own words are not so good as those of the Magician himself. I understood, so I suppose that you who hear me will understand the Magician, as did I.

I was now able to make out what the Commandant was saying. The sepulchral sound began to be coordinated with the lips; the words were being formed in a reasonable fashion. I will not repeat these words, but give the gist of what was said, since I needed to strain very hard to hear him, to attend to the agonies of this man. What was needed of me was a very great feeling, a sensitivity to his pain: to attend to his words would have been too much, too wrong, too narrow and one-sided, just as he had been.

The Commandant admitted that he had been narrow, judgmental, a tyrant and hater of men with his strict rules, moral righteousness. He admitted that he had been totally consumed with the picture of the kind of figure that he would cut in the world, oblivious to the true feelings of his wife or others. He did know, however, that he loved his daughter, would have done anything for her. When he heard that Don Juan, the rake, had seduced his daughter—and this information had come from his erstwhile friends, the Franciscans, who had lied to him—he grew insane with rage and horror at the act of Don Juan. He rushed to his daughter to find out if this dastardly event had occurred. The daughter wept and pleaded, neither denying it nor admitting it, wishing the father only to calm himself. The Commandant took this as admission of the truth that she was seduced. He failed to see that the daughter was trying to protect her mother. The enraged man then set forth to find Don Juan and, not only rightly castigate him—as Don Juan admitted he should—but also to threaten his life. The Commandant challenged him to an immediate duel, which was attended by the Franciscans. These keepers of the spiritual keys allowed the duel to be held in their convent. As the duel progressed, Don Juan taunted him in return, telling him, the poor Commandant, about how he was unable to love, how his wife hated him. The Commandant grew very weak in his knees, felt the truth of what Don Juan had to say, and almost cooperated in his being killed by the sword of Don Juan. He wanted so much to die, to flee from the horrors of this accusing tongue, that he grew utterly weak and impotent. In his final moments he became aware of the split nature of his life and his being. Here in Purgatory, the Commandant was trying every way to recover a certain wholeness, a realness. He was only too ready to beg Don Juan's pardon, to reconcile himself with his erstwhile enemy.

With this news, Don Juan re-appeared, in the person of the Magician, and was equally eager to reconcile himself with his former enemy. I applauded the Commandant's apologetic attitude, his readiness to recant and come to wholeness; I applauded, even, Don Juan's eager willingness to embrace his enemy, but I smelt something rotten in this. What of the Franciscans, I thought? What was their role? And what of the women, of mother and daughter, wife of the Commandant, and the girl who was-wasn't seduced? What was their view of this?

The Magician looked at me with a half smile. "Not so foolish, this time, Grandson of the Knight, not so foolish, after all. You are right to be suspicious of this great and noble, goodhearted and sublime attempt at reconciliation. That is far too easy, isn't it? You are right to want to know more. And you are right, also, in looking to those Franciscans as the carriers of more information, more truth which will clarify, explain. Search for them"!

I accepted without further question the Magician's command to search and his half-complimentary support. But how to search for the Franciscans?

As an answer to my question, there appeared before me a Franciscan priest. He was neither a sketch on the page as the Commandant had been, nor as the Magician, but a man. He was dark, slender, aquiline of feature, gentle. The look of his eye was enormously gentle and deep, yet I had a sense of the possibility of anger and violence, of deep passions, controlled, yet not controlled. As if many years had been spent in a struggle with instinct and passion, with pride and humility, and what now appeared was a mixture of these, a quiet strength which was compelling and trust-evoking, yet also somewhat uncertain and even frightening.

Even though slightly daunted by the appearance of this Franciscan and his surprising countenance and demeanor, I addressed him. I openly questioned him on his role in the affair of Don Juan and the Commandant, on the behavior of the Franciscans. Did they, in truth, bring Don Juan to their Monastery precincts by a ruse, as history claims? Did they kill him, as some wonder? Or, as they said—or claim to have said—did the statue of the Commandant come to life and slay the man called rogue and rake, who was not that or only partly that?

The Franciscan spoke slowly and carefully in answer to my questions. He was matter-of-fact in the beginning, trying to answer the "facts" as best he could, but then warmed up to his topic as these were disposed of. He said, first, that the "facts" were true, but in a symbolic sense rather than a literal sense. It was concretely true that the Franciscans had invited Don Juan into their precincts, and precisely, as the Commandant had averred, for the purpose of reconciling the two, Commandant and Juan, Authority and Lover, but not, as he had said, for the purpose of a duel or battle. It was true, symbolically, that the Commandant had been a statue and killed Don Juan. For he had, under the duress of the combat unwanted by the Franciscans, been "killed," only to come out of his hard, cold, statue-like state of being encumbered by rules and morality, to come to life and in turn "kill" the rake and rogue and deceiver that was Don Juan. In truth, however, both men were something more than—and less than— Authority and Lover, Tyrant and Rake. Both were men. The sad truth is that both were killed, concretely, in the duel. As both lay dying, both repented and vowed to spend as much time in Purgatory as necessary to repair the sorry state of their one-sided souls. The stories told were partial truths, and symbolic truths, but not whole truths.

"And what is the 'whole truth?' " I asked of the Franciscan. Listening to this wise man, I wondered also of his truth, if his vision were any better or deeper or truer than the Maniness of Love of Don Juan, or the Oneness of Authority of the Commandant. As I looked at the austere face of this Franciscan, as I say, I wondered what was he serving? Family and order like the Commandant? Sexual love like Don Juan? The Franciscan could easily guess what I was thinking, and said:

"You wonder perhaps what I and my fellow monks have to gain in all of this, what we serve. You want to know what we serve. Why, it is service, itself, really. We are celibates, voluntary eunuchs of God. A celibate, when he is a spiritual man, voluntarily sacrifices an individual mating in order to be able to love all of God's people more generously and intensely and fully. We sacrifice and sanctify our sex in order to love not one person, or one family, but to love and serve the many. Celibacy, in union with God, is the highest form of creativity!"

As the Franciscan spoke these words, with rising intensity, I saw that he, too, was a man possessed, a fanatic, like Don Juan, like the Commandant, and, unfortunately, like myself. . . . I remembered what a wise man once told me: fanatics do all the damage in the world, not fools or rogues. Now I saw that both Don Juan and the Franciscan were loving the many, but oppositely, and were enemies. I saw that the Commandant was with the One, but with the family, one law, one country, not one person. I saw, too, that all three men were impersonal, really, in service of a principle and not personally connected at all or, if so, only to a limited extent.

These three Spaniards: for the One, for the Many, at war and at peace with each other . . . strange. I remembered then that other great Spaniard, that romantic and visionary, Don Quixote. He was for the One, after all; one love, one ideal, gallant, free, a mixture, perhaps, of Franciscan and Commandant. Equally well, I suppose, could he be a mixture of the Commandant and Don Juan. But no, he was an original, different from these. These four made a cross, did they not? All arms of a totality, but all different.

For love in the one (Quixote) and love in the Many (Juan), spirit in the one (Quixote) and Spirit in the Many (Franciscan), Service in the One (Commandant) and Service in the Many (Franciscan). I saw that all were needed. I saw, even, that a part of me was like each of these men; I, myself, was a Juan, a Commandant, a Franciscan and Quixote. And I was just as fanatic with each of these, when I was like them, as they were in themselves. Nor was this just an intellectual partition into parts for me! How often had I felt the inner war between family man and lover of many, between romantic idealist and the reality of life, between spiritual sacrifice and desire: all warred and jostled. Among the four there existed in my soul an orderly chaos, or jumbled regularity, depending upon how one looked at it. Seeing this, I grew sad, as all men are sad when they are forced to face their inner diversity, their inner conflict. . . .

All four men faded now back into the Magician. I was silent, for I had nothing to say, nothing to add. I, myself, was many, and longed for an inner unity, which could not be. I sat down near the figure of the Magician and remained silent. I knew the advantages and disadvantages of each, the union and disunion in each, the order and chaos in each. All of them, in their four-fold union and disunion felt it also. For they were men, were they not? They were living beings and complex, just as I was, were they not? And they, did not their fanaticism do damage to the other parts of themselves as well? They, too, suffered from inner diversity and lack of union with each other. They, too, were silent. For what more could be said? What man, having faced the impossibility of his inner diversity, his inner contradictoriness, his inner tornness, and, like they and I, having lived this contradictoriness to the fullest, what more could be done than to remain silent. So, silent we sat.

After a time, I once again heard words from the Magician. I was
startled, since the voice that I heard was that of a woman, even
though it came from the Magician. I looked up to see a handsome
woman where Magician had been. She spoke softly at first, telling
me that she was the wife of the Commandant, that she had suffered
much in her years of loveless marriage. As she spoke, however, her
voice grew harsh and irritable. She complained bitterly that all the
men were impersonal, really, more involved with their ideas, or with
their roles, or with their spirit, rather than with a real person, the
concrete woman, the flesh and blood being that they professed to be
so involved with, to care about so much. She almost spat these words
out, she almost choked with the bitter feelings these words accompanied, she almost grew rigid with it.

I remained silent. I agreed with the woman, and knew that what
she said was true. But this viewpoint also was one-sided, and was—for
me—an old story. More feminine complaints, more female demands,
more female bitterness; but where was the love in turn? Where was
the spirit? Where was anything that would help resolve the confusion
of tongues, the pain of rivalries, the dross of bitterness? Nothing!
Only more demands . . . I sensed at that moment my own bitterness
in life, in love. I recoiled at the realization that the wife of the
Commandant was just as much like me, a part of me, as the four men
of the cross that I had struggled with before. I was just as bitter and
demanding and complaining—and needy. I was just as much in need
of love. What use more words? What use other than to know that all
five were like me? I would sit, now, like a Buddha, silent. I would sit
under this tree and move no more. I would ask for no more, question
no more. Neither would I help nor remedy. I would sit in silence.

So I sat . . . After some days, the daughter came. She sat next to
me, in silence. I nodded, and was grateful, for she came to sit, to be
quiet, to be near. She demanded nothing, she gave nothing, she
simply endured. And I saw that she, too, was like me, a part of me,
just like the rest. Had I not waited, asked for nothing, given nothing,
merely endured? Yes, I answered myself, I had done this thing.

As I sat in silence, knowing that all six were I, and I they, the
others came and sat with me, one by one. First the Daughter, as I said,
and then Don Juan, Commandant, Wife, Franciscan. Even Don
Quixote came, though until that point I had not spoken with him,
had not seen him in the flesh. He had only been a memory, a book
read, a feeling felt, not a reality. Now he came as a reality, and he,
too, sat in silence. We all sat, waiting, waiting; waiting for the God
who would unite us or release us, awaken us or do away with us,

assuage our bitterness or make it so impossible that we would all choke to death, soften our despair or make it so unbearable that we would cease to exist.

I waited. But as I waited for the God or Demon to make an end, I realized that I, only I, was alive. I, only I, was living as a flesh and blood being in this world. I, only I, now had flesh. All these others were in the Purgatorial place of memory, of history, of fantasy and image. I, only I, could live there, with them, and in the flesh and blood life outside of them. They were real, only too real, both in history and in their effects on men, and in fantasy and memory as well, but now they existed only in me, in my soul. "Only" I said! What a word! In truth, they were more real than myself, yet illusion! They were both more real, since they encompassed the parts of me, and less real, since they existed in my psyche and apart. Oh, what illusion and deception! It made even that of the romantic Quixote seem quite harmless in comparison!

At that moment, I realized why I was sitting in silence under that tree, and felt myself like a Buddha. Was I not like the Buddha, after all? Was I not suffering the assault of the images and demons that also assaulted him? Was I not in the midst of the struggle over sickness and disease, old age and death, immortality and mortality, just as he was? And was I not doing so with different words, different images, but just as real as were his? More even, perhaps, since these were not just some vague and esoteric demons but living realities of my soul that I had experienced. But I knew that I had created them: I was the Magician who could summon them, speak to them, enquire of them, abandon them. I was their God! I was, just as those foolish people who know nothing of Buddhism say of Buddhists, an atheist! Little do they know that what is meant when it is said that the God, the Buddha, dwells within: we create our own Maya! And yet, I also knew that these, all six, created me. They, too, were my God; I was a figment of their imagination. They had more reality in the world, in history, in their effects upon men, in their living ongoing being, than that little "I" that I was, who so seriously examined them. The Magician was I, and I, the Magician. And the Magician was all six, and the seventh me.

With that, as a strange man, as a Magician whose face could change and move and glow, I felt as one. I, Grandson of the Knight, Son of the Knight, no hero but an ordinary man, was enlightened. A quiet event, a peaceful event, no light-making, gun-sounding event. I was enlightened . . . at peace.

Grandson of the Knight II

The enlightenment that I had experienced as a consequence of the silent sitting, the no-mind kind of Buddhist waiting, had an impact upon me which was firming and quieting. It was, of course, not at all a final Enlightenment. Does anyone achieve a final enlightenment after all? As long as he lives? As long as he continually must re-work, re-experience, as well as be open to new events, new situations? Of course it is so.

My further reflections taught me that I had learned not only about the four kinds of love from Don Juan, but that each of the actors in that famous event were themselves representative of different kinds of love. Don Juan carried the experience of the passion in the flesh—a maniness of love; the Franciscan embodied the passion of the spirit—a maniness of love of mankind; the Commandant was loyal to love of forms, of institutions and structures, such as family and clan, nation and tribe, church and religion—a oneness of love in the concrete and real; Don Quixote embodied a love of the vision, of the dream, of the romantic quest, of those loving dreams and the knightly heroism without which there is no meaning in life, a oneness of love in the abstract and fantastic. All of these male loves were necessary, a cross of oneness and maniness, of flesh and spirit, of concrete and abstract, of reality and fantasy. All were very satisfying. And yet, as the wife of the Commandant had revealed to me, all these male loves are impersonal or, if one may use a less judgmental term, they are transpersonal; they leave out the deeply important necessity of the personal, the individual, the particular. Without the personal, the unique, the particular, there is no individuality after all, and that, as my Grandfather and Father, Knights #1 and #2 had clearly shown me, is the highest value of all!

So, the personal love of the Wife makes all those male loves individual, "really real" and unique. And the devotion, the personal and private and enduring love of the daughter is the juice, the energy, the softly stubborn commitment in personal relationship which makes it all possible, makes change occur, makes love fulfillable. I had, therefore, learned much about love from my experience with Don Juan and his companions. I had learned not only the four loves of Connection, Adoration, Caring, and Mutuality, I had learned four more male loves of Passion-Flesh, Passion-Spirit, Love of Forms, Love of Ideals. Besides these I had learned the feminine cross of the Sensual-Individual Love, and Personal Devotion.

All this I had learned, and I had even felt a measure of wholeness in it, despite the diversity, despite the differences and obvious oppositions of one to another. It all came together in the form of the enlightenment. But I was soon dissatisfied. Are we not always so? Is it not true that we can hardly ever rest more than a moment, hold what we have only briefly? Is it not true that something drives us further, to include more, to test what we have, to make ever larger, greater, or simpler wholes? So it was with me.

I returned to where I had encountered the Magician. I descended the steps and found myself in a different kind of place. Before, I had seen a very colorful library, filled with books of all descriptions, a writing desk, and the Magician was a cool and clever man who melted into shapes, wrote and sketched, ignored me and encompassed me, taught me and scolded me. Now I saw only a cave-like room, with dark, hewn walls, very little light. It reminded me of the stories that had been told me by my father, for he had spent much time in a cave. He knew caves, darkness, and purgatories of the underground world.

Now, there was only a ghostlike quality. I saw no one, but felt the presence of the great Magical Man. I felt a tug at my sleeve which led me back into the cave. Before I knew whether the cave went on farther and deeper, I was shoved by this Presence against the wall. The shove made me jostle a stone and I saw that one could take out this stone. I did so and a knob to a door stood revealed. I turned the knob and found myself in a forest. It was a beautiful spot with big trees, colorful plants and shrubs. An intuition, like the sweet smell of frisia flowers, came into my nose, and I knew that just as the cave had been like the one dwelt in by my father, this Forest was like the one where my grandfather went to meditate and where the Angel had come to him.

I was terribly pleased, for I felt that I was truly a spiritual son to my father and grandfather, that I walked where they had walked, and felt and could feel the spirits and presences, Gods and Demons, just as they had. And I knew that I, Grandson of the Knight, but ordinary mortal, could trod these sacred places just as they did and that they would approve.

I sat down by a large tree and felt quite peaceful. I had achieved enlightenment by a tree, had I not? No enlightenment came now, only the outline of the shape of the Magician. Now he spoke to me gently, in a dreamy voice, one in which he could speak also to nature beings, to elves and dwarfs. The Magician said that I had more to learn about love, for one never stops learning about it, just as one never has the final enlightenment while he lives. But now, the Magician said, he was going to tell me a story. It was a story which had several versions and was very old. Indeed, over the last thousand years or so, the story was gradually changing in its form. Earlier versions ended rather badly and destructively, but more recent versions were showing some change. We would talk later about these changes, for we were not only going to tell and listen to stories, we were going to try and understand them. For to learn about love is not only to be dreamy and poetic and to float among feelings, it is to understand, to know in the spirit as well as in the soul and the flesh.

I nodded in agreement and the Magician began his tale.

The Wizard's Tale

Once there was a wizard who would take on the shape and quality of a poor man and go begging from house to house. At these houses, he would catch pretty girls and take them away. Just how he did this was not entirely known, but it was common knowledge that as he begged for bread, he would touch the girls and they would be compelled to jump into the basket on his back. He thereupon hurried off to his house in the midst of the forest.

One day the wizard appeared at the door of a man who had three (or seven) pretty daughters. The eldest gave him bread, was touched by him and carried off to the forest house. Everything within this house was magnificent and he gave her all that she desired. After a few days, he needed to journey forth, and he gave her the keys of the house, telling her that she could go everywhere and look at anything except into the one room which the smallest key would open. That room he forbade her on pain of death. He also gave her an egg, enjoining her to carry it carefully and continually.

With the departure of the wizard, the daughter examined everything, up to the forbidden door. She wished to pass by, but her curiosity would not let her rest, so she used the smallest key, opened the door and was shocked to see a huge bloody basin with many human beings therein, dead and hacked to pieces. She was so alarmed that she dropped the egg into the basin. She retrieved it, but found that she could not get the blood off. No matter how hard she washed and scrubbed, the blood would return. In some versions of the story, it is the key which is bloody, now on one side, now on the other.

When the wizard returned from his journey, he asked for key and egg. When she gave them to him, he saw by the blood spots that she had been in the bloody chamber. "Since you have gone into the room against my will," he said, "you shall go back into it against your own." He thereupon dragged her in, cut her into pieces and threw her in with the rest.

The tragic consequence was repeated with the second daughter (and, in some versions, up to the seventh daughter, or more). The youngest daughter, however, was clever and wily. She put the egg carefully away, instead of carrying it about. When she entered the chamber of horrors, she saw her dead sisters, but carefully put together their limbs and heads and bodies, in as good an order as she could. Miraculously, the limbs joined themselves together and the maidens were alive once more!

Upon the return of the wizard, he asked for key and egg. Finding no trace of blood upon the egg, he told the youngest daughter that she would be his bride. He was also now in her power. This youngest maiden required the wizard to bring a basket of gold to her parents while she prepared for the wedding. Instead of gold, however, the maiden hid her sisters in the basket and the wizard had to carry this heavy burden back to the home from which he originally took them. Ordered to continue without stopping, the wizard found the burden too heavy, but as soon as he would stop and rest, one of the daughters would call out that she was looking from her little window at him. The wizard, thinking that it was his bride speaking to him, continued walking, and finally he arrived at the parents' house exhausted.

The wedding feast was prepared by the bride, and invitations sent to the wizard's friends, but the maiden took a skull, put some ornaments and flowers upon it, and let it look out from the upstairs window. She then covered herself with honey and with feathers, so that she looked like a wondrous bird. She deceived the bridegroom-wizard into thinking that the skull was the bride and that she was herself a bird.

Once the wizard was inside the house with his friends, the brothers and kinsmen of the bride arrived, locked the doors of the house and set fire to it. The wizard and his crew had to burn.

Thus did the Magician end this tale of the wizard and the maidens. He looked at me as if to ask me for an interpretation or a reaction. I responded at once that I recognized the tale as one about the infamous Bluebeard, that blackguard and violent man of myth and tale who not only was interested in the many, as was Don Juan, but was cruel, vicious, violent, and murderous.

"So many epithets, Grandson of the Knight," said the Magician. "You judge very quickly. Have you not forgotten how you misjudged Don Juan? Are you not too ready to add to the opprobrium of that also heaped upon the unusual man? Are you not too ready to condemn? Did you not discover that things are not always as they seem?"

I had to admit that this was certainly true of my experience, through the Magician, with Don Juan, but it was hard for me to believe that there was some redeeming virtue in such a murderous and violent figure as Bluebeard. I had learned enough from the Magician, however, to be open to what he would have to say.

The remarks of the Magician were in the nature of an interpretation of the tale, I was somewhat startled to find out, for now his instruction was taking this form. I shall try and reconstruct what he said, though I cannot with certainty claim that I heard all, nor do I vouch for the full accuracy of what he said. The gist of the interpretation, however, is quite definite, and subsequent experience has made me convinced of this. The shadowy character of the Magician's form, at this time, is what accounts, I think, for my inability to formulate with total accuracy what was said. Hear then, without further disclaimer on this point, what the Magician said:

"The wizard, Bluebeard, far from being a mere sorcerer, a dark and peculiar villain, is none other than the dark God of Love. This may startle you, but it is true. Consider; is not the dark God of Love a rejected and poor figure in the course of the last thousand years of western history? Does he not seek the bread of life, the flesh of food? Is it not love, in its dark form, which 'touches' and captures girls, especially pretty girls, and beyond doubt when they have fed this demon the bread-flesh of their bodies, their desire and passion? For, once touched, once awakened, pretty young girls are 'captured' by the demon love, they are carried off by him to the dark forest of nature, of the magnificent house where all wishes are fulfilled! And Bluebeard is that dark, but spiritual (blue for heaven, for spirit, for the blue-bird, even) force which has been rejected but comes back for food, for power, for vengeance. He seeks a bride who will obey him; one who will submit totally to his bidding. But, no; no woman can. Nor can the soul itself, whether male or female. Because love is not enough. One always is curious to know, to understand. Eros is always insufficient, one longs for Logos. And the curious aim of the forgetful soul, the vulnerable heart, is to investigate, to find out. And, of course, one is then exposed to the horror of love! One is clearly at the mercy of that dismembering experience of love, for one is torn apart!

"Is not love, when dark and passionate, tragic? Are not most songs, songs of love? Are not most songs of love, songs of pain? Does not creativity sing of love, out of an agony? So it seems. Furthermore, the dismemberment is like that of a witch. One is torn apart, bathed in the blood of passion. The key belongs to man, of course. It is always the free choice of man, is it not? Consider that other figure, the God of Adam and Eve, who also gave them freedom and all good things, enjoining only one taboo. Consider also that this God must have wanted Adam and Eve to taste the Tree of Knowledge, to know. For he wanted company, he needed someone to be as conscious as he, or more conscious, perhaps. And, in his 'no,' like to a small child, he was also encouraging a 'yes.'

"Think, now, of this Bluebeard, a form of the God of Love. Is not his province the egg, just as in the myth? Was not Eros, Himself, born out of the World-Egg? Was not Love there before even the Gods were there? And is not the egg, the primordial beginning, bathed in the blood of pain, of passion, of dismemberment? And is not the experience of love one in which the nascent, unbroken God bathes in man's pain and passion? Thus the story, and the myth.

"And, consider further. Man has the key, but he is not clever, usually. He defies the will of God, and pays the price in pain or work or both. But, consider the wily daughter; consider the cleverness of the last, the youngest child. She, the one who also defies the will of the God, she is the most wily, the most conscious of all! She is so clever, so knowing, that she is more clever than the God of Love himself. Harken, she deceives him. How? By carefully taking care of the egg of love. She carefully puts it aside. She must have had an inkling of the inability of a person to handle love carefully when he views the pain and horror of the witch-state, of the devil-state of dismemberment. So, she takes care of love while she looks to know. Does she not love her sisters? Even in the horror of seeing their dismemberment she controls herself, tries to bring order. She brings an order of meaning into this horribleness of passion. In so doing, in trying to arrange all the parts in a way which is human, handleable, in being able to persist in the midst of the blood, she arranges the stage for the miracles to occur. She, the soul, the woman, is human, she cannot arrange a miracle; but she can, like us, like man, arrange the parts and hope for a healing, a whole-making. And it occurs: life returns, there is rebirth. Death is illusory, the soul is reborn.

"And thus is the demonic, violent character of love harnessed. Thus does the devilishness of love lose its hegemony and now the soul in man—and woman—has power. What then does she do, this wisest and youngest Maiden? She makes Love, himself, submit. He, now, who carried the power and made the soul suffer, he must now carry the burden of the soul. He, this demon lover, must hold that heavy weight of the soul; he must be responsible. He must feel the weight of it, and he does. And the soul looks out, for love must become conscious of itself! Just as that God of Adam and Eve needed, a thousand years after them, as Job foresaw, to become aware of himself. God must see as well as act! And so He does.

"But he is deceived once again. It is true, as we have seen, that the Maiden goes right on deceiving him, this demon-lover. She pretends to be death itself, she pretends to be full of flowers, and looking out the window, seeing, seeing. In truth, however, she has tried to sweeten herself with honey, and to don birds' feathers! Does she not become like a bird herself, a spirit which can soar just as love, a bird with feathers, soars in the spiritual world? Love itself is deceived by Death, we are told. And man can become aware of his spiritual nature, and deceive the immortality of love itself.

"At last, love is trapped, and burns. The soul has been bathed by the blood of passion, the life force of warmth and pain. But now love must suffer the hell of passion turned back upon itself. Is this not a true suffering? Should not that violent and cold and hard love of the tale transform itself in that fire? Should not that Devil, that rejected aspect of love in the Divine Itself undergo transformation? It should, but it is still languishing in Hell, in the fires of its own violence and misery. For love is still not accepted, valued, treasured, submitted to. It is merely banished.

"And so, Grandson of the Knight, you know something of this tale. I have taught you. But you, yourself, must descend into that hell of Bluebeard. You must go into that fire and speak with him, redeem him, and find out what it means that Love lies in a burning fire!"

Thus ended the interpretation, as best I can render it, of the Magician, and thus was I compelled to carry this tale onward. Thus was I, poor mortal and man, Grandson of the Knight, enjoined to be a hero like my father and grandfather. Much against my nature it was, to enter into the fire of the myth, the heat of this state, and encounter the Bluebeard, the rejected demon of the dark love!

Bluebeard

Having spoken these words of interpretation and exhortation, the Magician's form, already only vague in outline, melted altogether into the green and yellow, the brown and red of the forest, all darkening and softening. Light faded and, as darkness covered all that was visible, I began to feel things, to hear things and, even, to touch things. In short, other senses as well as sight were awakened. I thought: this is right; for just as that demon God of Love made his presence felt by "touching," by reaching into the marrow of the bones, it is meet that I not only "see" with my Logos light of consciousness, but that I feel and sense and touch and be touched, if I wish to learn about his reality. I therefore submitted myself to experience whatever might occur.

I felt the cool of evening as a moist breeze which pleasurably tingled the perspiration on my forehead into wavelets of shivering pores. But then it got cold. I breathed in the frisiac smell of scented coolness, and the green-smell of nature, too, but then it grew heavy and musky, as if from decayed flowers and over-damp. I heard the soft sounds of wind-in-trees, of small animal movements, of heartening water stream. But then I heard ghost sounds and wild animal sounds, and I grew afraid. The senses gave me fewer pleasurable messages and more painful ones. I was also receiving less and less light. Finally, there was total darkness. The ghost-sounds became horrible cries; the smells became the stench of skunk, of privies, of pitch; the cold became a pain and bite of pinched flesh, of hurt nose and ears. My senses from within began to send bad messages as well: my muscles were sore and aching; my belly growled in hunger and fear at the same time; the residue of dried sweat, of unbathed flesh, was added to by traces of my own feces, urine, flatus. I stank to myself. So, from inside and out there was bad hearing, bad feeling, bad smelling. And, withall, bad thoughts and fantasies, fear.

Thus was I prepared for the living presence of the demon God of Love. Now I saw him. Suddenly, in the midst of the darkness, there appeared a circle of fire, surrounding a dark figure slumped on the ground, huddled up as if a wounded animal, a retreated and withdrawn soul. He was not hurt by the fire; indeed, rather than in a fire-hell as I was led to expect, I saw a figure protected and warmed by it. He, at least, was free of the cold that I had been suffering from.

I drew close to the fire and felt warmed by it. I noticed that the figure was a dwarf, and not the huge, dark man of my imagination. His upper body was large, but his limbs were small, his legs particularly. He looked to be powerful of arm and chest, but weak of leg and foot. He looked neither up nor out. Rather he was so closed up that he seemed to be fully inside of himself. When I called to him, he did not seem to hear me; whether this was because of the hooting racket of ghost-sounds all around us or because of his deafness, I did not know.

Nor did I know how to contact this figure, this dwarf, this demon. I knew that the Magician, who had been my friend and guide, meant me to encounter this demon, but I did not know how. I smiled then, for once again I felt a spiritual connection with my grandfather, the Knight. Was he not summoned and guided by an Angel, just as I was by a Magician? Did he not find himself confronted with Gods and Demons, as did I? Did he not have to use his wits, his feelings, all his powers, in order to cope with them? Did he not have to find and experience his individuality, his wholeness, his God? Thus, of course, must I, who wanted an understanding of love and life. But my wholeness and individuality, I recognized, would be different from that of my grandfather, the Knight, and my father, the Son of the Knight. I had to find my own way in it, even though, unlike them, I was no Hero.

I resolved, therefore, to get closer to this demon-God, if such he was. I needed only to brave the fire. In truth, this was no heroic act for the fire was no wider than a hedge, and the flames no higher than a large dog. I could even leap over it without too much difficulty. This I did. I stood back, ran a few steps, leapt over the flames and found myself inside the circle with the demon-God.

The most dramatic change was that of silence. As I penetrated the circle of the demon, all sounds, all ghost-noises, all whirlings of winds, all cries of pain vanished. There was silence. Now I noticed that the fire was very warming. My ears and nose thawed quickly. The hardened dirt-sweat melted and I felt only my warm-blooded body. I was natural and at home. Even the bad smells vanished. What had been the stink of skunk, now seemed like only a pleasant and somewhat pungent man-smell. Whatever was left of the stench of feces, of urine and sweat, were now gone or covered over by the pleasant smell of wood burning, as if in a hearth or fireplace.

I knew that I was in the magic circle of the demon-God of love and, to be sure, this was no terror that I was experiencing, but rather the transformation of horror into pleasantness, of evil into good.

The dwarf looked up at me. He seemed sad, with deep eyes, knowing much.

"It has been ever so," said he. "Men think that love will bring pain and destruction, that the love in the flesh has in it the seeds of horror and terror. The truth is that once in the full precincts of love, one is redeemed, the terrors assuaged, the evils transformed."

"What you say is true, Demon of Love, if such you are, for I have experienced such redemption, such transformation, in love. But I have also experienced the hells, the terrors, the dismemberments. And, if men think that love is also hell, then they are right, too."

The Demon put his head down and folded himself back in upon himself. He wrapped himself more fully and closely in the dark cloak of which I had been unaware until that moment. He closed himself off from me, but not for long. A few moments later, he pulled away his cloak and there was revealed before me a figure of death, a skull such as that portrayed in the tale of Bluebeard that the Magician had related to me. The skull kept its form for only a moment and then metamorphosed into a most fierce and frightening face of a dark man, more as tradition had represented Bluebeard himself, a face violent and cruel, vicious and bitter. I held my ground, not fleeing before these transformations, and a final face revealed itself. This time, I saw a figure in great pain, one suffering fires of hell, but from inside himself. He did not—or could not—cry out, nor make a sound, but his eyes were those of agony, itself. Once again the horrible smells, the terrifying sounds, the creeping sensations, overcame me, and they all seemed to come from this demon. I cringed, and withdrew.

In my withdrawal, however, I understood something. I grasped something that perhaps this demon of love was trying to tell me. Was he not trying to say that there was, indeed—though he did not first speak of it—an agony of love, a horror and fear, a hell and dismemberment, just as everyone who had loved deeply and conflictedly had known? This awareness did not require words, for it was an experience of love in the flesh, in the living and being, in the fire of life. Did he not also say, in words, that there is also redemption, there is beauty and fulfillment in love and that everyone knows that, too. That, after all, is why they seek love and value it. But I also realized that no one wants to be touched by the dark side of love, of jealousy, possessiveness, revenge—all the stinking, painful, conflict-ridden parts of love— and that the soul runs from that like the plague.

All these things I realized as I looked at this transforming wizard-dwarf, skull, terror-face. I understood, for so it came to me, what these changes meant. Dwarf, with his big chest and arms, small legs: Is not love an experience of the chest, of the heart, with its bigness of feeling? Does it not always rest on a poor and enfeebled footing, a questionable reality? Are not the arms, the embracing and containing of love always larger than the forms and vessels and containers for it, whether of institutions or of person? Such is love a dwarf!

And skull. Is not love a death's head? When one loves, does one not want to love for eternity, feel it as eternity, know it as eternity? And yet does not one fear that death will come, to oneself or the loved one? Is it not the worst thing in the world to imagine being alive when the loved one is dead? Remember the mourners in all the churches and temples! Remember how they look when they mourn the loss of one loved. Is it not horrible? And is not loving such a vulnerability to death?

And terror-face. Think of the brutalities done in the name of love. Think of how those who love each other hurt each other. Think of how when love is great, need is great, of how love hurts as well as heals, tears up as well as mends. Is not that terror-face of love known to us all?

These things I understood. But I understood them in terms of myself, of what love had done to me. I suddenly realized that I was sensitive only to myself, or more to myself than to the other, more than to love itself. I was what I hated most: self-involved. I sadly realized that it was love itself who was suffering. Love was dwarfed, was rejected and hurt. Love was death, and dies each time, a million deaths, whenever rejected and betrayed. Love was the terror born of bitterness, of frustration at lack of its fulfillment in every poor soul who has loved and been unfulfilled, or worse—has never loved nor been loved.

So, I now realized not my own suffering in love, nor the suffering of others in love, but the pain of love itself, the suffering of the demon-God of love, as he goes about, trying to participate in peoples' lives, trying to touch them, to be fed by them. In so doing, he does indeed welcome us to a great castle of riches, to the fulfillment of all our desires. But we disobey him, we do go against love, in a million ways. And perhaps we must embrace the fact that love also murders, dismembers, hurts, that love is horrible. Most of all, perhaps we must embrace him not for ourselves alone, but for the suffering of the demon-God himself.

With these feelings, I moved forward and embraced this dwarf, this terror, this demon. I felt great tenderness for him and his suffering. I knew how he felt to be heir to a great gift and fortune, eager to share this with men, needing also to be fed by them. I embraced Love, and touched Love, just as I had been so many times embraced and touched, dismembered and rejected, transformed to heaven and hell, by love.

I embraced Love, and felt him as a youth, as a cherub, even, small and peaceful, and I understood that there were those who knew love as a tender child. And he wept. I felt Love as a son to me, as a pained and rejected son who needed all of my warmth and love. And then I smiled. For I realized that Love needed my love! That insight came to me! Can you imagine it? The God of Love needs man's love! That overwhelmed me and it threw me flat upon my face! I called out to my grandfather, the Knight, and said that I knew something, found something, just as he had. My grandfather had found out that God, the God of Light, of Consciousness, of Logos, needed man's light and consciousness, and now I was finding out that God, the God of Love, of Relatedness, of Eros, needed man's love and relatedness! It was all so natural and spontaneous, and true. As if there truly was an order to things, not just chaotic chance.

It also came to me that this order must be similar to what the youngest daughter must have felt when she could look with compassion upon the dismembered limbs, upon the blood and gore. She looked carefully, arranged them in a natural way, and the wholeness was restored. Thus did I feel now, with this enlightenment about the God of Love.

I was deeply moved and rewarded by this chest-filling, dwarfing experience of love. I was filled to bursting with it, and dwarfed by the enormity of it: that the God of Love needed men's love. It was enough, I thought, but only almost. This "almost" was not the continuing proviso of which I have already spoken, that man is always greedy for more, more love, more light, more of everything, until he dies. Even greedy for more enlightenment until the last. It is not that "almost" of which I speak. No. The "almost" of which I speak has not to do with the chest-filling, the dwarfing, nor even the pain of love. I was unsatisfied with the violence of love.

The tale of Bluebeard had revealed love as an abbatoir, with its butchering violence, tearing asunder, blood and gore, hot rage and cold rage. The Magician explained—and I hardly needed the words of explanation since my own life had taught me such things in the flesh—that love and its conflicts of duty, of passion, were dismember-ing, were as horrible hells, as well as heavens of delight. The Magician said that, and I certainly believed it, knew it. But there was something more to the violence, the rage, the tearing apart, the power struggle in the story of the demon demanding submission, the daughter craftily and unfeelingly getting her revenge upon the demon love. There was something more heartless, violent, loveless, and sinister in all that. And I would not rest with a superficial explanation of this horror. I had seen too much violence, betrayal, senseless death, compassionless hurt of man for man, to rest with the skin-deep explanation of this violence in both Bluebeard and the Maiden who conquered him.

I turned again to the figure in the circle of fire. I had been meditating, reflecting, turned in upon myself for what seemed like a long time, but in the timeless place of closeness to the demon, it was probably only moments. When I wanted to address the demon, to question him, he was gone. He had vanished altogether. Not even an outline was there, as there had been when I had previously seen the Magician. Where had he gone? And what was the significance of this fading from sight of both Magician and Bluebeard, after one had truly grasped and felt their reality? Were love and magic so evanescent, so transient, that one could only see them in moments, and was then doomed—or perhaps lucky—to be out of sight of them?

I turned, then, to the circle of fire around me. It, too, was gone. I was sitting alone, on the ground in the forest. Night was replaced by day. A rainy, cold, sunless day it was. But quiet. No ghost-sounds, only the gentle fall of rain, and a light, tender breeze. No bad smells, only the moist-clean smell of freshness upon trees and flowers. No fear-terror-horror, only the quiet, timeless feeling of no-mind, in the meditation of stillness. No hunger-need, only a free-floating openness to fantasy or to life.

In that quiet state, my thoughts wandered back to memories of the stories of my Grandfather, the Knight, of how he would come to just such a forest and meditate, of how he heard in such a place the soft singing of the Daughter of the Goddess, the Granddaughter of the Great Goddess, and of how he, and they, were raped and overrun in just such a place. Poor man, and poor women, too, tied up, humiliated, torn apart, by men and demons, by the violence of life itself. But finally, were they not affrighted by the rage of the Great Goddess, of Mother Nature Herself, furious at the rule of men, of the male principle of reason, power, science? Thus it had been for my Grandfather. But he had lived in a timeless age, a heroic age, an age of Knights and of a quest. My age was no such time, there was no such easy access to Gods and Goddesses—except, of course, for the demon, Love. And I had known about love, its demonism, its violence and horror. I had been raped, too, but differently from my Grandfather.

As I sat musing in that place, so like the forest of my Grandfather, I wondered about the violence anew. What was that power struggle?

Bluebeard and the Muses: Kleio

As I sat meditating upon this experience of violence, knowing that life—and men—do very heartless and vicious things, I was aware that there is an unanswered question about cruelty and insensitivity, done even in the name of love. As I sat meditating upon this fact, I found myself curled up, turned in upon myself. I was withdrawn and cold in the misty rain; I was weak and inept in the chill wind; I found myself like a dwarf. I looked down upon my legs and saw them weak and fragile. I looked at my chest and saw it big, but capable only of heaving, of large breaths. I saw my arms long, like an ape's, and I embraced myself. I turned in upon myself, just as had the God of Love. And I asked myself—not God, not others, just myself: Why the horror, done in life, by others, by me? Why?

For an answer, I gave myself only tears and sobs. For answer, I only wept. For answer, I felt only a rack of pain, a heaving chest, wet eyes, torn heart. For answer, I had no answer.

I rocked myself and wept. I hugged myself and hummed. I sang myself a lullaby, as if I were a father-mother to myself; as if I were comforting myself for the pain and horror of life and love, both giving and receiving. Quiet, quiet, Grandson of the Knight, I said to myself, quiet, quiet. You live, it is enough; you love, it is enough.

As I rocked myself and stilled myself with humming, I heard another humming. It was a female voice, as if in harmony with the remembered fragment of childsong that I was singing. The voice echoed mine, went around mine, penetrated mine, made mine deeper and richer, as if it were an organ. The voice was sweeter, then louder, then more resonant. I stopped my song, astonished. The voice stopped too. I looked around to see where this singing creature could be. I saw no one. I waited quietly. The voice did not resume. I began singing again, the voice resumed. I stopped; it stopped. A puzzle.

Now there appeared, once again, the figure of the Magician. He was big and gorgeously dressed. He looked at me and laughed—not sneeringly or hurtfully, but with a certain pleasure at my perplexity and astonishment. I sighed, remembering once more the plight of my Grandfather with his Angel, of always being somehow thrown down, puzzled, humiliated. What a fate for our family, I thought. Then I smiled, too, and laughed.

The Magician spoke softly to me, and kindly, as if he knew that I had suffered much and that soft words and kind words were needed to dull the pain of ghost-cries, witch-screams, and tear-sobs that had been in my ears.

"Grandson of the Knight," the Magician said, "You know that voice. You have heard it. So did your Father, the Son of the Knight, and your Grandfather, the Knight. That voice is the same as that heard by the Knight in his forest, she that sang so sweetly in many tongues, in many registers. That voice is the same as that which spoke to your father, the Son of the Knight, as Shepherd and Swineherd, the voice that made him speak as poet. It is the same voice that came to him from Lancelot of the Song, of the Knight at the lake where "no birds sing." You know that voice, for you have heard it, through them. But now, having suffered much, you will hear it for yourself. You, yourself, will hear and speak with that voice, just as they did. But you will know, even more than they, who that voice is, what it is. Because of your struggle with love, because of your pain, because of your dogged persistence, just as they, and, above all, because of your humanity, your longing to love, and not only to know.

"The voice" continued the Magician, "is not just one voice. It is sometimes two, often three, and, indeed, eight or nine. For the voice is that which has been called Muse. It is the voice of the soul, of the psyche which sings in response to pain and deep hurt. It is the voice which sings and speaks when touched by love. Know, now, the secret: the voice is that of the wives of Bluebeard! Those maidens, those girls, those three and eight and nine wives of the demon-man-God are none other than the Muses, known by every man whose soul has been 'touched' by the demon-God! The daughters are the maidens, the speakers who are trapped and broken by the God, but also inspired by him. And they, in turn, inspire man to speak, to sing, to proclaim. For such a man must speak and proclaim. He—like you—is silenced and reduced to inarticulate weeping. From this, from the breakage of ego, of self, of man, comes the inspiration of God. And the soul speaks. Hear it speak. Hear the voice and attend!"

The Magician left off from speaking. His handsome and smiling countenance faded once more, until there was only a vague form and then nothing. Instead, there appeared a light-complexioned, young woman with lighter hair. She seemed northern, cool and frozen, serious. Very beautiful, quietly intense, eyes deep, far-seeing. She spoke in clipped tongue, short.

"Kleio, my name, 'giver of fame.' But rhymer am I not. For fame am I, and history, too. All know me. All poets do, and writers, and artists and musicians. All those who seek for fame, for recognition, for immortality. As soon as touched by that dark Blue-God, as soon as words, or images, or musical sounds begin to flow, they think of me. History am I, the story of the past. Fame am I, the story carried into the future. All long for me."

I heard Kleio's self-introduction, and believed it. I knew of what she spoke, could not deny it. And she was attractive indeed. How woo her, how gain her love, her care? She, the first of the Muses, the first of the soul-images to arise when the Blue-God of love-passion is touched. What to do with her? How win her, how please her?

"Do not ask, Grandson of the Knight," Kleio said, knowing my thoughts, of course. "Fame comes unbidden, fame comes unsought. It comes as dark fame, too, you know. Do you not know that fame is history? That history is rewritten all the time? Think of it. Do you not rewrite the facts of your life with each passing decade? Do you not understand, hence remember, differently each big event of childhood and youth, of adulthood and age? Is not history rewritten with each breath?"

"It is true, Muse Kleio," I said. "But still, there are facts, there are unerasable events, unforgettable people, unchangeable transitions. There is eternity, even though re-interpreted. And there is fame, undeserved at times. And there is anonymity, undeserved, too."

I did not know why I needed to argue with the Muse. I smiled, for I realized that I was probably doing exactly the wrong thing if I wished to woo this Muse of history and fame. Arguing with history, arguing with a giver of fame seemed likely to produce results opposite from that which one intends.

"But perhaps you are getting just what you intend," said Kleio. "Perhaps you wish to have fame reject you, pass you by." Kleio said these words matter-of-factly, not assertively, but as a possible 'just-so.' I reflected: perhaps she was right. If so, why did I undermine myself, argue with history and fame, so as to preclude its acceptance and recognition? Was it because I guessed, as the famous have said, that once one has fame one sacrifices privacy? Was it because I secretly knew that I was not worthy of fame? Was it because I knew the worth of myself was such that it merited nothing of the sort? Or was it that I enjoyed re-creating history in my mind, just as I enjoyed re-creating my past, and that this play of imagination would be taken away if I were famous? The famous have to be serious and responsible after all, do they not?

The Muse turned away from these speculations. She said, "You are not ready yet." Now I asked her straight-out. "Why, Mistress Muse,

Kleio of fame, why am I not ready?"

But Kleio would not answer. She turned away. Her blond hair covered her face, and she turned in upon herself, as did the God of Love as Dwarf, as did I, in my pain and need of a mother-father to comfort me. She turned in upon herself and did not speak. I sat near her for some time, and then moved away. I could not look upon this creature, this beautiful being, as if she were some stone, devoid of feeling or care. I could not sit and suffer. I needed to walk, to see the trees and flowers, the moist places where the rain had fallen. As I walked, I knew that just such a place was one where my Grandfather had walked. I knew that he had met this Muse, or one like her, and had been raped by the Goddess. I knew, too, that he had sat with the Goddess, in stillness, in quiet, in pain. He had absorbed her pain, as well as his own. But that was my Grandfather, the Hero. That was the Knight, of no time and place and of every time and place, for he was timeless and of eternity, though real and concrete, my ancestor. But I did not want to dwell in pain any longer. I had had enough pain in my life. I had had enough pain in my multiplicity of loves. I had had enough pain of rejection, of misunderstanding. I did not want to follow my Grandfather's lead and bow down to the pain, the violence and cruelty.

Nor was I like my father, the Son of the Knight. He, poor thing, had known no mother, was not loved as he should have been, and had to wander and find himself, who he was. I was not like that. I was loved, had loved. I needed only, perhaps, to love myself better, to embrace myself as the Dwarf-God had done, as I had done in my sadness and now . . . I thought once again of the Muse . . . as she was now doing Herself. I hastened my steps and returned to the place where I had seen the Muse, Kleio.

There she was, sitting now with arms crossed in front of her chest, embracing herself, but now looking square at me, and smiling. I smiled, too, but somewhat wanly, since I did not know why she was smiling, or, indeed, why I was smiling.

"Smile, Grandson of the Knight," she commanded. "Smile!" Then she started to laugh aloud. "Do you think that fame is merited? That history rewards the just? That only what is true and beautiful survives?" She laughed once more, now uproariously. I did not know why she laughed so hard, as if she had some private joke. I only thought that I knew that there were those who were great who had fame, and there were those of no greatness who had it also. And vice versa. But why this talk? Why was I confronted, and puzzled, and a bit foolish? I felt a little ill in my stomach. I sat down and started to weep, not having any idea why I was doing so. I also tried to embrace myself as she had done. I found it empty, without pleasure or solace . . . I could not embrace myself with pleasure. . . .

A small light began to fall upon me. I repeated my own thoughts in words: I COULD NOT EMBRACE MYSELF WITH PLEASURE. Deep thought this. I did not like myself, please myself, enjoy myself. What a strange and true thing to find out. I knew that this was the "just so" of which she hinted before. Of all my talk of love, of all my search and questioning of love, of all my battle, encounter, struggle with love, I could not love myself. And, because of that, I needed fame. With fame, I could find, perhaps, that I was worthy of love, of adoration, even. For, if so many could love me, adore me, value me, then I was surely worthy of love, is that not so? How sad for me! How sad for anyone in such a predicament! But, I thought, is this the situation of all those who seek fame? Do all those who seek the plaudits of the world feel, deep down, that they cannot love themselves? I suspect so. Recognition, yes, that is natural—everyone wants that from another, or many others. But fame? That is the longing of those who do not love themselves. "Kleio," I said, now turning to the Muse, who sat looking at me with a great smile, just as she had a moment before, "Kleio, is it true? Do those who seek fame, who seek your aid, who seek your blessing, even, limit themselves just to those who do not love themselves?"

Kleio nodded, still maintaining that wide smile that seemed to me to be strange, beside the point, unnatural. . . . I did not know what word to use for that strange smile. It was just inappropriate, I thought.

"That is right, Grandson of the Knight," said Kleio. "Inappropriate. That is the word. That is my smile. That is the smile of fame. That is the thing that drives men to puzzle with the Muse, describe the Muse, paint the Muse, fight the Muse, embrace the Muse, love the Muse: the Inappropriate. The Mad, the Insane, the Irrational. Those men touched by the God . . . or by the Goddess . . . have to do that. They just have to. As your Grandfather did, as your Father did, as you must. But you, poor Grandson of the Knight, you poor, sweet, dear man, you have hit on something that they did not know. You have found out that the search for fame is because one does not love oneself, has no fame in one's own house, so to speak. Queer, isn't it? Strange. One might say, 'Inappropriate,' no? Your Grandfather had lost his God, had no God, had to find his God, but just because he was such a total self, a total mother-father, and such a whole man. And you, Grandson of the Knight, you have had to search for the meaning of love, the quality of love, just because you have loved so much, been loved so much, yet have not loved yourself. 'Inappropriate,' paradoxical, even. But such is the curse of the Muse, of the

God. Welcome, Grandson of the Knight! I dub thee Knight number III, scion of the generations, Seeker, like Father and Grandfather, and particular friend of the Muse!

"Embrace me, Knight III, for you are my friend, my spouse, and my lover! I laugh, for I embrace you, I love you and will bring you fame! And you will know, well enough, that love and fame are different indeed!"

I laughed, too, but not so freely as did the Muse. I was glad to be embraced by her, though not so sure that I would, thereby, become famous. I was, however, dazzled enough by the realization of the statement that the seeking of fame is because one does not love oneself, and that the Muse is the Goddess of the "Inappropriate," the smile that forces one deeper, further, better! That was enough. So, I reached forward to embrace this Goddess, this Kleio of history. She embraced me, but turned her cheek to mine, and kept her lower part from me, still laughing. "Not yet, my dear, not yet," she said. "First you must meet my sisters."

Having said that much, she gave me a sisterly peck upon the cheek and vanished. The peck upon the cheek which she gave me also gave me a slow kind of enlightenment. I realized that Kleio, Muse of History, had also touched me in my desire to explore the past, to go into Purgatory and Heaven and Hell of Myth, of Imagination, of History, as well, in order to know the truth, to ascertain the totality of what the whole truth was, like a scientist, or like a poet, or like . . . and here, I, too, smiled, as did the Muse, like a Seeker, which were my Father and Grandfather. Seekers follow the Muse, I saw. Seekers after truth, after reconciling the paradox, straightening the Inappropriate smile. Kleio, my darling Goddess, my sister, she of the Inappropriate Smile! I recalled now, as would anyone with such a thought, the painting of Da Vinci, and knew who, indeed, Mona Lisa really was: the Muse of the Inappropriate Smile; the Muse-Goddess who pushed and inspired that man to be artist, scientist, poet. And all he tried to do, I realized, was to straighten the Inappropriate Smile!

I laughed aloud and welcomed myself to the fraternity of Seekers, to the foolish men of the Inappropriate Smile! I embraced myself as Knight III and laughed. Well, I thought, if I cannot love myself, I can laugh at myself, and call myself a brother of the Seekers!

Muses II: Euterpe

Having been kissed by Kleio, Muse of Fame and History—kissed, mind you, not embraced totally—I felt a certain joy and pleasure, an acceptance of myself. I even was ready to settle for a little fame until such time as I could love myself better! I also smiled at the realization that the touch of the Muse had brought me enlightenment, but different from that which I had experienced with Don Juan, or with Bluebeard, himself. I now found a certain confidence in myself, however, as a brother to seekers, and a worthy descendant of my father and grandfather.

So it was not surprising that I did not have to wait very long for the appearance of the second Muse, without even needing the intervention or aid of the Magician. The second Muse, Euterpe, "Giver of Joy," appeared just at the spot where Kleio had vanished. She, too, was light of complexion and hair, though darker of eye. Where Kleio had seemed Northern (Scandinavian, maybe, or German), Euterpe seemed Northwestern (English, perhaps, or Irish). She appeared light and gay, holding her flute, but not playing it. Then, just as she appeared, she vanished. Just like that. No apparent reason, no cause that I could see. How like joy, I thought, she appears for a moment, gives you a taste of good things, and then vanishes without leaving a trace of awareness of how she came, why she went, where she went, or when she will come back. And then I laughed. These Muses, I thought, are making me more a philosopher than a poet! Their comings and goings make me reflect, rather than express in song. My father could do that rather well, I know. Perhaps he was meant to be the poet, and I a philosopher. But, no matter, I shall not wait to see if Joy in the form Euterpe returns. No, I shall go about my business. Did not someone say, a wise man, I think, that one does not seek after joy, it just comes to one, unbidden? I think he was right. In any case, this I will do, be about my business until the Muse returns.

No sooner had I decided to be about my business, to attend to all the duties and responsibilities one has in daily life, when I was yanked back to the place in the forest. I grew annoyed, wondering if this was the sort of thing that drove my grandfather to his fits of rage. If the God was a nuisance in His demands and complexity, the same could be said of the Muses, I thought.

Yanked back to the forest by tugs which pulled me away from my responsibilities, I expectantly looked around for Euterpe, the Giver of Joy. But no Euterpe. I sighed deeply. It was no joke, now. The frustration led to an awareness that Joy, like Kleio's smile of fame and history, is irrational. Joy pulls one away from duty and responsibility and then drops one. Or, perhaps, the need for Joy pulls and tugs, but does not necessarily fulfill. So I sat and did nothing . . . Is that not how it is, sometimes? One is pulled away from the tugs of responsibility and duty, but then one cannot really go with the joy. Or is it, as it now was with me, that Joy pulls but does not come to one? Bah . . . I was simply growing dull with my thoughts, and not a bit joyous. Go, then, seek joy among friends, I thought. The Muse abandons you, then do not be so passive! There is joy in friendship, in marriage, in all those deep relations of the soul; I can go there, and not only await the Muse to appear, to inspire!

At that moment, the Muse, Euterpe, re-appeared and leaped into the air with a quick sort of Irish jig, saying, "Bravo! Bravo, Knight III, Bravo, Bravo!" With that bit of approval, she vanished once again. And so, I accepted her vanishing, and I went off to seek joy among my friends.

The joy that I sought, however, was not forthcoming. I went to a friend whom I loved, with the prospect of just being together, of walking together, of a warmth in each other's company. Instead, I received from my friend a litany of troubles, and a repeated list of grievances of where I had done harm. I listened to this for a time, and began to feel myself grow pale, my muscles to ache with tension and soreness, my belly and heart to feel a bleeding of a wound reopened. And this more so, since for the previous several times I had seen this person, I had listened to the list, had tried to repair the hurts, caused by me or not. But now I could stand no more, and I went off, saying that I felt as if a large pail of refuse had been dumped in my face. I felt strongly the one-sidedness of this relationship at this time: we shared in her pain and turmoil, her feelings, and I gave solace and understanding as I could. She wanted both parent and friend, but gave back only in the limited doses of which she had energy. I understood, but I was wounded, bleeding, and returned to the forest where I had seen the Muse.

I sat upon the stump of a tree and held my belly and wept. There was no joy. Euterpe was not to be found with my friend that day. And whenever such joy was to be found, it was paid for dearly in subsequent pain and loss. "Well, Euterpe," I said aloud, "Where are you? Where is joy in the midst of such pain of frustration, despair and repeated re-opening of wounds?"

"You seek joy in the wrong places," said a voice from somewhere behind the trees. "You know that there is darkness there, and that joy is not a frequenter of that place and that person. It has always been so."

I assumed that this was the voice of Euterpe, though I did not see her. I nodded my head in agreement with what she said. The particular relationship, it is true, had brought me much darkness and challenge, but little joy. Perhaps, I did seek Euterpe in the wrong places.

"Where then, Euterpe, if such it be who speaks to me from behind the trees—where then can I find joy?"

"In yourself, Knight III, in yourself."

"But how, Euterpe?"

"Just so, Knight III."

The voice then took on substance and I saw, once more, the figure of Euterpe. Her blond hair was long and loose, her dark eyes were soft and wet now. She held a flute and began to play. She improvised a sad tune, doleful and melancholy. Was this Euterpe, the Muse of Joy? To sing so sadly? She sang this song:

> Joy is my name
> Euterpe my fame.
> All seek me.
> All find me.
> But moments alone.
> Alone.

I did not like her words or her song and felt only my pain and my bleeding. "I am in terrible pain and I cannot express myself or hear your song . . . Help!" I called.

At that moment, another friend came by and knocked on my door. This friend, a man, had had a sad and bitter life, was often depressed and frustrated. He had often consulted me on matters of his sadness and failures. Earlier that same day, I had been walking in the street with another acquaintance and had seen my sad friend coming toward us. Remembering how hurt the latter had been at a previous encounter, when he had felt slighted and affronted by a less than cordial greeting from me, I openly and effusively embraced him, laughing all the while, knowing that both of us were aware of his previous complaint. But now my sad friend was knocking on my door. He came in to say that he did not know why, but that my cordial and playful greeting of him had made him feel very good indeed, had given him much joy, and that he was calling to express his gratitude! I replied that I was very happy for this, had worried that I might have embarrassed him, and that his taking the trouble to thank me gave me, in turn, much pleasure. He thereupon left and I felt a much reduced pain. My cry for help had been answered by him, by the man whom I had helped.

What did this mean? Help came from one whom I had helped. Should I try to get solace from my pain from she who had wounded me? I looked at Euterpe, hoping for an answer. But she only stared at me with her great dark eyes, soft and wet, not joyful at all. The pain in her eyes distressed me and I reached over to her, to comfort her. That joy should be saddened seemed strange, unnatural, even, but there it was.

I took Joy's flute and tried to play to her. I thought of the painting by Rembrandt of David playing the harp before King Saul, while the latter wept and wiped an eye with his drape. What a magnificent painting it was! I tried to play this flute to the sad Euterpe, but found that I could not. Try as I might, no tune came out of the flute as I played. So, I could not be David to this Queen of Joy who was sad. I, myself, was sad like the King, and could give no solace.

"Euterpe," I said, "I can give no solace, I can give no joy. I need it. Joy came to me for a moment where I had given joy and care. But not enough. I do not know where to find it inside myself. I do not know where."

For reply, Euterpe just looked on sadly, saying nothing. I put my head in her lap and wept, feeling her physical warmth, but no comfort. I felt no joy from Joy. I embraced myself once more, and tried mightily to give myself comfort. I squeezed hard. To my surprise, a very tiny creature then walked out of my mouth. It was a fully formed woman, a very close replica, indeed, of Euterpe herself, but no bigger than my middle finger.

This little figure, as I say, walked out of my mouth, as if she had come from my belly itself, and jumped onto my outstretched hand. She looked up at me and smiled, then yawned.

"I have just been born," she said, "That is why I am yawning. It was a hard job, getting born from inside you that way, and I am sorry if I have caused you lots of pain. But births are like that, as every woman knows—and some men do, too—and it can't be helped. Anyway, here I am, and we can have some fun."

Thereupon this little creature, who was clearly my own, personal, small and just born capacity for joy from myself alone, did a little dance of joy for me. She smiled and sang and danced. She hopped around, popping into my ear, my nose, my mouth. She made me smile, too, just by her presence. No words, even. I had now witnessed the birth of Joy in myself! I looked, now, to the larger Muse, the Goddess Euterpe, who was large as life, and, once again, smiling and happy. She nodded to me, and needed to say nothing. I realized that she was painfully quiet and not helping because I needed to give birth to a Euterpe of joy in myself, and not be dependent upon her. She was with me, in her silence and sharing of pain. So Joy was a good mother and sister; she let me find and give birth to joy within myself. A great gift of self, a great gift of joy. And I was surprised by Joy, and knew that it comes like that, unexpected, from without, and that I had now given birth to her from within. She would have to grow, this little Euterpe from within, but her presence alone made me smile.

Muses III: Melpomene, Terpsichore & Erato

My encounter with Joy, and the birth of the little "joy" within me was welcome, but I knew that I had to move onward. I was aware by now that I was engaged in an encounter with the Muse, or Muses, and that I was going to meet them, one by one, until I could learn from them, or make my peace with them, or love them, feel them, unite with them, just as Bluebeard had; but no, better than Bluebeard had, because I would have to redeem-be-redeemed by them, just as Bluebeard needed to redeem-be-redeemed by me. I intuited that this encounter with the Muses would be like a circumambulation of the world, a succession of compass points. I had gone North with Kleio for fame and history, and Northwest with Euterpe for joy. I expected, therefore, that now I would go West and meet the Muse of Comedy.

I was surprised, therefore, when there appeared in the forest a handsome woman, dark-brown of hair, green of eye, and clearly of the Mediterranean climes, from Spain, say, or Italy. But her handsome face was marred by a sadness of eye and even more by a turning downwards of her mouth. There were lines there which bespoke sadness, bitterness, even tragedy. Now I knew the Muse with whom I was in contact: it was Melpomene, "the singer," Muse of Tragedy.

Melpomene looked at me sadly, with bitterness. Was there reproach in her eyes? Was she finding me at fault? Was I, were all men, was life, the fault? Did tragedy always look like that? For answer, Melpomene began to sing those deeply sad and moving Flamencan songs, those gypsy calls from throat and belly which combine the lyricism of Moors, the wailing cries of Jews endlessly persecuted, the passion of Spaniards, and the gypsy drone with haunts of India. What a wailing, singing, crying calling thing is that! That is tragedy expressing itself, knowing itself, calling out in the knowing, but expecting no surcease, no help, no relief. Perpetual pain, feeding on itself.

I sat down and wept, knowing this voice of Tragedy, knowing its Flamenco flame in my soul and my life. What else is to be done with Tragedy, Muse of Life?

The soul calls out its cries in the tragedy of life, in the playing out of those dramas which end in frustration, in bitterness, in the loneliness of old people, in the loss of vitality, of sapped strength, of withered beauty, of drained life, ending in the dry brittleness of emptiness, sorrow and death. Life is a fatal disease, say the pessimists; you die a little every day. And they are right, of course.

But life is more than that, I said to myself. I spoke out against my own pessimism. Not only is there tragedy in life, there is also joy and fulfillment. There is gaiety, growth, and deepening. At every point of my life I am glad that I am where I am; I do not wish to go back to any point and live it again. That must indicate that I have lived my life, have accepted my tragedies, that I realize that much tragedy is simply life unlived, grown sour with unfulfillment. Thus say I, to tragedy, to the Muse, to Melpomene, the singer, the soul who lives in South and Southwest.

She looked back, did Melpomene. She looked back at me. For answer, there were no words. Nor did she sing anymore. She merely looked with sad, bitter eyes at me. Without words, I came forward and put my tongue to those sad, bitter eyes. I licked away the tears. I put my tongue to those dark engraved lines which moved down from nose to mouth, licked away at the lines of age and bitterness. It matters not how they were caused, by me or by another. It matters not to my soul if I have inflicted my own tragedy upon myself or if they are to be blamed on another. What matters is that I lick up the tears of my own suffering; that I accept and soften the lines of anger and bitterness and frustration of my soul, whether from my own hands or from another. I accept my Muse within, I accept my tragedy, my Melpomene. You are within, great Goddess, great Muse! Though I do not sing with your voice, I hear you. Though my words do not wail in the fiery Arabic-Hebrew-Spanish-Hindu magnificence of your fantastic Gypsy being, I know you within me! I lick your pain and adore you. And now I reveal to you—and to myself—the secret joy of tragedy: Tragedy does indeed feed upon itself. I feed upon my pain, I transform it into song, into depth, into growth. I grow handsome with it; I grow attractive with it; I grow deep with it; I grow! That is the secret of Tragedy, Oh Muse! We both know it!

Having said these words to the Muse—and to myself—and having licked away the tears of pain, the lines of anger and bitterness, I half expected to see her face change. I thought the lines would soften, the eyes shine, the tears turn hardness into softness. And they did do that for a moment, but only for a moment. But then, when I thought that Tragedy might change, there came back into my life the same friend who had treated me callously and bitterly, the one with whom I was forced to find Joy back inside myself. And now, it was similar: a focusing upon self, a non-giving, a withdrawal, leaving me hurt, enraged.

How now to cope with my own bitterness and rage, my own tragedy of life? How now to lick away, from myself in my pain, my own downturned mouth, my own wet or enraged eyes? I have done this for others so much in the past. I have also done this for myself, but in ways which were not enough, not successful. Why? They were always designed to help. It has always been so: one loses one's self in the help of another's tragedy, losing one's need for help and care; or, one loses the other in the care for one's self. The Tragedy: one is either together and lost; or apart and lonely.

That is the Tragedy of Life: Either/Or: I am lost in my uniting with another or I am lonely in uniting with myself. Is that your message, Melpomene? Is that what your silence wants to communicate?

No answer. And within me I feel the silent opposites of rage and need, of love and hate, warring. They fight and I, poor I, am the battleground. I, poor I, am the tragedy. Let me wail like a gypsy, let me wail and sing a Flamencan song!

I wailed for a time, was bitter for a time, was hard and sentimental by turns, dryly sour and sweetly self-pitying until—at last—I said to myself to leave off from tragedy. I had enough of tragedy, of despair, of listening to complaints, my own and others, of hearing the impossibilities of life, of the downturned mouth of darkness. Enough of that mask, said I, enough!

And then, as if in answer to my silent command, my silent rejection of the endless Musings about Tragedy, the final saying No to Melpomene, there appeared before me a very different creature indeed. Without needing to be informed, I knew at once that this was Terpsichore, "She who enjoys Dancing," she of the lyre and the lyric poetry of flesh moving, in rhythm. I knew that Terpsichore was here not as a consequence of any great intuition on my part, for anyone would know it, anyone who had a taste for dance, for movement, for the sensual gyrations of flesh in motion. There, before me, was a gorgeous creature from a truly Southern clime, for she was black and comely, dark of hair and eye and skin. She moved with a natural grace, not only like a leopard or panther—for of course she moved like that as well—but more like a human being, a woman after all, who knew and enjoyed the vitality in herself, the flow of life, the pleasure of living.

She did not speak to me, nor did I need her to. I felt that an answer to Tragedy, an answer to Melpomene, was to be found in her sister, Terpsichore. An answer to pain and grief and to the end of words, an end of complaining and bitterness is to go with the movement of life, the pleasure of the wordless gestures of the life flow. So, I got up and danced, wordlessly, with Terpsichore. It was of no importance

whether I danced well or not; it was of no importance that I expressed
myself beautifully or badly. What mattered was that I went with the
flow of life, that I moved with it, that my own gestures came out of
me, naturally. So, I, too, became like a leopard, or a panther, or
better yet, like a human being, who moved from within himself, who
danced the dance of life while listening to his inner rhythms, his inner
flow and lived from there, from bones and muscles and skin, and
danced with the Muse. End of Musings, beginning of the Muse-dance.
End of reflection on Tragedy, beginning of the living, the active living
of life.

Terpsichore continued her dancing, but now, beneath her, in that
rain-swept forest, there appeared what looked like a compass or map
of the world. The circle etched itself and Terpsichore began to change
shape and color. She moved from her Southern place of African heat
and sensual pleasure, from the natural dance of the expressiveness of
life, up and over. She danced back and forth between Greece and
Israel, finally settling in the Holy Land itself. The settling transformed
her: Terpsichore had changed her skin from black to olive, her hair
from black to dark red, her eyes—a dark-dark brown remained the
same. But now Terpsichore was no longer Terpsichore: the Muse had
changed. Just as tragedy gave way to the joy of expression, Terpsichore
gave way to Erato, "Awakener of Desire," Muse, too, of the Dance.
But here was a different dance. Not the dance of expression, of the
movement of life in the bones and muscle and skin, now was the
Dance of Desire. The rain-forest changed, too. Now there was a
dryness, a desert, a hotness. Is desire always from a desert, a hotness,
a longing for water? But no, for there were also trees of sweet odor:
oranges and lemons, dates and pomegranates. There was sweetness
and a dry, soft warmth of night air, of moon with gentle coolness.
And now, the dance of Erato was different. Here the movement was
one of awakening, not expressing. She was not alive to the currents
inside herself, she was not moving as the life force moved within her,
no. She stood very still and gazed deeply at me. She moved her hands
toward me, magnetically, as if to awaken me, awaken a desire in me,
but for what? For life? For love? But I . . . I was dry. Drier still than
any desert. I had been drained by tragedy, exhausted by Terpsichore,
and now I was dry. I could not be awakened. Nay, I wanted not to
be awakened. Let me be dead, I thought, for life and awakening and
desire mean pain. They mean frustration as much as fulfillment, agony
as much as pleasure, impotence as well as power. Better, perhaps, to
be unawakened, be a dead virgin in the life of desire than to experience
all the opposites as the battlefield of life . . . I was worn out. I resisted
life, I resisted desire, I resisted awakening. So be it. Erato, awakener

of desire smiled. She could wait. So she waited. She stopped her dance and stood leaning against a tree, enjoying the smell of lemons, and waiting for me to move toward her or—at least, allow her to move toward me.

For my part, I moved away from her, away from the place altogether, going about my daily life and business. In this, I was similar to my Grandfather in finding myself unable to cope with the forces that emerged from my encounters in desert and forest, but different from him in that I was resolved to find my way in both worlds, to bring them together and not have the one more important than the other.

I experienced my deadness and lostness; I experienced a re-awakening from music, which made me weep and feel pain once more. Music—of course, the realm of the Muses. But the music I heard was of others, born of their pain and suffering and joy, and it only reminded me of my own. I could not and did not want to hear the Music of my own encounter with the Muses. For answer, then, dryness. For answer, then, desert heat and angers: volcanic stirrings of rage, of impotent frustration, of thirst. Then I knew: the Muse Erato was there whether I summoned her or not, whether I wanted her or not. She was there, Desire Awakener was, without any prompting from me. I felt her in my desire, and my lack of desire; I felt her in my fleeing from desire and fleeing toward it. I felt her in my dryness and wetness. What to do, what to do? I held my head; I held my heart, I held my belly. In so doing, I knew the experience of Desire in all three realms: the desire to know, the passion of my Fathers; the desire to feel and love, a passion of theirs, but awakened from without and become within; a passion of hungers, and these were mine. I hungered for love, for understanding, for a food and drink of the soul which would nourish and soothe, which would delight and pacify, which would entrance and make merry. For these I longed. But they came not. So I sat in misery, hands on head, on heart, on belly.

Thus retreated and broken, the figure of Bluebeard came to me. I looked at him, as one would to such a hard, quizzical creature, with his blue beard and dark, fierce eyes. I looked just as quizzical and apart.

"Now you know why I break the soul—and women," he said. "Now you know."

"What do I know?" I replied. "I know nothing. I know only that I am tired of being a battleground of desire, a field upon which the forces fight. I want peace, and love, and surcease. Above all, I want understanding so that I can survive, if I must. At least give me that! At least, if you are, indeed, an avatar of the great God, give me that which was vouchsafed my grandfather and father: understanding. I need love, care, of course, but in lieu of these, help me understand!"

For answer, I received a slap! For answer, I received a sneer! For answer, I received a blow on the head, a blow on the chest, a blow on the belly! But I gave answer for answer: I held on to him. I did not return blow for blow, slap for slap, sneer for sneer! I did not shout or rage at Bluebeard, or Eros, or God, whoever he was. I simply held on. I grasped his ankle, his leg, his arm, I held on like a worrisome hound.

"Bless me," I called out, "Bless me!" I startled myself with this cry and demand. Was I like Jacob with the Angel, or was I like the devoted, plodding, unyielding Knights of my family? I did not know, I just held on.

"I will hold on to you, God, or God-Man, or Demon, or Fiend, whatever you are! I will hold on! Until you bless me! Blessing I want, blessing I demand. You do not give me love, nor understanding, then blessing."

With that, the Demon Bluebeard shook me, whirled me. He leaped high into the air, and shook me like a cat with a bird in its mouth. He dug deeply into the earth, and shook me like a groundhog with a field mouse. He dove deeply into water and shook me like a shark with a blow-fish. But I would not let go, I would not let go.

He took me onto land, and took me to his place, his castle in the forest. He locked me in the room, filled with the bones and blood of previous victims. He made me sit there in the stench and horror of it. He made me let go of him physically, since I was no match for his power, of course, but I would not let go. I sat in that room, holding on to him. "Yea, though you kill me, Oh Lord, I, Son of Knights of Devotion, will not let go of You!"

And now I saw the weeping of the great Bluebeard, Demon-God of Love! Now I saw Him weep! And now I saw Erato, awakener of Desire, the Israeli Muse, the red-haired, dark-eyed passion flower, go toward this Demon-God and embrace Him. I saw how the soul longs after and will not let go of God. I saw now, my heritage of the Fathers, and the true desire of my soul: Never let go! Though He kill me and betray me and roast me and cut me, I will never let go. The love and lust of my soul is a hunger after God, and will not be appeased. I will hold until God relents, until God weeps, until God reunites with her! This is my answer, Oh Lord, this is my answer: no counterbattle, no trickery, like the soul of old, no wiles: only a holding-on.

Thus I sat, in my dryness, and sadness, in my misery, and frustration, in my agony and tears; but once again dryness and sadness, misery and frustration, tears. Was this how the Buddha sat? Was this the flow of demons known by avatar after avatar? Or like Jacob holding on to the Angel? No matter, I will not let go.

I sat so, for some time. And then I smiled, for I thought of how I had held on to God! I remembered how I said that I held on in the air, like a cat in a tree with a bird in its mouth, or deep in the earth like a groundhog with a field mouse, and deep in the water like a shark with a blow-fish. But who is it who holds in such examples? I felt like bird and mouse and blow-fish; but I held on like cat and ground-hog and shark! Holder-on and held-on are One, I thought! I hold on to the Lord, but He holds on to me! So be it.

Then again, I thought: I demand the blessing of the Lord, but I cannot tell who is the holder-on or held-on-to. Perhaps I must bless the Lord! Perhaps I must give that which I need! Perhaps I am he who can bless, as well as he who needs the blessing! With that, I fell upon my face. With my face flat upon the floor, I said these words:

"Lord, I bless Thee! Lord, God of Love and Understanding, I bless Thee. I bless Thee for all Thou hast given me in life. I bless Thee for the joy, for the pain, for the tragedy, for the pleasure. I bless thee for the flow of words and the halt thereof. I bless Thee! For I know that we two are as One, the many of the two are like the one of One! I bless Thee, my brother, my hounder, my tyrant, my friend. Just as did my forefathers, and fathers, I bless Thee!"

Muses IV: Ourania, Polymnia, Thaleia & Kalliope

Many days went by before I could again find my way into the forest, because after my Hebraic-Buddhistic type of enlightenment with the Muse, I found myself back in my normal pursuits, my average everyday situation. In time, as I say, however, I sank deeply into myself, submerging lower than the "library" of Magician, and emerging in the rain-forest of my Grandfather, the Knight.

Sitting on the trunk of an old tree, as had been my custom, I peered at the place where I had seen the Compass of the Muses, the many-sided direction-finder of the wives of Bluebeard. As I stared, the Muse again revealed herself, but not, as I had anticipated, from the East. Just as the Muse of the West was bypassed in the counter-clockwise circumambulation, now was it so for the Muse of the East. Instead, the Muse of the Northeast made herself known.

A slow, heavy beat of music accompanied the Muse this time. Now I saw Ourania, "the Heavenly," Muse of the stars, of the astronomes. She came as the ruler of the heavenly laws, as astronomy, and as astrology. The beat of her step was slow, deliberate, peasant-like, as if in balance to the wide and airy sweep of her heavenly task. Her skirts were many and thick, though made of linen, and she was covered all over, except for her face and a bit of hair. But such a face: smiling and warm, open, not mysterious. Her cheekbones were high, her eyes had more than a trace of the Orient, though they were blue. Her hair was brown and I thought she might be a Finn, or north Russian, or perhaps even a mixture of Eskimo and Indian. A blue-eyed Eskimo is the closest I can come to describing her. After her brief, heavy dance, Ourania looked at me with a pleasant smile. Was my fate so positive? Were the stars good to me? I doubted it. I had had my horoscope cast now and again, and, though my stars were not irretrievably negative, I could not claim a beneficent fate from the gathering of the forces upon my birth date.

Ourania, able to read my thoughts, of course, said, "Your fate is neither good nor bad, Grandson of the Knight, it just is. The stars do not judge, nor complain, nor put you irretrievably into any fate, good or bad. Like the body, or inheritance, they provide a vessel, a structure, a pattern, a framework, into which the soul flows, finds its place. And, like a river, the structure of the moment both forces a bed of life, of experience and meaning, and is forced, is contained and molded. Can you understand that?"

I could understand that. I had plenty of opportunity in my life to know the interplay between inner and outer, between structure and function, between form and content. I had even gone beyond that! What, indeed, had I learned from my encounter with the Muse in her previous form, as Erato of Desire, who had led me to experience Bluebeard as God-Himself? Did I not learn that container and contained, holder-on and held-onto were two aspects of the One? I had learned that deeply in my bones. For that, indeed, was what the Buddhistic-Hebraic experience really was. I, therefore, could understand what Ourania was telling me: I understood that my fate was both "given" and "possible," I was both molded and could change it. Knowing this, I nodded to Ourania. Satisfied that I understood her on this point, she continued:

"Think, Grandson of the Knight! Think of your horoscope. Meditate upon the fact that your Sun is in Gemini and that your Moon and Saturn and Lilith are in Scorpio. The sun gives you light and air and quickness, full of mercurial brightness. It also gives you the heroic, like your father and grandfather, and, above all, it gives your Maniness, your continual flitting about, your versatility and variety. But the Moon, the Moon: your Moon is dark and deep, finding its death-like darkness and passion in the Scorpionic depths. Its sting and poison work deep in you; deep, deep, ever deeper, ever darker. And, if that were not enough, there, too, you have Saturn, Lord of Structure, of the depths of Tradition, of form, of the baleful limitations of the past and its laws, of the Father and his strictures. And that, in the dark depths of the Oneness of the Scorpionic House makes him very deep and dark and demanding indeed. Look then, poor Grandson of the Knight, look how your maniness of Gemini encounters your oneness of Scorpio!

"Nor is it only the Moon and Saturn in your Scorpio with their deep darks that bring you down into earth, the depths and fixity. No. For Lilith is there, too. That dark moon, which no one can see, that black blackness, so black and dark that she is a force only, a witch of the occult and passionate mistress of the Kabbalistic fates, she dwells in the house of the Scorpionic state for you.

"Such a fate, poor Grandson, such a fate: to be a light in the airy Maniness and to be a darkness in the depths of the deep Oneness! Thus, then, you can see how your fate has been a struggle between the One and the Many!

"But more! For you live, too, in a grand cross of conflict, a battle of squared opposites which would have killed many another, but which your physical constitution, thanks to Father and Grandfather, enables you to endure. You already know about that, of course, have even revelled in it! But that cross is lucky, Grandson of the Knight, for you can realize much, know much, bring about much."

I heard Ourania so describe and explain certain aspects of my horoscope, and I received some serenity from it. Somehow, this explanation of the forces as beyond my poor ego, beyond my ordinary condition, gave me solace, made me understand how I was plunged into this never-ending conflict of One vs. Many. I understood that the conflict that Ourania described was the counterpart to the happy, pleasant place of the union of Mars and Venus in my chart, matching that of my good and loving wife. I understood that my strange fate, my dark brooding, was my own, and not like hers, nor any other's, indeed. But how reconcile such a struggle, I thought? How live the vagaries and pains of such a moment of time and place, of such a concatenation of forces, inner and outer, which produced my pattern?

Ourania looked at me with a half-smile. Throughout her words of instruction, she at no time seemed sad, even when she used the words "poor Grandson." She seemed only to be reporting the facts of the situation, showing its aspects. Now, however, with her look, she added something more. Now she did not speak in words, but she gave me to understand intuitively that I was also under a beneficent streak of Uranus, her twin-brother, really. This Uranic streak brought me into the modern, the new, the ever-changing. I would be continually with the imagination of the future, too.

So I was faced with a strange prospect: I was to deal with the Many and the One, the Gemini-Sun and Scorpio-Moon. I was to cope with the furthest and most conservative tradition, of Saturn-Moon, with the most forward-looking and anticipatory influences of Uranus gazing upon it. I needed to continually be with the particular and the individual, and at the same time to reach to the universal. All this was given to me, Ourania was telling me with her eyes. All this, she conveyed with her blue-eyed Eskimo gaze, was what I had already been living with in a myriad Gemini ways.

And the mode, the mode of continuity of this struggle, I wondered? The way in which to survive, to continue, to realize this peculiar fate?

Ourania stood very still and faded. She faded as if the individual cells of her body evaporated into the air, as if they were dematerializing and going into the heavenly space from which she had originally come. As she dissolved, I realized that even the stiff, heavy, high-cheeked, earthy Finnish being which she revealed was only a temporary container, a real, though illusory, vessel for her endless being, for was she not the Muse of the Heavenly? I understood, too, how I was only a temporary vessel for those energies coming into being with me, those forces finding a concretization in the matter of me. I was stilled.

Very soon after Ourania faded away, however, there appeared in the due East position of the compass a very beautiful brown-haired, dark-eyed creature of olive skin as lightly clad as Ourania had been heavily clad. Her clothes were thin and diaphanous silk, she wore jewels and bangles. She was Persian in appearance, out of a tale of the Thousand Nights, perhaps, or an houri of Omar the Tent-maker. Yet her eyes had that almond shape which linked her farther East, perhaps, or even China or Japan. She was of the East and, indeed, due East!

She looked at me and smiled. She danced and sang, but in a humming way, with words of the East, in the throat like a Persian, in the nose, like an Oriental, but above all, from the heart. I did not know her words, I did not understand them, but I knew that she was Polymnia, "she of many hymns," Muse of Story-Telling.

I now understood in a deeper way what my grandfather, the Knight, had experienced here in the forest when he spoke about hearing that marvelous young girl sing in songs of all languages! I now understood that he was compelled, after this experience of the Goddess, to speak of what he had heard! He had known her as Daughter of the Goddess, and Granddaughter of the Great Mother, the Great Goddess. Now I was seeing her in her true light as Polymnia, she of the many hymns, she who sang in all languages and told endless tales of the feelings of life. For Polymnia is singer and story-teller, and my grandfather was enchanted by her, had to serve her.

My father, Son of the Knight, had known her too, I think. Did he not know her as a singer, as Iambe? Did he not pursue her and bind her more deeply, even, than his father? Did he not delve into Demeter and Persephone, into Mother and Daughter, which made him a poet like the Shepherd, Swineherd of the depths? Yes, it was so.

And now, true to the tradition of the fathers, I was faced with the Muse, as well. I was faced with Polymnia, the story-teller. Now I knew why my fate was as it was: Polymnia would express for me the story of the struggle between one and many, between old and new, between dark and light, between good and evil, between all those warring opposites of my soul and of life, for such was my fate, and for such was I born. Like father before me, and grandfather before him, I would serve Polymnia, and she would serve me. Together we would serve that great One and Many God which was beyond us all. She and I would serve and she would give me words. I would be her vessel, and she would be mine!

Knowing these things, I sat back to enjoy the songs and dances of Polymnia, the gorgeous one. She entranced me. Her lips moved, her throat sang, and I heard myriad tales, so many that it would take all my life to relate them. She danced further and further east until she vanished from sight.

But no, she did not vanish from sight, she only went all around the world, further and further east, until she appeared from the west, from the westernmost reaches of the compass, coming close at last, close enough to see that she was different appearing.

Now, in the West, she was Thaleia, "the festive," Muse of Comedy. Now she was like an American, brown-haired and blue-eyed, laughing all the time. Her mouth was joyous and laughing, she was healthy and strong and athletic, and moved with a verve and grace as if she had drunk in all the elegant bodiness of the black man and red man. But she laughed, how she laughed! She laughed at the Comedy of life. She laughed as if to say, as someone once said, that if you felt all the pain of life, it was tragedy, but if you thought about it all, it was comedy! But Thaleia was "festive." She laughed, all right, but she laughed as if to neither feel the pain of life alone, nor think about it alone. Rather she celebrated life. Celebrated, that was the word. For to celebrate is to make festive, to make holy, to proclaim and value. Festivals commemorate, they re-tell, they relive and make sacred that which was painful and pleasureful, sad and joyous. Thaleia was Muse of the celebration.

And I saw that Polymnia could become Thaleia, that to tell the story is also to celebrate. And that is the fate that the Muse wanted from me. I saw that the Muse in every form, whether as the Erato desire for the union with God, the African dance of passion from within, Terpsichore, the Spanish dance of Melpomene, the tragic singer who felt the dark scorpionic moon, the joyful play of Euterpe who celebrated like Thaleia, the fame-seeking, recording eye of Kleio, the blond, all under the fateful, heavenly eye of Ourania, the Heavenly, all of these Muses, all these fantastic eight were aspects of the One Goddess, the Many Muses in the One Goddess!

As if to verify my realization, there appeared in the center of the compass, the Greekest Greek of them all, Kalliope. "She of the beautiful voice," Muse of heroic song, the greatest and best of the Muses, as Hesiod said, was really none other than an incarnation in a Oneness of all the other Eight. The Ninth, the singer of the heroic song, was also a teller of the heroic tale. And she spoke for all, for Erato and Euterpe, for Melpomene and Ourania. She spoke for Kleio and Terpsichore, and finally, for Thaleia and Polymnia.

The One and Many, the Muses and the Muse, the Goddesses and The Goddess: these were the wife-wives of Bluebeard, Magician of Love.

Now I sought for Bluebeard once again, aware that I had known his wives, known his soul. Now I searched out the Magician once again, for I had tasted the depths of his realm. Now I longed to embrace Bluebeard once more, for I knew him to be my brother. I had tasted the clash of opposites, had grown deeper in myself and, thus, deeper with my ancestors, and knew the Magician was magical because of his touch of the Muse!

Bluebeard II

I looked for Bluebeard in the subterranean place of the many-colored library. I searched him out in the lower region of the rain-forest, where my grandfather had lived. I sought him also in the parallel place of the cave, of the underground haunts where my father, Son of the Knight, had been born and lived and to which he returned. In all these places I looked for Bluebeard. I realized that I had known Bluebeard and his loves, that he was of the same stuff as Don Juan and the Magician. I knew, but I could not find him.

So I selected the place in the forest where grandfather had come to reflect, think, be happy and at peace. I sat down upon the stump of the tree, and I wondered where Bluebeard the Magician, Bluebeard the Lover, Bluebeard the Don Juan could be.

My mouth parted in a smile, all by itself. I felt the Muse of the Inappropriate Smile, I felt the laughter of Joy, because an answer came at once: Bluebeard the Magician, Bluebeard the Lover, Bluebeard the husband of Muses, was inside me! I felt him in my head, in my heart, in my belly. The God of Love was indwelling within me, as knowing, as feeling, as desiring. He now took up residence inside me! I laughed very loud. Grandfather had experienced his guide, his Angel, as ultimately finding a place—as both angel and horse, as spirit and instinct—inside himself. Now I was experiencing something similar: the Magical One was inside me, too, in a triangle of centers, in a trinity of divinity.

I looked into the stream and saw my eyes. They were dark and deep and fierce, like Bluebeard. But they were also soft and warm and gentle, like Bluebeard. He was my friend, within. I needed nowhere else to seek him than within myself. Library and forest and cave: they, too, were like head and heart and belly, were they not?

I looked out at the Compass of the Muses, with its eight points and center. As I looked, the center began to rise, but as if attached to the rim of the circle like a transparent cloth or paper. It rose to make a cone, stretching high up toward the sky. At the same time, the center opened up into the earth, reaching down to make a cone as well. The cones above and below made a beautiful form, glistening like a diamond. I thought of the Tree of my grandfather, of the great Kabbalistic Tree of Life which he had discovered, though it had existed before he had known of it. He had come to know and experience that Tree of Paradise, and his symbol, as I had long since known, was the sacred Star of David, the Seal of Solomon. What strange symbol was I now experiencing? The intertwined triangles of my grandfather were now appearing as touching at a round common base, one reaching into heaven, the other reaching into the depths of the earth. They came together in the common circle of the Muses, a different symbol for me.

I mused: Grandfather had a different guide, after all, an Angel. Mine was a Magician. But was it, perhaps, the same guide? I could not tell. All I could guess was that each of us had experienced and had to cope with different aspects of the divine, of God, and that was all that we knew. My grandfather could rest with his vision of the Star and of the Tree, but there was something unfinished in my quest. Thinking, now, of my struggle as a "Quest," I realized that I was, in fact, Knight III by dint of the Muses. I remembered also that my father in his Quest had joined two and three, had come to himself in a union of One and Many in the Charioteer. But my quest, as I say, felt unfinished. Something was lacking. The Magician was within. I could just enquire as to what was lacking, could I not? So I did.

The Magician told me very simply: I had not yet gone to the top of this pyramidal cone, nor to its base. How could I know it, realize it, until I had done so? Before me was a tree like that which my grandfather faced, but this was no tree of nature. I did not know what it was, exactly, but I realized that I would have to do as he said. I had an inkling that I had to know the God of Love more than I had thus far. Head, heart and belly had I known, but how about those places, above and, below, top of the head and in the genitals? Had I penetrated those places of the God of Love? Perhaps not. Or not enough. For answer, the inner Magician said "Yes. Climb and descend. Ascend and come down."

Conveniently, there now appeared steps in the material of the cone, and I began my climb. I climbed up, out of the forest, into the air. I climbed up and up, into the clouds, moist and wet, into the night, cold and stark, into the light, hot and clear. I climbed from the belly and heart and head of things, the circles of desire and feeling and reflection, up to the top of the head, the Sahasrara of Kundalini, the lotus place which was beyond my heretofore deeply experienced Hebraic-Buddhistic love. I climbed to the God of Love in Heaven.

Heaven turned out to be a simple Christian Church. Heaven was not heaven as I had thought, with angels and streams, trees and pretty girls—that sort of heaven I had already known as the Paradise on Earth, the heaven of my grandfather and of my experience with the

Muses. This Heaven, here at the top of the pyramid, at the apex of the cone, sitting serenely without force of gravity, without place in time or space, was a simple Christian Church, such as those one knows from Romanesque times. St. Francis might have worshiped in such a place. Simple, not elaborate, one that everyone in the Western world has seen.

I went inside this church, and knew why I was there. For, besides the altar, the cross, the pews with simple seats, the only wall decorations were the Stations of the Cross. I knew that I was here to see, to reflect and understand, to take-in these stations, that end-life of Christ. I was here to experience the God of Love anew: Not Hebraic, not Buddhistic, but Christian. The Passion of Jesus, the man, Jesus, the son of God, Jesus the Christ, Jesus, the God of Love.

Jesus I

Who is this God of Love whom Christians call "Lord," "Son of God," but also "Brother"? Is this portrayal of suffering, of crucifixion, of being torn apart between opposites, a picture of Love? And love as Lord? Surely, it is true. And surely have I, who is no more a Christian than was my grandfather, the Knight, or my father, Son of the Knight, surely have I known this to be true. For I have known the cross of the suffering of love, of the conflict between love as caring and duty versus love as passion and desire. I have known deeply and intimately all the states of love of Don Juan, of Bluebeard, and the Muses. And, too, I have known the spiritual love, the *agape*, the brotherly love of Christians. So though no more a Christian than my grandfather and father, I am no less a Christian than they either! Did they not know the depths of the Christian experience? Did not my grandfather know that he was also Christian in his heart, as well as pagan and Jew? Did not my father?

Was not my father a friend of Dog, who had witnessed the Crowning of Thorns? Did not my father find his mother and grandmother who were present at the Crucifixion? Did he not see and know the things of Christ in other forms? I think so. Indeed, I know it to be true, for he was friend and servant of Lancelot and Arthur, of Guinevere, as well as mother and daughter, of Dog. And so he knew Christ through them.

But I am of another generation, after all, and it seems my task is different. I am, by dint of Muse, Knight III, and so must I now see the Christ differently, in my own way. So, then, let me about the continuing business of my father and grandfather, let me about my own redemption, let me follow the Christian path of the Stations of the Cross. Let me meditate, as they do, upon the Passion, upon the Via Dolorosa, upon what it means that a God of Love suffers.

I will begin with a prayer, just as do the Christians. I will ask, as they do, not to be separated from you, and to be delivered from sins and evil, to "cling to your commandments." What was his commandment, this God of Love? What did he say that Passover time, when he knew that he would die?

"This is my commandment," he said, "that you love one another as I have loved you. Greater love has no man that this, that a man lay down his life for his friends."

That was the love of this man. Thus do the Franciscans serve him in their brotherly, spiritual way. Thus the *agape* of love. Brother Christ, I accept you, I embrace you. Spirit of brotherly love and compassion, spirit of self-sacrifice, accompany me, do not depart from me as I meditate and try to understand, to take in, to become one with your Passion, like a Sacrament, a Communion for one who is not a Christian, but would know its love. This is my prayer to you, as I begin your Way of the Cross.

Jesus II: Stations of the Cross

First Station: Jesus is Condemned to Death.

Jesus was unjustly condemned by Romans, abetted by Jews. I know what it means, Jesus, to be unjustly condemned by narrow and rigid men: that is an old mark of our history. I know how it is that a narrow stricture of negative conscience, rigid rule of law, can condemn one, cannot permit that God became Man, that love can be human, that one can proclaim the divinity from within. We Jews can do that—to ourselves, and to others. And the Christians can, too. And have. How unjust they have been to Jews and in your name! Condemnation in the name of conscience, of justice, in the name of the right thing! How horrible! Forgive me, God, for condemning. Forgive me, Lord, for being righteous and judging others whose way, whose morality, is different from my own. Let my own strictures be gentle, let my inner judge be kind, let my own authorities allow a God of love, a human God, to live in me, in my heart—and in mankind.

But, Jesus, you were condemned by Romans, after all. It was Pilate, servant of Caesar who condemned you, washed his hands of you. What was this Rome that condemned you? Was it not Babylon all over again? A place of lusts and loveless passions in which lived only cruelty, brutality, exploitation? Was it not the end of an era, a loveless time when a sick animal dwelt in men's hearts? Yes. And was not Caesar so jealous of his own power, of being thought of as a God, as the only God on earth, that he could not abide you? I think so. Roman power-God: brutal, exploiting, sick animal. He condemned you.

And so, Jesus is condemned by right and left. Crucified by sick animal and vengeful morality. No love. No wonder you let yourself die between them. No wonder you proclaimed human love, Godly love, brotherly love, and in man! No wonder you proclaimed self-sacrifice as love, for this neither sick animal nor rigid conscience can do. Jesus, Lord, I salute you. I salute you as brother, as one who tried, as the Christians say, to bring "kindness and good deeds (as) our answer to injustice and hatred." Let it be so, also, in me.

But let me not any more allow myself to be condemned by others. Let me not be the paschal lamb, the sacrifice for others or for that judge or Roman in me! The time has ended for that. If, indeed, you live in me, then you are to be honored as a God-Man, not be crucified again! For now, oh God-Man, I too, am a God-man! No sick Roman animal shall dominate me, nor sick Pharisaic conscience. The two shall be as one: the morality of love, the health of the animal, united as one—no longer to be condemned, no longer to be crucified! End of condemnation.

Second Station: Scourging, Crowning with Thorns, Acceptance of Cross.

"And they clothed him in a purple cloak, and plaiting a crown of thorns they put it on him. And they began to salute him, 'Hail King of the Jews!' And they struck his head with a reed, and spat upon him, and they knelt down in homage to him. And when they had mocked him, they stripped him of the purple cloak, and put his own clothes on him. And they led him out to crucify him."

Oh, Jesus! I said that I saluted you. Let me not salute you as did the Roman soldiers. Let me not mock and have contempt for the loving God-man in myself and others. Let me not mock the weakness in me, let me not humiliate that in me which is not strong, cannot stand up for itself. Let me not falsely give away the purple cloak, the royal-passionate-mystical color so easily. Purple cloak: Red of passionate-feeling-animal combined with blue of spiritual conscience: Let me give it to you, indeed, God of Love, one who will unite them in his being.

Jesus, I, too, have been humiliated. All my beliefs and principles and loves have been pushed aside, and by the rough and brutal treatment of myself, by the uncaring warrior part of me which serves harsh judge and brutal power just for the money of it, the energy which it gets.

But no more, Jesus, no more, God of Love. No more shall I mock my own love, my own God-man, who will unite red and blue! No more shall my own power be in the service of self-destruction! No more shall I mock another or myself who tries to serve his own God-hood. Lord, the prayer says that we may share the glory of Jesus, by sharing his cross. But I say, after you, that I will come after you by taking up my own cross, daily, and with inner pride that I, too, am a God-man. Jesus, my brother, I adore you and bless you.

Third Station: Jesus Falls the First Time.

Oh, my God, how I have fallen when I have tried to carry my cross! How many times have I fallen and cried out in pain, in exclaiming against God for my fate! How many times have I done much worse than that, for I have hurt and offended those whom I have loved. I have, in my guilt and pain, flailed out against the innocent; I have damaged the feelings and hearts of those close to me. And, I have fallen for lack of humility. I have fallen in the arrogant belief that I was a chosen God-man, an especial one, more than others.

And so I am, Lord. So I am. I, too, am a God-man. But God-men are sons of God, serving the same Father, the same all-encompassing spirit which transcends us all and would become us in the every act of daily life. What was it that I learned from my father, the Son of the Knight? That God is man becoming, and that man is God being? Thus do I believe. And thus, too, do I believe in the ever-transcending God of the Fathers which dwells beyond. Just as I now believe in the ever-immanent Son of God-Man being, carried first in our history by Jesus the God-Man, Jesus the God who fell! He fell, Lord, just as I do. He fell, his burden was too great, too painful. Even God can fall, even God cannot carry his totality, his double-natured being of divinity-humanity!

Thus, Lord, I adore you and bless you. For by your holy cross, by carrying and falling, you have redeemed the world. And how redeemed, Lord? By showing us the way. We must carry our own cross of divinity-humanity, and fall and rise up again to go onward.

The Fourth Station: Jesus Meets His Mother.

How did it feel, Jesus, to meet your mother on your painful way? Did it not feel horrible? Was it not a worse burden for you to see her suffering because you were suffering? But were you not also filled with tenderness for her? And did you not—come now, if you are a man, admit it—did you not long to lay down your cross? To kneel at her feet, to hide yourself under her skirts? To feel the tent of her being all around you, to protect you from the pains and hurts? Thus would I feel, Jesus. And such, no doubt, did you feel, too. Even though you said that all who took up their cross were your father and brother and—mother. For a God-Man needs a mother, after all. Especially when he takes up such a big task, he must needs be very little. He must also feel the child in him, afraid, foolish, unable to endure, unable to stand the pain, foolish. Was that not the first fall, Jesus? I think so.

And what did Mary feel? Was it not even worse for her? Was it not worse for her to see the fruit of her womb, her beloved child, her God-child, struggling and suffering and being humiliated, and she could do nothing about it? Was it not always thus? The suffering of woman, in her powerlessness? The horror of what men do to each other, and to her? Was she not pierced by a sword in her soul? Did not Scripture say so?

Indeed, it did, oh Lord! And beyond Mary and Jesus, Lord, beyond mother and son, beyond male and female: Is it not the agony of life to have the God-man born out of one's soul, to feel pierced by the spirit of God, to have one's own being the place for this birth of the divine, and to feel it suffering and burning and agonizing, when one is powerless to relieve it! For such is the child-God within and without. Such is the man-God within and without! And such is the soul, mother of the God, who must bear it all in patient, dumb, devoted, love. The love of devotion. A different love, Lord, but as great as your own. And you know it. I know it.

The Fifth Station: Simon Helps Jesus to Carry His Cross.

As they were marching out with you, Jesus, they came upon an ordinary man, Simon of Cyrene, and he they compelled to help carry your cross.

What a mockery of you, Lord, and what a mockery of him. "Compelled" him to carry your cross. Worst humiliation of all. Lord, King of the Jews, has to be helped to carry his cross, and some other man, ordinary, has to be compelled to do so. How many would have helped with joy! How many now would help with gratitude! Many, Lord, many. But I know what is meant. I know that I have had to learn the ignominy of having another carry my cross for me. I have needed my brother, not only to carry his own cross, and not burden me with it, but I have needed my brother to help me with my own. How hard it has been in my life to say "help me!" How hard it must have been for a King, a Savior, a humiliated God-Man to ask. But you so asked. And they, the Romans, even forced another to help. The brutal forces make us drop our burden and make another carry it. I know it. When I have fallen, as I have said, I have flailed out, I have blamed another, I have made others carry the burden of my own conflicts. And it has been the brutal burden, too much for me, that has forced it. But I am grateful that there are brothers and sisters, to whom I can call out. Let me call out easily, as I need it; let me be a brother in need, rather than a brutal imposer. Let me ask for care, and let me give it, without the burden. For, as Paul said, we are many parts of the one Messiah. We need each other. "Just as the body is one and has members, and all the members of the body, though many, are one body, so it is with Christ. For by one Spirit we were all baptized into one body—Jews or Greeks, slaves or free—and all were made to drink of one Spirit. For the body does not consist of one member but of many. If one member suffers, all suffer together; if one member is honored, all rejoice together. Now you are the body of Christ and individually members of it."

Thus spoke Paul, even though he finally rejected the body. We need each other, individuals in a community, parts of one man in the community of the man, as well. I acknowledge it, I proclaim it, I embrace it.

The Sixth Station: Veronica Wipes the Face of Christ.

I know how you felt, Jesus, walking along your path, not knowing if it was hopeless or foolish or not. Thinking that you were Son of God, but by now fully aware of your helplessness, your need. You spoke, said Matthew: "For I was hungry and you gave it to me; I was thirsty and you gave me to drink; I was a stranger, and you took me in; naked and you covered me; sick and you visited me; I was in prison and you came to me." I know that you went on to say that he that comforts and feeds and clothes and visits the lowliest of men also does so to Christ. I know and understand and appreciate. For in doing that, one feeds, comforts, clothes the Christ in the other. It is Christ feeding Christ. I know that.

But I think of you, Lord. I think of you, as a man, a God-Man, in need. Mother Mary stood looking on in paralyzed agony. The mother of the God suffered the pain of helpless impotence to reduce pain. And now, Veronica; not a mother, but a sister. The sister comforts, she touches, she wipes the face, and the legend is that the image remains everlasting, a miracle of a face printing itself upon the cloth. Is it so miraculous? Does not the face of the divine preserve its image on the woven cloth of our souls? Do we not carry it always?

But the woman, Jesus, she comforted you. She loved you, touched you, soothed you. God needs woman. God needs Mother's care, sister's touch. He needs the woman present and the woman active. Oh, Jesus, teach me! Yet I know. I know because you have shown me. I adore you.

The Seventh Station: Jesus Falls for the Second Time.

"And going a little farther he fell on his face and prayed, 'My Father, if it be possible let this cup pass from me; nevertheless, not as I will, but as thou wilt.'

"Again, for the second time, he went away and prayed, 'My Father if this cannot pass unless I drink it, thy will be done.' "

Jesus falling again. Oh, my God, how many times have I asked that my suffering be taken from me; how many times have I fallen? You show me, Jesus, you show me by your humility. You did not cling to your Godliness. You did not cling, even, to your pain. You asked that it be taken away, but you also accepted it. You accepted that higher God in yourself. You accepted that Father of which you were Son. Christ Jesus, my brother, you have shown me the way. Help me to emulate you in this path. Help me to be the man that you were. For here you showed yourself to be a great man, not a God-man. Here you showed yourself mortal, needing, in pain, ready to give up your task, but submitting. Would that I could do this. Would that I could emulate you in this. Jesus, son of God, I believe in you, I hope in you.

The Eighth Station: Jesus Speaks to the Women of Jerusalem.

You change, now, Jesus. Before, so human, so needy, so broken in spirit, so ready to go on your way humbly. But now, now. After suffering the vision of a mother dying for pain of your pain, after feeling the need and solace of woman wiping your face, now you speak to the weeping women, the Daughters of Jerusalem, not in pain, not in need, but in pride. You speak:

"Daughters of Jerusalem, do not weep for me, but weep for yourselves and for your children. For behold, the days are coming when they will say, 'Blessed are the barren, and the wombs that never bore, and the breasts that never gave suck!' Then they will say unto the mountains, 'Fall on us'; and to the hills, 'Cover us.' For if they do this when the wood is green, what will happen when it is dry?"

Jesus, you said this. You also said, "I am the vine, you are the branches. He who abides in me, and I in him, he it is that bears much fruit, for apart from me you can do nothing. If a man does not abide in me, he is cast forth as a branch and withers; and the branches are gathered, thrown into the fire and burned."

How powerful you are, Jesus! Now you speak from the Christ within you, you speak from the Messiah, the great light, the potent force that knows most of creation. Creation is where Christ is, says Jesus. He says, even, perhaps that even he, Jesus the man, must die and not be wept over. One must weep for one's own barrenness, one's own dryness, one's own lack of creativity. One must weep when one is cut off from the Lord of Creation. "Do not weep for me," says Jesus. Does he say this out of pride again? Or out of feeling that he is now only a stick, a dry bone which must also die? I think both. For now he has regained his pride, his feeling of grace, his conviction that the grace of God must and will bear fruit.

Thus do I also believe, dear Jesus. Thus do I entrust myself to the same God as do you. Thus do I stand for the growth of the vine, and the consumption of the dead branches. Let the dead in me be consumed by the passionate fire! Let the new and green thrive and grow and bear a testament to the grace of God. Let the Muses serve Christ, as they served Eros!

The Ninth Station: Jesus Falls for the Third Time.

Oh, Jesus, how many times do we have to fall? How many times do our poor mortal bones have to bring us low? From a height of pride, you fall again. Was it then that you said, "My God, my God, why have you forsaken me?" Tradition says yes. And I believe it. Does not the Psalmist say it better than anyone?

> "I cry with my voice to the Lord, with my voice I
>   make supplication to the Lord,
> I pour out my complaint before him, I tell my trouble
>   before him. "

. . . and again:

> "I cry to thee, O Lord: I say, thou art my refuge, my
>   portion in the land of the living.
> Give heed to my cry; for I am brought very low!
>   Deliver me from my persecutors;
>   for they are too strong for me."

You knew it, Jesus. Is it true that without suffering we cannot help in the work of love and redemption? Has there not been suffering enough? Have you not fallen enough? I am tired, Jesus. I want to fall no more. I want to walk gently upon the earth, modestly upon the earth, honestly upon the earth. I want to fall no more. I want to sit down, not fall down; lie down, not be thrown. Jesus, help me to make the "Yoke light" as you say. Jesus help me. Jesus, did you not cry out to your Father? Did you not complain of having been forsaken? Remember me, then, and do not forsake me.

The Tenth Station: Jesus is Stripped of His Garments.

They took you up to Golgotha, that "place of a skull," of the dead, and there they crucified you. They gave you wine to drink, mixed with gall, but you would not drink it. But then the soldiers divided your clothes and made of them four parts, "to each soldier a part, and also the tunic. Now the tunic was without seam, woven in one piece from the top. They therefore said to one another: 'Let us not tear it, but let us cast lots for it, to see whose it shall be." That the Scripture might be fulfilled which says 'They divided my garments among them; and for my vesture they cast lots.' "

Thus were you stripped, Jesus. Thus were you robbed of your last human dignity, made the ultimate scapegoat and bearer of ignominy. Just as your cross was four, all your vestments are divided among the four warring elements. How well I know that one is divided into two and then four and each part wants it all. But your wholeness they could not divide, Jesus. The tunic, the vesture, the one thing left which was without seam, woven in one piece, that could not be divided. And what was that, Jesus? I think that it was your attitude, your wholeness in being of one piece, knowing yourself to be a God-man, whole and one, divinity and humanity, son of the Christ which dwelt within you. And so, you were stripped and allowed yourself to suffer ignominy, but praise God, you did not drink of the wine mixed with gall! You did not do it! Those who spoke of Jesus as a fool, a victim and scapegoat who let everything happen to him are wrong. You did not drink of the spirit mixed with the gall of complaint, of humiliation, of degradation. You, Jesus, I know, kept your image of wholeness without gall! For this, I look to you, salute you, praise you, and wish to be like you. I wish not to carry crosses any more, but to hold and wear an unseamed tunic of wholeness which cannot be ripped asunder, cannot be divided among the battling elements of my soul. Most of all, I want to taste the gall of battle no longer, no more have the beautiful spirit of the wine and blood of the emotion of life turn into the gall of complaint, of bitterness! Jesus, I salute you. For this makes the rest of what you say possible of understanding, acceptance.

Luke tells us that you asked us to love your enemies, do good to those who hate us, to bless those who curse us, pray for those who abuse us. "To him who strikes you on the cheek," you say, "offer the other also; and from him who takes away your cloak do not withhold your coat as well. Give to every one who begs from you; and of him who takes away your good do not ask them again. And as you wish that men would do to you, do so to them." Thus you spoke.

I think I understand. Jesus, I cannot follow all that you say, such as offering the other cheek, or giving to everyone who asks or steals of me, I cannot do this. But I understand. For you, also, Jesus, refused to take the gall! You refused to be humiliated in your own spirit, you refused to let the warring parts tear you apart. You gave up everything of yourself, except your deep perfect pride in your own spirit, your own wholeness, which made you know that you were a God-man. With that knowledge, you could give up everything else. Everything. Wonderful. I cannot do that—at least not yet. Nor do I want to. For in your day, there was so much arrogance of spirit, so much material-ism and hardening of heart, that your example was the right one. I think that now it is different. I think that one must, as you did, respect oneself, love oneself, even love some of one's possessions, at least those that one needs, or thinks one needs. It is no failure to do so. And yet, and yet. In that day, when everyone has what he needs, your example will be right.

Above all, oh Christ, I, with you, will try no longer to swallow gall. I shall not allow myself to be bitter, to be cheated, to cheat myself of the real spirit, the real wine, the real blood of life and emotion, and have it mixed with gall, with the gall of not knowing my own wholeness, my own divinity-humanity! For this, Jesus, I thank you. For this, Jesus, for showing the way, I adore you and praise you.

The Eleventh Station: Jesus is Nailed to the Cross.

Nailed to the cross, between the two thieves; beyond possibility of change; forced to stay totally, fully and agonizingly in the conflict. Poor Jesus, none can save you now. None but you can know in that moment what it means to be nailed on the cross between the opposites of heaven and earth, between the divine and human, to be both God and man, to be both eternal and temporal, to be proud and humble, to be . . . two in one, or four in one. One in many, and many in one: Oh, God of Love, I know thee, and bow before thee. For you did submit to the Christ, the God who dwelt within you. And now I understand when you said, "Father, forgive them for they know not what they are doing." It is true. They did not know that you had already freely accepted the cross of divinity-humanity, that you were a God-man, and longed for them to be so also. They did not know.

Nor did they understand that you said, "I am King of the Jews." The Jews, of course, denied that you were their King, and, in fear, said that only Caesar was their King. But there, on the cross upon which you were nailed, was written in Hebrew, in Greek, in Latin, "The King of the Jews." And it was so: The Christ in you was King, and a revelation and development of the spirits of Israel, of Greece, of Rome! The Christ was King. The Jews, of course, were right, because only Caesar, the dreaded tyrant, was their outer King. The Jews were right, too, because the real King of the Jews is always God; beyond that, every Jew, like you, is his own King! But they did not know that you were the first of the Jews to accept his own Messiahship, his own Kinghood, his own indwelling of the God-spirit. So they were right . . . and wrong. They did not know. And yet, it was so: you, Jesus, inheritor of spirits Hebrew, Greek, and Latin: King of the spirit, shower of the way to the western spirit to find the God, the Christ, the Messiah, the Savior, within.

These are only words, Jesus. Only words. Pray that I may understand

without words. That I may be among those who will not need to be
forgiven, that I can accept your divine kingship, and that of everyman,
and, at last, of my own.

The Twelfth Station: Jesus Dies on the Cross.

You died, Jesus. Man that you were, mortal that you were, you died.
Luke tells us:

"It was now about the sixth hour and there was darkness over the
whole land until the ninth hour, while the sun's light failed; and the
curtain of the temple was torn in two. Then Jesus, crying with a loud
voice, said, 'Father, into thy hands I commit my spirit!' And having
said this he breathed his last."

When you die, Jesus, the sun darkens. For you are a light, a sun, a
bringer of consciousness, a helper to show us the way to live and die,
and follow the Christ within. When you die, our holy oneness is torn
in two, our older forms of worship die, too. For now we are thrown
back upon ourselves, upon our own spirit, upon our own Christ. In
this we no longer are one with the temple as Jews, nor with Jesus as
Christians, we are thrown back upon ourselves. And you, Jesus,
showed us simply, for you said unto your Father, the Christ who dwelt
within and beyond you, that unto Him you committed your spirit.
You surrendered and died, giving up ego-hood, manhood, mortalhood,
for the divinity.

But they say to us, Jesus, that you laid down your life for all of us
sheep; so that there should be one flock and one shepherd; that God
gave His son for the redemption of men's sins; that He voluntarily
became their scapegoat. Who spoke thus? The Jesus, or the Christ?
Or were the two indivisible? Jesus died, for the Christ; man dies, for
God. But God tells us that God dies, for man. So that the many shall
be One. Hear, Oh Israel, the Lord our God, the Lord is One. He is
undivided. Thus the proclamation, when it is felt, when experienced.
But it is not always so. We—and God—are often divided. We are cut
off from each other, split, separated, in despair. And it must needs
be so. For was it not said that one must die in order to be born again?
At every level of being?

Jesus I accept your death—and my own. "Because by your holy
Cross you have redeemed the world." You have shown us the way of
a God-man, you have shown us the way to serve the God within us
and transcending us on every side. And you must die so that we can
find the Christ within ourselves. By your showing of the way, you
have redeemed the world.

I adore you, Jesus, and I bless you.

The Thirteenth Station: Jesus is Taken Down from the Cross.

When the soldiers came to you, Jesus, they did not break your legs, the way they had already done with the thieves. They lanced your side, so that blood and water came out. And Joseph of Arimathea, your secret disciple, took your body away.

They did not need to break your legs, Jesus, for you were already broken, you already had let yourself be broken on the Cross. But the blood, the blood and water from the lance! Why? Luke tells us, from that last Passover, that last feast of Liberation:

"And he took bread, and when he had given thanks he broke it and gave it to them, saying 'This is my body which is given for you. Do this in remembrance of me.' And likewise the cup after supper, saying 'This cup which is poured out for you is the new covenant in my blood.' "

Thus did Jesus speak on that last Passover, feast of liberation. Thus did he break the Matzoh, and become it, and thus is the body in the Eucharist. And thus the wine, the last cup is his blood. It was the Christ within him which spoke, the Divinity which carried the Jews out of Egypt, the Divinity which brought body and soul, the spirit which transcended and created and found its being in bread and wine, body and soul. Thus do we take in the God; thus are we, human beings, cannibals of the spirit, for we take in the divinity-humanity of the God-man, in himself and ourselves, when we treasure the miracle of spirit incarnating in body and soul. Jesus, I understand. I understand the mystery!

And did not my father, Son of the Knight, understand? Was my father not present and did he not hear the Knight, Lancelot? He of the lance who felt in human, loving flesh, the pain of the body and blood? My father knew it from Lancelot, but now, Jesus, I know it from you and your crucifixion, directly. Thus, Jesus, does the Passover liberation continue: From the liberation of the many Jews, to the liberation of the one God-man to the liberation of the many God-men. So be it. Amen!

The Fourteenth Station: Jesus is Laid in the Tomb.

So they bound your body in linen and spices and placed you in a new tomb in a garden. And they rolled a large stone against the entrance and departed.

Abandoned, dead. Wrapped in a shroud for no one but yourself, and made to smell sweetly, as well. Alone. What does it mean?

Your Apostle Paul told us that all who have been baptized into Christ Jesus (does that mean taken on the same water that flowed from his insides when pierced, the same water of life which comes from Christ to Jesus to us?) were also baptized into his death. St. Paul says that we are all buried with him, so that we, too, can become resurrected, raised from the dead by the glory of the Father, "walk in the newness of life." Thus speaks Paul. Just as Jesus and Christ are one, so Christians and Jesus are one, through the Christ. Thus does the saint speak.

What Paul says makes sense to me. But I am more moved by a prayer of your priest who spoke, at this station, to the Father, Christ:

"Almighty and eternal God, on the edge of sadness when all seemed lost, You restored to us the Saviour we thought defeated and conquered. Help us, we beg You, so to empty ourselves of self-concern that we might see Your hand in every failure and Your victory in every defeat. These things we ask in the name of Your Son, Jesus Christ, who lives and reigns forever with You in the unity of the Holy Spirit."

I can say amen to this, oh Lord. This priest asks for us to empty ourselves of self. Like Buddhists. Let us be empty so that the Christ, the Buddha, the Divine, can fill us! So be it. So let our ego die. So let our humanity die, ever to be reborn anew, ever to be filled by divinity being reborn in the flesh and blood of this life. Ever for divinity to fill life so that it is totally sanctified. For ever and ever. Amen!

Jesus III

Jesus, for most there is no fifteenth station, but there is a "closing," a prayer, or an indication of the resurrection. The Risen Christ appears to his disciples, they say, and ascends to heaven. They say that the women came to his tomb, and found the stone rolled away. A young man told them not to fear, for Jesus of Nazareth who was crucified was not there, but had risen. And they say that Jesus appeared unto many of the disciples, telling them:

"Thus it is written, that the Christ should suffer and on the third day rise from the dead, and that repentance and forgiveness of sins should be preached in his name to all nations, beginning from Jerusalem. You are witnesses of these things. And behold, I send the promise of my Father upon you; but stay in the city, until you are clothed with power from on high."

So the disciples were led out, and then did he part from them and go up into heaven. And they worshiped him and returned to Jerusalem with great joy, and were continually in the temple, blessing God.

That is the story, Jesus. I know of it, because for the Christian, you are the Risen Christ and you appear in the sacred sacraments, the liturgy of the Mass, and the sacred Scriptures. And I, though no formal Christian, believe them, for the word of God continues to unfold, the Spirit continues to incarnate in flesh, in blood, in the creative word of pious men and women.

I also know the story, Jesus, from my father, Son of the Knight, and his mother and grandmother. For they, Mother and Daughter, were there at the Crucifixion, and they were there, at the tomb, at the opening to the dark Underworld, to the hell where the Saviour went. They were there, suffered, and were sanctified. So, I know from my father, from my grandmother and great-grandmother. But I do not know for myself.

Jesus, I have made these meditations upon the Stations of the Cross. I have gone your holy way. I have abided here in this holy church, high above the clouds. I have come to the apex of this inverted cone, whose base is the great circle of the Muses and at whose apex is your simple church. I have experienced love in the deeply Hebraic way, the deeply Buddhistic way. I have experienced love in the Christian way. But show me now, Jesus, show yourself to me. I have identified with you, suffered as you have suffered, have dis-identified with you and tried to know you for yourself. Show yourself to me, as Jesus, as the Christ. Speak to me, sweet Jesus. Let me hear your words and do not only pour forth the words from my own mouth!

I see you, Jesus, I see you. Just as the artists have seen you, thus do I see you. Like Durer, Gruenwald, Rembrandt saw you. As a strong man, a deep man, a gentle man, but firm. No sentimental man, no saccharine, emasculated man, but one touched by divinity. Speak to me, Jesus, and tell me.

"What do you wish to know, my son?"

"You speak of me as your son, Jesus. Just as your father was the Lord, the Christ, you appear to me as a Father. Are you then a Christ, or Jesus, the man?"

"The Christ am I, and no other. That bundle of bones and flesh and blood which was Jesus is no more. He exists only as the images and fantasies of those who live on. Just as I, who appear before you, am a bundle of images and fantasies, which dwell in your imagination."

"Is that all you are then, Jesus? Just a conglomerate of my fantasy? Of my wishes? Of my intentions and gatherings?"

"Just that, my son, just that. For what else is the Christ? What else is the divinity except an unformed vision, a concatenation of images potential and actual, waiting to be incarnated in the creation, man? Thou art God, my Father told me, and I understood. Now you understand, and now the many will understand as well. Incarnate me in you. Live me in you. In so doing you will be living me—and you. For what else can incarnate from within the soul of man, other than what he is, is meant to be? What else can the spirit do except wind itself into the soul and form images? And what else can the soul do except weave these images into forms and become realized in the flesh of pictures, in the flesh of body, in the flesh of words, in the flesh of blood? And, when it dies, this picture, this image, this word, this body, it does not die, but returns to its source, the spirit, and waits to be incarnated again. The Christ is everywhere and nowhere, within the One man and the many men. But you know all this already, Grandson of the Knight, you know all this."

I know it, Jesus, but it helps to hear you say it. For these words have come from other places for me, from Hebrew images, and Buddhistic images, and even from Pagan images.

"What is it, then, that you want of me, Grandson of the Knight? What is it then that you want?"

"You speak of wanting, Jesus, you speak of my desires. What a difference from the words attributed to Jesus of old, to give up desire, to give up the flesh, to give up worldliness. Only, of course, I now understand, to give up the ego desires and serve the Christ desires. But now the Christ wants to know what the ego wants!. . . . You laugh. It is good to know that a Christ can laugh. It is good to know that he that suffered the cross, embraced the cross, willingly underwent suffering, can now laugh. For I understand that we are brothers, that brothers need to help fulfill the need of the other, I understand it. For fathers sacrifice for sons, and sons for fathers.

"Ah, Jesus, your laugh has brought me an awareness, an understanding of what it means that Christ will now become brother, that this will be a religion of brothers and sisters, rather than of fathers and sons alone. For, as I said to myself, the religion of fathers and sons is one of sacrifice, one for the other, as well as fulfillment, the realization of the one in the other. But that of brothers, that is a mutuality where both help each other. Brothers in Christ will then have a new meaning, will it not? And sisters, too, and sisters. For sisters and brothers in Christ will also have a new meaning, a loving meaning, a helping meaning, a union meaning: Brother to brother is shoulder to shoulder, brother to sister is face to face! Yes!

"But what do I want, you ask, Jesus, what do I want? I want the Christ to live in me. I want the Christ to live in me with an easy yoke as you promise. I want to feel whole, to feel united, to know that the father and son and brother are united in me, and that I live my life and my love and my meaning. Not without some suffering, for I know that some is necessary for growth, for redemption, but out of an essential wholeness. That is what I want. I want my life to be full of intensity, of diversity and unity and of serenity. Can you hear? Intensity and serenity, diversity and unity. All of these opposites, like your cross. But I want them in a harmony of flow, in a way that brings the minimum of hurt to those I love, and I want others to have these things, too. For alone I am nothing, on a mountain, and I need my brothers and sisters, I need my lovers and friends, I need my fathers and sons, mothers and daughters, my neighbors and strangers. All this I need."

"And all these you shall have. And you shall have them because you give them. Blessed are those that give, I have said, for they shall receive. And exactly so, for they shall receive that which they give. You have given intensity and serenity, diversity and unity, you shall receive them. You have given your wholeness, you shall receive it. Thus is it more blessed to give than to receive, for one then receives the fruits of one's best gifts. It is just so, not a moral thrust, not a law to be obeyed, but a natural morality of the soul, a natural morality of the flow of life."

"But it is not always so, Jesus. The wicked do receive good things, and the good are unjustly punished."

"In life it is so, Grandson of the Knight, in life it is so. But there are other lives, other deeds, other bodies. My Father's house has many mansions, I have said, and it is true. There are the many of the lives, and the oneness of the being. Look to repair injustice, look to heal the wounded, but trust in God. For those that repair and heal will be treated justly and healed."

"I see, Jesus. But what of love, Jesus, what of love? I have loved the many and the one, in spirit, in soul, and in the flesh. I have loved as a man. What do you say of love? You who had not known woman? You who had not known children? You who had not known wife or lovers?"

"Is it so, Grandson of the Knight? Is it so? Are you so sure? Is the whole of my life known? Are there not stories of my having gone to the east to learn from the sages? Did not the Wise Men come from east and south and north? Were they not of all colors? Was it only the star that led them? Or was it not also that I had traveled there and learned? And are you so sure that I knew not woman? Perhaps it was only in the present Scripture that this was not included. For, was it not a time when it was more important to love spiritually? To love all mankind? To love and embrace, but not carnally 'know'? Was this not the answer for the sick animal of the time? You know that is true. So a truth was promulgated. But must you assume that because a truth was promulgated, the whole truth was there? Are there not truths which one is ready for? Are there not truths which unfold? Was this not the realization of your Grandfather, the Knight?"

"It is true, Jesus, it is true. We know of you only what is written, and what is written leaves much room for other experiences of you. I will not ask, I will only accept that it is possible for a Christian God of Love not only to have preached love, but to have experienced it!

"But if you know, Jesus; if you know what it is for a man to love, to love deeply and passionately, in the flesh, and to be rejected, to lose his love, to lose the significance of his life, his being—if you know these things, then tell me, answer me, how is a man to turn 'the other cheek,' to love his enemies, to endure the pain of the loss of a loved one, to endure the horror of the loneliness, of being cheated, of feeling the fool? Can you answer these things?"

"I can answer, Grandson of the Knight, I can answer. But you will not like my answer, you will not abide it. You will need to know more, you will need to know from my brother, the Eros of the depths, you will not be satisfied with my answer!"

"Try me, Jesus."

"Well, then, hear me. Whenever we love in the flesh, whenever we love carnally, we love wholly, totally. And, when we love, we demand, we crave, we desire, we cannot let go. All who love thusly are human and natural in it. And it is based on the divine, for that too is the way God loves, the way the Christ is embroiled and engaged with the flesh of mankind. But do not confuse the one with the other. The desire for union is intense; the desire for incarnation is intense; the need for love is intense; the experience of love at every level is intense. All these are intensity, just as you asked. But so also is the pain of loss intense; so also the pain of frustration, of lack of fulfillment. And here is the painful point which you will not accept. Love for any particular human being will never suffice for the love of God. Love of Christ will never be fulfilled for the love of any man, any woman, any child. Any of these, and all of these, man, woman, child, are where the Christ is; but, at last, the Christ is within, and that union cannot be found in the world. Thus did I say, abandon father and mother and follow me; abandon the things of this world and follow me. The 'me' of which I spoke was the Christ, that God which transcends every incarnation, every love, every bit of being."

"I hear you, Jesus, and I understand. But you also spoke of love in the flesh, as love of man, and of the community of loves. And I have believed in Christ 'among' you, as well as Christ 'within' you. What of that?"

"I knew that you would not accept, nor understand. For, you are in pain of loss, and this always precludes understanding, acceptance. Know only, that I love you, my son, that all will be well."

"I trust, Jesus. I do not understand; I do not accept; but I trust. I make an act of faith, I trust."

"Then you are Christian, my son. Faith in God, that is the Christian leap, that is what I did when I committed my spirit, that is what I did when I gave up the ghost. For I, too, did not know, I only trusted. Welcome, then, to the community of the faithful of believers! You do not have all, but you have faith. You can walk upon the earth, as you wished, modestly, courageously. You do not have all, but you have faith. Arise then, Grandson of the Knight! Arise, Knight III, arise and know the Christian spirit of Arthur and Lancelot, Knights also. And, know, at last, the Christian spirit of Guinevere, know it in yourself. It was given to your father to know it from them, to participate with them. Now you know that spirit in yourself. You are blessed."

Thus did I unexpectedly receive a blessing from Jesus, the Christ. Thus did I quietly and beneficently receive the Christian spirit: Faith. I had known the Hebraic love of devotion, of "holding on." I had known the Buddhistic love of acceptance, of emptying oneself, of allowing the demons to plague one and neither moving nor desiring. Now I was experiencing the Christian spirit of faith, of acceptance, of trust. And I suddenly felt that Hebraic devotion, Buddhistic acceptance and Christian faith were all the same. The three Gods and three spirits were, in truth, the same: God the Father, God the Son, and God the Holy Spirit; The Fathers of Israel: Abraham, Isaac, and Jacob, and the trinitarian compassion of the Buddha. One spirit of devotion, acceptance, faith. It was beautiful.

But, also, it was not enough. Just as Jesus had known, I was not satisfied. It was not enough. And so, from heaven, I sank down. From heaven I fell, slowly and heavily, down inside the cone, I fell all the way back to earth, I fell to where the Muses were, because all I had heard, Hebraic, Buddhistic, Christian, did not reconcile me to my own experience. For the Goddess was left out in all these. I had known God, but it was not enough. I awaited the Goddess—Aphrodite, mistress of Muses, of men. "Aphrodite" I prayed, "Come and help me; come and tell me; come and show me your love."

Aphrodite I

I had not long to wait. Within moments of my utterance of the prayer for her, the Goddess of Love appeared, just in the center of the circle of the Muses. Here on earth she appeared, just as any mortal woman, of average size and appearance. Average did I say? Yes, of course average, for is not her name Aphrodite Pandemos? Ordinary love she is, common love, or, really, the love which appears among all ranks and conditions of life. Just as her light olive coloring and dark hair are no different than the thousands of women along the Mediterranean Sea, or the Indian Ocean or the Pacific Ocean, for that matter; in short, most of the women of the world. And her shape was not so extraordinary either. She was rounded and pleasant appearing, but so are many women. In short, God and Love are Woman, are they not? But then: I looked at her, and she smiled. She smiled, this Goddess of Love, and I knew that Love is ordinary, but extraordinary. She smiled and I was enchanted. I saw the glow of her glory about her, for she is called Golden. I smelled the scent of her, the scent of Aphrodite, which was like the choicest bamboo, the most intoxicating incense, the balsam of Indian treasure boxes. As I smelled, I also tasted and felt her flesh, for all sensory pleasure and ecstasy were as one: it was the taste and touch and smell of a woman in love, or love of a woman. The many in the one of her, the many smells and tastes and touches of her in the one Goddess. I sighed and closed my eyes, for she also moaned softly and all senses were enthralled. Oh, my God, this is the touch of love, this the love of which the spiritual passions of maleness of Hebrew, Buddhist, Christian love can only guess! I fell to the ground, shivering and moaning. The many pains of all my loves, the agonies of abandonment, of love lost, of love unfulfilled, of love fulfilled in guilt and terror, of love as rape—all of these became bearable in the one moment of experience of the Goddess as the sensual, sensory love of woman. All was worth it, all tragedy, all despair, all the horror of love, for the one moment of carnal, fleshly, marvelously sensual love. Oh, the smell of her—woman-love; oh, the taste of her—woman-love; oh, the touch of her—woman-love; oh, the sound of her—woman-love; oh, the look of her—woman-love! I wept and I sighed, in joyful remembrance, in sorrowful loss, in painful need, in happy acceptance!

"Aphrodite," I prayed: "Thou art Love. I, Hebrew, Buddhist, Christian, spiritual man, passionate man, enlightened man, I a man, bow before you and worship you as love incarnate! I worship you, for I have known you, in the One Woman, and in many women. You come and go, incarnate in a woman for a time and leave, perhaps forever. You are fickle: you come as you wish, stay as you wish. You even incarnate in a part of woman, and not the whole. Your totality of scent and sound, of touch and taste, and of the look, appear here and there. Sometimes you are in the lips of a woman, so that you taste like the softness of the inside of the thigh. Sometimes you are in the breasts so that Solomon can speak of gentle does. Sometimes you are in belly or ear-lobe, all of these. But in the parts where you mostly are: Are you not called Kallipygo, "she of the beautiful buttocks?" And are you not in the holiest of holies, the soft tender place where your name itself, "Foam-born" comes? For is not the liquid of vagina the foam of which you rise, and is not the channel of our entrance into you the same from which we are born? You, Goddess, you Aphrodite, command me!"

Thus did I speak to the Goddess, in words that came to me just by being in her presence, and on the sacred ground where the Muses had come to me. The Goddess answered only with a smile, and a gentle laugh. But then she touched me. My God, she touched me! She took my hand, and looked deeply into my eyes. I knew then why it was that she was called kindest and merciful to mankind. I knew that I had often felt her dominion over sweet lust, for I had known that sparrow bird of hers in my passions. I knew that she was mistress of the whispering of maidens, for from early adolescence I had shivered at that sound, which intrigued and beckoned but also made me shy and fearful—and that is how one ought to be about love. I knew that she was mistress, too, of laughter and hoaxes. Is not love full of mirth and tricks? Are we not deceived by illusion in love, and overcome with the laughter of union? But now I knew, from the tender look in her eyes, that Aphrodite was also mistress of loving kindness: for there was compassion in them, not like the Buddha, perhaps, but surely like the Kwan Yin, the most compassionate feminine, that the East knows, too. I looked and saw the depths of the Goddess, and I was comforted for the many pains I had suffered in love.

Aphrodite's look told me that I must go deeper into her, as she had gone deeper with her look into me. She wordlessly told me that I should meditate upon her life, the stories of her, just as I had with Jesus, and Bluebeard, and Don Juan before them. For, if one would know the meaning of the experience of love, one must reflect as well as experience, one must ponder as well as live, one must think as well as feel. Aphrodite smiled again as I accepted this charge, and she slowly disappeared. I knew, though, that she remained nearby, as I would reflect upon her, come to understand her maniness, her fickleness, and come further in my need to understand love.

So, then, in my acceptance of the "stations of Aphrodite," the story of the passion of the Goddess, let me begin at the beginning, let me begin with her birth.

Kronos, the God, castrated his father, Ouranos and the phallus fell first to earth and was then cast into the sea. There it roamed and tossed for a long time. White foam, "aphros," gathered around it, formed a skin and a maiden sprang up and grew within it. She rose up out of the water, this shy and beautiful Goddess, and young grass sprouted at her feet. She is called Aphrodite by Gods and men because she was fashioned of foam. Thus the tale of the birth of the Goddess.

Aphrodite, you are fashioned of foam, but your being is that of a phallus. Imagine! The Goddess of Love is, in reality, made up of the phallus of God! Is that merely the transition of a culture, changing from matriarchate to patriarchate? Is that only a male vanity, that love is, in reality, not even feminine at all but related to his manhood? No, there must be a deeper truth in it. Kronos, the God of time, of the need for realization in life, in everyday being, takes the power of his heavenly Father, Ouranos, depotentiates him, and brings his essence down into the depths of the psyche. Not even the earth of everyday life is sufficient. So, the need for time, for becoming, for measuring and quantifying, takes away the power of the eternal and casts it into the depths of the psyche, into the unknown waters where it wanders. But, from it, from the male potency of desire and love (Eros and Himeros, love and desire, accompany Aphrodite from the beginning in the tale), come the Goddess. But she, too, is called Ourania, Aphrodite the Heavenly, knowing that love in its female form has its own heaven, its own eternality, its own spirituality which comes to earth as Aphrodite Pandemos.

Goddess, you are born from the union of male phallus and foam. The foam of the waves is surely like that liquid of love in the sexual organs, that spiritual-physical essence which is both an originator of love and its consequence, the flow of passion and the resultant thereof. Surely the foam is that. But what else is the foam? Is it not the union of water and air? Of the depths of the soul with the air of heaven? That is what true love is: a union of the desire and instinctual passion of the phallus along with the airy foam of the spirit on high. Well, then, Aphrodite Ourania and Pandemos, you are love spiritual and love carnal, love eternal and love realized, you carry within you love male and love female. What a sacred and strange mystery, that the

most feminine, the most female, the most womanly, the most woman
of all Goddesses should be born of the male organ, and of that in union
with the spiritual waters, the divine depth and heights! But was this
not true of another great female, Eve? Though not a Goddess, she
was born of a male part, too. But here, the form is clearer: man's love
is created from the falling away from the power of eternal heaven (just
as with poor Adam), into the earth and pain of life, into the depths
of unknowingness, and finally, to be born and experienced as the
feminine triumphant, as Goddess. Love must be born from the heights,
fall into the depths and be realized as divine. She is born and arises
in the grass of the living spring, in the beauty of nature on earth,
which is neither the eternal heights unchanging, nor the eternal
depths unknowing. Aphrodite, Goddess, idea become flesh, maleness
become femaleness, I adore you and bow before you.

The myth goes on that Aphrodite was received and clothed by the
Horai, the daughters of Themis, Goddess of the law and order proper
to the relations between the sexes. The ancients thought that the
love Goddess had to be clothed, adorned, and part of the law and
order of things before brought before the other Gods. I understand,
Aphrodite. You are so magnificent, so inspiring, so consuming, that
it is dangerous to see you naked, uncovered, in your true state; every
God and mortal would desire you, want you only for himself if that
were so. But time changed, Aphrodite, did it not? In time, Praxiteles
and other artists were able to see you naked and whole. Are we there
again, Aphrodite? Are we advanced again to the place where we need
to see love unabashed, love in the flesh unadorned by rules and
regulations? Are we sufficiently ordered in ourselves to worship you
and adore you and experience you without all the rules of Themis?
Well, perhaps some of us are, Aphrodite. Help me, Goddess, help
me to treasure you, whether clothed in the laws of Themis, the
measured relations of love, or in the nakedness of your true being.
And help us all, Goddess, to adore you, worship you, as you are!

The myths of the Goddess after her birth are mostly concerned with
her love affairs. I suppose that it is fitting and proper for a Goddess
of love to be so involved. What higher work is there than to live in
the play of love between men and women and what better way to
demonstrate this than by the example of one's own life? Did not the
Greeks know, fair Goddess, that the Gods and Goddesses are the face
of experience? That when the experience happens, the God is there?
They knew it, fair one. So, let me look to you, to know what the
experience of love is.

Before you became a Goddess, Aphrodite, before you became
embroiled with your loves, before Zeus summoned you to be among

the honored Olympians, the story is that you abided in pleasure and peace in the water with Nerites, son of Neueus. That honored and only son among fifty daughters was the fairest of men and gods. You were perfectly content, Aphrodite, to take pleasure only in him, to love only him, as you lived in the water. When the time came for you to be summoned to the Olympians, you implored your one and only love, your comrade and playmate, to come with you. But he wanted to stay in the sea with his sisters and parents. You wanted to bestow wings upon him, but he had no desire for this either. So, Goddess, you changed him into a cockle, and took as your companion the young love-God, Eros, to whom you gave wings.

Aphrodite, I know you in this, for you are truly woman. In the beginning, you loved only one man, lived for only one man, you were naturally and totally monogamous, and with a chosen one among men and Gods. You accepted the task of coming out of the depths, of love no longer being only unconscious and unaware. You accepted that love must be worshipped and adored as Divine, in consciousness and in power. You were aware of this Goddess, I know. And you wanted to take your consort with you, to be your faithful and exclusive lover. You wanted to give him wings, to spiritualize him, and have your monogamous love be elevated to a spiritual principle. But your lover was not up to this; he wanted to remain with his family, to be the happy boy. He was not fit to be your partner and spouse. So you made him into a shy shell fish, unconscious, unawakened, safe, in no pain. And you took the once and future God, Eros, with you. You must have known, Goddess, you must have had that fantastic wisdom of nature to know.

Perhaps, Goddess, it was necessary for you to leave that ideal state of natural oneness and bliss, natural monogamy, so that you could discover and portray your maniness to all humankind. Perhaps you needed to be born into the spirit and flesh of the Greek Gods to show us what love is all about. We, too, need to see the maniness which has arisen out of your oneness. But I wonder, dear Goddess, how you felt when your deepest love, your most darling partner, could not accompany you on your spiritual task. I wonder how it was with you. The story does not say, for the story only tells us the facts, the situation, not the feelings of those involved. But I can guess, Aphrodite, I can guess what you felt. It must have been painful and awful. You must have felt lonely and broken, desperate and in despair. For, once having been happy, it must have been painful to change your state, to develop again, to become conscious and aware, to participate in the many and thus lose your love. But you tried, and your consort was found wanting. Thus love must develop, grow, it must spiritualize

itself and become a conscious value, once it has fallen from eternity
into the depths. It must come back again. Goddess, I know what it
feels like to be torn from one's love into a maniness, into a need to
carry love, its pains and pleasures. Goddess, I know. The story does
not say, but we can guess.

Again I see your face, your eyes. You look, and smile. Your eyes
tell me that what I say is true. Goddess, I hold your face. Now I look
as deeply into you, as you looked into me. I am overwhelmed and
adore you, my sister, my lover, my Goddess, my friend.

Aphrodite II

From her birth and elevation, let me proceed to the next "station of the Goddess." The life of this Goddess, like that of some women, is not generally considered remarkable in other than her men. So it was in the ancient days, and this was certainly true of Aphrodite, who was more woman, more feminine, more Herself, than the Goddess in any other form. In short, from birth and initiation into Herself, the next tale we hear of her is that she has wed. Who is the great God who becomes her spouse? Who could possibly be worthy of such a fantastically attractive and challenging creature? Why, it is Hephaistos, the smith and master craftsman! Of all the Gods, of all the possibilities that existed for her, Ares and Hermes, Poseidon and Apollo, Dionysos even, only Hephaistos, the crippled dwarf, the God content with his smithy, the least romantic or attractive of the Gods, is the one chosen to be the Love Goddess' spouse! Why is this, I wonder, why him? Is it simply, as one often sees, that the most attractive of women, the most gorgeous of creatures, are often wedded to ugly men? Is it that loveliness needs its total opposite, and the reverse? Perhaps these are true reasons, but they are shallow. There must be a deeper truth here.

To understand, I must go deeper into the figure of Hephaistos, what he was and did. We are told that this master craftsman created young virgins made of gold who moved as if alive. They thought and talked and worked. He even fashioned the first woman, Pandora. So he is the creator, par excellence, and particularly the creator of the feminine. In some tales, just as Aphrodite is wed to Ares, Hephaistos is wed to the youngest of the Graces, Aglaia, "the glorious." Why, then, is this ugly crippled creature so close to the feminine, so close to creation?

Hephaistos was a child of the great secret love of Zeus and Hera, during the three hundred years of their secret relationship. Hephaistos was a premature birth, and his soles and feet were turned back to front, not fit for walking. He was rejected by his mother, and cast from up on high into the sea, just as Aphrodite had been. Sometimes he is said to have been fatherless, or born from Hera's thigh. The Goddess who later became so annoyed at her husband's affairs, Hera, was herself ashamed at her own affair and the child from it, and cast him out. He was caught and held by two other sea-goddesses and cared for, himself fashioning jewelry for them. It is also said that Zeus rejected him and cast him down from the place of the Gods, and this at a time when Zeus strung his wife Hera on a golden cord between Heaven and Earth in punishment for her persecution of Heracles.

Hephaistos, then, is a rejected one. Like Aphrodite, he is cast from above into the sea, to find his temporary protection and then welcomed back into the group of the Gods. But he is born of the Mother, Hera, just as Aphrodite is born from the Father. Both result from heinous deeds, father castration and mother rejection; crimes against nature. From the one, true Love is born. And the other? Is it not creativity itself? Is not the fire which attached to Hephaistos the fire of creativity? It was forge and metal which fashioned gorgeous images. Is not creativity also wed to the charm of the feminine? It is impossible to be creative unless one is wed to the Goddess, to love, I think. And is it not also true that the heels and soles backwards are the mark of the inward-looking, inward-walking, depth-seeking principle of masculine passion which is necessary for creation? This is the natural spouse of Aphrodite, who continually walks out among the people of the world, stirring them up into loving each other, being involved with each other. The opposites wed here: love with creativity; beauty with outer ugliness; inner-peering with outer living. Both are created from above, rejected and fall into the depths of the psyche, then are reunited with the divine. I understand it now: Love-in-the-world-Aphrodite coupled with Creation-in-the-soul-Hephaistos. The one, rejected by the male, yet part of it, the other rejected by the female, yet part of it. Love-in-the-world has many children, as does Aphrodite, but with Hephaistos, none is mentioned, or only sometimes Eros. For such a union, of love and creation, can only beget total Eros, nothing more, nothing less! So, I salute Hephaistos, rejected by the Gods, feared by the Gods, respected by the Gods, and spouse of Love!

But some tales also say that Ares was the spouse of Aphrodite, that war was wed to love, and that there were numerous children, Phobos and Deimos, "Fear" and "Terror," Eros and Anteros, "Love" and "Answering Love," and even the beautiful Harmonia, "the Uniter." One can understand these results of the union of the Goddess of Love with the Lord of Battles. Does not love—when the product of two such passionate natures—bring such things as fear, terror, love and answering love, as well as the beautiful second Aphrodite of harmony and union? We all know that such love brings these things. But why is Ares also considered the husband of Aphrodite? We all know of the famous tale of the deception of Hephaistos by Aphrodite and Ares, and how the master craftsman caught them in his invisible net. But, before I examine that tale for what it tells of love, I must understand how it is that Ares is the rival of Hephaistos. It is told that Hera, so ashamed of her misbegotten son, cast him out, and that Hephaistos then got his revenge by sending the Goddess a throne most beautiful, but bound with invisible chains. Hera accepted the gift, and thus was bound between heaven and earth by the chains. The Gods could do nothing to free her. Nor would Hephaistos. Ares, the mighty war-God undertook the task, but was defeated by the flames of mighty Hephaistos. The power of war and conflict ultimately retreat before the fire of creativity. The power of creation will always be greater than the power of destruction; if not, none would be here to speak of either of them!

It was Dionysos, who gave Hephaistos wine, who was able to bring Hephaistos to Olympus. Such a spirit, such an intoxication by another God can temporarily becloud the creative God, but only temporarily. Hephaistos set his mother free only in exchange for marriage with Aphrodite. And so was he rewarded. Creativity, sometimes clouded, knows its mother, knows its power, and can only be assuaged by love! Aphrodite, your ways are not so mysterious as I enquire of your stations.

Now one knows why Ares, deceiver of Hephaistos when he is wed, came back. He was defeated by Hephaistos once, and surely needed revenge. But more than that: in the deep fires of the binding of the Mother, creation is not to be denied; in the passion of love, in the battles of involvement of love and life, creation is sometimes impotent, deceived, even stupefied. But this is true: Love must unite with both Gods, be married to both Gods, for She requires both the inner products of union—art—and the outer products of union—relationships— to make her happy. She is wed now to the one, now to the other. Perhaps, Eros is indeed a son of both fathers, Ares and Hephaistos, the passion of conflict, and the passion of the forging of new things. I see, Aphrodite; I see how the soul of the Greeks knew you, understood you.

But speak to me, now, Goddess. Before I proceed with your "stations," before I continue trying to understand you by means of your loves and your life, speak to me. Tell me, in your own cool and warm words, give me solace in my own need for love in . . . I almost said bereavement. For the loss of a love is like a bereavement, is it not? I feel as if dying, for a love of many years and much depth has gone away, and I am desolate. It is good to understand your story, Aphrodite. It is good to know of the truths of your initial union, of your marriages with conflict and creativity, of your only hinted-at depths. But show me some mark of kindness, some mercy. You are said to be merciful, Goddess, but thus far, in your treatment of Nerites, and even of Hephaistos, you are not merciful. Nor do I, poor Grandson of the Knight, dubbed Knight III by the Muses, feel mercifully treated. Speak to me, Goddess, I implore you.

"Do not implore, Knight III," said the Goddess. "Do not abase yourself before me. I do not respond to abasement. I respond to a swelling of love, a pride of love, an exclaiming of love. Look at my fullness! Look at my richness of flesh, the flow of blood and warmth, smell and taste! You know these, Knight III! I have not deprived you of them. You have known them fully and deeply, more than most men, for you have worshipped me. You have recognized, served, supported, and adored me. For this, the rewards and gifts to you have been great. Yes, I said gifts! You have loved long, loved many, and been very deeply loved in return: those are the gifts. These are yours, plus the gift of tongues, of hearing and knowing the languages, having the Muses respond to you. Have you not already divined the union of Hephaistos with myself? Have you not already understood the union of Ares with myself? I tell you that you have. Well, then, make use of your knowledge, love, and gifts. Much have I given you, more still will I give. Stand up, then, for your love, for your gifts. Stand up and be a man! Stand up and be a God-man!"

These words of the Goddess solaced me. They allowed me to straighten my back. I was reminded of what my good and beautiful wife had said to me, that all things come in time, that my impetuous soul had difficulty knowing that, keeping that. Good wife, server of Aphrodite with her deep love, she knew that. Goddess, in loving her, I serve you! Goddess, in her loving me, I feel your love, too. And with others also . . . ! Lord, I almost said, Goddess. Lord! I almost called you Lord of Love! Like a male! Like the loving Lord of Heaven, like the Lord of Jacob, the Lord of Buddha, like the Lord of Jesus! But you are a Lord! Are you not born of phallic flesh as well as foam? Are you not called Aphrodite Ourania, Love as Heavenly, worshipped even by the men-loving males of Plato's time? Are you not, then, also Lord? Even though so feminine, so female, so womanly, so woman, so Goddess, so human, you are Lord, too. Goddess, I adore you. And in loving you, I find myself!

I continue your Stations, Aphrodite. I continue my meditations upon your story and thus understand love more deeply. In this, I pray to you, just as the Christians pray to Jesus in doing the Stations of His Cross.

I have spoken, already, of the adulterous union of Ares with Aphrodite, when Hephaistos had gone away. Once again, Hephaistos, who had entrapped his mother in the almost invisible steely-web, did it again with the adulterous pair. Then the husband, in terrible voice and wild rage, summoned the Gods to see how Aphrodite had made a mockery of him. He complained bitterly of Aphrodite, who shamed him because he was a cripple, and loved Ares because he was fair and straight-limbed. Yet, it was the parents' fault, he said, who should never have begotten him. Poor Hephaistos, understandably humiliated as cuckold and proclaiming his misery. Poor Hephaistos, who did not stand up for himself. But he could not. The inner-searching, image-forging, creative-wielding principle is always humiliated by the more beautiful, more attractive, more enticing involvements of life. It is only successful in its creation. But hear, how he complains! How he makes a fool of himself by demanding back the gifts from his adoptive father Zeus! Can those marriage gifts be returned? Can humiliation be repaid by a return of gifts? Aphrodite, Hephaistos shows his smallness here. It is meet that although Poseidon convinced Hephaistos to set Ares free, in promise of atonement, that none was ever made. Zeus was disgusted with Hephaistos for making such a public spectacle—he only humiliated himself, really, as the Father God recognized. But the truth of the myth is that nobody paid Hephaistos because he was so much in love with Aphrodite that he never would divorce her anyway! That is the deep truth, Aphrodite, and that is the deep truth, Hephaistos! The creative spirit is so enamored of the Goddess that it will suffer any pain, any humiliation, because of it. Love leaves creativity and goes off into the web of life and involvements. The web of creativity is no more powerful than the web of the witch of life which magically involves conflict, passion, people. No use to complain, Hephaistos, though you must. No use to demand redress and justice, for there is none. Love is wed to Ares as well as Hephaistos.

Oh, Goddess, deeper and deeper do I understand you. Deeper and deeper I go in my understanding of my own love of two women. It is you, Goddess, it is you in me. For I am Hephaistos, desiring you, and I am Ares, desiring you. And you are the women, Aphrodite, you are in them, desiring both. Oh, Goddess, by what mystery can you be wed to both. By what mystery can you go back and forth and make both happy? Apparently, from the myth, it is not possible, for one is watered down, adulterated, caught in adultery. Creativity or life, inner or outer. Goddess, I implore you, find your way in my soul so that neither is chagrined, neither is adulterated! Can it be so? Not in the myth, not in your tale. But Goddess, eternal one, Aphrodite Ourania, as well as Aphrodite Pandemos, dream yourself onward, come to us from the Greece of long ago and find a new way to enter into our lives, a new way to reconcile loves. In your Oneness, help us to find peace in your Maniness.

Not just Ares and Hephaistos were yours, Goddess. I continue with your tale and want to know the other Gods who wanted you. The Goddesses, wisely, stayed at home, but the Gods all came at Hephaistos cry and confronted them. In came Poseidon, Hermes and Apollo. They laughed at Hephaistos' cunning, but were enamored of the Goddess at once. Apollo asked Hermes, "Would you like to lie in such chains with the golden Aphrodite?" And Hermes answered with an oath that he willingly would, even if the chains were three times as strong. Hermes, the clever and wily, Hermes, ancestor of mind and magic, would gladly enthrall himself with love, with the Goddess, and suffer any humiliation!

Oh, Goddess, how right you were to love and respect this God. With Apollo you did not sleep, of course. Love cannot wed itself to cool reason. Apollo can only observe you and marvel at you! That is fair and right enough for reason, even when a God. But Hermes, that wily and airy spirit who is mind more than reason, magic more than science, he knows your value. Is it not Hermes, after all, who is the God behind the alchemy of transformation? It is Hermes who is the Lord of the creation of the philosopher's stone, the merging of male and female, making a new self, which puts them on par with Hephaistos. You knew that, Goddess of Love, and so united with the great Hermes. And your offspring? The Hermaphroditus: the union of male and female which was the goal of the alchemist's art! Aphrodite, Goddess of love, your goldenness is here, there and everywhere! Your love united you with creation, with life, with the magical mind which produces the golden stone, in which you partake! Goddess, words desert me. Like a dumb-male alchemist, lost in his projections on matter and metals, I see you and am dumbfounded!

But clever Poseidon, that God of the sea and earthquakes, he also lusted after you. He, who is usually straightforward, turned wily and clever. Aphrodite, men and Gods change in your presence, we turn into our opposites, we transform ourselves in desire of you. For you are the sparrow and dove, the birds of lust and love!

And what did Poseidon do? He concealed his jealousy of Ares and pretended to sympathize with Hephaistos. He claimed that he would see to it that Ares paid for his release with the equivalent of the marriage gifts. He—goodheart that he was—offered to take Ares' place under the net if he did not pay and even marry her! Hephaistos accepted this offer, but Ares never paid. Nor did Poseidon. But you were appreciative of Poseidon, Goddess, and you slept with him, too.

Deception, hurt, betrayal, ending. Oh, Goddess, why is there such pain in love? Why is the sparrow there with the darkness, with the pecking-out of eyes, with the loveless end of care, with the cruel misuse of feeling? Why is compassion spoiled by sourness? Speak to me, Goddess, tell me, solace me! Or, if there is no solace, then make me understand, make me see clearly, make me transform my whimpering soul from the place of need and pain, into one of compassion and caring!"

"You, yourself, have said it, Knight III. Have compassion, if you can. We Gods have so little of it. We have so little for man, for each other. I am called the kind and merciful, but often I am not. I go where the passion is, do I not? Am I not wed to the God of war, and the God of creation? And, as you have seen, am I not coupled with Hermes, the magician, and Poseidon, the Earth-shaker? I am, I am. Have, then, compassion! Have, then, more than I."

"How can I, Goddess? I who need it so much more, I who am a mere mortal? I, who am resentful, bitter, greedy, truculent at what I have given and not received sufficiently in return. I who suffer in belly and heart and head. Goddess, you have known of my suffering! Help me!"

"Weep, my son. There is relief in that. I, who have been lover, can call you son. I, who have been called callous, can have compassion for you."

"I know. I feel it. But I feel it in the drawing away from erstwhile love. I feel it in the . . . but no. I weep. I feel the emptiness of words. I feel the emptiness of solace, the pain in the belly which shows the depths of my hunger, my hurt, my continuing agony at your hands, or . . . love."

"Love is Music, Knight III. I stand here, at the center of the magic circle. I stand here, where Kalliope has stood. I stand and know that the words and sounds and visions and images and feelings and thoughts and sensations and intuitions of the Muses are the Music of the soul. Thus are all songs, songs of love. Of love desired, love lost, love fulfilled or unfulfilled. And, do you think that because I am the Goddess of Love I am unaffected? Do you think that because the stories of me show me as playing, as enjoying, as being wholly lover, that I suffer no pain, that I suffer no feelings of loss, of guilt? That I cannot also be Mother as well as Lover? Compassionate as well as passionate? The tales would make it seem so, I know. For it needs the poets to speak of me. It needs the men of Greece to be born again. And they are, from time to time, everywhere. And you, Knight III, though neither like your Grandfather or Father, you, too, are a poet, though you disclaim it. And you are poet because you attend, you listen to me, you search me out, you find me.

"But Knight, I need you. We Gods, we all need you, you men. Without you, we have no food of sweet sacrifices—your emotion, your spirit, your lively instinctual nature—yes, all that! But much more important, we need you to transform ourselves. What do we know of the human condition unless you tell us? What do we know of ourselves unless you mirror ourselves to us? We need you. I need you. I need, too, to be reborn, to come back into life. And this act, this loving and pious act of the attention to my mystery, the worship of my tale, that is an act of bearing me, once again, within you. But do not forget, oh Knight, that just as was told to your Grandfather, and to your Father, I am in the world, everywhere, not only inside you! You have and will know me in every woman, every love, every passion, every moment when you say, 'Aha, Aphrodite is here!' You will know in your tears, in your heart, in your phallus, in your belly, and yes, even in your head. For love is everywhere or nowhere; I am everywhere or nowhere."

"Goddess, I know this. And I hate to lose any part of you, anywhere. I want all of you, everywhere. Does that mean, as one told me, that I cannot have all of you in one place? That you are, indeed, the One in the Many, and never the One in the One?"

You are silent . . . You do not speak to me here . . . So I contact another love, neither the one who is eternally with me, my wife, nor the one who abandoned me. I contact a friend, a loved one, a dear one. And she assuages me, she hears me, calms me. Are you there, too, Goddess? Of course you are. You are there, everywhere! And I shall seek you and find you, and accept you wherever you come. But I shall also know that each person is a person, not a Goddess. Each person is an incarnation, a Goddess, yes, but not the whole of you. But no, they are the whole of you, but a part of you. Oh, Goddess, you know what I mean. I seek you, to find you, but keep my humanity, theirs, yours!

Aphrodite III

Following this meditation with the Goddess upon the hurt, betrayal and pain of love, following the reflective concentration upon Her love for Hephaistos, creation from within, and Ares, creation in relationships, I had a dream. The Goddess answered me with her words, but then a dream came. This dream and what happened with it, Goddess, I offer up to you. I give it, as a sacrifice, to you. I present it as a work, as a devotion of love, as a way of mingling with you. Now hear it, Goddess, and what came of it:

I dreamed that there came to me a couple, a dark-haired man and an equally dark-haired woman. Both were very handsome, well-formed, but both had sour or sinister or sneering looks in their faces. The woman, full of breast, came toward me and asked of me where she could find a Jewish lung. The man, sneering of face, took my hand and forcefully pushed it down to his penis, as if demanding that I attend to it. I felt the peculiar demand of the woman as puzzling, impossible, and the unfeeling pressure of the demand of the man made me angry. I awakened from this dream and felt compelled to reflect upon it, to stay with it, to solve it as if it were a Buddhist Koan.

First the woman. She seemed at once like those many attractive but bitter women of all races and creeds: those who are totally devoted—or want to be—to one man, one love, but unhappily. They are aware of their gifts (the full breasts), but they are bitter because they are unfulfilled in their deeply monogamous wish. This is because the man they love is not available, or the love dies, or the man is unfaithful, or the myriad other reasons which hurt and make bitter this deeply monogamous need of the feminine soul. Everything in one place; everything in one relationship; all or nothing. Is it not natural that this woman would seek a Jewish lung, a Hebraic spirit of the One God? Hear oh, Israel, say the Jews, the Lord our God, the Lord is One! Thus the longing of this woman for that spirit. And she asks it of me.

Now the man. Here he is, a man very aware of his phallus, the deep masculinity of his spirit-in-the-flesh. He wants the natural polygamy of his masculine nature accepted. Does not the phallus respond to many women? Does not the desire for union go to more than one place? It is natural that in serving love that he go where his deepest nature leads him to go. The God is there. He demands my attention as well. With his own power, greater than my will, he forces me to attend to his masculine striving.

These two, Aphrodite, have made their claims on me. These two, who had a history of intense love for each other—these two demanded of me. I know them, Goddess, I know them, from deeply in my own soul, and in my life. Have I not always felt the tremendous need for the one love, the perfect union, the ideally monogamous marriage which would be deeply right under the law of the Testament, Old and New? And, have I not felt the pull toward the many loves, the many experiences, the many involvements? I have experienced both; the love of one woman, the love of many. Each principle has violated the other.

Goddess, I have known and felt and lived these all too fully, all too well. Yet, not too well, but with pain and agony, with stupidity, with doggedness and stubbornness, as well as their opposites of pleasure and joy, with consciousness, with devotion and persistence. And, Goddess, are you not there in these two? Is it not you, in two forms, who speak to me? The man, for example. When he points and persists in making me attend to his phallus, are you not there in that phallus? Are you not born of it? And are you not the living representative of the maniness? The woman, too, Aphrodite: are you not present, as you have said, in every woman? Are you not full of your gifts of love, of kindness and compassion, of care? Were you not, in the early days, totally at one with your love for Nerites? Were you not also desirous of maintaining this oneness from the depths of the soul-sea to the heights of the spirit-sky? And did not Nerites choose to stay with his many sisters? So, Goddess, you are in both. The love in the chest, which is compassionate, hearty, caring, full to bursting with the desire to give, to assuage pain, to make full and rich. And the love in the phallus, longing to penetrate, to complete, to fulfill, to go deep in love and fructify the many. Goddess, you are there in both, just as you married both Ares and Hephaistos. Oh, Goddess, they have warred and battled in me, in my soul, in my life. And I am not alone, so many are like me. So, then, Goddess, tell me, how I can serve these two. How can I give the Jewish lung, the monogamous devotion to the woman who needs the one, and, at the same time, serve the phallic pressure of the man, to take hold of it?

Goddess, tell me, I beg of you. I present my thoughts, my service, my devotion to you, tell me, guide me, I pray you!

"Knight III, you are doing it! You have been doing it! And you will continue to do it! Because you are a Knight, like Father and Grandfather, and because you are Buddhist and Christian and Jew. You have, are and will, I know it. You will serve both, just as in the past. You will serve the inner union, the marriage of Hephaistos, the deep mystery of love as the oneness inside. And you will serve the outer union, the marriage of Ares, the deep passion of the union outside. And Knight III, as you already glimmer, you will serve the one and the many in both places. From within, you continually seek the many, for ever greater union in oneness. You seek to unite with the all, in a great circumambulation of the soul of man. So, like Hephaistos with me, you seek that perfect and creative union of the Many in the One. And outside you are devoted to where I manifest, in every form of relationship in which heart-feeling or passion-desire appear. And you pursue them, each relationship, relentlessly, to bring each one to its natural wholeness. You seek, outside, the One in Many. Inside: Many in One. You are doing it, Grandson of the Knight. You are devoted to each relationship and you are devoted to the soul. What more can anyone, even a Goddess like myself, ask of you?"

But these two, Goddess, this couple. They are not Gods or Goddesses, but human beings, I think. They demand. Or are they Gods? Are you saying that I can answer to them that I am doing the best that I can, that they, too, must love each other, respect each other. For they, too, long to unite, long to be whole, long to find each in the other . . . How do they unite? Like Hermaphroditus, perhaps, who, in one form, has breasts and phallus? Perhaps, Goddess, perhaps. But that is found in the marriage of alchemy, a proper union for the inner work, but a monstrosity in the world.

Do they unite then, as Priapus, your son, Goddess, with the passionate spirit of Dionysus? That great ugly figure with huge phallus can be found only in orgies, in great dyonisiac, impersonal celebrations of the phallic. That, Goddess, can occur in the moment, the special religious celebration, perhaps, but that surely is not the symbol of union. Nor, Goddess, can it occur with Terror and Fear, the natural consequence of your union with Ares. These surely occur, but they are not satisfying. Even Harmonia, the uniter, who is, as they say, a second Aphrodite . . . ah, Aphrodite, I know. Only Eros, your stories say, is the common product of your union with Hephaistos and with Ares. Only Eros, your son, and also your brother. Did he not accompany you when Nerites would not? Did he not take wing, become spiritualized? Just as the true Hermaphroditus is winged, spiritual? You nod, Goddess. Again I am driven to Eros, that God who dwells in the depths. You drive me to him, Goddess.

Though not yet ready to pursue him in the depths, though not completed in my meditations of the Stations of Aphrodite, I find myself sinking down into the earth. I sink down, deeper and deeper.

But I am holding on to the hands of the woman seeking after the Jewish lung, and the man seeking to have his phallus held. I hold on to them, sinking deep into the earth. I hold on to her breasts, I hold on to his phallus. We sink. Down, down we go. We go past forest, we go past library, we go deep, beyond caves, beyond light, beyond darkness.

Down in that darkness, as I was falling, I remembered another dream, of long ago. Just as the present dream, with its hounding of the man and the woman, came to challenge me, this old dream now came to haunt me, but also quieted me. Long ago I dreamed:

I had been on a long journey and had come deep into the earth, where there was a cave. I entered the cave and found a room with a light in it, dim, from an unknown source. A tapestry hung on the wall, very beautiful. On it, was a figure like Columbus, but this one was a Knight, accompanied by an Indian. They were discovering a new world. In this new world was a powerful being like the Mercurius of Alchemy, a Hermes-like sun-figure giving off a halo of light. The God and spirit of Alchemy was here. And then I saw, not as a tapestry, but as a living gigantic being, a figure, chained to the floor. He was huge, powerful. This was a God of Love, I knew, chained here. In my pocket I had the key to unlock him. I hesitated for a moment, in fear, but then decided to unchain him. I did so, and we immediately began an arrow-like voyage to the City. We came to the City, the Center. Thus the dream.

Since then, many years before, I had, like my fathers before me, pursued the knightly vision of the Alchemical Art. I had discovered, as had others before me, a new world. But I also found the living reality of the chained God of Love. The Once and Future God was here, and I had unleashed him, accepted the task of coming with him into life, the City and Center. Indeed, I had been with him ever since, had I not? I remembered dreams of such a figure forcing a woman to lick up the remains of love-making, thus teaching her to love. Had I not suffered and struggled to contain it? Had I not, as well, felt the enormous power of this God, in heart and phallus, in head and belly? I had. So now I knew who it was that I had served these years: Eros, Son of Aphrodite. But also her brother: product of relationship and creativity, but also equal to the Goddess; spiritualized, elevated, but also made human in the struggle. Goddess, I know your son-brother. And I know that my Father knew him as Charioteer. The Son of the Knight knew him, indeed, as that wise and passionate union of Many in the One, One in the Many, did he not? Was that not what he had known on the Ship of Solomon? His story had told me so. And my Grandfather? Had he not known Eros as the Messiah, that once and future God-man? Reconciler of Christian and Jew and Pagan? I think so. I had not known that I, like my fathers before me, was serving the same God. I was, and did not know it. Knowing this, I had the instinct to leave my two friends, man and woman, there in the depths of the Earth, in the home of Eros. I knew that I, with my own ego and its limited powers, could not unite these two. I hoped that would I but leave them here in the depths, in the deepest place of the soul, that they would unite of themselves, or that the God-beyond-all-images would unite them. In this act of mine, was the faith of the Christian, a trust, the acceptance of the Buddhist, sitting firm on the earth, the devotion of the Hebrew in the God beyond all images, and the bowing before the pagan, for did I not acknowledge this Lord to be Eros, a pagan God?

Thus, in my act of devotion to Eros, my trust in Love by action and surrender, by devotion and letting go, I put the opposites of the soul into the hands of the One and Many God. In so doing, I came up, once again, to continue my devotion to Aphrodite. I came back to the circle of earth to further attend to her story, the Stations of the Great Goddess. . . .

Aphrodite, Goddess, a miracle has happened. While meditating, while working and searching, while struggling with the opposites of male and female, of many and one, a change has happened. Outside, there has been a change: she whom I have loved and hated; she to whom I have devoted alchemical care and who asked for the monogamous devotion which I could not give; she who after long suffering and pain separated from me; she with whom every contact was passion of union or passion of estrangement; she has heard me. Goddess, it is more human. She remains with her monogamy, caring for me, but from afar; I am with my wholeness, caring for her, for others, staying with the love. It is a change, a humanization. I thank you, Goddess, for your help in this. I felt your compassion in her, my eros in me.

This brings me to another station of your devotion, Goddess, the story of Pygmalion. This King, this man, was an ordinary mortal like myself. Maybe he was something of a dwarf, like Hephaistos, for a variant of his name was Pygmaion, which means "dwarf" and may have meant the same to the ancients. And he was a creative man, as all know, Aphrodite. He fashioned an image of you, Goddess, he molded and formed an ivory idol. But, in another tale, it is said that he made a statue not of you, Goddess, but of a beautiful woman. He fell in love with his creation and, taking it to bed, prayed to you, Goddess, to take pity on him. The statue, whether Goddess or woman, is said to have come alive, and Pygmalion married it. Some say that it is only after this act of Pygmalion that you, Love-Goddess, were truly worshipped.

Goddess, I know this man, Pygmalion. I know him, as a man like myself, not a God like Hephaistos. I know him as one yearning to create, forced to create, and desperately wanting his work to bear fruit, to be made alive, walk around in the world with its own life. He wants, too, to unite with it. But I know this Goddess! Again, how I know that you are both the Goddess which is created, in one tale, and the Goddess which blesses the creation. Goddess, you are like the Gemini of my own nature, two-sided. But you are more, Goddess, much more: for you are like the Christ, both divine and mortal, both God and human. You are the matter created by man, the hungry thirsty driving man, into a living image. And you are the Goddess that creates the actuality, changes the lifeless matter into the reality of life. Goddess, you are God-woman! And Goddess, you, in wonderful ways, make Pygmalion and me, we hungry men, into God-men. You and we, we need each other. We make you human, you make us divine! And, in the doing, we create each other. Goddess, I adore you, I bow before you and worship you! Love is the beginning and the end, the God-maker and the human-maker, and love is a God-woman, just as was Jesus. Goddess, I wed you and make you mine!

Goddess, in this tale, in this act, in this devotion, I complete this station of your life, your tale, your nature, your being. We are wed, within and without.

Aphrodite IV

The story of Adonis, Goddess, begins when Smyrna, daughter of a king, was compelled by you to sleep with her father. Smyrna's mother had boasted that the daughter was prettier, even, than you, fair one. Enraged, you made her fall mortally in love with her sire. Many days did she sleep with him in his drunken state, until one night he awakened and saw you with a lamp. Mad with anger, he pursued you with a sword, eager to destroy both his daughter and the child to which he would be both father and grandfather. At the top of a hill, he overtook Smyrna and was about to kill her. You, Goddess, feeling pity, turned her into the tree that weeps its fruit in spicy gum. The king split the tree in half, and from it there was born Adonis.

Adonis, "lord," was so beautiful that you hid him in a chest, Goddess, and gave him to your sister, Persephone, Queen of the Underworld, for safe-keeping. The Dark Goddess, in her curiosity, opened the chest and fell in love with Adonis, not wanting to return him to you, Aphrodite. The dispute between you, brought before either Zeus or Calliope, resulted in Adonis dwelling a third of the year with you, Goddess, another third with Persephone, and a final part alone, in relief from your great demands. But it is said, Goddess, (is it so?) that you tricked Adonis with your charms and magic, and persuaded him to give up his own free third to you. Persephone, aggrieved, told Ares of this and the jealous God of Battles turned himself into a boar, wounding Adonis mortally. The Lord's blood flowed and turned into beautiful anemones, and some ran down like a river in Lebanon. You, Aphrodite, witness to the event, were compelled to mourn for your lover before you could truly possess him. Despite your holding on to him, despite your tears and love, he suffered one day and then soared away through sea and air. Some say that he is still alive, that Zeus permitted him to live and love both you, Goddess, and the world, in the summer. And some, in Eastern lands, celebrate him by bringing little "gardens," their femininity, by lying with strangers in their temples. Thus the story, thus the rite, what the significance?

The story begins with mortal pride. Goddess, you cannot abide human inflation. You want to create men in love, be created by men in love, to make us Gods, even, but you cannot accept the hybris of men—or women—who feel themselves superior. The punishment: a proof that men's will or pride is nothing compared to your power. The ego will and hybris is broken by your passion, the passion of love coming in a form which is painful, horrible, terrible. But why is incest so terrible? It is natural for the Gods, but so against the laws of men that they usually do not even make such laws. Why? Is it, Goddess, because incest is the prerogative of Gods and whosoever breaks such laws finds himself among the Gods? I think so. It is as if you say, angrily, "So, man (or woman), you think you are as great as the Gods, do you, even greater? Well, then, try on the intimate, painful, lawbreaking which will crumble and kill your mortal pride. See how it is to be God, and see if you can survive it!" I think so, Goddess. The human, when arrogant, thinking he can break the tribal law, must suffer the fate of being a God! If he survives, so much the better. If not, he suffers woe and death. Goddess, I see in this the hardness of your nature, and your compassion as well. How much better, though, to be like Pygmalion, who loves you, worships you, longs for you. He, too, would be with the Gods, as creator, as lover, but his deep devotion, his prayerful attitude, these spare him from the horrible fate of the prideful one, the arrogant one.

So Smyrna is smitten and unites with her father. The latter, symbol of the ruling consciousness, the king who governs, loses this conscious-ness, loses his awareness by the gift of Dionysus and commits the deeply in-breeding sin. With the hidden lamp, with another form of consciousness and light, he discovers his deed and, enraged at the deception, vows destruction. The sword of discriminating conscious-ness, leadership, will destroy the feminine soul which is overcome by love and desire. But you Goddess, in your compassion, spare her from this. Did she not ask to be nowhere, neither in heaven, nor in hell? And you turned her into her natural state, a Myrrh Tree. Is this the Tree of Life? Is the tree like that in Paradise, which knows of immortality? Cut in two by consciousness, Adonis is born. Adonis, the lord, lord of spring and renewal. Is he not also Tammuz, beloved by you as Ishtar, Goddess? And, is he not Adonai, Lord of the Hebrews? Does not a new image of the Lord emerge from the Tree of Life? Jesus died on a Cross of a Tree. Adonis, the nature lord beloved by you, was born from it. And so beautiful, so beautiful. So beautiful is the spirit of vegetation, that gorgeous animated something which springs from all life of trees and plants, of the world of nature reborn. No wonder you love it so, Aphrodite, no wonder love is also forever longing to be united in nature. But so does your sister, the hard underworld Goddess, long for him. Death also claims the spirit of nature. Death claims life. Love claims nature and longs to unite with its spirit, but so does death. There is always life, death, and rebirth. But what, Goddess, is this deep, dark longing of yours for this mortal creature, this spirit which results from the incestuous union? His beauty fascinates you. Man, Goddess, in the deepest beauty of his soul, of the fundamental spirit of his vegetative, plant-like nature, fascinates you. Even though you rage, you know that he is as beautiful as you. Ordinary mortal life has a secret essence, a vitality, an intimate quality of greatness that even the highest Goddesses want and seek.

But the humanity of it, as well. The humanity of it. I have known those who would be happy to have a triangle of loves: a man with two women, spending part of his time with each, part alone. I have heard of it, and often. Just as often as mortal men also commit the crime of father-daughter incest. Done, but not often spoken of. The suffering of such a conflict: and the apparent impossibility of it, Goddess. For you always seek more, I know. Love and life always want more, and, at the expense of death, the underworld hells of pain, dismemberment, unconsciousness. But Goddess, nature does not permit this. Neither nature, nor the highest spiritual principle of maleness, Zeus the Father. The highest and lowest converge to bring balance, and their just claims. And so, Goddess, your beautiful hero is lost. Jealous Ares, Lord of Battles, sends his truculent, dark-mooned, crescent-tusked, pig-boar of the nether regions to crush him. And is it not so? Does not the greedy and dark nature kill such a hero? Does not the conflict finally send a blood bath to one who would love two Goddesses? Two women even? Is he not then, a rival even of the Lord of Conflict? And oh, the blood flows, the blood of pain and emotion, and agony, and the tragedy of the classical love affair, of the triangle, occurs once again. Poets know this, and writers of all the songs. Must it always be so? Must the spirit of life be crushed in this conflict? Must the blood flow and become the beautiful flower-feelings expressed in song and verse? Must it survive like that, while its soul joins with the heights and depths, doomed to be unrealized? Oh, Goddess, the spirit dies but, like Christ, it will and must be resurrected! The women, offering their femininity to the dark impersonal Gods in men try to bring him back to life. As a religious devotion, sexuality as a rite, as a devotion, can bring back this beautiful spirit of nature which dwells in man.

But Goddess, I mourn with you. For I have known such pain of conflict, such horror and violation in having two loves. I have known the blood of feelings that flow from the agony of the boar of battle which compels these passions. I know Adonis' experience of the flower-feelings emerging. But I know your feelings, too, Goddess, mourning for the loss of a loved one. For that is the other part of the tragedy, the loved one dies and is mourned, even by the Goddess! Fair One, it is said that you have compassion, but here you show it. You show your mortal pain at loss, you show your mortal need to hold on to your love. Goddess, I am with you, I weep with you. Oh, that the spirit would come back and stay! Oh, that the loved ones would never die! Oh, that conflict might not, ultimately, destroy the great and beautiful spirit that emerges from the secret love, the forbidden pleasure, the sacred unions permitted only the Gods! But, Goddess, there is death-in-life, but also life-in-death. Is not the agony of Adonis like that of Jesus? He dies and is mourned after by the feminine. And he, too, is resurrected. If the highest spirit, that of God-sacrifice for men's sins is resurrected, then surely the nature spirit in man will be reborn. It will sink into the depths of the psyche once again, rise to the heights of spiritualized sublimation once again, and be reborn in every act of sacred love in which woman offers her deepest femininity.

Here, Goddess, you show the way to the woman, and to men's souls. The feminine will offer up her depths, her love, her deepest feelings to this great spirit and treasure it in all men. Goddess, just as I came to see that you dwelt in all women, the women must come, by your example, to see that Adonis dwells in all men. No father-consciousness can kill it, finally, and not even the greedy lusts of life in battle nor conflict can, ultimately, kill it. This spirit, dwelling in men, will be deepened, refined, and be reborn, in man after man, generation after generation, until it will once again be treasured, adored, and valued, just as you do, Goddess. For was not that Tree of Life transformed by the Hebrews into the Tree of Kaballah? Did not the spirit of the ancients die, fall into the depths of the soul, rise to the heights and re-emerge as the Adonai of the Tree of Life in Kaballah? And is this not true, right this instant, as I worship you, Goddess? Let Adonis find his way, once again, from the ancient places of the Greeks where he was once fully alive and where the myth died, into the soul of a modern man, who would again worship, again celebrate, again adore the Gods in man. Let my celebration be like those of the poets and singers, those who pick the flowers of the blood of the fallen Adonis. Are we not partakers of this feast, so similar to those who celebrate the Mass, partake as of the blood and body of the divine Savior? Are we not all powerfully drawn to the deep cannibalism of the soul, to transform and be transformed by the Divine Son, be he Jesus or Adonis? It must be so, Goddess, it must be so. And I adore your love for him, I worship your care for him, I participate in your mystery of both precipitating the horror of his conception, the grandeur of his being, and the mystery of his death and rebirth. For such a man is elevated into a God, that which we will all one day do. Bless us, Goddess, as we celebrate with you, partake with you, sorrow with you. The passion of Adonis is over. He is dead, but will rise again.

Aphrodite V

The final station of your passion, Goddess, the last story of which I have record, is that of your love of Anchises. Again a mortal, and your final tale concerns a total mortal, not even one with divine and mysterious origin like Adonis. Anchises, though a king, was a very mortal king, and was known as a simple herdsman. He pastured his cattle high up on a mountain, but was known for his beauty, as handsome as the immortals, some said, though there was no boasting for it. No; Anchises was not, like Adonis, a victim of human pride. Rather, Goddess, his being the object of your love was owing to your own battle with your adoptive father, Zeus. Few were the Gods or Goddesses capable of fighting your great power, only your sisters Athene, Artemis, and Hestia. Even Zeus was compelled by your immortal power, Goddess, to fall in love with many mortal women and neglect his own loyal sister-wife, Hera. Thus, the greatest of the Gods, the highest spiritual principle, was compelled by you, love-Goddess, to forsake a oneness and succumb to a maniness. He had to love and unite with many mortals: such is the power of love. I know his feeling and fate, Goddess, for I have often spoken of it.

But to you, Goddess, in revenge for his inability to keep power over you and your domain, to you he also compelled love, and, in sweet revenge, to fall in love with a total mortal, at that. The spirit, compelled by love to unite with mortals, to incarnate in the flesh of life through love and passion, can compel the same of love. It can compel the concreteness of love, the humiliation of the divine-love to come to earth. Is there not conflict in the divine sphere, in the realm of the immortal spirits? And does not this conflict then require them to come to earth, to unite with us? It seems so.

Goddess, I do not think that you were humiliated, as your adoptive father had hoped. Unlike Smyrna, the mortal, you accepted your falling in love, even relished it. You annointed yourself with your immortal oil, whose fragrance clings to you. You clothed yourself in gold and impassioned red and you came to the poor herdsman, Anchises, in mortal guise. Behind you came wolves and lions, bears and leopards, in great hunger for the cattle of Anchises. You, Goddess, rejoiced at these beasts, and filled their hearts with love, so that they all lay down in couples and made love rather than war and devouring.

You entered Anchises' tent, disguised as a beautiful maiden, and claimed that you were a Phrygian princess, ready to marry Anchises by divine order. Anchises, dazzled by you, Goddess, fell more and more in love with you, and could not wait, as you requested, to sleep with you only after the usual wedding celebrations. He would rather have died than waited, and so he took you. He slept with you on soft sheets made of the hides of bears and lions that Anchises himself had killed, and bees buzzed all around.

Later, Goddess, you showed yourself to poor Anchises, in all your true form and beauty. Your lovely eyes dismayed him. He turned away and begged for you to save him, for no mortal man remains in good health for the rest of his life when he has slept with a Goddess. True enough; it is said that Zeus sent poor Anchises a thunderbolt and lightning. One tale says that he was lamed by this lightning; another says that you protected him, Goddess, that your magic girdle deflected the shock, but that he was weakened, all the same. But you also told Anchises, Goddess, that you would bear his son, who would be the founder of a great new nation, and so you did. You encouraged him and softened him, but there are also tales that he was punished with blindness for having seen you naked, Goddess, bees stinging out his eyes.

Goddess, what is the meaning of this tale, the final story of your passion, the stations of your story? That the highest spirit and the highest love, Zeus and yourself, compel each other to incarnate, to come to earth with mortals, I have understood. The strange, powerful mystery of the battle in the divine sphere, their need of mankind, that I have understood. That you relish this involvement with man, with life, that, too, I understand. For what more can a Goddess of love appreciate than loving, mortal and divine, union, mortal and divine, ecstasy, mortal and divine. That you cherish and are delighted by the animals, those wolves, bears, lions and leopards—that, too, I understand. For are not the animals more totally pious, even, than men? Do they not portray the divine nature of instinct and flesh as much as the Gods? Is not the power of love the only thing that can calm animal lusts and hungers? Just as it is for the animal in us and in you, Goddess? I understand this.

But why, Goddess, do you tell the tale to Anchises, as if to deceive him that you are mortal? And why do you suggest that he tarry, that your love fulfillment wait until the ritual is fulfilled, the proper wedding vows proclaimed? Are you, indeed, as in your earlier station, still deeply desirous of monogamy? Are you, indeed, very eager to be clothed in the rules and rituals of Themis? Do you desire to be fully mortal, fully whole with one man? Or is this only a ruse, which awakens even further desire from a totally amazed, enraptured man, only too ready to take you at once? Goddess, should you truly want it, few men have the awareness, the consciousness, to restrain their desire, once inflamed by you. And, those that do, more often than not, are servants of Apollo, hardly touched by you at all, except to admire you from afar. What is it, then Goddess, that you seek to show us by such a fact in your tale? What is this message?

I think it is that you, too, would welcome not just laws and customs and regularities, but the restraint of passion, the forming of desire, the differentiation of lust into love, of passion into relationship. For, if a man can restrain the passion and desire which arises from the same regions from which you are born, does he not then spiritualize his love? Does he not give it wings, just as you did when you rose from the depths of the sea to the heights of Olympus? And that, no doubt, is what you wish. And some of us can do it—at times. We can wait, we can spiritualize, we can suffer, we can try to contain our love in the established forms. Oh, Goddess, how I tried to contain your passions in the established forms of love, of marriage, of friendship, of healing, of all those structures which curb love, transform love, and—at best—give love a vehicle, a vessel for expression. And that, it would seem, is what you would want, in truth.

But we are like Anchises, Goddess. In the face of you and your power, we go beyond forms, we transgress structures and rules, we break the vehicles and vessels. And so, we unite with you. And you do not stop us, Goddess, you do not stop us. In truth, you are co-guilty of going against your own desire for Themis, for order and structure. Do you not gladly submit to Anchises, as well as excite him beyond belief, just by your being? It is true. And so, you show us your dual nature: wanting order and spiritualization, and desiring disorder, fulfillment, passion—free and profoundly spontaneous. Goddess, I know you so well, in your many-expressioned twin-nature. So many times have I seen your doubleness, in every act, every station of your being. Here again, Goddess, Aphrodite Urania of the Heavens, and Aphrodite Pandemos of the Earth, you are two and one, and we suffer-enjoy you gladly.

Anchises, who finally realizes he has slept with a Goddess, grows afraid. He begs to be saved, for he knows that he can be killed, or at least will suffer bad health. Zeus sends his thunderbolt, his flash of powerful hurt, rage, justice, which makes such a man, who has experienced such a love, aware of the consequences. And I, too, Goddess, know what that means. How often I have suffered in the soul and in the flesh, the rage of the spirit, that vengeful cry of guilt to be expiated. I have even known the near madness of the conflict that could have drowned all vision, the many stings of the buzzing bees of thoughts, fears, ideas, that took away all perspective. For Anchises was blinded, it is said, even though you blocked Zeus' worst blows.

Oh, Goddess, must it be so? Must it always be so that one who follows you, worships you, is overcome by you, must always pay the terrible price in pain, in tragedy, in guilts, in blindness? Love is so often tragic, they say. And they are right. Must it be so?

I hear your sigh, but I hear no words. Only buzzing of bees and a lack of vision. You shyly drop your eyes, as if to say to me that if one survives the bolt of lightning, the noise of the thunder of the great Father spirit, if one can live through the agony of the bees, of the many-stinged ideas, and thoughts which will drive one mad from fear, guilt and rejection, if one can admit and survive the blindness, and still be true to the love, then, perhaps, redemption is possible. Oedipus found redemption only as an old man, and through his daughter. Canny Odysseus fared better, but who would choose his fate? And Anchises, Goddess, who unknowingly broke the deepest taboo, who broke the barrier between God and man, who slept with a Goddess? What of him? His end was, it is said, that you lost your passion for him.

Goddess, I think I understand. For you ask, down deep, for a marriage, for a union, for a devotion and long-lasting relationship which does not pale, does not die, but survives the exigencies and vagaries of love in the battle of life, love in the fire of creation, love in loss and weakness and blindness. Goddess, I, a man, Grandson of the Knight, have wed thee. I have known thee in all forms, and I praise thee. Like Anchises, I have been wounded, blinded, broken, but I have held on. Goddess, I will hold on. Goddess, I have proved my natural devotion in a Christian, Hebrew, Buddhistic way, for I have held on. I have maintained my oneness by wrestling, by accepting, by faith, by trust. I will do so with you. But help me, Goddess, help me to hold on to you, as I have held on to the spirit. Goddess, I have known love in marriage, in friendship, in parenthood, with you in Themis—in order and care— and I have been with you in Dionysus, in disorder, transgression and unconsciousness. Goddess, I have known and held on. Help me to hold on to you; to love when the loved one leaves, when the love hurts, when the love vanishes. Help me to hold on, not to illusion or delusion, not to fantasy or desire, but to the reality of love lived, of love fulfilled, of love in the living forever, whether incarnated or not. Aphrodite Ourania, heavenly and eternal, incarnate in Pandemos, in the loves of my life, never leave me. Or if you leave me, come back, and help me to love when you are gone. For such is the wedding that I offer, such is union that I seek with you.

Aphrodite VI

Aphrodite, Goddess of Love, I have completed the six stations of your life, your tale, your passion. I have loved you, understood you, wedded you. I have been there at your birth, united with you, as did Nerites, as did Ares and Hephaistos. I have known your passion and being in the love of life, in the love of creation. I have been created by you and created you, as did Pygmalion. I have suffered your maniness, and been tormented to death—and life—like Adonis. And, at last, I have known my humanity enveloped by you, blinded by you, mortified and saved by you, as did Anchises.

I have even known the Rose of Rhodos, born by you as a result of the union with Poseidon, God of Sea and Earthquakes. That wholeness of the rose, that flower which is part Christian, part Buddhist, part Hebrew, and part Pagan, born of the union of you with the God of the depths of the soul and the reality of life, that flower of life I have known, too, though I have not spoken of it. My sons have not become leaders like Anchises, but I know that will be, too, Goddess. I know, Goddess. I know and I feel. I am conscious and I have loved. Speak to me, Goddess, speak to me, wife! Speak to me, mistress! I implore and command it! I desire it and expect it! For I, also, am one in two, I am Gemini; I am Grandson Ourania and Grandson Pandemos, I am a spirit man and an earth man, one who dwells in the heights and depths. So then, speak to me, Goddess!

And, Goddess, by your smile, I know you! By your laugh, I know you! By your fragrance and deliciousness, I know you. For I need not implore you to speak, for you are me, and I, you. We are as one. You speak within me, as I do for you. The twoness of our being is wedded in the oneness of our speaking. I speak for you and live for you. You speak through me and live through me. Goddess, I am yours, you are mine!

With that realization of the union of the spiritual loves of Christian, Hebrew, Buddhist, there comes, on earth, the love of Aphrodite, Pagan, who dwells on high and on earth. And the four meet in the cone of the one. One triangle united with a circle, making the cone of heaven and the base of earth. A wholeness.

But now I descend, now I fall to where the couple of my dream went. I fall to the depths under the earth from which will arise that which will complete, reconcile, make full and manifest the love of the cone above. The inverted cone, the cone of the depths, must now receive me. Eros, Once and Future God, receive me!

Eros I

I sink down, down. I sink past the library of the Magician, the Cave, the Forest. I go beyond the forms of Bluebeard, and fall in the empty space of earth. As I fall, with the endless purgatorial sadness of The Fall, I carry with me the knowledge that what I have lived is over, what I have suffered is over, what I have carried is ended. I came to this place, I, Grandson of the Knight, with the problem of Love. With the One and the Many, came I. And now it is over. The second love has gone away. The second abandoned the struggle, abandoned the pleasure, abandoned me. It is over, and I sink into the depths, not knowing why, how, where, what. I sink down to Eros, called Charioteer by my Father, the Son of the Knight, called future Messiah by my Grandfather, the Knight. Where is he, this once and future God? Where is he? Will he speak to me, console me, inform me? Will he close that gap of understanding? Will he heal that ache of loss, the wound of betrayal, the agony of the maniness become oneness, and yet lostness?

I sink through the air of earth and come to the fire of earth. I come to the heat of the pain of lost intensity, of lonely aching in the pit of the belly, of searing bowels of passion turned sour, turned bitter, turned acid. I think of the Woman, the bitter woman of my dream, rancid and grim, seeking a Jewish lung, but I do not see her. The fire burns me, scalds me. Does it purify me? I do not think so.

I sink through the fire of earth and come to the water of earth. I sink into the cooling watery depths which make me moody, sad, like a woman possessed by the menstrual moodiness of the watery flow. My head and nose and eyes water with tears, followed by dryness, followed by deadness, followed by tears. Anger comes, and I think of the Man, the demanding man of my dream, raging and bitter, wanting me to recognize, take hold of, his palpitating need. I think of him, but do not see him. The water drowns me, overcomes me. Does it cleanse me? I do not think so.

I come to the earth of earth, rock bottom. But neither is it rock and ending. For it gives way, it softens and becomes mud, then fine sand, gravel, as I sink through the earthiness of earth. It is the facts of my life, the many endings and experiences, the many places, memories, which say, "this has happened," this is not to be denied, interpreted, transformed. This you are, this is what you have done, this is what has happened to you. With earth of earth, space hardened becomes time remembered: memory makes reality.

Finally, there is an end to the earth of earth, and the gravel becomes rock and the rock becomes stone. There is an end, and one sits on the stone of stone, surrounded by the gravel and the sand and the traces of black earth. One moves no more. One is dead and buried in a tombless tomb. One dies. Does Eros come here? Does the God come when summoned? When petitioned? When prayed to? Apparently not. For he does not come.

The aridity of the depths is all that comes. I perk up, for this is what is asked for the interior contemplation of the Christian. Is this not what the saints and Church spokesmen speak of when they say that the aridity precedes being filled with God? That the dryness is the prelude to infused contemplation? So speaks John of the Cross, so speak the others. But the darkness persists. No light appears.

"Let it all go by" comes to me also. Do not attach to the hope, to the expectation, nor to the lack of hope and expectation. Empty the mind, empty the soul, empty the self of self, and let neither aridity nor desire hold sway. Thus the Buddhist, thus quiet mindlessness which could precede enlightenment. But nothing comes and nothing goes. This is not the Void of which they speak. This is the Void of barrenness.

"Hold on," I think, "hold on." Like Jacob with the Angel, like the Hassid in his dance, do not let go of the Eternal God, and He will bless. Summoned or not, prayed to or not, He is always there. But He is not there. Here among the rocks and stones, among the debris of broken vessels, of ended hopes and expectations, of loyal devotion unrewarded, here there is nothing to hold on to. A loose stone? A bit of gravel? A pebble? Enough air only to breathe for a time, and then no time? Nothing and no one to hold on to.

Love, finally, love. Aphrodite, of the soft and passionate eyes. She is there. She does not abandon. But she does abandon. For she is born of air and water and lives on the earth. Here among the stones, among the gravelly bits where nothing grows, nothing is seen, nothing is felt, even Aphrodite does not live here.

So I sit. Not holding on, not empty, not loving, not trusting. I sit. No. Negation. And negation of negation. Stillness.

This stillness persists for some time. It is interesting how one can be alive and dead at the same time. It is interesting that one can continue in the tomb at one level, and survive at other levels. Has not everyone known this of himself? Has not everyone continued upon his daily round, flourished, even, in the routine of life, and yet felt dead, been away in limbo, or, in a hell of stillness? Most have felt this, as have I. But, in my sitting, I realize that there are the one and the many of me. I am one who can be in the depths of the still void, and still continue on a daily life, a human round. So, then, why can I not leave a piece of me there in the void of the depths, the gravelly ruin to where I have fallen, and rise up? Rise up, at least, to the library, when one can read about the Eros God who does not come. For he existed once, it is said, and people have written about him. Besides, the one who abandoned me spoke of the silliness of being victim, the idiocy of allowing oneself to be a passive onlooker, bystander, and waiting for the good thing to happen. I cannot will it otherwise, but I—or a part of me—can ascend, can rise to the library, or cave. So I rise. I fight my way back up, through stone and gravel and earth, through water and fire and air. I struggle back, inch by inch.

I come to the library of the Magician. It is easy to raise the trap door, to come inside and see the many colored books, the shelf upon shelf of the riches of thought, of expression, of life. And I come upon the Story of Eros.

In the very beginning, it is said, before there were any Gods or anything at all, there was only Night, Nyx. There was only the darkness of Night, as a great winged black bird. This Nyx conceived of the Wind, and laid a silver Egg in the great lap of her own darkness. From the Egg sprang Eros, a God with Golden Wings. This Eros, this Love, was son of the wind and the night, no more. He was Protogonos, the "firstborn" of the Gods. Love is the first and last of the Gods, it is so. How to understand, how to take in?

Darkness in the beginning, darkness and the wind. The unknowingness of this, impregnated by the spirit in its first formless form. From this, a totality, the Egg, comes first, and then the God. Oh, God of Love, product of the union of Night and Wind, they call you many names. Eros-love, and Protogonos-Firstborn, I have said. But most of all, Phanes are you called, "He who reveals" and "He who appears": you are the light and light bringer. And that, the story says, because you brought into the light everything that had lain previously hidden in the Egg. Above: the void, sky; below: the rest, an orderly confusion, Chaos. But, from this you brought forth the earth, and the sky and earth married.

"In the beginning" goes another tale, "God created the heaven and the earth." That creation, too, showed the earth without form and void. Are you that same God who said, "Let there be light?" Are you that Adonai, to whom one prayed? Are you that Father who preceded the Son? Is The Light-Bringer the same as the Love-Bringer? The tale says so. The tale speaks of the beginnings, of the marriage of Heaven and Earth, and the continuing creation which goes on after the beginnings of Night and Wind, and their immortal son Eros-Phanes-Protogonos.

Thus the story, or the beginning of it. But, in the half of me which dwells in the depths, waiting for the Eros-God to appear, I sit in a void. The tale speaks of the void above; for me, as I sit, the void is below. It is an awaiting. I think of Wind and the Night. And I think of the dark woman, waiting, asking for a Jewish lung. Does she not wish the wind? Is she not some Greek or Mediterranean, asking for a spirit which will make her alive, fecund, breathing, like the Goddess night? And does not the spirit of the Wind impregnate the bird, like the eager phallus of the dark man? Unite Bird, unite Wind, unite man and woman! Come together, come and hatch an Egg from which Eros can emerge. Out of the Chaos, out of the Void, let the light and love come forth.

But it is only I who sit in the void. It is only I who sit in the gravelly nothingness of the sub-earth. Only I. And I do not feel like a God. I do not feel like a love, or a light. I do not feel, even, alive.

So, the words do not help. The library only points . . . I sink back to the cave, down. Here, too, are words. For Eros is called the dweller in the Cave, the Shining One whom no one can look at, for his light is bewildering. He created sky and earth, and sits in his cave; the Father, with the three-fold Goddess, Night. Night, the Mother and lover and Daughter of Eros, gave the Oracle, she spoke of the truths of future. But she also became the wife, the ravished one of Phanes. And her third form was also the mother of justice. So, he is wed, this God, to the vision, the ravished soul, and the law. Before the Cave sat a Goddess with brazen drum, to hold the justice in men's eyes, to compel the bees to swarm elsewhere. Eros is a loudly buzzing celestial bee, bringing honey when ordered, and stinging out men's eyes when the order is disturbed.

Thus your ancient forms, oh Eros! Thus did the ancients know you. Thus, even, did my Father, Son of the Knight, know of you in the Cave. Thus, were you known to him as not only Light-Bringer and Love-Bringer, but as Charioteer, One and Many! I know that. This was the form in which you showed yourself to him. But not to me, Phanes, not to me, Eros. For I know you, too, as Son and Lover of Aphrodite, as son of Hermes, of Ares, of Hephaistos. You are even said to be son of Zeus. For, thus, you are father and first-born, as well as son of . . . product of . . . love, creation, wisdom. You are all these things. But you are not these things to me. For I sit, in the void, created and destroyed, product of one and many, defeated.

Where are you, God? Where is the wholeness of love, of light, of wisdom? Only in books, only in caves. Only for Grandfathers, only for Fathers. What then of the Grandson? You do not speak.

"I do not speak for I have spoken. Once have I spoken. Twice have I spoken. I will not speak again."

These words come to me. But they come from within me, from a weak and painful place which is both in the pit of the belly, and in the soft flesh about the eyes. These words come as words from a child, a hurt, a pain. They come from no hero, no God, but a poor impotent mortal.

"Twice have I spoken, thrice will I speak, I will not speak again."

The words repeat. A child is there, a youth, but he does not appear. God is a child, a mortal, a poor youth. No hero, he. God is weak, with weak Eros, weak limbs . . . sometimes. The weakness is the God? Is Eros a weak thing, as well as a passion? Is it a vulnerable, frightened, uncertain, human, frail thing, as well as a powerful light and beacon? It seems so. If so, oh God, if so, oh Phanes-light-bringer, if so, oh Eros, then I know thee well. For I know my depressions, my weakness, my sadness, my pains in belly, and tears of eyes. If that is where You are, I know You.

"You know me well, Grandson of the Knight, you know me. Have I not spoken as Bluebeard? Have I not been Magician? Is not Love, as you have found, both the tyrant and husband of Muses, the Magic of Love and Life? And am I not Son-lover-father to the Goddess? And have you not reveled in your new-found wisdom of my origin and place with Ares, with Hephaistos? All these things you know. All this you know and forget. For you know, too, that I am brother to Jesus, and to Jacob, and to Gautama, too. Three above and three below, it is said, and it is said truly. For, in the upper cone dwell Jesus, Jacob, and Gautama. In the lower cone dwell Bluebeard, Magician and myself. And we come together on earth with the Goddess, mistress of Muses. Is it not clear?

"And is it not clear where we all dwell in you, Grandson of the Knight? Do you not know the centers of love and consciousness in yourself? Jesus on high, the light between the eyes, the love-consciousness of agape, of spiritual sacrifice which is high and far-reaching, the vision which looks to the Father, above and below. Jacob in the heart, the all-feeling, all struggling, all encompassing light and love of devotion, of Israel wedded and passionate with the Father. Buddha, in the belly, the neither-inward-nor-outward-looking dedication of the No Mind, of the reality of what Is, the Isness of Being. Bluebeard in the throat, the Master of the Muses who speak through the sounds and murmurings of music and word. Magician in the depths, in the nether regions where all magic, all life, all matter begin. Aphrodite in the phallus, in the benignly creative and seeking, in the searching and desiring, and Aphrodite in the eyes, in the soul of beckoning and following, of feeling and reaching.

"And I, and I? Eros in the Diaphragm. The region of Aha, where reality is One and Many. The region where Love and Light converge. And I float up and around the centers, for each is part of me, and I part of it. Each is true, each is right. Your task, Grandson of the Knight, Knight III, would you know me, would you live me, and find me, is to take those two whom you have let go: take the dark woman and dark man. Take them on a journey of the centers. Take them from below upward, and from upward below. Take them to the centers and heal them, unite them. Would you serve Eros, would you serve Love and Light, then take them. Be neither victim nor fool, be neither scapegoat nor hybritic, but take them upon a journey through the spheres of the Gods."

Eros II

These words of Eros gave me conviction. These words did not come like the great dreams of old, they did not come as the powerful and overwhelming light-love I thought of. They came as almost human, as greatness and littleness. What is best, they came as good sense, as if Eros did not despise Apollo. And they came as a way of healing, of making whole in me that which I craved.

And so I took the dark woman and man of my dreams. I took the bitter lady and angry man. I grasped them close to my bosom and sank down into the depths and sought the Magician. Love as Magic, as the creator of beginnings, of occult and dark light. To the Magician, the beginning of my quest, to him did I bring the man and woman. To him at the anus of the world, the Muladhara of my being.

The Magician took them as so much clay. He breathed deeply into the lungs of the woman. He breathed and breathed, as if to fill her lungs with spirit, with the wind of creation, as on that first day. As he breathed, the woman breathed, she lost her hardness and bitterness. She seemed to sense the magic in her own soul, her own spirit. She felt that she, too, could be free, could be whole. And the Magician took the phallus of the man. He kneaded it as if it were clay, he molded it and made it as if it were a statue. As indeed it was. It was in the image of a God, and the image of a man. For it was the spirit of a man. And the man knew that his phallus was the image of his own spirit, his own Godhood, his own manhood, not to be despised, nor to be neglected. But to be kneaded and molded, the God made man, and the man made God.

I took them, then, the man and woman, up to the lower belly, where sat Gautama, deep in meditation. I took the two to him and waited for what he would do. He only sat, and motioned them to sit. They did sit. We all sat, the man, the woman, the Buddha and myself. We sat and sat. For eternity we sat. We sat until a breath emerged in the woman, a sigh emerged in the man, a wind emerged in the Buddha, and a cry emerged in me. We began to breathe in unison, sway in unison. From the depths, from the deep-within-which-is-also-without, there occurred a unity of spirit, a unity of being, an isness of light-love which swept us and kept us peacefully on the ground. No words, no deeds, no action: an enlightenment of love-breathing.

I took them then, the man and woman, beyond Eros, up to Jacob, in the heart regions. Jacob, the wrestler, the climber of the ladder to heaven, the devoted; I brought the man and woman to him. He embraced them, each and each. He cajoled them, each and each. He berated them, each and each. He loved them, each and each, and enjoined them to look up, as well as down, pray and entreat the God on high. He spoke deeply to them and said that like Job they should look to Heaven for answers to their bitterness, their anger, their sorrow. They should look to the One. And they did look, these two, the man and the woman. They looked. They looked and they saw, way up in the air, the Throne of Heaven upon which sat the just God, the benign God, the loving God. But they also saw the hard God, the angry God, the God who was unjust. And above it all, they saw the Tree of Life, the tenfold Kaballistic Tree of the Living God, the Adonai. They were enraptured and their faces shown of what they saw. They fell down upon their faces and wept the Shema.

And I took them, the man and the woman, I took them up beyond Jacob and lifted them to where Bluebeard stood. Bluebeard motioned me downward, and we fell, past Jacob, past Buddha, to the region of Aphrodite, for she was both below and above, both Pandemos and Ourania. She smiled a smile upon the man, and smiled a smile upon the woman. She laughed and her laughter was infectious. When she laughed, they could not help from laughing, and from the magnificence of the divine image and the shining throne with Jacob they felt, now, the magnificence and shining foam of Aphrodite, the love in life. And they were lifted up, and, with Bluebeard, made to go the round of the Muses, to suffer the effects of each Muse, to feel the horrible-beautiful tyranny of the wives of Bluebeard, and their voices began to speak. They spoke as if they were poets when they had not been, they could take tongue where they had not been able. The woman spoke from her breasts and chest, the man from his creative God-phallus, and the words were like statues and milk, like air and semen.

And then I took them, the man and the woman, up to Jesus, and he only put a hand on each of their heads and blessed them. He called them sainted, he called them God. He spoke and touched them and they were silent in tearful joy and humble gratitude. They felt their humanity and divinity, brotherhood and sisterhood, their apartness and union.

And I fell with them, the man and the woman, back to the center, the place between belly and heart, where Eros dwells. Eros Phanes, Love light and revealed, did nothing with the man and woman, nothing at all. He simply embraced them in his golden wings and embraced me as well. He embraced us and sent us up and up, up beyond the centers of heart and throat, of eye and head. He sent us up to the lotus-leaved place where the Gods come in and go out, where the potential becomes real and the material becomes spiritual. He took us and sent us, the man and woman and myself and took us up to the many-petalled lotus where they joined, the man and woman. They joined in a holy union of divinization, an apotheosis of their humanity-divinity. And I saw this. I, Knight in my own right, I saw this divinization of man.

PART II
The Pairs

Guinevere's Daughter

The story I am about to tell has to do with my experience of love, with my search for understanding, just like the Grandson of the Knight. I will speak, in a moment, about how we differ, but first I want to speak of . . . oh, Lord . . . I started to break down again, just with the memory and pain of it . . . Let the pain wait, too. The Grandson of the Knight suffered from a conflict between one and many women, between his love for One and Many. He resolved himself in the many Gods, the many centers of his being, the varieties of love and consciousness which were united in the One that was within him. I have heard and understood. That is fine for him and that, I know, brought him peace.

But my place . . . my place. Not many, not a surfeit, nor an overabundance; not a multiplicity due to my own complexity, as it is for the Grandson of the Knight. My place has been with the pain of the loss of love, the loss of a loved one, the impossibility of the realization of love, the limitations in lack of fulfillment. I have been with love frustrated, love lost.

I must explain, first, who I am, and a little of my history. A daughter of Guinevere, I was born during the period of her love for both Arthur and Lancelot. In truth, I do not know my own father, for he may be either King or Knight. In that fact, I resemble the father of the Grandson of the Knight, for he had two fathers also, although he did not know it at the time. The Son of the Knight had both a God-Father and a Father-God, in real and symbolic ways. I, however, had only one biological father, and quite a human one at that, but which, which? Furthermore, my mother, Queen Guinevere, like the Grandson of the Knight, had several loves, and felt them in conflict. I have felt only inner pain, not outer conflict. I have wanted to love fully, totally, either one or many, but have gotten restriction, hurt, rejection, frustration—or split. Is this the natural consequence of being the daughter of my mother? Do I suffer the pain of her sin of loving and being fulfilled by many? Must I suffer the agonies of her unlived life? Of being never fulfilled? So have I believed, at times.

And so do I feel now. Oh, friends, you there who read this, I had hoped that I could, in a masculine way, like the Knights, tell a story of the past, of a successful conclusion of a quest, of realizations arising from adventure, but it is not so. I am still embarked upon this path, and I do not know its outcome. I sit here, aware of the dull pain of the loss of love. . . .

I am aware of rage and frustration with my emptiness. In all my struggles and failures, I have not had to cope with the loving of two people or more; I have not had the temerity to seek Gods or Heroes and confront them. Mine has been the horrible experience of being ripped apart internally. I have been a wretched battlefield of warring opposites.

For example, I have felt a continual difference between the feelings of my heart and of my belly. My heart goes out towards people, to love them, care for them, connect with them, to get angry with them sometimes for not letting me come close to them, unite with them. But these feelings war with those of my belly, which speak to me of hungers, selfish desires, my emptiness. The belly wants to take in, not give out, wants to go inside, not out. Just these two opposites have been enough to drive me to distraction. Grandson of the Knight has been able to expand above and beyond, to many centers. Just these two have been enough to kill me.

Grandson of the Knight believed that he had to take a pair of warring opposites, the angry male and bitter female, up through all the centers, up to the very top of his skull where the human beings meet the Gods. He says that he witnessed the divinization of man. I do not doubt this. But what about the other half of what he speaks? What of the humanization of God? What of the coming down of those same two figures? What of the bringing down of the spirit, of the descent of those two transformed ones into the lower centers, into life, into love? What of that? And how to contain the spirit, if it does descend? That is my dilemma. I am not a seeker, I am a poor container. I am not one who wishes to confront, expand, seek out, reconcile, but one who dies from being unable to contain what there is inside of her, reconcile the drives, powers—call them Gods if you wish—which threaten to destroy her. And, more specifically, it is the conflict of these same forces, the loving-out and the needing-in, that threatens to cut me off from all that I love, all that I need, both outside and inside. So I scream. Or I open my mouth in agony and cannot utter a word. In that, I am like some horribly suffering witch in hell, burning in the fires, who can neither help herself nor call out. That is my state.

Oh, Eros, whom the Grandson of the Knight found; you who dwells between heart and belly; you who goes among them all, come and aid me, I beseech you! Come and show me a way!

"I am here, Daughter of Guinevere, I am here."

So, speak, then, tell me. Bring back my love, bring me some measure of peace, bring me . . . show me . . . I weep.

"The tears are mine, Daughter of Guinevere. I, Eros, weep in you. You are I, and I, you. Do you not know that? You are God—or Goddess, if you prefer. Your tears are my tears. Love weeps, love is hurt, love is frustrated, love is burned. Love is wounded by its own daggers. I, Eros, though the first of the Gods, there in the beginning and in the ending, I, Eros, am not omnipotent . . . not in bringing about my desires, or your desires. I am merely omnipotent in feeling, and even this power is all-ranging, all encompassing, not all-containing, for I need you. You, Daughter of Guinevere, have lost your love and you weep. It is true. We did our best, you and I. For I was there with you. You have not been alone."

But, what now, Eros? If you are me, and I am you, we are one, how is it that we can speak at all?

"Can one not speak to oneself? Cannot one have a dialogue with oneself? Of course one can. I am your partner, your other half. When you are one-sided, off-balance, I bring in the other side. I should think that you would be glad of such a thing. Where you love wrongly, excessively, I balance. Where you reject love, I balance, too."

But what of fact, what of reason, what of reality?

"What of it?"

Do you provide those things, also?

"Only if it exists in you somewhere, for I am you, as I have said. The part not available to you at that moment. So, here I am, use me."

Are you Eros, really?

"You can call me that. Or anything else. I am . . . call me other-half. Wife to your husband, husband to your wife; I am son to your father, father to your son; I am daughter to your mother, mother to your daughter. I am lover to your lover. Together, we make a whole."

All right. I will test you. Green.

"Red."

Yellow.

"Violet."

Not an opposite!

"Right. I supplement, not complement. Violet is red and blue, which complement you. Opposites are too narrow, too ending. For I would lead onward. When you want to settle things, then I have to lead onward. You are mostly feminine, after all, and thus concerned with Being. And I, as mostly masculine, after all, am concerned with Becoming. But, as I say, I can be wife to your masculine, too."

Talk! Talk! Show me how I can cope with my longing, my need, my tears, my feeling!

"All right, Daughter of Guinevere. Here is how you can cope: take them in. I will help you. Take them in, inside yourself, take in these pairs. Take in sister and sister, mother and daughter, husband and wife, lover and lover. Let them speak inside you. Let the heart and belly both have their say. Let dialogue occur. Do not despair, but listen to me as your other half. Be the vessel yourself. And I will help you, I will be there! Just as I was there with the Grandson of the Knight, in his Oneness and Maniness, just so will I be there with you, with your pairness, your duplicity, your splitness. And just as I aided—even directed—the Grandson of the Knight to raise up a pair, I will now help you bring down the pair, incarnate them. I shall help you be a container for this. Are you willing?"

I am willing, Eros. Let me be the vessel; let me contain them, if I can!

"So be it. I bring, you contain. I will bring them from above and from below, from beyond. And you, Daughter of Guinevere, will contain within you, be a vessel for reconciliation. Prepare, now, for the succession of couples! A new Noah's ark will you be. Are you ready?"

I am ready.

"Then we begin. First are Heart and Belly. Listen how they come: the warring sisters!"

Sisters: Heart and Belly

"Sister of the Belly am I, hungry, needy. I need, I want, I desire. I long to take in, to fulfill. But, in my fulfillment, I am ruined, for the more I take in, the more I want. This is no abstraction, no mere thought-form which comes out in paradoxes: this is a reality of my life, of my love. Yes, I have loved. I have loved such a man as Eros, I have loved such a creature in the flesh. And the more I have loved him, the more have I wanted him. More, More, More. More of him, less of me. Fill me up! That is my cry. Selfish, some say of me; but that is not true. For to love is to need. To need is a consequence of love. I need only those I love, no others. And my love makes me more needy. I need to give, too, though those around me may not think so. I need to give of myself, to fill up the need of others. But I speak from my intensity within. I speak from a passionate, lust-thirst-hunger-emptiness-longing-desiring. Fill me or kill me, lest I devour you, kill you! Oh pain, I am the Sister of the Belly, in agony."

"Sister of the Heart am I, searching, connecting. I give, I seek. I, too, desire, but to connect, to engage the other, to find his spots of being and becoming, to see his need, his state. I long to solace him, care for him, to connect with him. I long for union. People do not see me as selfish, they see me as giving, but I am just as selfish as my sister. My need is as intense as hers, but it is for uniting with the other, recognizing his uniqueness and becoming whole with him. But I am kind, I do not pressure, I do not devour. My loving is a going out, not a taking in."

"I, Sister of the Belly, am again in pain. My belly aches because I am not understood. Not even by my sister am I understood. She sees me only as greedy, which I am, selfish, which I am, and devouring, which I am. But she fails to see that she is the same, everyone is. I am the devil; I am the witch. But I, alone, acknowledge that I am dark and devouring. So are others, but they will not admit it. Feed me, feed me. Feed me the blood of others' emotion, the passion of other's love, the milk of connection with me, my dreams, my fantasies, my desires! Feed me! But give me no ersatz of non-emotional, non-sensual foods which only bloat the stomach and do not feed the center! Feed me!"

"She screams, that belly-sister. Always here, always here. She can see no other except herself; she can connect with no other except through her own fantasy, her own lust. She has no empathy, no understanding. She offends me. She calls me liar, she calls me innocent and self-deceiving fool. I call her cut-throat, selfish bitch, insatiable harlot! She impugns my motives, my caring, my way. She does so because she does not understand it. She is lower, she is less aware. She claims a consciousness of dark depths, but she is unconscious of herself and what she does to others. What is worse, she interferes with me when I seek out another. She intrudes into my deep desire to connect with another; she filters in by keeping up her incessant hunger for union. This becomes a devouring, a rage, if they retreat from the pressure of her vulture—like hunger and I am left with the pain. I am misunderstood, misinterpreted, left and abandoned because of her!"

"She talks, she complains, she blames me, that heart-sister. She, so unaware of her own need, continually goes out and absolutely overlooks me, my hungers. Continually going out, she is unconscious of herself, and I pay the price! I despise her . . . and I envy her. I envy her because others like her, think well of her, and blame only me when there is need expressed, something demanded. But, without me, there would be no intensity, only a passionless connecting without sense, without individuality."

I, Daughter of Guinevere must speak. You both war and battle in me! I am the victim of you both! You quarrel and despise each other. And my poor being goes from hunger to frustration, from rage to impotence. Is there no solace for me?

"No solace for you. On that we can both agree!"

I, Guinevere's Daughter, collapse. I fall down and weep. Oh, Eros, now you see it. These two sisters, of Belly and Heart, they battle, they seek their own way, each at the expense of the other. And where do they agree? Only in that I shall have no solace, no peace, no rest. Oh, Eros, you brought them to me, you allowed them to exist in me. Can you quiet them, tame them? Can you get them to cooperate a little? To let off from tearing me apart? Eros, Eros, I beseech you! Help me to cope with them!"

"Why do you give up so easily, Daughter of Guinevere? Why do you collapse when they simply provoke each other so? Why do you not respond when they agree that there is no solace for you? Should you not ask them that question as I ask you?"

I had not thought. But then, I do not think sufficiently. I feel, I intuit, I sense, but I do not think so much. Eros, you ask me to think, to reflect, to confront them. But they do not think either. So, Sisters of Belly and Heart, you agree to give me no solace, but why? Why do you agree only in that?"

"We must each have our way; we must each have our say."

You may have your way, you may have your say. But can you not give a little? Must it be all or nothing?

"Right! Right! All or nothing! Thus say I, Sister of the Belly! All or nothing! I would prefer having all, a totality of ingoing, incoming, loving intensity with one man, one God-man, and I must have all of him, as well. No rival will I brook! Until I have it, better nothing."

"All, all! I, Sister of the Heart, I will give my all, not demand it! I will give my all to the one God-man, to the one man whom I love. I am not possessive and jealous and devouring, like she is, I am totally devoted. True, I will cry and suffer if the love is not returned, but that is all. All or nothing of me do I give. But, better all than nothing. And, all of me in each place, if I can."

I, Guinevere's Daughter, am dumbfounded, puzzled, perplexed, impotent, helpless. I would have to be a great All to encompass you both! But I feel like a Nothing because I cannot. But you two only unite in agreeing to give me no rest. All right, then, you will each get Nothing. For if I am ruined by you, devoured by you, depleted by your yearnings and taking in, giving and going out, then there will be no one left at all. Indeed, then you will have nothing!

"Bravo, Daughter of Guinevere! I, Eros, applaud you! Let them answer that!"

"I will speak to that, Daughter of Guinevere. I, Sister of the Belly, will speak. Nothing, then nothing, is my answer. I do not fear death nor nothingness! I have been half-suicidal most of my life anyway. So, such threats are of no value to me, no importance."

"And I, Sister of the Heart, will speak also, Daughter of Guinevere. The threat of Nothing is also no threat to me, for I am glad to be obliterated! I would be glad to lose myself, to fade away. For, if I cannot unite myself with the Other, if I cannot have total union, better to have nothing, better not to exist at all!"

"Do you see, Daughter of Guinevere? Do not weep and be so servile! They, Belly and Heart, are willing to die for their Oneness. They want all, but are ready to be Nothing. Can you not see?"

I see only that I am torn apart. They want all or nothing. I cannot be all, so I must be nothing, yet I cannot abide that. I cannot rest in death alone. So I continue to be torn apart. I continue to dwell in the foolish, unknowing, tearing, painful state of sisters who are opposites, yet similars. They both want the One, the one God-man who can satisfy them. Well, then, Eros, I offer them you! I offer them the One. I will not be a sacrifice, a ruined battlefield for their war-games of devotion, I will offer them you!

"You laugh, Daughter of Guinevere. You think it is better for a God to be a sacrifice, a victim for the opposites than poor, mortal you, eh? Well, then, let them come to me if they can. Let them find their One in me, if they can! But they will not because they both want me exclusively, permanently, possessively, individually, and they cannot. They will not!"

They both nod, Eros. They hear you and they know that what you say is true. They nod, and agree only in hounding me, not submitting to you. Well, then, I feel something like my Mother, Guinevere. She, the Queen, had two loves. I have two as well, but two enemies, two sisters who do not love me, they fight to dominate me! Well, then, I shall smash their heads, their hearts and bellies! They will submit, they will submit!

Do you hear, Sister of Heart? Do you hear, Sister of Belly? You will not have hegemony! You will not have all. You will submit to a higher center, a higher oneness, a higher union. You shall not have your own center as the ultimate, as the only way! I shall insist upon it. You may die, if you wish, that is your choice. But I shall serve a totality, which is what my Lord, Eros, serves! I proclaim it: I, Guinevere, a soul, will serve a totality of all centers. I shall let no one center have total domination. In this, I shall serve my God and myself. In this, I shall feel right and whole. I proclaim it, in pride and humility.

"Daughter of Guinevere, do you not see? You have reconciled these two Sisters in yourself. By serving yourself and serving God, you serve both of them. By serving the God within both ways, and the God without both ways, you have transcended them. Look now! They, the two, meekly bow. Belly, Sister of Desire and inward-looking, weds herself to Buddha, Lord of the Belly, Lord of the absence of desire, of the non-seeing. Sister of the Heart, the Serving-Seeking-Caring, unites with he who struggles, devotedly pursues. She weds herself to Jacob, he who wrestled with God. So, it is Belly-Belly, and Heart-Heart, uniting. And they unite, Daughter of Guinevere, when you do!"

So be it, Eros. Let them unite in their centers, and let them reconcile themselves to you, too, for you, in the Diaphragm mediate between them, do you not? You, who speak to me, mediate them for me. And I shall serve you and them. In so doing, I serve myself, just as you say.

Following this realization from my Lord, Eros, and following my assertion and achievement of some independence from Sisters of Belly and Heart, I felt the need to reflect upon what I had learned. It had stung me, earlier, to realize that I had not reflected enough. I had been too much the creature of my feelings and impulses, just like Heart and Belly. I needed to think about what had happened. For if Belly were to be truly wedded to Buddha, there would need to be some Sutras, would there not? Some Dharma, some order, some understanding takes place, even if one lives in the moment, in the Being. And if my Sister of the Heart were to be wedded to Jacob, to the Israel who was united with God, there would need to be some understanding—some rules, perhaps, some grasp of the word. For, if Jacob-Israel is not related to the word, what then is he?

So, I reflected. Belly Sister: you are aware of hungers and desires, and of the need for oneness; that must be fed inside yourself. What better union for you than to be united with a Buddha Belly? What greater union for you than to be with the one who is totally with the moment, with Being, just as you are, but who is utterly egoless, selfless? He is like you in his belly-centeredness, but opposite in his ego-hood. He can selflessly examine what is happening, he can give objective statement to what is. He can be impersonal, vast, totally One. You, Belly-Sister, can be personal, as narrow as you want, one with yourself. A good union, one that will worship the Oneness of Being, attend to what Is, in the inner depths of Being, yet not be devoured by selfishness nor selflessness. Now I see her, Sister of the Belly, sitting, facing the Buddha, herself in a meditative posture. She is as important as he, as vital as he. She does not just serve him, she is ready to unite with him. I watch them uniting, as they sit in their meditative posture. They meditate facing, in Rinzai fashion. But they come close, they come closer and closer, as if they are doing a kind of Tantric Yoga, a meditative sexual union. They unite and become One. With this, my belly breathes freely. The image of the sitting, meditating union of Buddha and Sister of the Belly equals the Service of the Lord of Being, and this silences the raging hunger.

I turn now to the Sister of the Heart, she who reaches out in love, in need for union with another. She is active, warm, outgoing. Can she be, then, a fit spouse for Jacob, who is, in truth, he who wrestles with God? Can she, who longs to unite, who feels and cares but does not battle, can she, like the Ruth of the Old Testament, unite with that devoted, single-aimed, contender with God? She reaches out for the God within the other person. Jacob reaches neither in nor out. Like Buddha, he is at One with the Lord-without and the Lord-within. But he is impersonal, even with himself. Does he not become Israel? He carries the symbol for a whole people, a chosen people, as an instrument of God. He serves, he loves, but he is impersonal in his raging and battling and loving. Like Buddha, he is at one with his devotion. Sister of the Heart is devoted, too, but she is personal, individual, she wants that uniqueness of that person out there. Can they unite really? Can Sister-Heart and Jacob-Heart unite? Of course they can, just as Sister-Belly and Buddha-Belly united! And similarly, for here the male is vast, impersonal, devoted. And here the female is specific, personal, unique. Let them unite. Eros, my heart opens and I breathe freely as I proclaim the need and beg that they unite.

How do they unite, Eros? How do these two, Jacob-Heart and Sister-Heart unite? They come close, they stand close. They do not sit and meditate like Buddha. They stand and they embrace. They are chest to chest, heart to heart. Just as Buddha and Sister of the Belly united in being organ to organ, belly to belly, now Jacob-Heart and Sister-Heart unite in being chest to chest, heart to heart. He feels the warmth of her breasts, nourishing, feeding, needing to find and feed the need of the other. She feels the beat of his heart, passionate, deep, strong, rhythmic, the flow of life and blood flowing in his veins and arteries, repeated throughout his body, in head and phallus, in throat and toe. Above all, in his center, the Chest. They unite in the embrace, and their love is romantic, passionate, caring. They are assuaged, and I can breathe freely. The Sisters are united with Brothers, and I, Daughter of Guinevere, who must contain them, can breathe freely.

Eros, my love, my center, who dwells between belly and heart, who mediates Sister and Sister, Brother and Brother, Eros, I adore you, worship you.

The Sisters are united, not with each other, to be sure, but united all the same, to the spouse of their center, to the brother of their being. United, and not warring—at least for this moment. But last night I dreamed:

I dreamed that I was upon a ship, or in a room, and I saw that this was also some sort of school. There were numbers of children being taught by men and women. The teaching was a special thing, a hard thing, and—as I learned what it was—an incredible thing. The children were being taught to feel nothing. These cold, clever teachers were teaching these infants to feel nothing! I watched in horror as a little girl of perhaps five was told that her Mother had died. She paid no heed and went right on in a bright, cold way, talking with words beyond her years, with intelligence beyond the norm, but with no feeling at all. No heart-feeling was there, of care, concern or sorrow, and no belly-pain was there, of hunger, of longing, of loss. I awakened aghast and horrified.

What manner of dream was this, I wondered? Oh, Eros, where are you? Is this an answer to the solution of Belly and Heart? That the separation of the warring sisters should be followed by the mournless, feelingless death of a mother? Eros does not answer, so I reflect upon the dream. The five year old girl is the product of a union I have had, a love which has died. Only some days ago did I realize that there was no love there, no care for relationship. The love had died and the lover gone away. The little girl, the inner child of that relationship, remains alive, but motherless. And those teachers, cold and impersonal and intellectual, they teach it not to feel. Have no more feeling, child, for to feel is to feel pain; to feel is to suffer. To suffer without surcease is horrible; better not to feel at all! Perhaps so speaks my head, so speaks my mind, so speaks those seemingly care-less, feelingless parts. But that, too, is horrible! What say you, Eros! What say you, Lord of Love, Brother and Lover to me? Reconciler and redeemer?

"Speak not to me, Daughter of Guinevere. Speak to Aphrodite, Goddess of Love, who dwells as Mother and as Daughter, as well as Sister and Lover. As Mother she dwells in the Eyes, those fierce and caring, intense and luminous mirrors of the soul. As Daughter, she dwells in genitals. For was she not conceived from the Phallus of the God? And is she not Woman and Lover of the first and last? She is those; enquire of her. Anyone who would know of such matters, who would seek answers to questions of Mother and Daughter, of life and death, of soul and body, must speak to her."

But how will I find her, Eros? How will I be able to speak to your own Mother-Daughter-Sister-Lover?. . . My words to Eros are as nothing, for he vanishes as he came. Instead I find myself looking into very warm and luminous eyes. Two open and warm orbs reach out and take me in. They seem to envelop me with their care, their warmth. There is an invisible web of tender cotton threads which reach out around me. And then I see that it is a bird which weaves these threads around me. It is a dove. The dove takes these threads and weaves a softness about me as if it were a blanket. It weaves and weaves, in a play and feeling of love. But now, as it weaves, I feel choked and suffocated, for I am alone in my love. I am alone in my need. I have lost my lover, my partner, he who would accompany me on a voyage through the lands of the sea. I am alone and choke in the web of love. For love alone in the web is like the fly in the web of the spider. He dies, is suffocated and devoured. And thus, I suppose, is my experience of the Goddess when I am alone: I am without my love and know the Goddess as a witch, as a weaver of webs which only suffocate and kill, do not satisfy nor fulfill. Oh, Goddess, in your wordless way, you tell this to me. With your warm and luminous, yet fierce and passionate soul-eyes, you inform me, as woman to woman, being to being. You tell me that your Center of Eyes is to unite soul to soul, being to being, and that your wish is for the two, the two eyes, two loves, should see and unite as one. The two eyes give breadth and depth to vision and to love. But the love which has gone away leaves me like a lonely child, suffocating and in despair.

So it is that the teachers come, these cold and calculating teachers of the mind. Like machines they dispel feeling and thereby dispel love. Is this help or hindrance? In some ways, Goddess, I see that they wish to free me from pain, and I would want that. But, to be freed from feeling? Never! Horrible! Tell me, help me!. . . You do not answer. Your eyes only continue to look.

But now, my eyes go down. My eyes descend and I hit upon the genitals of the Goddess of Love. The roundness and softness, the mount, so rightly named after her Roman form, her star shape, as Venus. Does not the Heavenly Aphrodite, the Aphrodite Urania, descend and become Aphrodite Pandemos, love in the world, love among mankind, love not spiritual but carnal? Surely it is so. But, as I look at this immortal vagina, this gloriously soft and round and fresh cave into which the spirit of Gods and men enter and from which the creative children exit, as I look I see that here is a third Eye, a receptive opening which does not look out, it looks in! It receives and takes in, it responds to inner movings and rhythms.

Now I understand again through the wordless instruction of my Mother and Sister, Aphrodite. She tells me that above, in the Eyes, she is like the Sister of the heart, looking out, seeing, caring, but also fierce, loving in an active, conscious way. And below, here in the vagina, she is like the Sister of Belly, looking inward and desiring. Here she looks with the one eye inside herself, attuned to the rhythms of the womb, attuned to the moonlight within. Above, one can see the light, the sunlight; with the eyes one can see much, how men feel, where they hurt, what they are like. But below, one can receive men, one can assuage them, one can cool their ardors. Love from the soul above, Urania Aphrodite, and love from the flesh, below, Aphrodite Pandemos. Thus does she teach me. Thus does my Mother, the Goddess, speak to me, another woman like herself. She tells me in the womanly way, without words, but with symbols and feelings, with intuitions, with looks and soft gestures. Oh, Goddess, speak on, speak on and tell me more!

She further explains that, at times, the Mother dies. There is no longer soul, only body. This is the horror for a woman. When she dwells only in the flesh, only in the vagina, then she has no soul, she is dead. That is a hell, that is an agony of a Daughter without a Mother, a feelingless death of a lack of union. Then there is only cold brutality, mind and no spirit, flesh and no body. For union is the thing. Above and below, right and left, union is the thing. Splitness is the horror.

But think, Aphrodite tells me, think. The lower is daughter to the upper, to be sure, but only when there is a movement from above to below. When the Gods move from the highest heavens above down into the soul and flesh of man, it is so. Then Aphrodite moves from being in the Heavens above (was she not the organ of the father on high?), as Mother, down to Daughter, down to the deeps of the psyche and the vagina of the flesh. But is there not another movement in the story of the Goddess? Indeed, there is. For the Goddess as a girl and little playing daughter, with Nerites and many sisters, once again rises into the heavens. She rises and joins the Gods, is elevated. Now she becomes more than Mother, more than Daughter, she becomes Woman, and Goddess! Having descended from the heights and gone into the depths, now she rises once again, and unites with many Gods, and becomes the archetype of the Woman and Woman in Love. What other thing is there for Woman to be, pray tell, than to be in love? What, indeed, is there for the soul to be, than to be in love? That is what the soul is for: to unite with another and to unite with God! To unite! With oneself and with another; is that not the highest form of love? Of Being?

And now, having conveyed her wordless message to me, I see the Goddess leaving. She goes away, leaving me to be Mother and Daughter, Goddess and Woman. She leaves me to understand, to cope, to love, in union and alone. She leaves me to decide if I would suffer or die in feelinglessness. Would I accept pain, and thus become Woman and Goddess? I would, and I will.

Oh, Eros, who was son and brother to Aphrodite, who was father to her as well! Eros, I have heard the wordless message of the Goddess. I understand that she once wed Hermes the Messenger, and moves like him, for she has moved so in my soul and I am grateful. I feel more than ever a woman. For now I have felt the centers of Eye and Genitals, I have felt the active movement of the Eyes going out, loving and caring and searching, and the receptive, inward-looking eye of the Vagina, reaching in, making a womb, a nest, a place for new births, whether in spirit or flesh.

"It is not enough, Daughter of Guinevere, it is not enough." Thus spoke my Lord, Eros; thus did he speak, but I did not understand.

Father and Son

I have dreamt again. Again I have slept and again have I dreamt in pain and horror. I dreamed that a father stood, with other fathers, outside a circle. The circle was large and there was a charm or magic whereby they could not enter it. Inside the circle were many children, largely boys, I think, about the age of ten. These boys were being systematically and rhythmically beaten by some very muscular and powerful men. They were hit and cuffed repeatedly, not enough to drive them unconscious, but causing pain and hurt, leaving hard marks. The father was, in the strange way of dreams, a man close to me, known to me, loved by me, but also unknown. I watched in anguish as this father stood helplessly by while his son was being beaten. One could see that he hoped that the son could survive this beating, might even grow stronger with it. His agony was that he could do nothing, could not intervene, was powerless to change the terror. I awakened aghast and horrified.

What manner of dream was this, I wondered? Oh, Eros, where are you, once again? I have dreamt of the brutality of the mind teaching children not to feel, and now I dream of the brutality of the flesh, the beating of young children! Oh, Eros, speak to me, explain to me! Come as your Mother-Daughter-Sister did. With words or without, please enlighten me!

"I can tell you, Daughter of Guinevere, when you request it. For my nature is of words, words of love and light. Just as my Mother-Daughter-Sister spoke to you, enlightened you about the love of Mother and Daughter, Demeter and Persephone, Aphrodite Urania and Pandemos, just so will I speak to you about Father Son, about the love—and hate—of father and son. Just as there is a Mother-Eye, a loving, caring, and fiercely concerned Mother Eye in Heaven, looking deeply and widely in double vision, just so there is a Father-Eye in Heaven, looking just as widely, as deeply, as caringly. But he looks with rules, with ideas, with principles, does this father eye. He looks impersonally, vastly, widely. Just as the Buddha is impersonal, and Jacob is impersonal, and Jesus is impersonal, just so is this Father-Eye in Heaven impersonal. Better, perhaps, to call it transpersonal. For his Eye is wide and deep on eternity. It is not that he cares not for the individual and personal and unique—he does care. But he cares for the eternity of things. Think of the Buddha, unmoved; think of Jacob, wrestling in service; think of Jesus, gladly sacrificing himself for the Father. Thus is the Father, seeing from above and beyond, relating to what is yet even above him, in the heights of that which has not yet been, has not yet incarnated, has not yet occurred. He sees, too, into the depths below, to the child, the plant, the son who dwells below. Who is this father in Heaven? Who is this spiritual rector who rules, governs, sees? Is it Zeus? Yes. Is it Apollo, cool and reasonable? Yes. It is all these careful and moderate father Gods. But it is also a fierceness, a rage, and a passion. Is it then, like Dionysos or Priapus, or even, like me, Eros? No. For we are sons, are we not? So, look to us below.

"There, we are below, in the phallus of the man, in the waxing and waning organ of love. Sensitive, flexible is she, this organ (for is it not Aphrodite?); and hard and penetrating is he (for is it not an incarnation of me, Eros?). The phallus is sensitive; a hard and flexible, sensitive and penetrating organ of love. He-she sees with one eye. For there is that one eye below which senses very differently from the eyes above. You know how he-she senses? He-she responds to all the centers above, from head and upper-eye and heart and belly. He-she responds, rising in desire and anticipation, settling in disappointment, fear and disgust, in frustration. Sensitive is he-she. Penetrating is he-she. Thus is the Son, the Eros-carrier of love.

"So there is between Father and Son, between Zeus and Eros, between spirit of eternity and rulership above and spirit of love and connection below, a union and a disjunction. For the Eyes above cannot stand the irrational rule of the Eye below. The Eye below cannot abide the continuing frustration of the Eyes above. They quarrel, they fight, they do battle. You, perhaps, as a woman, do not know that battle of the male spirits, of order and mind versus disorder and desire. Buddha knew it, Jacob knew it, Jesus knew it. And now, at this level, Zeus above and Eros below know it. We know it.

"We know it from the ways of your dream. Though father and son battle, though they war and struggle, they also love. Just as the Father is the predecessor of the Son, when one comes from above to the below, from heaven to earth, just so is the Son father to the Father when there is an ascent from below upwards. The upward-seeking spirit of the semen of love in the son below rises and teaches the Father in Heaven what it means to love. Did not God learn from his cherished son, Jesus? Did not God learn from Job? Does not the father learn from the son, become renewed by the son? It is so. Therefore, what is father and what is son can vary whether one moves from above to below, from spirit to flesh, or from below upwards, from flesh to spirit. They need not war . . . but they do.

"And so your dream, thus the hurt. The father would strengthen
the son. The father would prepare the son and make him strong. The
father would wish that his son would be hurt by none, but he is. The
father hurts the son, yet he is hurt more by being cut off from him.
That is the worst of all. Just as in your other dream, the evil thing is
not that the mother dies, but that there is no more feeling—that is
the horror. And now, too, the sad thing is that the father is powerless
to help the son. He must stand by impotently while the great
impersonal power of the stupid and mechanical forces of masculine
nature beat this child, this new and needy thing. Thus, again, it is
the impersonal, unfeeling forces which sometimes help, sometimes
hurt. You agreed, Daughter of Guinevere, to suffer pain. You agreed,
for the sake of feeling, of connection, to endure pain. Let it then be
that the Son, the new spirit, be beaten into shape, be formed, be
molded and made strong by the impersonal forces of nature. Let it be
that the father, the old spirit, should suffer the pain and frustration
of impotence, too. Let it be. But fight it, too, Daughter of Guinevere.
Fight it too! For the Gods need humans to fight, as well as submit,
to complain as well as accept.

"And finally, Daughter of Guinevere: from Son to Father, from
Father to Son, is to become a man, a true union of above and below,
of spirit and flesh, of rules and freedom, of impersonality and personality, to become a God-man, just as there is a God-woman. Do I not
make a home in the center of the two, as well, between Eyes and
Phallus? Is not the Diaphragm the place of the union of the Tree of
the Phallus with the Branches of the Eyes? Are not Above and Below,
Father and Son united in Eros, God-man? Is it not so, Daughter of
Guinevere, Daughter and Mother of Aphrodite, God-woman?"

My Lord, Eros, left me with this question and went away. He
informed me, loved me, but went away. But that night, I dreamt
again. I dreamt that I was visiting a wise man, who was both a father
of wise men and a grandfather of wise men. Before I could engage this
wise old man in conversation, I was summoned to help an Italian man
who had some difficulty. This fellow proved to be husky, good looking,
warm-hearted. We chatted briefly and he felt better. I moved then,
to speak with a most interesting woman, a kind of priestess in the field
of the occult. No sooner had I begun, however, when I was once again
summoned to see the Italian man. Now, he was lying on the floor in
agony. I tried to wrap my arms around him and comfort him. He
screamed and cried. It was with great difficulty that I could put my
arms around him and I needed help to put him up on a bed where
he could be contained, warmed, comforted. As I arranged him upon

the bed, I found some drawings and paintings, some writings and poems that looked familiar to me. They looked like efforts of my own that I had done many years ago, when I had come to a period of wholeness. That totality did not last very long, and I was soon broken by the exigencies of life and pain, of relationship and conflict that come to most people in one way or another. The dream ended with my caring for this man.

Who was this man? And what did it mean that my writings and paintings were connected with him? What, too, of the wise old grandfather, and the priestess? Until now, Eros had been with me, to help me to both understand and to feel. Now he was not with me . . . Or was he? In a lightning-like way, I suddenly understood my dream. The understanding came in a wordless way, and it is hard for me to express it, but here is how I understood:

The Italian man of the dream was none other than Eros, himself, but as an Italian, not a Greek, a kind of Amor. But he was human and ordinary, not a God. In that form, he was pained, for he had suffered love, had suffered the invasion of the Gods, being racked by opposites like Sisters of Belly and Heart, a going-out of feeling and a needing thereof. He was human and ordinary, and suffered. I understood and knew that the Italian man was just a human being, like myself. He belonged to the center of centers, the diaphragmatic place which is the center of the person; the place between belly and heart where we all live, where all of us human beings struggle. We all are caught between our desires and our carings, our longings and our helpings of others. We are all born from below and are attached by the umbilicus to a concrete parent which makes us real, flesh and blood. And that navel is the center of us and, like the Omphallos of Delphi, the navel of the world. For the world is based on us, ordinary mortals. Oh, Italian, oh feeling, husky, handsome, but ordinary man who suffers like me, I belong there with you, in that center, in that middle, umbilicus place which suffers, which mediates all the spiritual and soulful places from above, and all the spiritual and soulful places from below! I embrace you, Amore, Italian Eros who is an ordinary man, who is a physical man longing for pleasure, love and happiness. I embrace you, my man, who is a union of father and son, a union of the above and below, and a sufferer of the union of these!

And, in my embrace of you, Amore, I rediscover my own images, my own poetry, my own union of image and word, of flesh and spirit, my own wholeness. Best of all, I rediscover my art, a union of feeling and sensation, a place of creative resolution of above and below, inside and outside. In embracing you, Amore, I embrace my own spirit, my own love! Speak to me, Amore, tell me of your pain, your love, for I would unite with you . . . You do not speak, you do not come forward. Your dark eyes are still in pain, they reveal woundedness, brokenness, silence. But I will keep you here, in the bed of my heart and belly. I will guard you, with the Eyes of my Mother and the Eye of the Daughter. And I will ask that your broken union of Father and Son be healed from on high . . .

From on high . . . With that thought, I went on with my dream, and realized that I needed to speak to the grandfather, the old wise man, and to the priestess as well. For these two spoke to both higher and lower centers of being. Were I, Daughter of Guinevere, to fulfill my task and become the soulful place of union of all these centers, all these Gods and men, Goddesses and Women, then I must go onward with my dream, onward with the task.

Father and Daughter

Just as I was prepared to continue my dream onwards, to talk deeply and meaningfully with the wise old man, I was interrupted in the strange, irrational way that dreams are, that fantasy is, that life is. I realized that there was, indeed, a union of Mother and Daughter, of Father and Son. Father Eros and Son Eros, Eyes above and the Phallus below united in the figure of Amore, the ordinary Italian man. There was also a union—in that same center—of Aphrodite above and Aphrodite below and that union was none other than in myself, the mortal, suffering, Daughter of Guinevere. I could see that in just such a place was the Grandson of the Knight, ordinary, mortal, seeking, dreadfully concerned with the One and the Many, just as I was involved with the Pair. And now, just as my concern was ready to shift above and below, I saw that there were pairs where the Grandson of the Knight saw only One and Many. Pairs I had already seen, in Belly (Buddha and Sister of Belly), and in Heart (Jacob and Sister of the heart, like Ruth). But now I saw the pairs of the Eyes above. For there in the Eyes, in the loving, searching, fierce, penetrating vision from above, was a union of Aphrodite Urania, as Mother, with Eros as fiery spirit. And, below, in the genital place, was a union of Aphrodite Pandemos of the Earth, as Phallus and Vagina, with Eros. Below, the earthy, loving union of flesh with flesh, love with love. Mother-Father above, Brother-Sister below. Was it not so in the story of the Goddess, and did not the God say so? Aphrodite was alone with her Eros-lover below, in the depths, and was with the Many in the heights.

I returned to the wise old man of my dream. He dwelt in the third eye, that forehead vision of time and space which sees beyond the ordinary and the everyday, beyond people even, beyond time and space, into the eternity which awaits us all and from which we all come. This wise old man was like the old man in the cave of the Son of the Knight, who was father, in turn, to my friend and companion, the Grandson of the Knight. The Son of the Knight, after all, was like me in not knowing who his father was. He had two fathers, it turned out, the Charioteer of the Cave, an immortal Eros, and his very concrete father, the Knight. But was he born of the one, or the other, or both? Not to know. And I, with two fathers: the mortal, but heroic King Arthur and the mortal, and equally heroic Sir Lancelot. Two fathers, one finds out, is like having no father. Thus did I know what it meant to be fatherless, just like the Son of the Knight. But this is different for a woman, after all. So it was with trepidation and pleasure that I approached this wise old man.

He looked at me compassionately and was far from cold or impersonal, or speaking from vast, empty places. Rather, he looked at me and said that he knew about me, knew my effort to become a proper vessel for all that dwelt within me, and a proper mate, after all, for my Lord Eros, himself. He knew all that, and commended it. He knew it because where he walked, to and fro, those things were known. He said that perhaps I had, indeed, been too personal, too limited in my view, even though I had experienced Sisters of Belly and Heart, Eyes of Aphrodite and Eros, all of whom transcended the personal. He said that perhaps I should follow the example of the Grandson of the Knight, and, if I wished to understand, I, too, should attempt a "stations of the cross." I, too, should try and relate to these bigger Gods and Goddesses, but in ways not understood by the Grandson of the Knight, with his One and Many psychology. I, for example, could cope with Father and Daughter, and achieve understanding where he could not.

"But tell me," I asked, what story or myth could help me in this?"

"Zeus and Athene, naturally," he replied.

He was right, of course. But could I, a non-intellectual woman, have a dialogue with Gods and Goddesses as did the Grandson of the Knight? Why not? I thought, if a man can do this, so can a woman. But how? Grandson of the Knight made use of a cave, a library, his magician. I knew only Eros, and dreams. But Eros is a God, is he not? And he came to me willingly, frequently, and desirously. I will, then, follow the example of the Grandson of the Knight, and sink, in my own way, into the place where the Gods are found. . . .

I do not sink. I rise. I rise within myself. I rise from the region of the diaphragm, from the intermediate place between belly and heart. I rise up beyond the throat, beyond even the eyes where Aphrodite dwells and where Eros has his fierce vision. I rise to the place in the forehead of the third eye, that all-seeing, one-eyed place where, I am told, live Father and Daughter. There dwells Zeus, the all-seeing, eagle-eyed, father-king, first-spirit, consciousness-God. There resides he who became Lord of the Gods, he who made a community of Gods, and related to men.

Yes, I can rise there. I can slip inside my own forehead. I can see him even, the One-Eyed Eagle, the All-seeing Zeus. He seems like a Grandfather of men and Gods. A spiritual father is he, perhaps, beyond my own dual fathers of Arthur and Lancelot. But this Zeus is not loving. His is not a vision of care and love as was that of my two fathers, or as is of my beloved Eros. This Grandfather has a consciousness, a Greek Logos, rather than an English or French or Italian love. Or even a Greek love. So, Grandfather of Gods and men; so Eagle-eyed Zeus, I see you! I see the white-bearded, non-bearded, one-eyed, double-eyed, apparent-transparentness of you. Tell me, oh conscious one! Tell me, oh Father of Gods and men!

"Tell you what, my Daughter?"

Now I have to laugh. For, with all my proclaiming, asking, searching, now that I have arrived at a place of high consciousness, now that the God of Gods, the Logos-Center wants to know what I want to know, I have nothing to ask! Why came I here? What do I want to know, indeed? What vision do I need? I suppose I need another vastness than the vastness of love. I suppose I need another vision than the vision of love. I suppose that I need to see, as the wise old man of my dream told me, a larger impersonality, a transpersonal place, even though I was committed to coping with the two, the pair. I suppose that this higher place can look down upon the pair of eyes, and see the Aphrodite-Eros pair. I suppose so. But can it? Is it not also a pair? Zeus and Athena? But what can that cold-eyed daughter of Zeus, born from his head, rejector of nakedness, fierce warrior who slew, what can she have to say about love?

"Love isn't everything," says the Goddess. And now I see her: a fierce Amazon, but with long golden curls. She is tall and stately and lithe, as light as Aphrodite was dark, but with her comes her dark owl, a wise bird of the night. Just as Aphrodite, with her dove and sparrow, could be dark and passionate, just so does Athena, light and lover of culture, bring a dark bird of the night, seeing into the dark depths.

"Love isn't everything," she says. Perhaps so, perhaps so. I have been so wounded by love, so hurt by the loss of loves, so disillusioned, that perhaps a dark bird of the night can see better than I. Perhaps a wisdom of the mind, a love of the spirit, of culture and civilization, can help heal the wounds suffered in the love of men. Perhaps so. So do these thoughts come to me.

Athene smiles. For she, too, thinks these thoughts. Perhaps it is she, herself, who thinks these thoughts through me. For is she not a female like myself? And is not the female, even if head-born, always one with love? Love of culture, of knowledge, of civilization, after all, is also a form of Eros. We know this is so, or we should know it. And so, Athena, daughter of the Grandfather God, born of the forehead, I can come to you. From you I would know things. You I trust, for you are female, and you will always have that female something, that feminine longing for union, whether you acknowledge it or not. Is it not true?

Athene nods. She does not speak. She smiles, but I know that she, too, wants me to know her, to visit the stories of her life, just as the Grandson of the Knight needed to visit the stories of Aphrodite. Well, then, Goddess, I shall do so. But let me pray to you and to your wise Father. Let me pray. I can examine your stories, study your tale, Goddess, only with your help and that of your Father. For I am a seeker after union, after the pair and, with your help, perhaps I can see more, better understand that which I need to know. You nod agreement. So I will begin.

Father and Daughter II

Athene the Goddess was born of her father, Zeus the all-seer, as everyone knows. That she sprang, full-grown, from the peaked brow of the Great Father—that, too, everyone knows. But is it so generally known that Athene had a mother? Is that a secret, hidden? It is told in some tales. Her mother, the great first wife of Zeus, was she whom he wed before even his everlasting, ever monogamous, ever complaining, ever jealous and narrow-viewed wife, Hera. Before even Hera, Zeus pursued and wed Metis, she of "Wise Counsel," she who was Zeus' equal in wisdom and courage, she who was born of the Titans, and already in alliance with the all-seer when his brothers and sisters were devoured by his fearful father Kronos. Metis it was who gave the dreadful Father Kronos the potion which put him to sleep, which compelled him to yield up the Gods he had devoured. And Metis, too, it was who changed into every creature and shape as Zeus pursued her. She was his first wife.

And Metis conceived of her husband and Lord, Zeus. She conceived but had no pleasure in the birth because Zeus swallowed her, put her in his belly. This great and glorious first wife of his, she of wise counsel, was devoured by the great Zeus, just as his own dreadful father had devoured all his brothers and sisters, and why? For the same reason. It was fated that Metis should bear exceedingly wise children: the first an owl-maiden Athene Tritogenia, equal to Zeus in courage and wise counsel, like her mother. After this maiden, however, a boy would be conceived, a male of all-conquering heart, King of Gods and men. And Zeus, great and wise, devoured his wife, lest she bear a son who would depose him. Thus is the first tale of the conception of Athene, the Goddess, the head-born daughter of the great Father.

What do I understand by this gruesome tale? What do I grasp? Only that men are endlessly competitive, endlessly battling, endlessly fearing from Father to Son and Son to Father. If it is so with Gods, this sacred battle and great fear, how is it then with men? Just so, the same. Are we women doomed to forever look upon this horrible war? Must we, like mild does or vapid cows, simply watch as the old and the new collide? Must we sit by and be mere passive spectators to this battle of spirits, taken possession by that which triumphs? Are we

Europa to Zeus the Bull? No, the tale says—or hints. For now, a daughter is born, a daughter of wisdom, equal to her mother in both wisdom and courage, and even a Tritogeneia, an owl-eyed chieftainess of armies, awakener of battle, rejoicing in tumult and strife—for such is the meaning of the Tritogenia, she born by the river Triton, she daughter of the three-pronged spirit of battle.

Does this, then, mean that a new spirit is born out of the head of the Father? That a female, a Goddess, a Daughter of spirit, both wise and courageous, can appear? It seems so to be. This, for me, makes the dire and doleful act of Zeus in swallowing his loving and wise wife more acceptable. For he did not kill the wonderful Titaness, Metis. He devoured her, integrated her, took in the great and wonderful wisdom and courage of his first love. True, this was not out of tenderness and deep desire; true, this was done out of sheer fear that he would be deposed by her son; true, she was not consulted if she so wanted to be devoured. But it is also true that she did not fight it very much. She, after all, this Metis of wise counsel, this female who knew as much as Zeus himself, this creature who had been able to take every shape in eluding Zeus, she allowed herself to be devoured. Perhaps she knew, in truth, that she would love to be inside her lord, always there with him, always there to love him and advise him on matters of good and evil. And I would guess that she knew that her daughter would be a unique Goddess, born of the head of the Father, and ancestress of all those women, thousands and thousands of years hence, who would want their own spirit, have their own courage, sport their own wisdom. I think that she knew this, this wise Metis; I guess this from my own feminine intuition. In so guessing, I forgive Zeus, I accept this wily and canny Father who saved his brothers and sisters, saved himself, and gave birth to the great Daughter, wily and canny as he! Zeus, I salute you!

The tale continues that some say that just as Athena was born of the father, so Hephaistos was born of the mother, Hera. It was a contest of spouses. Is it so? Is the creative God born of the monogamous mother? And alone? Is the wise and courageous Goddess born of the Father alone? Yes, I think so. For such an incest of the spirit, such a deep and rejected and *contra naturam* event must needs be so: creativity is always an incestuous union, is it not? Mother and Son? And wisdom is always an incestuous union, is it not? Father and Daughter? Is it not so? No . . . it is not! For this is only one form of union. Did not Hephaistos wed Aphrodite? And give birth to Eros, my Lord? And was not Eros also a child of Ares and Aphrodite? So love emerges in both the creation of man alone, and in the battle of relationship; that the Grandson of the Knight learned.

But Athene? She, the product of father alone, but with a secret mother? She united wisdom and struggle, but she is the Goddess of civilization, as we know, ancestress of all culture, patroness of the symbol of the highest city-culture of all, Athens the great! So, then, she must needs be virgin, away from all the feminine needs of love, warmth, closeness. And the great Goddess is compensated for this loss by being wisest of all, greatest of all, and in an everlasting union with the Father. That incestuous union, that amalgamation at the Eye of the forehead, that union of the spirit, is, indeed, worthwhile. I embrace you, Goddess, you who had to surrender the warmth and joy of the lower animal levels, the pleasures of love, the feminine joys of nakedness and vulnerability. I embrace you, as a woman, as one who values your devotion to spirit and father, to culture and freedom, to wisdom and civilization. I embrace you and love you, for you need my love, you need the love and approval of men and women, just as your sister, Aphrodite, needed their understanding.

So Athene sprang full-grown from the head of the Father. Hephaistos or Prometheus, or both, struck the great lord Zeus in the head with the double axe, relieving him from his most fierce of all pains, and out she sprang—mighty, wise, fully armed, and with a great shout!

And so it is: The creative God must assist the Father in his great, birth-giving, creative act, and even that Titan who is totally loyal to man, willing even to suffer having his guts devoured in order to bring man fire and light, even that man-server must be present! What an event! Oh, how I salute the ancients who understood the story, how they must have known in their depths! The birth of Athene, savior of the spirit, is such an event that both the server of Gods and the server of men must assist in the two-headed, forceful, hard work which both need! And both need it because of the ever-recurring, ever-senseless, ever-brutal competition when male animals battle, male spirits struggle, and one or the other triumphs. Both need it because a female spirit can fight and not have to triumph for herself; a female spirit can fight for culture, for the emergence of higher forms, and not have to bellow for her own power, strut her own prowess. Because, as a woman, in her heart she knows the value of love. It is not so, Goddess? Do not I as a woman speak truly of you?

She nods. The Goddess nods, and bids me continue with the reflections on her life, a meditation on the events of her marvelous tale.

The Goddess is said to have had other fathers as well. She was, of course, a Father's Daughter, a warlike virgin more related to the Fathers than the Mothers, so that it is understandable that several other fathers can be claimed for her. Among these was the giant,

Pallas, which can mean, in Greek, either a strong young man, or a strong virgin, a *virago* in Latin. This same Pallas was said to have tried to rape his daughter. The Goddess overcame him, took his skin from him, as well as his wings, and wore them herself. Understood. Such a Goddess can and must be strong enough to prevent an animal father-daughter incest, must be capable of overcoming the mere brutality and acquisitive, power-hunger, sex-driven character of the untamed giant spirit. But she, too, must be able to take that skin and those wings and wear them for herself. What does that mean? That she can show such a fierce outer garment as a protection of her feminine nature, she can be fierce and warlike and invading, if necessary, and also as much a winged spirit, a creature of higher realms as any father. This is her shield, her protection. And so does Pallas Athene overcome the negative, raping, unfeeling father, and carry her victory as a triumph of defense.

A third father was said to be Brontes, the "thunderer." Zeus had been told that there was danger that Metis would bear something stronger than lightning. That flash of Zeus', his powerful and light-filled electrical wisdom, something more than that? What then? Why, thunder! Thunder, the province of Zeus' equally powerful brother, Poseidon, the thunderer. The universe had been divided up, had it not? The sky to Zeus, the underworld to Hades, and the sea to the Thunderer. So then, Athene, ancestress of the female spirit, must needs have a relation to the Thunderer as well. It is said that the phallic primordial beings were to teach her. So these creative earth beings, associated with the Lord of the Sea and Earthquakes, brought their earthy, sea-wisdom to the great Goddess. How else could she become so wise? Are not all these fathers necessary? Zeus, her real father of the spirit, Pallas, her negative father of the masculine rape, meant to be overcome and used as a protection; the Thundering phallic beings, who taught her truths other than those known from the higher spirit alone. It is right and just that these fathers should belong to our great Goddess, Athene.

But there is also a fourth father, Triton, the River-God. Triton was one of those who educated Athene, and he had another daughter, named Pallas. Athene and Pallas played the war-game, since both were daughters of fierce warriors. As Pallas was about to strike Athene with her javelin, Zeus, fearing for his daughter, interposed his fear-awakening goatskin, the Aigis. Pallas turned aside her gaze and was mortally hit by Athene. The Goddess mourned for her, and made an image of her, the Palladion, around which she hung her Aigis, and set it beside the image of Zeus, her Father.

Oh, Goddess, I think that I understand this tale, and I feel for you. Is not this Pallas a girl who is like you in fierceness and courage, but more like her namesake, an animal earthy creature, who could lust after men? Is she not your feminine opposite? Zeus feared that you would succumb to such a fierce sexuality, like his own, so he had to protect you from it. And you did kill it, raising it up as a spirit, enshrined alongside your own father. It must be so, Goddess. For you have never gone against the fierce needs of the animal, the needs of union, you have had only to forego them for yourself, to have that as a shield against the entrapments of love, like those from your sister Aphrodite. Oh, Goddess, you are deeply Pallas Athene in every way. Oh, uniter of wisdom and courage, spirit and culture, I know how you sacrificed, how you must have suffered and mourned. Oh, Goddess, I, a woman, Daughter of Guinevere, she who was even more your opposite than Pallas, I, Daughter of Guinevere, mortal woman who has had to suffer for her spirit, I embrace you, have compassion for you, but I also salute you in your largeness, your capacity, your sacrifice.

Father and Daughter III

Athene, Goddess, I address you anew. Each time that I have desired to approach your stories, to perform the stations of my meditation upon your life and deeds, upon your nature and significance, each time that I assay to do this, I grow tired and sleepy. Something deep within me says "no" to this and "no" to you, Oh Goddess. I report this to you; in chagrin and shame I tell you this. But now, as I lay down, as I fell into a reverie which was neither dream nor sleep, but a quiet consciousness which was far, indeed, from the heights of vision of your Eagle-Eyed Father, and far, as well, from the vision of your concentrating, city-building, culture-evolving self. It was, rather, more like an owl-eyed vision, a glimpse into darkness, into the night, into the feminine depths from which you escaped and which you fight. For you abhor unconsciousness, you abhor the non-seeing, the lazy, the merely biological and earth-bound. I know this, and part of my feminine nature rebels at you, rebels at your need for consciousness, your need for culture. And so, I grow sleepy and lazy. And so, I almost sink into the depths of your opposite, the Gorgon Medusa, she the Witch-Goddess of the lowest levels. But I do not, Oh Goddess, for your owl comes to aid me. A few moments of the reverie-sleep, the waking-darkness, the night-vision, and I can return to you; I can return, with your owl-eyed servant, to your worship and to the meditation of you. I know that you gave your hero the wisdom and cleverness to not look directly into that dark-Goddess of nature, lest he turn into stone. I know that you flee from the merely biological; but I know that you have your owl, that natural night spirit that can see in the dark depths. So, Athene, I can accept my need to sink down, and I can trust that your owl will guide me, wake me, and return me to your worship. I, Daughter of Guinevere, can serve you and find you, and not do violence to my own deep darkness, my own animal nature. In serving you, I serve a high spirit, one of day, but I do not abandon night.

In all the stories of Athene, she is always styled Parthenos, "Virgin," for such she is. But she is also invoked, at times, as Meter, "Mother." I know that she was a Daughter of the Father, but how is she also Mother? A Virgin Mother? Like that other who came much later? What is the tale?

It was told that Hephaistos, creator God, demanded, as a reward for his assistance at the birth of the Goddess, that she should be his bride. Indeed, she was given to him, and he led her into the bridal chamber. But when he lay down beside her, it is said, the Goddess vanished, and his semen fell to the earth. Of this semen, the earth Goddess, Gaia-Chthon, bore Erichthonios, the divine child of the Acropolis, of the great city of Athens, and handed him back to Pallas Athene to be cared for.

It is also told that there was strife (Eris) between Hephaistos and Athene, and that is why the child is called Erichthonios. Yet a third tale relates that the God pursued Athene to rape her, but even when he overtook her, he could not penetrate her and his semen fell upon her thigh. The great Virgin Goddess used wool (erion) to wipe this away, or was it dust? In any case, the newborn divine child is also called Hersos or Erros, offspring of "bridal dew."

Again, Great Goddess, the masculine comes to you, at you, in various forms. He comes now as the creator God, yearning to unite with you. He comes as the one longing to marry, craving to rape, and in battle with you. And you repulse all of these. Unlike your sister, Aphrodite, you do not wed the creator God, Hephaistos. Your female consciousness turns away from marriage, turns away from that form of union which includes mating. And, of course, you also turn away from his rape, his wild and hungry passion. Oh, Goddess, just as you ran from the raw animal passion of the Father-incest on an animal level, you now run from it also on the mating level! There is strife between you and Hephaistos, just as there was between Aphrodite and Ares, God of War. But you, Goddess, are your own warrior, and you will not unite with strife. What then, oh Goddess, what then? You cannot escape the semen, you cannot escape that great powerful male spirit which wants to unite with you. You cannot escape it, but you can force it away from its biological union, even away from marital union. And you take it upon your thigh. Just as your father carried your wild brother, Dionysos, on his thigh, you, too, receive the wild passion, material-spiritual, upon your thigh. And you give it to Mother earth, you present it to her, the Chthonian female, for birth. Not to abandon it, oh Goddess, I know, but to have him born and come into earthly being. Only then will you care for him.

I think that I understand, Goddess. You, most spiritual and longing for the great city, require that the mortal dew, the dust, shall be your hero. I understand that the longing of the creative God for you must be deflected, that the energies must first go into something watery and earthy, something concrete even. Only then can your spiritual care and concern, your instruction and guidance take over. I know, too, that there is war between you and the creator God, strife. But from this strife, even, there is born a new creature. And so Erichthonios, divine child and mortal child, of dew contrived, of water and dust, he comes forth, and he it is who will serve your greatest urge: to create in the spirit, in the city, and for the community.

Is that why you will not unite with Hephaistos? Are you only against biological union? Or are you also against individual creativity? Are you only for the city, for the society, for the group?. . . You nod. But you were also the patron of lonely Odysseus, so you must also serve the wandering hero, who is alone, and trodding his own path. Perhaps you are meant to be a Goddess for us, for women, who need to trod our own path. Perhaps, in your rejection of the merely biological, the natural, you can help us, can serve us, can aid us in finding our own spirit. You nod vigorously to that, Goddess, for I suppose that in serving that spirit, we serve both you and ourselves. Is it so? Again, a wordless nod. You do not speak, but you agree. In this, perhaps, you show me that you still are female, you serve the spirit, but your night-owl vision is wordless and deep, and like women, can silently let the moonlight do its work. Is it so?

You nod and smile. It is so.

Your story continues, Goddess. The tale related the course of events set into motion with the love that the smith, the creator God, Hephaistos, had for you. It was said that you, Goddess, received from Mother Earth the child Erichthonios and that you sought to bring him up in secret, so that the other Gods should not know of it . . . Why not know, Goddess? Is your Motherhood a shame? Is your virginity so precious that none should know? I do not believe that. Rather, Goddess, I think that you sought to protect this young divine child, you sought to keep the other Gods from knowing of him, lest they seek him out, hurt him, take him from you. For was he not special, this divine son? Was he not your only-begotten, not-begotten son? And was he not then a prey, a possible victim? I believe so, Goddess, for the story says that you put your son into a round basket, like those that you used in the Mysteries. Or that you laid him in a chest, just as your sister Aphrodite had lain Adonis. Ah, is that not it? Did you not know the efforts of your sister, the Love-Goddess? Surely you knew the lamentable fate of Adonis, the Tammuz, the dying God who suffered so. And were you not deeply aware that such a fate could come to your only-begotten? Aphrodite, at least, had children aplenty, and from many lovers. But you, Goddess, you committed to the spirit, to wisdom, and to the building of culture, only one child had you, and that from the spirit. Hence your care, your overabundant con-cern . . . You nod, once again.

But it is also said, Goddess, that your child was a serpent. Some say that you gave birth to a serpent, or that in the basket-chest was a child guarded by a serpent, or even by two serpents, or yet a child with serpent feet. I shall wait to understand that, but first I must know and understand that you gave your child into the keeping of the daughters of Kekrops, the first King of your city, Athens. These three girls you chose, strictly forbidding them to open the closed chest.

Shades of Bluebeard, Goddess! Memories of the story of my mystical brother, Knight III, who understood the tale that the many sisters were enjoined not to look into the forbidden room. The many sisters of the soul, all Muses, broken, creative, inspired by the dark, magical, creative God of Love, such was the mystery ascertained by Knight III.

What, then, is your mystery, Goddess? You are no Bluebeard; you are no dark Magician; you are no Eros. What, then, are you about in this tale? No answer from you, so I shall continue.

The tale says that one of the sisters, Aglauros, could not contain her curiosity and opened the basket or chest. Another sister, though which is not said, shared her guilt. Each of the two sisters who espied the secret, went mad and leapt from the high rock on which the Acropolis stood.

Why is that, oh Goddess? What did the sisters see in that basket which drove them mad? It must have been the serpents; the serpent nature, perhaps, of their own father, Kekrops, the first King of Athens, said to be himself half serpent, half man. Did they see the darkest depths, the foul-witched, evil-natured serpent-being of the Gorgon, Medusa, herself? I think so, for what else drives a person to madness except that she witness the darkest depths of the witch-soul, the serpent being of the great dark-Goddess, that Gorgon of the Underworld, of the lower centers which are farthest from you?

Other stories confirm this, Goddess. For Perseus, your hero, fought the Gorgon Medusa and was advised by you not to look directly at her many-serpented head, upon pain of turning into stone. Does not one turn into stone, become hard and lifeless and dead, when under the direct vision of that dark feminine principle of Nature? (For Gorgon, too, was said to be a child of the Earth Mother, Gaia.) The serpent nature wants darkness, not light, the natural dark flow of nature, and not the light of consciousness, as you desire, oh Goddess. So Perseus did not look directly at the Gorgon, but slew her, cut off her head by looking at her through the reflection upon his shield. He saw her image, rather than her dark being; he reflected and looked indirectly, using a shield of self-protection, a way like your own. Did not Perseus do as you did with your dark Father, Goddess? He faced the horribleness of the destruction of consciousness by feminine darkness, took its own dark power and used it as a shield, a defense. Just as you slew the dark Father-God who would have raped you, so did he use her skin as shield, her wings as spirit.

From the Gorgon's head sprang the winged horse, Pegasos, the great poetic horse whose spiritualized animal nature was close to the Muses. Did not Poseidon have Pegasos touch his foot to the ground and produce the fountain *hippou krene*? Just as the Muses were in battle with the false Muses? Pegasos, the soaring spirit of nature transformed into the heights, is born from the slaying of the dark Gorgon-witch, together with the hero Chrysaor, "he of the golden sword." From those abysmal depths of darkness which fight consciousness in every form, there is born—by your adopted son-hero Perseus who produced it—the poetry of the soaring animal spirit and the heroic gold-consciousness-discrimination which are like your own, Goddess. In that act, you are not Daughter to the Father, in that act you are Mother. What does that mean? Does it not mean that at the heights of the third-eye, the Eagle-Eye of Heaven-Zeus, you are Daughter to the Great Father, but that as one descends, beyond the eyes of Aphrodite-Eros, down to the throat, the Bluebeard region where the Muses live and revolve around their mother, dark Mnemosyne of Memory, and look up into the Eyes of Aphrodite, there in the throat and the art of the voice, there is where you are Mother to a Son.

I begin to understand, oh Goddess, I begin to understand. In your high-level place of consciousness, you are the great and far-seeing Daughter of the great Father. But you touch back down, do you not? You are touched by the earthy creator God, you take care even of mortal heroes like Perseus the Gorgon-slayer, and Odysseus, the first great human adventurer of your favorite people. You must dip down to us, to mortals, men and women, and in that, Virgin Goddess, you are Mother, Parthenos-Meter, a Virgin-Mother to us all. But you are Mother to a creative spirit, a poetry of culture.

To return to your tale: who and what are the daughters of Kekrops? It is clear enough that the daughters perhaps spied something of their own father-nature in that basket. They, poor mortals, had a glimpse, perhaps of their own human father-incest, and, unlike you, Goddess, could not abide it, went mad with it. But I think that there is more. For only two of the three went mad; one did not. Which then?

Aglauros, "dweller on tilled land," the most curious, was surely driven mad, for it is so stated. But whether the other who leapt off the high rock was either Herse or Pandrosos, meaning "dewfall" for the one, and "all-bedewing" for the other, it is not said. But the stories can help.

Aglauros must die, for she is always tragic. Did she not play such a role in the story of Hermes and Herse? The great Mercurial God fell in love with Herse and asked Aglauros to help him with her sister. "The dweller on tilled land" demanded gold, and then grew so jealous that she would accept nothing. Hermes turned Aglauros into stone. Just as Gorgon, the witch, could turn a hero into stone, into a dark-nothing of feelingless unconsciousness, just so could the dark, changeable God, transformer of the psyche, do the same to the dark feminine. For is not jealousy, the possessiveness of the poor mortal woman, an aspect of the dark feminine Goddess? And can not Hermes-Mercurius, as dark as the Magician and Bluebeard himself, do the same? I think so. The results prove it, for the ancient God who is ancestor of the alchemical change of souls, guardian of the theft of cattle, of valuables, and of dark consciousness, loved Herse and fathered a beautiful son named Kephalos, he of the gorgeous head. From the union of the dark God with one of the sisters, the "dewfall," there appears a new golden-headed son, a new consciousness, a new wisdom which cannot be destroyed.

So, then, it must be Herse who was spared, beloved as she was of Hermes. For Pandrosos, though "all-bedewing," was patron of the sacred olive, of the caring of the sacred trees. Goddess, I glimpse what it is that happens; the three daughters are aspects of ourselves, are they not? Aglauros the curious, "dweller on tilled land," wanting culture above all, grows dark like her sister and jealous, but she cannot survive her jealousy and goes mad. The feminine longing for wisdom, for civilization, cannot survive the darkness of its own one-sidedness in the face of love. Furthermore, it grows dead and dormant, feelingless in its mere lust for riches of wealth and golden consciousness, and cannot cope with the dark God who produces transformation. Aglauros surely goes mad in the face of the deepest darkness of the serpent.

Something similar must be true of Pandrosos, the "all-bedewing" patroness of orchards. The green-eyes one must represent that in us mortals which does not build culture, as in tilled land, but in tilled trees, in the growing of culture as the fruits of life, as a gatherer of the poetic food, she, too, must go mad. Oh, Goddess, it must be true that only Herse, she who is "dewfall," allows herself to be loved and penetrated by the God, she who is so human and vulnerable, and ready to experience love, only she can look at the serpent and not grow mad. Is she not your counter-heroine to the great Perseus? Do you not, Goddess, secretly treasure both consciousness and love? Of course, or you would not be feminine! So, then, it must be Herse who survives and who creates the new head, Kephalos, the darling golden one, who unites passion and cleverness, who forms a new consciousness, which, in truth, can be claimed as your Grandson.

And so, Goddess, in proof of what I have learned, I go on with the tale and find that when the crow came and told you of the tragedy of the fall of the two sisters, you grew wroth. In your anger, you dropped the stone you were carrying, which was to be the base of your great city and the citadel of its heights, the Acropolis. This great stone, instead of being the base, fell and became a mountain, Lykabettos. And the crow was turned black, when formerly white, was banished from the Acropolis, and rejected by you.

The stone, that which could be the foundation and basis of culture, of the building of cities, like the philosopher's stone, the whole self-wisdom that you desired, fell back into nature, back to mother earth Gaia. And that, Goddess, from your anger; for your anger links you up, again, with the dark beginnings, with the dark depths of your secret sister, the Gorgon, and you know that culture cannot survive that darkness. Oh, Goddess, only a new consciousness born of love can survive, and only that, Goddess, is worthy of the great stone, the solid foundation which you would wish to give us.

The crow, that bird once yours, that harbinger of bleak intuitions, that knower of the secrets, must perforce then be banished into depths and be black, for the lightness is no longer with him. And so, Goddess, you remain in your upper regions, helper of man, servant of consciousness and culture, but you became a wrathful Goddess when crossed, so you are still linked to the lower reaches. Is it so, Goddess; do I understand you? Have I served you, in your stations, in your story, the way that my mystical brother, the Grandson of the Knight served your sister, Aphrodite?

You smile, Goddess. Your olive-green eyes sparkle, your golden hair flows smooth beneath the eagle-crown on your head, and your glorious Aigis shines, too. You smile upon me. You smile a golden smile and shine, and now I understand another part of your story: when you sprang from your Father's head, he let fall a golden rain. You, Goddess, are the golden one, the one of golden light, like sunshine, but like the water, and you, yourself, are a Herse, a bedewed female who is open to love in the spirit and servant of love in the spirit, because open yet, to that Father-consciousness, that eagle-eyed seer who, himself, is always seeking after union, after ever-renewing, ever-rebirthing, ever-creating unions with Goddesses and mortals. You, Goddess of the upper center, that third-eye, you are ever being born of the Father, ever looking down on your heroes, ever secretly attending to your daughters, ever a carrier of that search after light and golden wisdom. But, Goddess, mostly you want the wholeness of the stone, mostly you desire that the dark be fulfilled within the light, mostly you want our culture to be based on the stone, and your anger at our failure is eternal as well. Until Kephalos is born, and your son, Erichthonios, also contrived of dew, of water and dust; he, the divine child who can create in the spirit, in the city, and for mankind.

Sisters II

After my encounter with the Goddess, Pallas Athene, after my realization of the meanings of the culture-building feminine consciousness from above, I expected that I would rise still higher. I expected to ascend, just as my mystical brother had ascended, to the top of his cone. I thought I would rise and meet the great Mother of the Son, that I would encounter Mary, Mother of God, just as I had encountered Athene, daughter of God. But I did not. Instead, I sank down from that high place of the third eye. Instead, I fell down, within myself, and I descended deeply, deeply into the lower places of my being. Past the warm-fierce-eyed place of Aphrodite and Eros of the Eyes, past the realm of Bluebeard and the Muses, lower yet than Jacob and the Sister of the Heart, beyond, even, Buddha and the Sister of the Belly, and beyond, at last, the Vaginal-Phallic place of Eros and Aphrodite once again. I sank to the region of the Anus, the Hell-hole some say, where my mystical brother, Grandson of the Knight, knew the Magician. I sank there and rested.

As I rested, I recalled my dream of the wise man, of the suffering Italian, my amore. I recalled that in it, I was going to speak to a priestess of the depths, of the occult and nether regions, but was interrupted by the calls of the wounded Italian. Now, perhaps, I thought, now I could speak to that lady, that priestess. Was she, then, a medium from those levels? Was she, in reality . . . As I asked these questions, I grew very weary, very lazy, almost paralyzed. My thoughts wandered to various kinds of occult events and groups that I had met. I felt unable to move, to continue, to meditate. In short, I felt paralyzed, like a fly in a spider web, like an ant in honey, like a mouse in a cat's paw.

In my paralysis, I had a glimpse of what I was, for these images came to me. I, myself, was the medium of my dream; I, myself, was a priestess of the occult—if I wished to be. And these images were from none other than the Queen of the Ghosts, the Mistress of the Dead, of Black Magic, the Keeper of the Keys of the Underworld, Hecate herself. For was not the spider and the web an image of the Dark Goddess herself? And is not the fly that weak spirit of human consciousness, easily snuffed out, and caught in the web of the dark mysteries of life, of love? I remembered that honey belongs to Hecate, too, and what more appropriate than that the ant, that careful, orderly, industrious insect be caught in it. I was like that in this moment. I was caught in a sweet, indolent, unmoving, fantasy world, wherein I could not work, not move, not feel part of the regular, ordered, community life. So, too, like the mouse did I feel, like the fecund, feminine, underground animal, played with by a larger feminine force, like the Lion of Hecate, who seduces us into thinking we are free, can roam away from pain and danger, but then we are devoured and descend into the black night of the Lioness, the great-cat Hecate, the dark-Goddess of the irrational, the occult, the sensual.

The three animals and states showed me well that Hecate was a mistress, indeed, of three levels: air, land and underworld, just as were the fly, ant, and mouse. Did not even almighty Zeus acknowledge that the Titaness could move freely at all levels? It was so, even though her greatest realm was in the underworld, that deep, dark place of the dead, of the ghost-spirits. I at once felt aware that this dark Goddess could roam where she wished. She could be in human life and relationships (on land), in the heights of the human spirit and its longings for greater consciousness (in the air), and in the depths of the magical places, of the dead, that all know about as her realm.

But I was paralyzed. I could only perform a "Hecate supper;" I could only feed the Goddess, as they did of old. I could only offer up a sacrifice of my own best foods, my own honey-sweetness of interest, of love, of care, and submission. Perhaps only these the great Mistress of Witches did not have. Witches did not love, it was said; neither did they care. And to submit? That was the least thing that a witch would do, for they were always plotting to have their way, were they not? And so, Goddess Hecate, Mistress of the Night, I submit to you. I will be a willing fly, a passive ant, a surrendering mouse. I will do this as the receptive feminine creature that I am. I will do this because I can do no other, for you are powerful, you are great, you are above, below, and around me wherever I move.

As I surrendered, I felt enveloped in a dark fog of night. I was covered with a moist web of warm darkness. It was like the black cloak that witches wear, but I felt it as a warm thing, a loving thing, a positive thing, and not to be feared nor despised.

"It is so, my daughter," came the words from my own anus. I almost laughed, for my anus, it seemed to me, had become a mouth with lips which was now speaking to me! I laughed, and then I heard a very loud, shrieking laugh, a cackling which was both fearsome and humorous.

"It is so," the voice continued. "When one is outside the Cloak, outside the Voice, then it is frightening, fearsome. But, if you are inside the Witch-Goddess, inside the Cloak, and know that the Voice speaks from you, then it is warm, pleasant, and even humorous. For is it not humorous that the anus speaks? Is it not laughable that there are spirits of the nether regions? Any woman knows this and laughs. And any man could, too, were he to submit to the Witch, to treasure the Goddess! But you now, Daughter of Guinevere, you now will know this, for you have descended here, have come here willingly and freely. You, now, will know what it is that the Whore of Babylon laughed at; you, now, will know the secret of the darkly ancient feminine. So, then, embrace your cloak, put it round you warmly, and listen to the anal voices of dark deep places."

I listened to Hecate and obeyed. My eyes grew heavy and I slipped off into another reverie. In this reverie, I was at a crossroads; I was face to face with Trioditis statue, a three-headed sculpture which faced in the three directions which I could now go: right, left, or straight ahead. The statue had three heads of animals, three heads of women, three heads of . . . And then I collapsed, for the third part of the statue stung me into unconsciousness. I could not remember anything that I had seen or felt. I lay, face down, on the crossroads and waited.

"Goddess," the words came to me, "Goddess, I implore you. I have given you the things which you desire: I have given you the black lamb of my submission to you; I have given you the honey of my sweet love and care . . . ah, I have not given you the dog. I have not given you the sacrifice which you love so well, the instinctive and deep loyalty of the animal in the service of man. Oh, Goddess, I understand. But it is hard for me to be in your service. Submission, yes; love, yes, but service? To serve the darkest occult, the deepest magical place? . . . Yes, I agree to serve you. Release me, please, from my paralysis, my unconsciousness, my own lovelessness, and I shall serve you."

"Daughter of Guinevere, do not deceive yourself. My service is not so terrible for those who understand. And you should understand. For have you not talked with my sister Athene? Have you not had the consciousness to see broadly and widely, and know the service of the feminine of culture? You have learned that even Athene is close to a dark feminine, that even Athene was close to Gorgon, Medusa, who also dwelt here. Have you not seen that when you wear my cloak from within, when you listen to my voice from within, then there is warmth and humor, and not only coldness and fear? Why, why, are people so afraid of my realm? Why do they see only the darkness of it, the fear of it? Why do they not see that when they take it up, take it in, submit and feed, they will be fed and warmed and made aware? Give me just the honey-sweetness of love, the lamb-gentleness of submission, and dog-loyalty of devotion, and these shall be yours. Am I not known to bestow wealth and success? Do I not give good luck and advice? Am I not powerful in earth, in the sea, and in heaven?"

"It is true, Goddess. It is true that you are powerful. Only a fool or a rationalist would be so silly as to think otherwise. But are not people right to fear you? Are they not right to fear your dark aspect, your lovelessness, your coldness and self-seeking, your power-drivenness?"

"They are right, Daughter of Guinevere," Hecate laughed, "and I am so to them when they do not submit. But, enough of talk, enough of the words from the head and upper regions. You have come here to seek me out, to understand me, to even love and submit and serve me. So then, do so."

She vanished, Hecate did, and I was faced, once again, with the three directions: ahead, right and left. But I could not move. Why not? It occurred to me that I had the dark cloak and I had the voice, but that I missed the other accoutrements of the witch: the peaked hat and the broomstick. Did one need these quaint instruments with the great Goddess?. . . Again, I collapsed. It seemed that the questions themselves paralyzed me. But I was not altogether paralyzed, for I had a realization: the peaked hat must mean a kind of wisdom or knowledge. This would be knowledge of the prayers and the incantations, a knowledge of the black arts of the occult, such as astrology, fortune-telling with cards—all those things which would require as much effort and time and devotion as all those other sciences, the white magic, had required. Now, too, I better understood the cone of my mystical brother, Grandson of the Knight, for this hat of Hecate, this peaked thing, was nothing other than the inverted cone of his heavenly pyramid and mandala. He had seen an upper cone and a lower one. Here, at last, in the depths, was the Hat of Hecate, the witch-knowledge of the depths for which he also longed, and of which he, too, had some knowledge, but from Magician, not Witch.

But how was his knowledge, his encounter with the Magician different from my encounter with Hecate? I thought I knew: the Magician was a Lord of Transformation. Could not the Grandson of the Knight, through him, go through all sorts of changes? Could he not transform into figures of history, of literature, of the world of Gods? That is the male magic of transformation. And the effect is direct: to change history, literature and the world of the Gods through direct action, by encounter, by struggle, by understanding, by battle.

But I, but I? I was meeting now with the Goddess of this region, the Goddess of Magic, and what was her way? Why, indirect, of course! Was not true magic indirect? Of course! Did not one get one's wish or desire or effect by the indirect means? The feminine way, the way of the Goddess, was indirect; not cause and effect directly, but indirectly. And how better indirectly than by working at one's self? How better to transform than by transforming one's self? How better be indirect and magical than by worshipping and changing those centers of love and consciousness within one's self? Is that not also an indirect way, a magical way?. . . This question brought a sense of yea-saying from the Goddess. I could not see her directly, but I sensed a yea-saying, a nodding of her head. And I laughed again, for I saw her humor. She was showing me without showing me, she was aiding me without aiding me, she was supporting me without supporting me! The Goddess was within; she was without image, she was without form, she was without . . . and now I felt a cone-shaped hat growing on top of my head! I was beginning to understand, I was beginning to have the consciousness of the witch. It was good. I understood that I would have to take much time to understand all that I must, and then . . . Then: I was aware that to serve the Goddess meant to go in at least two directions: To go right meant to study the occult sciences, to gather information outside from history, from wise men and women, from other witches; to go left meant to don the witch garb for myself, to listen to the inner wisdom of my centers, particularly the dark lower ones, just as I had now been doing. Both of these directions would make my cone-shaped hat grow larger and larger. Both of these would make the "lower cone" of the Grandson of the Knight greater. And, perhaps, if I so learned things, so devoted myself to the Goddess, I could be an ever greater partner for my mystical brother, Grandson of the Knight, my *amore* of the diaphragmatic center. It seemed good to me. We could grow together. But still . . . What of the third direction, straight ahead? And what of the missing broomstick? I had cloak and voice, beginnings of hat and understanding, but no capacity for moving, for traveling. I could quickly be thrown into paralysis, into passivity, into lethargy, and painful, loveless, stuckness.

"Goddess, I beseech you," I said. "You have helped me, I have understood. Help me once again. I have understood that to be in your service, to engage in your devotion, I must develop that hat that you have given me. I must take the paths to right and left, by study and by reflection, but what of the going ahead, and what of your broomstick?"

No answer was forthcoming, but by now I understood the ways of the Indirect, and I did not despair when it did not come. I felt, instead, a sensation of seasickness. I felt as if I were moving right and then left, right and then left, back and forth in wavelike motion, more and more quickly. As I did so, I was aware that I was gradually ascending into the air, gradually rising off the ground and was moving ahead. Now I was sitting upon a broomstick, and was gliding over the earth. How was this? I had gone left and right, right and left, in ever-increasing speed, and only then could I rise. Ah, I understood. Hecate was saying to me that as I gradually worked harder and harder with both the right and left, with study of the occult and of meditation upon her realm, that I would experience a wavelike motion of flow, but that I would gradually gather her kind of indirect power and find myself in the high-heady, spiritual regions which defy the natural scientific laws of gravity, and could move freely. I knew, too, that the vehicle of this work, this kind of study, was as feminine as the woman's activity of the broom. Did not the woman continually, for thousands of years, clean up the messes with brooms? Did she not tidy up her house, and actively work? The broom, then, was the active, phallic way of coming to the spirit by the two methods of right and left, study of the rejected occult sciences, and active work on the fantasy inside oneself. Thus would feminine power triumph and soar. Thus would it, too, one day, in me.

But why should this be seen as so negative, I thought? Of course, I realized, because these ways are different from the male ways. These ways of activity are different from what others say. Do not do those things, woman, they will say, be only loving and kind. Do not be conscious and powerful! They do not want this of women, do they? But my mystical brother is not such a one! Grandson of the Knight, server of Eros, understander of the Magician, he is not such a one! Where I will serve the Witch, he will serve the Magician. When I serve Consciousness, he will serve Love! Just as when I have served Love, he has served Consciousness. A good pair are we, a loving brother-sister alchemical pair are we!

"Oh, Goddess, oh, Hecate, I feel your goodness in me. I feel your indirect effect already. I bow to you, submit to you, love you. I shall be as a woman liberated, in serving you."

And then I ascended to her sister, Hera.

Husband and Wife: Hera

I think that I understand, Goddess. You are not only a sister to Hecate, a Witch in the highest as she is Witch in the Lowest, and three-natured as she is, but you are, in your uniqueness, Wife. You are Mistress of Heaven, if not Queen of the Gods, and you are monogamously married, servant of the single union. So, then, Goddess, what you desire is that I understand you and your service, by a contemplation of your life and deeds. You grow serious, you are silent still. Is it not so, Goddess?

"It is so."

Well, then, I shall begin. You it was, Hera, who chose your youngest brother as your consort and husband as soon as he was born. You sought him and served him. You married him in the depths, in the dark deeps and secrets of the Ocean where none could know. And there it was that you loved Zeus, your brother. You honeymooned and intoxicated him with love for three hundred years. What greater romantic union than this? What longer state of matrimonial bliss of the highest of the Gods and his spouse? And it is also said that you married not in secret, but in public, at the gates of the western region of earth, in your husband's palace. All the Gods came and brought gifts; Mother Earth gave the golden apples and the marvelous tree to you, great Goddess. And you kept it, guarded it with a serpent, in the garden of the Gods.

What does it mean that you marry both in secret and in the open? Your *hieros gamos*, your divine union, is deep in the depths, Goddess, an eternal, romantic, unknown union where you are forever with your spouse and God. A monogamy based on love endures, Goddess, I know; and even when it is broken and changed, when there is bickering and dissent, the union continues in the depths, it continues in the eternal place of no-time where such unions are consummated. And it exists, too, in the world, and is welcomed by earth itself, by the concreteness of life itself; for it is worthy to be the recipient of the bounties of the Tree of Life and Death, the tree of the great good fortune of love and creation, and of the dark, painful horrors of jealousy, of rage, of deception, and of death-dealing. That we know, too.

It is also said, Goddess, that once, after losing Zeus to another, you seduced him. From Aphrodite, the great love Goddess, you obtained a magic girdle, which you wore. Love, Goddess, is a different thing when the property of the magic of your sister, who serves a different love than do you. Is it true, Goddess, that your love is both ineffable in the dark depths, and open and abundant in the heights and in the world? But when your love withers, when it grows sour, it requires a different magic than your own monogamous loyalty, it requires the magic of the fickleness of Aphrodite. And you, Goddess, were not too proud to make use of it; you, who have been nasty and greedy and jealous, were not too vain to make use of the charms of your sister Goddess. For this, Hera, Queen of Heaven, I salute you. For, to win back your spouse, to recover a union, you served a love different than your own, a principle different than your own. That required a greatness that not every Divine can claim, I think!

One time, it is said, your consort and husband sought to seduce you, too. A tale is told that Zeus, before he was wed to you, came to you as a cuckoo, at a place of your temple, a place of Hera Teleia, Hera fulfilled and as Mother. Zeus came to your lap. You, Goddess, took pity upon him and covered him. As you did, the great Lord took his own shape and sought to make you his lover. But you struggled, since you were children of one mother, until he promised to make you his wife. This he did, and thus it was said that you, Hera, were the only woman ever to have had a man of exactly equal rank as a husband. Goddess, you are, indeed, a Mother of God when he comes as a spirit, to rest on your lap, when he submits to your kind mercies. But, when he seeks to have his union in his own way, you strive for your own principle, monogamous union, and, in this, you find the place of equality of man and woman. Such is your task, Goddess, and such your success.

But, Goddess, the tales are told that you often wandered alone, in solitude. It is said, too, that Zeus would not abide your anger. Despite your rage and conniving, despite your jealousy and plotting, your husband would not abide your anger, and you wandered afar, into the deepest darkness, where there was neither sunshine nor breath of wind. After each deception, each betrayal of your single union, you wandered in darkness and alone. You wandered and ultimately came back, to bathe in the spring where you were renewed, Oh, Goddess, you prepared yourself for a new mating with your husband. You were Wife and Virgin, ever wife—ever virgin. And so, in your three faces, three phases, you were Maiden and Wife and Mother. As Maiden, ever-renewing, you were beautiful, romantic, but also secret and in caring-love of your brother. As Mother, you were maternal most to Zeus, and not to your sons, Ares and Hephaistos. So, Goddess, though you are kind to women in childbirth, like both Artemis and Hecate, you are really both Maiden and Mother only in the service of your being as Wife. Hera, Goddess, you are Wife above all and everything, even in your solitude, when you wander away, when your principle is violated, when you grow dark and dreary, seek your aloneness. For you, Goddess, there is only the Divine Pair, the Syzzygy of Husband and Wife in One. Everything must serve it, everything must bow before it. That is your Magic, Goddess, that is your place of Maiden for Marriage, Mother for Marriage, and above all, Wife for Marriage. It is violated, other laws and unions take place, and you complain, you quarrel, you wander away. For you it is all or nothing; for you it is the one divine union or none. But, Goddess, though your rule is harsh, though you are dreary when crossed, though your darkness is insupportable, your divine wholeness is ever-violated, ever renewed.

I know, Goddess, by my deep nature I know you. I know that the longing for the one total union, where one is maiden, wife, and mother, to say nothing of sister, to the one man, is deep in the soul of every person, woman and man. I know that longing, and I know, too, how it is broken and blocked, and frustrated. I know how one becomes dark and dreary and in painful, witch-like solitude when that union is crossed. But Goddess, is it not a union within? Is it not a union of marriage of the male and female within oneself? You smile, Goddess; you give me a pale smile, with dark eyes; that tells me it is true, but not the whole truth. For union is within and without, in the soul and in the world.

There you exist, in that high center of the head. There, together with the union of Father and Daughter, of Zeus with his own creation, Pallas Athene, you exist in a painful triangle, a trinity of rivalry of Husband-Wife, Father-Daughter. And you hated his other union, his being alone and creating, from within himself, his culture-building daughter. But you took your revenge, Goddess, you made yourself a Typhaon, a monster who can be oracular. I know that in you, Goddess, and in me. In my dark states, there are only gloomy predictions, fears of doom, oracular comings of dark thoughts and anticipations which are worse than any which come from your sister below, Hecate. I know that dark state. I know, too, you in that dark state.

But you are also creative when alone, great Goddess. Did not the Latin tale say that when you were insulted by your Lord, that nature herself gave you a magic grass which could make the most sterile being fruitful and, touched by this grass, you became pregnant and bore your son, the great war God? Yes, you are mother of strife, of battle, of dissent, Goddess; and Mother Nature, herself, makes you this way, when your one and only principle is frustrated. It is then that you become so negative and the battle is born. But you did not love either son, Goddess. Neither Ares of Battle, nor Hephaistos of Creation. Why? I know; you long only for your own union. Battle as a consequence is not that which you seek, and creativity apart from your one true spouse is of no interest to you, rejected by you.

Oh, Goddess, what a power you are! What a force is that One, and the longing for it! But your Divine spouse is a Many, and even stronger than you. And you must dwell together in that high place: for there is a divine union of Father and Daughter, of the principle of the One and his creation, as well as with Husband and Wife, Sister and Brother. There are two unions in the three. And you, too, Goddess, in your own way, in the comings and goings of your nature, you are both united and alone. Do I speak truly of you, Goddess? Are you satisfied with my contemplation of your story?

"I am not! You speak nothing about my being raped by that phallic creature. You speak nothing of the destroyers. You say nothing of my being bound by my misbegotten son, Hephaistos, of my being humiliated and bound, too, by my arrogant husband, Zeus. You do not speak of this!"

"It is true, Goddess, I have not. But has not the Grandson of the Knight already spoken of the binding? And I, too, have spoken of your binding by Zeus. But what would you want of me, Goddess? I see, now, your wrath and frustration directed at me. I see how you are offended when I do not give you full and total satisfaction. I see that you are as much a 'Lord' and as arrogant, for your own principle, as your spouse and husband, Zeus! I do not like such rage and frustrated bitterness, Goddess! I, as a woman, I, Daughter of Guinevere, a Daughter of a woman who served and suffered for both your principle and that of Aphrodite, I, her Daughter, do not like your possessiveness, your limitation."

"Ah, then Daughter, speak to me of limitation, then! Speak to me of how one limits one's loves, one's life. Speak to me of how my beloved sister, Aphrodite, takes care of her loves. Does she not love, then leave? Does she not move on to new loves, new relationships? Does not my Lord, Zeus, do the same? Where then is the limit in their maniness? Where, then, is the care for what they have produced?"

"Where is your own care, Goddess? Where is there care for your own son, Hephaistos? Or for Ares, even? Perhaps the war-god would be less combative if he felt mother-love. And perhaps creativity would be less a pain and more a pleasure if there were mother-love in it. Do not speak to me of your care, Goddess. It is true that you are devoted as a wife, but as to care, I do not see it!"

"Daughter of Guinevere, well spoken, well spoken! I need mortals such as you. I need women who can speak up to me, confront me, be as difficult and one-sided, as angry and frustrated as myself! Do you not see, Daughter? You speak like me! You speak out of your anger, out of your expectation. You want me to be something that I am not, to be more mother than I can be, more maiden than I can be. I can be these, of course, but only as wife, as you know. But you speak, Daughter, you speak up, and complain, and thus, are like me. How does it feel to be irritable, demanding, crossed and unloving?"

"Not very good, Goddess, I must confess. Not very good. I lose my warm nature. I lose my caring disposition. I feel dark and dreary, and want to flee to my solitude."

"And so do I, Daughter, so do I."

And now, the Queen of Heaven, herself, Hera, accompanies me, a mere mortal, down into the depths of dark solitude. Hera, the Mighty Mistress, takes me into a deep darkness. It is a darkness where no sun is, no moon, hardly in the body itself. For it is not the magical region of Hecate. It is a darkness which must be deep, deep inside the skull. It is a place of death itself, perhaps, of timeless time, but not of Hades. I grow a little excited, for I think that Hera is taking me to a new witch-like place, a heavenly spiritual place where Woman is alone. A place of solitude where no birds sing, no moon shines. A place where not even the dead and ghosts are; it is a place of total solitude. And this is the opposite of the Goddess' total union!

Oh, Goddess, I shiver as I perceive it! Goddess, I tremble before your great power. It is not all or nothing! It is not mere possessiveness and jealousy and greed and anger. It is being totally united with one other, or being totally alone. And who can be totally alone? There no life is, nor is death there, either. Where is there absolutely nothing except one's self? Oh, Goddess, I can glimpse this, but it is vast and beyond me. When have I been totally alone? Without fantasy even? Or thoughts? Or memories, or wishes? Totally alone with myself? I cannot recall.

Then let me taste that solitude, Goddess. Let me sense the wonder of your great aloneness. As I do, I shall be able to grasp the darkness of your bitter face, as well. I shall perceive it, understand it. Dreamless sleep; consciousless awareness; solitary darkness.

With this prayer to Hera, great Goddess of Marriage, of Monogamous Union, of the Syzzygy, I grew quiet. For I saw her other side; I saw the place where she goes when not in union. I saw and I can speak. But there are no words there. There are no sounds, no lights, no lives nor deaths. Neither is there nothing there, for there is only solitude. Goddess of Union, you are Mistress, too, of Solitude, and I bow before you. From my aloneness will I also become quiet. From my aloneness will I also come back, and renew myself in the river of life. From my aloneness will I also join my Lord, and serve my desire for union.

In my aloneness, solitude . . .

As I reflected upon the greatness of the loneliness and isolation of the Goddess, I tasted the sweet stillness of no sound, no light, no pain, no smell, no sensation of any kind, I understood a deeper truth of a woman freed, a woman liberated from her total devotion to union. For she could, like the great Goddess, be totally alone, totally apart, totally separate. But her separateness, her individuality, must be experienced alone and apart, lest it be experienced by the world as a nagging, as a complaining, as a bitterness, as a petulance and jealousy. Her dark aloneness is even less bearable than that of her sister, Hecate, who, in her darkness, still is accompanied by howling dogs, by ghosts, by the hosts of the dead. In short, she is never alone, for she comes from a populated place of darkness.

Such aloneness, Hera; I am deepened in my understanding of your being called Chera, the Solitary. Now I grasp your three faces: Maiden, she who begins in the secret beginnings, and loves her true one husband before he is husband, but also she who can be eternally maiden in the sense of Virgin, of woman renewed, for you, Goddess, are renewed in your union with your God, and with your isolation and solitariness; Wife, she who is the loyal and true devoted woman to the one man, never dishonoring his bed or her own, ever in a syzzygy; Chera, the Solitary, ever alone, ever in the darkest dark of woman isolated, totally with herself and in fearsome union only with herself. Only such a one, Hera, can be a consort, a perennial spouse to the male God of marriage who seeks union with the many. I, Daughter of Guinevere, can understand you, just as the Grandson of the Knight could understand your spouse, Zeus.

In my quietness, I reflect upon all the great Goddesses of the Centers. I think of Hecate of the depths, of the magical region which goes right and left, to the dark sciences and the dark intuition of the indirect effect. I think of Aphrodite below and above, and her great loves. I think of the Muses, wives of Bluebeard. I think of Athene, and of Hera, too. Goddesses all. I think, too, of the not so divine, but equally profound Sisters of Belly and heart, different females all. And, as I think of them, I find myself rising to an even higher center than the Third Eye. I rise, just as Grandson of the Knight rose, in the upper conical hat, to heaven. And heaven is a small church.

Mother and Son: Virgin Mary and Rosary

Shortly after I had made the decision to rise to the highest center within me, the place where Mother and Son would share their paired Being, I realized that the way to relate to such a center, to grasp the significance of such a high place, open to God in the highest, would be none other than a meditation upon the mysteries of the Virgin. And that, of course, would be the same ritual, the same act of piety, practiced by countless people since long ago. Just as my mystical brother, Grandson of the Knight, had presumed to meditate upon the Stations of the Cross to achieve the highest, just so would I, Daughter of Guinevere, meditate upon the glorious Rosary, the "Bouquet of Roses" of that same Virgin Mother, who celebrated and experienced the highest mysteries ever given to mortal woman. There was she, a woman like myself, who gave birth to a God within her. Could I, who was no practicing Christian, dare to do this?

As I reflected upon the possibility that I might participate in a ritual for which I could claim no right, there came to me, as if by an act of grace, a gift of a beautiful Rosary from a loving and devout pair of friends, a priest and a nun. These two, whom I had only recently begun to know, presented me with one made in Italy, the place of my "amore." It had been used and blessed in the Holy Land, where Jesus lived, suffered and died.

If these two people—whom I had known to have lived their vocation in a devout and individual way—could see no barrier to my meditating upon the holy Rosary, then why should I hesitate? Had not my mother, Guinevere herself, become a nun? And Mary herself was said to be utterly merciful to all sinners, practicing Christian or not. Therefore, I resolved to recite the Rosary, and meditate upon those mysteries in my own fashion.

I held the lovely beads in my hand, made the sign of the cross; "In the name of the Father, and of the Son, and of the Holy Spirit, Amen." So I began. I next grasped the cross more firmly and realized that I could not, in good conscience, recite The Apostles' Creed, as I was expected to do, in the form in which it was given. It said:

"I believe in God, the Father Almighty, Creator of heaven and earth; and in Jesus Christ, His only Son, Our Lord; who was conceived by the Holy Ghost, born of the Virgin Mary, suffered under Pontius Pilate, was crucified, died and was buried. He descended into hell; the third day He arose again from the dead; He ascended into heaven, sitteth at the right hand of God, the Father Almighty; from thence He shall come to judge the living and the dead. I believe in the Holy Spirit, the Holy Catholic Church, the communion of saints, the forgiveness of sins, the resurrection of the body, and life everlasting. Amen."

All of this I could understand and accept in my own way, and with no violation, I think, to the spirit of those who proclaim this creed. My conscience balked only at the idea that Jesus Christ was God's "only" son. Secondly, though I could believe in the worth and merit and everlasting value of the Holy Catholic Church, I could not assent that this was the "only" Church, nor the only way to God, nor even the only way to Jesus or Mary, herself. Must I now stop here? Must I abandon this means, this vehicle, this vessel to come into greater communion with the lovely Mary, and with the mysteries of Mother and Son? I could only appeal to Mary, herself.

"May I, Mary, Mother of God," said I into the blue, "may I continue with the holy Rosary of your mysteries, balking as I do at the assertion that Jesus was the only son of God, or that the Catholic Church is the only way?"

For answer I saw a vision of what I took to be Mary, herself. She appeared, in her upper half, in a more or less conventional way, dressed in blue, her face open and loving. Unconventional, however, was the fact that she smiled broadly, almost amusedly, but surely benevolently. She smiled at me as if giving me permission to proceed, but not doing so in a way which would violate her church, or me. As if to say that both the church is right in its creed, but also a person like me, who has another way to her and her Son, is right too. How like a woman! How soft and flexible and understanding is such a mild-mannered woman, to smile in the face of such problems! Is it not more important that the prayer be said, the rosary recited, the meditations be made, than that the letter of the creed be minusculely followed? Was this not what her Son Jesus preached, and what St. Paul also said? That love would transcend the law, that the letter of the law would be overcome by the Holy Spirit? And, in this I surely believed. I believed, indeed, as the creed demanded, in the Holy Spirit. Nor can belief be demanded, I knew. The Holy Spirit bloweth as it listeth, it is said, and in this I, too, both believed and knew. If I were, in truth, in communion with Mary, in communion, too, with the Holy Spirit, she and it would guide my meditation and my ritual.

All this, of course, Mary knew, and she communicated it only with a joyful, even playful smile. Oh, Mary, I adore you. You are, indeed, as they say, "full of Grace." But before I make my obeisance to you, before I go on with your devotion, let me, at least, make my first obeisance, as the ritual demands, and as I gladly and reverently do, by grasping the first bead and reciting the "Our Father":

"Our Father, who art in heaven, hallowed be Thy name; Thy kingdom come; Thy will be done on earth as it is in heaven. Give us this day our daily bread; and forgive us our trespasses as we forgive those who trespass against us; and lead us not into temptation, but deliver us from evil. Amen."

And now, I grasp each of the following three beads, and say three times, the "Hail Mary."

"Hail Mary, full of grace! The Lord is with thee; blessed art thou among women, and blessed is the fruit of thy womb, Jesus. Holy Mary, Mother of God, pray for us sinners now and at the hour of our death. Amen."

Indeed I hail thee, Mary, and, before I proceed to meditate upon your first joyful mystery, I shall say, with the next bead, the "Glory be to the Father":

"Glory be to the Father, and to the Son, and to the Holy Spirit. As it was in the beginning, is now, and ever shall be, world without end. Amen."

I say the words, turn them over in my mind and on my lips, and understand that there is grace in the words of prayer alone, whether recited upon a wheel by a Tibetan, who endlessly repeats his mantra to achieve grace, or by me who feels grace from the words alone. Never again shall I scoff at those who pray words alone, not knowing even, what these words mean. For I feel them, I feel the potency of the holy words, whether Hare Krishna, or Glory be to the Father, for we mortals call out in prayer, we sing out the words when touched by God, and these are words which God and the holy ones speak through us. It is the divine in us commingling with the divine. So did Elisabeth also call out like the angel, from her own heart, "Hail Mary, full of Grace, the Lord is with thee." For the Lord was with her, too, and she spoke these holy words which came to her, from the Lord being with her. So do I respect and bow before the holy words of the prayers: Glory be to Father, and to the Son, and to the Holy Spirit. And it shall always be so, that the spirit speaks, quickens us, and we respond with the self-same spirit. "Hail Mary, full of Grace, the Lord is with thee." In my celebration of you, Holy Mother of God, let me be with your spirit, and your spirit with me. And now to the contemplation of your first Joyful Mystery, the Annunciation.

Mother and Son II: Joyful Mysteries

The First Joyful Mystery: The Annunciation

"The angel Gabriel was sent from God to a virgin, and the virgin's name was Mary. 'Hail, full of grace, the Lord is with thee. Blessed art thou among women.' When she had heard him she was troubled at his words, and kept pondering what manner of greeting this might be. And the angel said to her, 'Do not be afraid, Mary, for thou hast found grace with God. Behold, thou shalt conceive in thy womb and shalt bring forth a son; and thou shalt call his name Jesus. He shall be great, and shall be called the Son of the Most High; and of his kingdom there shall be no end.' But Mary said to the angel, 'How shall this happen, since I do not know man?' 'The Holy Spirit shall come upon thee and the power of the Most High shall overshadow thee. And therefore the Holy One to be born shall be called the Son of God.' 'Behold the handmaid of the Lord; be it done to me according to thy word.' "

Thus the beginning of the story; modest, humble, short of speech, like Mary herself. What was it that a good nun said to me, about her understanding of poverty, chastity and obedience? For these traits were surely what made Mary "full of grace," the worthy receptacle and vessel for a God-man to be born. Poverty, said the nun, is continuing modesty, lack of arrogance, quiet recognition that one is 'handmaid' of the Lord, open to God's spirit. Mary does not grow arrogant with this chosenness; nor does she falsely hang her head, either. For she knows that she is both a lofty one to be chosen, and a lowly one, an ordinary mortal of the most modest origin.

And chastity, continued the nun: Mary is pure and ever alive to the Holy Spirit. She is not pure as an angel is pure, because angels have no flesh, having nothing to be pure about. Her chastity is ever-renewed, just as was the Goddess Hera, for she was ever alive to the Spirit of God, ever open to the spirit of love.

And obedience: Mary is attentive to the Holy Spirit. She listens to the Angel of God and inquires how it is to be done. She does not fight nor fall over in submission; she is receptive, attentive, and, thus, obedient to the movement of the Spirit as it comes to her.

Oh, Mary, Mother of God! I see your humanness and divinity; you, too, are a God-woman, for you are become a vessel for the birth of the divine within yourself! Your soul is a home. I feel it and know it, yet my words are hollow shells. My words become rich and thick, full of flesh only as I ponder you. You who are of so few words, you fill the shells. You rarely speak, but you listen deeply and ponder the words of others, be they Angels or men. Mary, help me to be like you. Let my soul be a receptacle, a vessel for the birth of the Christ, the higher consciousness which descends from God and wants to find a place in me. Help me to be . . . like you? That comes to me and seems wrong. Help me to be more like one who is open like you. Show me. . . .

I realized that I was praying inadequately, meditating inadequately, that I could not . . . And Mary came to me, lifted me up, embraced me. She held me close, as a Mother to a Daughter, perhaps, or even, as a friend to a friend, or a sister to a sister. She held me and caressed me, and I felt her presence as if it were flesh. And she told me, without words, that she was just as mortal as I, just as failing, just as inadequate, and just as great, for she, too, was a sister and daughter and friend and mother of God, Himself! And, if she, a poor Jewish girl from Nazareth, could be all these mortal things to God, and, at last, become a lover and mistress of God, through the impregnation by the Holy Spirit, well then, why could not I? And why not, in time and in some ever-after eternity, why not every woman? Indeed, why could not a man's soul be also the birthplace for such a spirit? Of course, it could. For God is meant to be a companion, a sharer of divinity, just as He needs our humanity. And for these high-low events just so do we need our high-lowness.

Mary conveyed this to me without words. These thoughts were lovely, but I treasured more the feeling of her flesh, her warmth, her physicalness. I felt her emotion, and in this I felt an embrace of my own emotion. I felt as if with her in the depths of the water, in the warm moist place at the bottom of the sea, where woman knows the meaning of word made flesh. For the flesh, and the intensity of emotion, knows in its wordless way that which every male spirit-word tries ever to say and fails. We women—and we mortals—need not abase ourselves to the spirit, for the Spirit, with its words, needs us. It needs to be born in the flesh of the human. The divine needs to be mortal, just as our flesh and being need to become divine. Oh, Mary, just as Jesus was the first among the ever-to-become-many God-men, just are you the first God-woman. You, Mary, you knew, and know. Thus you are, as Gabriel said, to be hailed. For you are full of grace and blessed. This birth is in the soul, in your being, and you show us the way! Hail, Mother of God!

The Second Joyful Mystery: The Visitation

I clasp my Rosary to me, say the Our Father once again, and ten Hail Marys, a blessed decade of prayers for the great lady. Once more the Glory be to the Father, and I can now announce, with my beads, the second joyful mystery, the Visitation.

"Now Mary went into the hill country. And she entered the house of Zacharias and saluted Elisabeth. When Elisabeth heard the greeting of Mary, the babe in her womb leapt. And she was filled with the Holy Spirit. And she cried out, 'Blessed art thou among women and blessed is the fruit of thy womb! And blessed is she who has believed because the things promised her by the Lord shall be accomplished.' And Mary said, 'My soul magnifies the Lord, and my spirit rejoices in God my Savior; for he has regarded the lowliness of his handmaid. For, behold, all generations shall call me blessed; for he who is mighty has done great things for me. And holy is his name; and his mercy is from generation to generation on those who fear him. He has shown might with his arm, he has scattered the proud in the conceit of their heart. He has put down the mighty from their thrones and has exalted the lowly. He has filled the hungry with good things, and the rich he has sent away empty.' "

Mary, divine Mary, sings a song. She calls out from within herself a Magnificat, a magnification of the great event which has occurred. Mary, who speaks little, calls out in joy and great rejoicing. She proclaims this great event of God choosing her. And she speaks of him, his deeds, his attitudes. She speaks of the Lord as fearsome, but merciful, as turning things upside down, raising the low and putting down the mighty. This Lord changes the course of history. God in Heaven makes a whole new world, a brand new change in the system of values, in the goals of evolution. For God wants to become man, he wants to find a home in the human flesh and be born therein. That which has been kingly and proud, the kings of this world who have power, use power, exploit power only for their own ends, their days are numbered. No matter if they live on in the world as kings and tyrants for many eons, their rule is limited. For ordinary, lowly man is to become a dwelling place for the Lord. Man, ordinary man, is to become a God-man, sometime, at the end of days. And all of us lowly, ordinary creatures are so chosen. Thus does Mary, our human sister, the first of those like us to experience this event, thus does she proclaim. And thus is she blessed. And thus, too, Mary, are we blessed in you, for you are the first, the initial woman, to be initiated, to experience the changes in all those cosmic energies of the evolution of the universe. Mary, we embrace you, salute you, adore you. And like you, we, too, will be fed by this new spirit which you announce. We, too, will be fed in our old, weak, human, impoverished places which hunger after God. And we, too, in our false riches, in our power-hunger, our conceit, our foolish lust after things and dominion, in these we will be deprived, "sent away." For in our worship and devotion to power, we are, indeed, far from the Lord!

But what does it mean, Mary, that a "visitation" should be a mystery? How is it that a seemingly ordinary event should be a mystery? After becoming aware of your own pregnancy, you attended the pregnancy of your kinswoman, herself old and pregnant. Is it that this simple, ordinary, practical, loving care for our fellows is what we are being instructed about? Or is it that there is a divine and ennobling pairing of you and Elisabeth and of Joseph and Zacharias? Perhaps so, for Elisabeth is to give birth to John the Baptist, the heralded forerunner and spiritual brother of your Son. And it is also true that Zacharias did not believe and was made dumb by the spirit, whereas Joseph believed and waited patiently, devotedly. Is this foursome the mystery? Of how God affects the different aspects of the soul when he is ready to enter us? Perhaps so. For in part we are Mother, like Elisabeth, to the herald, the intuitive anticipation of the birth of God within us; we are the old emotion who adores and proclaims, but also needs full care to bring even the anticipation into reality. And part of our spirit, the old and critical, like Zacharias, is struck dumb, forced not to speak, so it, too, can come to a true and passionate proclamation of the great tidings. Part of our human spirit can only stand by, like Joseph, say nothing, only endure the events, and let the feminine principle carry the whole burden, the whole realization of this new message. Yes, all of this is surely true. All of these thoughts must be implied in this second Joyful Mystery. But, what more?

Mary, Blessed among women, tell me, convey to me, beyond what I have already divined, what is meant that this aspect of your experience, your holy bouquet, should be a mystery.

"Blessed are the weak, for they shall see God."

This does Mary say to me. And now I see her differently than before. I see more of her. Now she is not only an upper part, but I also see her belly. It is large and full of child, for she is pregnant. What is the significance of these words? How shall I understand them! Let me be like Mary, who tried to take in the words of the Angel. Let me take in her words. These words are familiar, yet different. The holy words speak of the meek seeing God, not the weak. But here Mary speaks of the weak. Perhaps again it is Mary's song, speaking of the rejection of power. Yes, Mary, I think I understand: when we are weak, broken like Zacharias, made only a witness like Joseph, but also soft and feminine and old and no more biologically creative, like Elisabeth, and, finally, totally open and receptive, proclaiming no personal power, like you, only then, Mary, when we are weak and powerless, does the power of God come into us and make us fruitful.

"Blessed are the weak," Mary, as you say, "for they shall see God!" Statement of fact; statement of experience; neither enjoined, nor finger-pointing, nor indicating, even, of an example. For how can anybody enjoin anybody else to be weak? We can only experience our weakness, take it in, and allow our powerlessness to be a receptiveness, not a complaint. And, in my weakness, powerlessness, receptiveness, my soul magnifies the Lord, not my own power. My soul wraps itself around and loves and enjoys the Lord, not myself. But neither do I demean myself, and put myself down: For I, like Mary, am exalted, am meant to be a handmaiden and mistress and mother of God. All that is put down is my claim to be a king, to be a tyrant, a ruler of my own life and that of others. In my riches, Mary shows me, I can love and serve others, particularly the God in them, the divine in them which is showing the way. That I can do. But the mystery, Mary, the mystery is the weakness.

"Blessed are the weak, for they shall see God."

Once more the Our Father; once more a decade of Hail Marys; once more Glory be to the Father; and I am ready to proceed to the Third Joyful Mystery: The Nativity.

The Third Joyful Mystery: The Nativity

"It came to pass while they were in Bethlehem, that the days for her to be delivered were fulfilled. And she brought forth her firstborn son, and wrapped him in swaddling clothes. And she laid him in a manger, because there was no room for them in the inn. And there were shepherds in the same district. And behold, an angel of the Lord stood by them. 'Do not be afraid, for behold, I bring you good news of great joy which shall be to all people. For today in the town of David a Savior has been born to you, who is Christ the Lord. Glory to God in the highest, and on earth peace to men of good will.' And behold, Magi came from the East, and entering they found the child with Mary, his mother. And falling down, they worshipped him. And they offered him gifts of gold, frankincense and myrrh. And Mary kept in mind all these things, pondering them in her heart."

Is God always born in the stable? Among the earthy animal instincts? In the smell of dung, of hay and earth? Is there always no room at the inn? I suppose so. For the new God, the God-man, never does fit in with the established order, he is always born at the place of the rejected, the animal and ordinary, the super-natural amid the natural. But of you, Mary? Nothing is said in the story about your labor or your pain. Is it that in those days these things were taken for granted? That the birth of anything from oneself was a labor and a pain? I suppose so. But as people grow and develop, they grow away from those old verities, and now we have to experience them anew.

But the Angel of the Lord was there, Mary. The Angel supported you in your travail, and announced the good tidings. And the Magi came. Those wise men from east and north and south, those ultimate wisdoms who have everything—everything except the incarnation of the God-man—they came, too. You took all this in and pondered. What did you ponder, Mary? What deep realization came from this experience?

"That all men knew, or would know. That it was true that which I had guessed."

So, you, too, had doubt, Mary? That you, embodiment of faith and trust, had doubt?

"True, true. There is always doubt, in the midst of the manger, in the midst of the travail, in the midst of the pain, there is doubt."

If you, Mary, can doubt, then I can, too: one needs all the wisdom that one can muster, one must give all that one has to this new and fragile birth of the God-man in oneself. For one is doubtful. One loses faith when driven from the inn.

Mary, Mother of God, pray for me! For I am doubtful. I am here in my travail and I do not know if a holy thing comes from me and my labor, or if I am, in truth, merely laboring amidst the dung of my own foolish animality. I do not know and I doubt. Pray for me!

And so, Mary, Mother of God, who in certainty and in wonder, gave birth to the divine within herself, kneels and prays with me. She does not know and I do not know. But she prays with me. She prays as do I, that the birth of the divine will be real and not an illusion, on earth, and not only in the fantastic realm of mind.

As I pray, I find myself at the gate of the womb of Mary, Mother of God. I find myself grown small and her large. I find that I am within her. I am contained by her as I contain that in me which wants to be born. She is my vessel and I am His. It is not only God that needs to be born, it is also I who need to be contained, loved by the Mother of God, and reborn myself! Oh, Mary, contain me, let me, in the act of giving birth to the God-man, become myself reborn, and, like you, a fitting vessel for the birth of such a One! For you have shown the way, you have shown the way!

Hail Mary, full of Grace! The Lord is with thee; blessed art thou among women, and blessed is the fruit of thy womb. For I, too, am contained in your womb. I, too, need to be made small and contained in your bigness; I, too, need to be blessed, and in giving birth, myself, to be born again.

Our Father, who art in heaven . . . Hail Mary, full of Grace . . . Glory be to the Father . . .

The Fourth Joyful Mystery: The Presentation in the Temple

"According to the Law of Moses, they took Jesus up to Jerusalem to present him to the Lord. Now there was in Jerusalem a man named Simeon and this man was just and devout, looking for the consolation of Israel. And it had been revealed to him that he should not see death before he had seen the Christ of the Lord. And when they brought in the child Jesus, he received him into his arms and blessed God. 'Now thou dost dismiss thy servant, oh Lord, according to thy word, in peace. Because my eyes have seen thy salvation, which thou hast prepared before the face of all peoples. A light of revelation to the Gentiles and a glory for thy people Israel.' And he said to Mary, 'Behold, this child is destined for the fall and for the rise of many in Israel, and for a sign that shall be contradicted. And thy own soul a sword shall pierce, that the thoughts of many hearts may be revealed.' And there was one Anna, a prophetess. She was a widow of about fourscore and four years, which departed not from the temple, but served God with fastings and prayers night and day. And she coming in that instant gave thanks likewise unto the Lord and spake of him to all that looked for redemption in Jerusalem. And when they had performed all things according to the law of the Lord, they returned to Nazareth. And the child grew and became strong and the grace of God was upon him."

Simeon and Anna, Mary, they understood. In the midst of the decay and rigidity of the old doctors of law and pedantry, in the midst of the unknowing ones, there appear a man and woman, old of years, and they know. Not just a maleness, Mary, not just the old way, but parts of the spirit which wait in patience and in hope. Such is Simeon. But even more so is Anna. She, the prophetess, the feminine, deeply awaiting consolation, deeply committed to the spirit, a light to the men, she was there, Mary. And your story once again shows that there are always a pair of the devoted in the midst of the rejecting. And the pair is male and female. For the Lord, in becoming man, must needs come out of the oneness of spirit into the duality of male and female. Father and Son, joined in the Holy Spirit, need, for their Trinity, a Fourth, Mary. and that fourth is you.

But Simeon warns you as well. He, too, is a prophet. He told you of the coming rejection of the God-man, and that your own soul would be wounded. For Mary, I see now that your doubt was because not all was revealed to you at once. How could it be? How could a mother know in advance the awful fate of her son upon that cross? How can the soul anticipate all the suffering that the divine undergoes within it? Divine and human, Christ and Jesus, Mary immortal and mortal. Simeon knew it. Your Son died for all mankind, Mary, but your wounds were so "the thoughts of many hearts may be revealed." Your wounds, your suffering, can help us know what it is that our hearts want, how we long for and desire the happiness of the love of God, the suffering of our witness to its mystery.

But what joy you must have had, Mary. What a proud mother you must have been to present the blessed fruit of your womb and to have it recognized . . . But you look sad, Mary, as I speak to you. This is a Joyful Mystery, is it not? You nod, but are still sad. You are sad because I do not comprehend it? You nod. What must I do, then? Close my eyes, meditate upon the image of the child, Jesus, being offered up, ransomed with the doves, but offered up. It is like the sacrifice of Isaac, you seem to say. One offers up the blessed fruit of one's deepest creativity. One offers up to God the Father, God the Son. The Presentation is but a way of renewing the old spirit, the old King, the old religion, the old consciousness, but finally the offering of the divine to the divine. That is what you want me to understand, Mary. A mother must already be ready to offer up her greatest joy, her child, very soon after finding it. Forty days, it took. Like the forty years in the wilderness of the children of Israel, and the holy four of your son. The four again; at the time of wholeness, sacrificed. And the soul, Mary, is witness, like you, to the event. The soul sees ahead like Simeon, prays and is devoted, like Anna. Again, Simeon and Anna, like Zacharias and Elisabeth, but now changed: for the male understands and foresees, no longer skeptical, and the female is spiritualized and profound. The drama continues, and the mysteries go on. Mary, I see now. It was the process and the sacrifice that you wanted me to see. And I do.

Our Father who art in heaven . . . Hail, Mary, full of Grace . . . Glory be . . .

And now to announce the Fifth Joyful Mystery: The Finding of Jesus in the Temple.

The Fifth Joyful Mystery: The Finding of Jesus in the Temple

"When Jesus was twelve years old, they went up to Jerusalem according to the custom of the feast. And when they were returning, the boy Jesus remained in Jerusalem, and his parents did not know it. They returned to Jerusalem in search of him. And after three days, they found him in the temple. He was sitting in the midst of the teachers, listening to them and asking them questions. And all who were listening to him were amazed at his understanding and his answers. 'Son, why hast thou done so to us? Behold, in sorrow thy father and I have been seeking thee.' 'How is it that you sought me? Did you not know that I must be about my Father's business?' And they did not understand the word that he spoke to them. And he went down with them and came to Nazareth and was subject to them. And Jesus advanced in wisdom and age and grace before God and men."

You hinted to me of the sacrifice, Mary. Now I see the other side: not the willing giving up, but the active search for the lost God. First the willing sacrifice, and then the unwilling? Is it not so? You nod. Yes. First I must willingly surrender the great fruit of the gift of God to God, and then I must go and search for it, too. I must feel abandoned and lost, and go and search. The soul understands and does not understand. For the work of God, the Son is in the service of God, the Father, and we mortals must bear this truth in non-understanding and in pain. But God, too, submits, the story says. He, after asserting his task, voluntarily is "subject to them." So, after we surrender and sacrifice, search out and suffer, know that the divine does not "belong" to us, but is shared with all mankind, only then does the divine submit, in turn, to us. A hard lesson, I think, and, Mary, like you, I do not really understand. Now you smile, and now I see that this is a joyful mystery, as well. For one loses, but one finds; one does not understand and then one understands. God confounds and is confounded; the soul surrenders and seeks out. But to lose a son and regain him, oh! To lose a love and regain it, oh! To lose God and find Him, oh! Hail Mary, Mother of God!

Mother and Son III: Sorrowful Mysteries

And now I begin once again. Once more do I begin a meditation upon the mysteries, this time upon the five Sorrowful Mysteries. I take that same Rosary in hand, saying the Our Father, saying the three Hail Marys, and saying the Glory be. And now I can announce the first sorrowful mystery:

The First Sorrowful Mystery: The Agony in the Garden

"Jesus came with them to Gethsemane, and he began to be saddened and exceedingly troubled. Then he said to them, 'My soul is sad, even unto death. Wait here and watch with me.' And going forward a little, he fell on the ground, and began to pray. 'Father, if thou art willing, remove this cup from me; yet not my will but thine be done.' And there appeared to him an angel from heaven to strengthen him. And falling into an agony, he prayed the more earnestly. And his sweat became as drops of blood running down upon the ground. Then he came to the disciples and found them sleeping. And he said, 'Could you not, then, watch one hour with me? Watch and pray, that you may not enter into temptation. The spirit is willing, but the flesh is weak.' "

Mary, Queen of Heaven, accompany me. Help me to understand your son. What sorrow is this, that God must suffer and be afraid like an ordinary mortal? That he calls out to us to share his prayer, his awful struggle to do that which he must, and that we fall into unconsciousness, into a sleep which leaves him to carry the whole burden? Where were you, Mary? You were apart during the enactment of this first sorrowful mystery. "Spirit willing, flesh weak." How often this is used as a statement against sexuality or hunger, or any of the other animal instincts! And how wrong it is! Was Christ not born in a manger, among cattle, in the midst of hay and dung? Surely it is true. So, then, the meaning must be that the spirit is willing to sacrifice, to serve, to die, to carry the burden of God, but the flesh, the human-animal-mortal flesh, with its instincts, grows fatigued, is tired, falls asleep into unawareness. It just is so; no blame, really. For Christ, too, was afraid of suffering, as he and we should be. Mortality-animality-Jesus-man fails the immortality-spirituality-Christ-God. But the two are in One, and we know it. Jesus, the Christ, knew it.

But Mary, where are you? What say you to this agony, this suffering of your only-begotten son?

"Let this cup pass from me."

You do not wish to speak? You do not wish to . . . no, you are saying something else. You say that you, as a woman, like myself, know more even than a man, what the limitations of the flesh are; what the suffering of the flesh is; what the fears, doubts, hurts, hungers of the animal-man-woman is. You know, Mary. And thus you repeat your son's words, "Let this cup pass from me." Even Mary, of immaculate conception, knows what it is to move from the agony of serving God in the Highest when it brings about awful pain, suffering, fear. Yet she did it, as Jesus did it. Oh, Mary, help me to be as steadfast and as human and as divine as your son and, as you.

Our Father . . . Hail Mary for a sixth decade . . . Glory be to the Father, and I am ready to announce and meditate upon the second sorrowful mystery:

The Second Sorrowful Mystery: The Scourging at the Pillar

They bound Jesus and delivered him to Pilate. And Pilate asked him, 'Art thou the king of Jews?' Jesus answered, 'My kingdom is not of this world. But thou sayest it; I am a king. This is why I was born, and why I have come into the world, to bear witness to the truth.' Then Pilate said, I find no guilt in this man. 'I will therefore chastise him and release him.' Pilate then took Jesus and had him scourged. Oppressed and condemned, he was taken away, a man of suffering. Though he was harshly treated, he submitted, like a lamb led to the slaughter. He was pierced for our offenses, crushed for our sins. It was our infirmities that he bore, our sufferings that he endured. Upon him was the chastisement that makes us whole, by his stripes we are healed."

Mark, John, Luke, and Isaiah all contribute to the tale, to this description of the mystery. But what does this mean, Mary, that God comes into the world "to bear witness to the truth"? The truth that God becomes human, and man divine? The truth that the kingdom of God is in the soul, not the world? All true. But Pilate, a king of this world, says he finds no guilt and, "therefore" will punish and scourge? Is that how this world is? Often true: the guiltless are judged unjustly and punished. Yet God voluntarily enters this state and is judged and punished unjustly, to bear our infirmities, for our sake. And most important, "to make us whole, by his stripes are we healed."

How does that help us, Mary? We knew that God was unjust to

Job, at the behest of Satan. We know that he entered into the human condition because of it. He needed to know how we felt, how it is to suffer unjustly the vast powers of God, of the universe, dark and light. Is he merely then a lamb, a scapegoat? I do not think that helps us very much. I am not cleansed by someone else taking on my sins, my breakings-away from God, from my own wholeness. How then, how then?. . . Thoughts come. Do they come from you, Mary? I hear that God took on the sins, the scourging, to heal us, to make us whole, indeed, but not by taking these things away from us, that is not possible. He took on our humanity, so that in exchange, we could take on his divinity. Or, better; for God and man both to know the other side. In this, both God and man are made whole. God, needing man, is no longer cut off from him in that vast, mysterious way of suffering and dying unjustly. When God knows that, he now knows all that it is to be a man. When God knows that, he has tasted our entire bitter cup. But his tasting it makes it less bitter, for now our suffering is sanctified, blessed, made whole because in the service of God. God serves man, and man serves God; but God also serves God, and man serves man. In this mutuality is the Holy Spirit; in this mutuality is Christ the King, not of this world, but in the world to come, both on earth and in heaven, both in everyday life and in the soul. This I experience, Mary, and is this from you? You nod. You do not speak, but you nod.

But what about Pilate? Could the mortal king of this world be such a total fool and such a graceless one as was Pilate and the Pharisees, too? Could they be so openly hypocritical as to say, "not guilty, therefore punish"? What does that mean? That our worldly, power side, that wants only peace, success, no suffering, is merely hypocritical? I don't believe it. For there must be a mystery here, a secret here in the unjust judge, in the punishing world which God and man need. Or is it, "did" need? I suppose that one needs to have this experience of injustices at least once in order to come to one's true aloneness, one's true separateness. But is that all? Mary?. . .

"God forgives."

That you say. And that, of course, is the small title that I forgot, "to forgive is divine." Ah, to judge, that is ordinary and necessary, human. Even God-like, or especially so, for what human can really judge another? Did not Jesus say, let him who is without sin cast the first stone? Yes, to judge is an act of raising oneself above, it is done. But to forgive, that is even more divine, more holy. But to forgive, one must understand ever more deeply. Oh, Mary, I need you for that! I have been harshly judged and wrongly. And I have judged harshly. Let me forgive and be forgiven. Was not Peter, the rock, deeply forgiven? And he the ground of a great church? And could not even Judas have been forgiven, had he asked for it? Let me forgive God for scourging me so, for letting my pain be so great. I do . . . You smile, Mary. You smile at my audacity. You can do that, because you know. You know that my audacity covers also my own sinning, my own poor judgment, my own injustice, scourging and hypocrisy toward others . . . But, Mary, I too, can now smile . . . and laugh. For I can forgive myself! That is the hardest thing, isn't it? For one to forgive one's self: God and human within, each forgiving the other! That is divine . . . and human . . . together.

Our Father . . . a sixth decade of Hail Marys . . . Glory be to the Father . . . and now I announce and meditate upon the third sorrowful mystery:

The Third Sorrowful Mystery: The Crowning With Thorns

"Now the soldiers led him away into the courtyard, and they stripped him and put on him a purple cloak. And plaiting a crown of thorns, they put it upon his head, and a reed into his right hand. And bending the knee before him they mocked him, saying, 'Hail, King of the Jews!' And they spat on him, and they took the reed and kept striking him on the head. Pilate again went outside and said 'I bring him out to you, that you may know I find no guilt in him.' Jesus therefore came forth, wearing the crown of thorns and the purple cloak. And Pilate said to them, 'Behold the man!' But they cried out, 'Away with him! 'Crucify him!' 'Why, what evil has he done?' But they kept crying out the more, 'Crucify him!' 'Shall I crucify your king?' And the chief priests answered, 'We have no king but Caesar.' Then he handed him over to them to be crucified. And so they took Jesus and led him away."

Crown of thorns and purple robe; degradation and exaltation. As king of this world of flesh: mocked and humiliated; as a wearer of the cloak of kingship in the spirit: elevated and royal. Just so. Just so is the God-man; that I already know. And of Pilate I know. The story continues, and seems the same as the second sorrowful mystery. For all is there, prefigured, pre-meditated. But let not my meditation be "pre-meditated." Let it not be all worked out in advance, with no chance of anything new coming into it. Let not my own view and experience of God be forced into rules and regulations, ideas and practices, beliefs and credos. For, Mary, was that not the true sin of the Pharisees? Were they not so embroiled in what they asserted God to be, God to perform, that they absolutely could not permit God to live and have a new being? Did they not preclude, with their "pre-meditation" all chance for renewal? And must not the Holy Spirit be free to blow where it listeth? It is so, Mary, for you nod once again . . . But speak to me. Tell me afresh, as a woman, what it is that you see in this crowning. Tell me, as a woman, what further understanding I need of the mystery of degradation and exaltation of God . . . You look at me quizzically. You look at me with a half smile, your arms under your breasts. What do you ask of me? Do I really care? Am I really interested? Or do I, too, wish only to keep the status quo? Want God to be safely contained in whatever vessels of belief and structure that suit me? Mary, I do not know. I hope that I am open, but I do not know . . . You nod. For you seem to say that in the not knowing, I can be open. One who "knows," who is king of the world, one who is clear and certain, cannot experience that degradation and exaltation of the spirit-flesh which is God-man. Mary, I take your hands. Mary, I look into your eyes and see a joy. And the joy is there because of our secret connection, our secret understanding. You, Mary, Mother of God, provide me with that living connection. You, Mary, Queen of Heaven, you quietly keep me open. You, Mary, contain me and let me be free.

Our Father . . . Hail Mary, with another decade . . . Glory be to . . . And the fourth sorrowful mystery is upon me.

The Fourth Sorrowful Mystery: The Carrying of the Cross

" 'If anyone wishes to come after me, let him deny himself. And take up his cross daily, and follow me.' And bearing the cross for himself, he went forth to the place called the Skull. And they laid hold of a certain Simon of Cyrene, and upon him they laid the cross to bear it after Jesus. 'Take my yoke upon you, and learn from me. For I am meek and humble of heart. And you will find rest for your souls. For my yoke is easy, and my burden light.' Now there was following him a great crowd of people, and of women, who were bewailing and lamenting him. Jesus, turning to them, said, 'Do not weep for me, but weep for yourselves and for your children. For if in the case of green wood they do these things, what is to happen in the case of the dry?' "

Clear enough. Take up my own cross, my own conflicts, my own struggle to carry my fate of being a divine and human creature, just like Jesus, and Christ. And right until death. And let another help me, like Simon. And be like Simon, in that I am suddenly forced into carrying such enormous conflicts, even those of God. But even these, he says, can be sweet and joyful and provide rest. How is that, Mary? What did your son mean by that? You tell me that I already know. That to carry my own totality of soul, to embrace my own life, even if it is crushing and painful, unjust and ruinous, it is still my own, and, if I follow the God within me—and, even, as it comes from outside, as it happened to Simon—then I shall also know a certain sweetness, a certain rest for my soul in it. But only if, like Jesus, I humbly accept that the cross I bear is my own, unique, and in it, I must deny myself. But what is it that I must deny? My own one-sidedness: my own animality-humanity or my own angel-divinity? One sidedness is to be denied. God-woman. Like you, Mary. But you shrink from that, modestly. Why? No answer. I must wait. I must wait, you seem to say, until the Glorious mysteries for an answer to that. Now must I "deny myself" in another way, and attend to the God-man. And what of you, Mary? There was a look between you and him, on his way. Oh, how you both suffered the other's pain! How a mother suffers when she sees her son in such agony, how much more a God-man, and the soul which needs to see it, and bear it! We know, Mary, and I shall say no more. Of love and connection, of care and comradeship, like you, and Jesus with the women, there is plenty. Of needing to lament and care for myself, when my time is also dry, and not green, that I must do, too. As Jesus said, take care of myself and look after my own daily cross. I accept it, embrace it.

Our Father . . . Hail Mary . . . Glory be . . . And now to announce the last sorrowful mystery:

The Fifth Sorrowful Mystery: The Crucifixion

And when they came to the place called the Skull, they crucified him. And Jesus said 'Father, forgive them, for they do not know what they are doing.' And one of the robbers crucified with him said, 'Lord, remember me when thou comest into thy kingdom.' And Jesus said to him 'Amen I say to thee, this day thou shalt be with me in paradise.' And Jesus saw his mother and the disciple standing by, whom he loved. And he said to his mother, 'Woman, behold, thy son.' Then he said to his disciple, Behold, thy mother.' And from that hour the disciple took her into his home. And the sun was darkened, and the earth quaked, and the curtain of the temple was torn in two. And Jesus cried out with a loud voice and said, 'Father, into thy hands I commend my spirit.' And bowing his head, he expired.

Such simple words, Mary! Such simple words from the disciples, as they witnessed this terrible, wonderful event. Jesus must have suffered more than most men in life.

"He had such agony at Gethsemane that he sweated blood; he was betrayed, denied, deserted, arrested, falsely accused, condemned unjustly; blindfolded, spat upon, beaten; ridiculed by Herod, scourged by Pilate; crowned with thorns; loaded with the cross and then nailed to it; enduring utter dereliction of soul in the midst of a terrible thirst; and even after death, his side was torn with a lance."

All this was how a loving priest put it in his own meditations, and it is all true. All this he endured. But what of you, Mary? What of you, observing this event, listening as he told you to be a mother to his disciple, and through him, to be a mother to all mankind, and not just your only begotten son? What of you, Mary? Speak to me, please; tell me, as a woman, what it was like, what you. . . .

"There was darkness. The earth was dimmed, even more than the sky. There was pain in each stone, there was agony in each leaf. There were screams of child for mother, unspoken, of mother for child, unspoken. There was a hymn of hurt; a rash of rended promises torn in two, as was the curtain of the temple. The end of days. What more, what more!"

And now I see Mary, Queen of Angels, weeping into her hands. I see her remembering that day, long ago. I see her participating once again in the visible agony, that time of the lowest low, the deepest depression. She weeps, and I, poor mortal, who has suffered hardly at all, comfort her. I presume to comfort the Great Mother; I feel compelled to embrace and warm her who comforts mankind. For you, Mary, also need my love and my care. Just as Christ needs the care and prayers of mankind, just so do you. Even you, Mother of us all in the soul. Mary, I weep with you, for you, I taste your tears and feel the throbbing pain of your heart. Mary, I have been within you, now I take you in me. I feel you, entering my own womb, filling up my own belly, being protected in me. And I am ready to let you live in me, in every way. Oh, Mary, Mother of God, I adore you, have adored you as my mother, my sister, and now I will be mother to you, and sister in a yet deeper way.

In the beginning was Eve, mother of men in the flesh. In the middle was Mary, mother of men in the soul. In the end there is I, Daughter of Guinevere, and every "I" who shall ever live, who shall make a home within for Eve, for Mary, and for herself. For just as there has been a trinity of God, the Father, God the Son, and God, the Holy Spirit, just so there is a trinity of God, the Mother, God the Daughter, and God, the Holy Soul. And the three plus three make interwoven triangles in which the star of David is fulfilled. And I, Daughter of Guinevere, daughter of one who suffered a crucifixion of two loves, bled in a triangle of pain, I, Daughter of Guinevere, live to see a redemption therein. For I know that the spirit and soul find a home in me, a living temple. I know that the temple curtain was torn in two, split, just as my mother was, as I have been, as men and women usually are. I know that my redeemer liveth and I know that Mary, Mother of God, lives in me, and I in she.

Mother and Son IV: Glorious Mysteries

Five joyful and five sorrowful mysteries have I announced, meditated upon. Many have been the Hail Marys, the Our Fathers, the Glory be to the Fathers, I have recited. Much help has Mary given me through this. And now, I begin once again: prayers, meditations, mysteries. I pray that Mary, Mother of God, who lives in me, as I live in her, will accompany me, as she has, and will warm-enlighten me with the special glow that she has, as I continue her bouquet, her rosarium of the Christ-consciousness, her rosary.

And so, once more Our Father . . . Hail Mary . . . Glory be. I grasp the rosary and announce the first glorious mystery.

The First Glorious Mystery: The Resurrection

" 'Amen, amen, I say to you, that you shall be sorrowful, but your sorrow shall be turned into joy. For I will see you again, and your heart shall rejoice, and your joy no one shall take from you.' At early dawn, they came to the tomb, taking the spices that they had prepared. And behold, an angel of the Lord came down from heaven, and drawing near rolled back the stone. 'Do not be afraid; for I know that you seek Jesus, who was crucified. He is not here, but has risen. Behold the place where they laid him. And behold, he goes before you into Galilee; there you shall see him.' And they departed quickly from the tomb in great fear and great joy. 'I am the resurrection and the life; he who believes in me, even if he die shall live. And whoever lives and believes in me shall never die.' "

". . . and your joy no one shall take from you." Is that what resurrection is, Mary? That one is joyously reborn into the spirit, into heaven, and one is never more thrown down, saddened, crucified? It must not be so, unless one is really never born again into human flesh at all. Or, indeed, was it not you who was so sorrowful in my last meditation, remembering that horrible day of the crucifixion? Was that only another illusion of mine, my own poor fantasy of you, not you? No, I will not even wait for an answer to that. For I will neither demean you, nor my fantasy. They—and you—are real. For what more does one know of life, of God, than what one truly experiences, from within and without? The rest is construction, important and necessary, but construction. And it is the construction that is subject to error, not the experience.

What do you say, Mary?

"I do not say. I remember. I remember days of longing, of sadness, of misery. I remember loss of faith, about which I did not speak. For, were I to speak of my own loss of faith, many, many would have been crushed. Better to keep silence, to carry my own sorrow, suffering, loss of conviction, meaning, than burden others with it. But I remember. And, lest others think me a Goddess, or some creature far from the laments, the pains, the doubts, the human frailties, then let them reflect again. For I was mortal and limited. My awareness of immortality came only with time. But I remember, too, the day of the resurrection. When my son came to me, and proved that all was not foolishness, ignominy, self-deception. I remember that day, too. Death is not life, nor the opposite of it. Death and birth are opposed, not death and life. For there is death in life, and, in the resurrection, life in death, and that I learned that day. The stone door pushed away, the empty crypt. I, it was, who annointed my son two times, as all know, both with the leper and on the day of his death. I, it was, who annointed him, and I, it was, who received him. For I am as the receptive soul to the spirit, who both comes to me and impregnates me and is born from me. And it is the spirit who annoints, who names and sanctifies. All this . . . all this."

"But you seem sad, Mary," I said. "We speak now of the resurrection, and you speak so much, more than ever before, either in the stories of you, or to me. You speak so much, yet are sad. Why?"

"Sadness is from the endless round of birth and death. Sadness is from the never-ending task of redemption, of resurrection. Sadness is for souls not saved. Sadness is for all of that. Not for myself. And you, Daughter of Guinevere, where is your sadness? Where is your sadness for all of those in such sorrow, bereavement, endless births and deaths? Where is your sadness for that?"

"I thought that I had it, had care for my fellow creatures."

"Then where is the joyful announcement? Where is your joyful proclamation of God-man, and God-woman? Where is your joy in life and experience? Transcending death and birth?"

"I have it, Mary, at least at times. But who wishes to hear me? I do not see people asking of me, and why should I presume on them? Their God-spirit will come in time, in one way or another."

"You are right, Daughter of Guinevere. You are right. So many want to hear me. At Fatima, and everywhere else. And my words are filtered through the particular soul. No matter, that is how it must be. Must be. 'I am the resurrection and the light,' he said, my son. And the Christ is exactly that. There is resurrection, rebirth in the spirit, and a new consciousness from that. And that was born in me, through me. Enough. I shall be sad no more."

With that, Mary left me, and I pondered over this strange event. The previous night I had dreamed that all was well in the world of mothers. There was great joy and homecoming—and this on the heels of my meditation in which Mary-in-me and I-in-Mary was fulfilled, the last sorrowful mystery. But now, Mary seems sad at the lack of redemption of others, and even a bit hopeless at the seemingly endless succession of death and rebirth . . . What is it?

Oh, Mary, now I see. For what else could be meant by the Sorrowful Madonna? What else could be implied by that glorious image of Mary, forever mindful of the suffering of others, forever open to their pain, forever available to the endless pain of death and rebirth? Oh, Mary, Mother of God, Madonna! Now I understand that the resurrection was the freeing from your final birth and death, that the Mary-life was your last on this earth. I understand, too, why you are Madonna to us all, as your Son said. I understand. Once again, I wrap myself in your arms, great Madonna. Once again I abandon myself to your care, your mercy, your ardent love of mankind. I, Daughter of Guinevere, who will need to be born again, I embrace and salute and bow before you, Madonna, woman who has finally transcended the cycle, and gone into heaven, transcended into a whole new level of being. You, Mary, initiated beyond all women, you are here to help us, be helped by us, and yet live in realms that we cannot even guess. For you, Mary, in the most high place, are open to that ever-beyond spirit of the God which is beyond being, beyond immanence, beyond our mortal awareness. Hail, Mary, full of Grace.

Our Father . . . Hail Mary, another decade . . . Glory be, and the second Glorious Mystery is at hand:

The Second Glorious Mystery: The Ascension

"Now he led them out towards Bethany, and he lifted up his hands and blessed them, saying, 'All power in heaven and on earth has been given to me. Go, therefore, and make disciples of all nations, baptizing them in the name of the Father, and of the Son, and of the Holy Spirit, teaching them to observe all that I have commanded you . . . He who believes and is baptized shall be saved. But he who does not believe shall be condemned . . . And behold, I am with you all days, even unto the consummation of the world.' And it came to pass as he blessed them, that he parted from them . . . And was taken up into heaven and sits at the right hand of God."

Jesus, fully contained in the Christ, is resurrected, rises up toward heaven. What is he saying? All power in heaven and earth is now his. Once totally contained in the Christ, once one's consciousness is at that level, then all spirit and matter is possessed, contained. He can then leave the world where man once fell, and now help us all to attain his state—at the right hand of God—redeeming, helping. But then the disciples shall be the whole world, not just one chosen person or people: ultimately all mankind will receive the message from Jesus. He shows mankind how they can save themselves, become Christed themselves. But first the baptism in water and belief. Baptism: an immersion in the depths of the water of life? To experience to the depths the total flow of being? Yes. But also an immersion in the depths of emotion, in the ever-encompassing waters of our tears, our joys, our sufferings, our pleasures. For emotion is what moves us, what we must relate to, participate in, be purified by, until we can be totally at home in our passions and our calmness, just as Jesus was. To be emotional, but not possessed. Only then can a person rise up to the ultimate heights of the spirit. It is as if genitals and belly and heart, the emotional centers, must be cleansed—by immersion—until one can rise to the highest centers of spirit, and, finally, leave the body altogether. So baptism is necessary. And belief, too. A cynic can't rise. Nor the skeptic. Our criticism will keep us in the head, not in the spirit. The cynic-skeptic will have to be fully immersed in emotion—then he will believe! Just so have I experienced, and, I suppose, all those who have been pulled into the waters of the path, felt the baptism of real emotion. The rest will be condemned to live the hells, the pains, the torments, until they willingly, freely, fully, can experience for themselves that total emotion—total freedom, total suffering, total joy—that Jesus experienced in His passion. For it was a passion, after all, not a quiet, placid thing. But, finally, ascension, rising beyond the mortal frame, at last, and being next to God.

But, Mary, you were there. You were there at the beginning, and at the end. At the inception of the helpless infant, and at the total redemptive, glorious Ascension. You saw the cloud. You saw. Tell me, then, Mary, Mother of God; please tell me what I need to know. Tell me how I can better grasp this mystery of the Ascension.

"You have grasped it. It has not yet grasped you."

"True, Mary, true. I remain in mortal flesh. I have a life to live. I have many lives and deaths before I would ascend."

"Not true. One can ascend once, twice, often. One can rise out of the frame, rise up to the Lord. Look now!"

I looked. And what I saw was a rising up from within me of a kind of ethereal spirit. It was as if from the lowest centers that a substance was gradually volatilized, spiritualized, so that it was both substance and not-substance. It was like a ghost-thing, which rose from center to center, until it reached that highest place in my skull. And I knew that Skull was skull, that all the stories were both true and allegories of the spirit-in-the-flesh. And I saw this same spirit leave my body altogether and rise up into heaven. And heaven was both a place and a state, inside me and outside of me. And I glimpsed, for a moment, the risen Christ. And the "I" that glimpsed was like Mary Herself, for the other "I" remained behind in that selfsame body into which I was born, in which I was baptized. And I understood what Mary meant. Hail, Mary, full of Grace.

And Mary smiled at me, as I returned, and she said, "Hail, Daughter of Guinevere, full of Grace." And I was astonished.

Our Father . . . Hail Mary ten more times . . . Glory be.

The Third Glorious Mystery: Pentecost; The Descent of the Holy Spirit

"When the days of Pentecost were drawing to a close, they were all together in one place. And suddenly there came a sound from heaven, as of a violent wind blowing. And there appeared to them parted tongues as of fire, which settled upon each of them. And they were all filled with the Holy Spirit and began to speak of the wonderful works of God. Now there were staying at Jerusalem devout Jews from every nation under heaven. And Peter, standing up with the Eleven, lifted up his voice and spoke out to them. 'Repent and be baptized; and you will receive the gifts of the Holy Spirit.' Now they who received his words were baptized, and there were added that day about three thousand souls . . . Send forth thy Spirit, and they shall be created; and thou shalt renew the face of the earth . . . Come, O Holy Spirit, fill the hearts of thy faithful, and kindle in them the fire of thy love."

Air and fire came unto them. The Holy Spirit initiated them from above, and there came down upon them the air-thoughts and the fire-feelings, the intuitions and spiritual passions from which they then spoke unto men.

First they had been baptized by water, by the emotions of life, and by being immersed in the waters of their own unconsciousness. They had deeply tasted of the primordial source from which all life comes. Some few of them had been able, even, to walk upon the water, to master themselves, their emotions, their own primordial being in such a way that they could do what few men could do: walk freely upon it, without sinking in unwillingly, without being drowned in unconsciousness. But now the Holy Spirit came to baptize them by the sound of wind and by fire. Now the immersion came from above. A new initiation of spirit; a new distribution of the energies of the cosmos so that a brand new order of being comes into existence. Those that are touched by the Holy Spirit know that God and man are partners, that brotherhood of men is the natural state, that everyone is hurt when one is hurt, that everyone is elevated when one is elevated, that the God-spirit dwells in men and needs only to be activated, that the task of men is to become like Christ, to achieve an awareness of their own divinity, to cultivate and serve it, until, indeed, the earth is transformed, and we are all one in Christ, all servants of the One God in whom we have our being and who lives in us. Thus the three thousand Jews from all nations, the representatives of all humanity, are touched, baptized.

All this I see, Mary, all this and more do I understand. But what must they repent? Why such an emphasis upon sin? Yes, one knows that the evil of sin is that it separates man from God. Yes, one knows that there is evil, ignorance, unconsciousness. One knows that the darkness of our minds must be purged by the water, the wind and the fire. But still . . . repentance? Of what should they—and I—repent?

"Repent that you might see God."

These are her words. Not because of sin, apparently. Not because of a "cause" at all. But "in order to"; so that one can see God. One repents so one can "see" God. Not just hear Him in the sound of the wind; not just feel him in the touch of water and fire, but see him. All right then, Mary, I want to see God. Of what must I repent?

"Of arrogance; of disease; of lack of love."

What a peculiar triad! Yes, of arrogance I do repent. False pride, not knowing that all creatures have the divine in them, of all that, I gladly repent. I know it is a vice, a natural effect of the puffing up of oneself when an aspect of God floods one, blows on one, and burns one. Yes, of arrogance I repent, and repeatedly. Of lack of love, too, do I readily repent. For I never can love enough, care enough, for others and, even, for myself. I am limited by my lack of love. For perfect love is always beyond, more, and as long as I am mortal I will be limited. Yes, Mary, I see: as mortal, as creature, I will always be limited by pride and lack of love. I know that we feel that because of Lucifer, the light-bringer. I know that egoism is our disease . . . ah! I did not understand that one needed to repent of "disease." But now I do. The disease to be repented of is egoism. I know that God really wanted us to develop an ego, and, in this he was secretly in league with Lucifer, but I know that our fall is that excess of it, that misuse of ego to be beyond God. I know the disease, Mary, and I am sorry. That, too, is the word, "sorry." That is even better than "repent." For one then is not judged from outside but one feels deeply within that one has hurt someone, something, or even oneself. Sorry. It is like your Sorrow, Madonna. I am sorry for transgressing, going beyond my limits; I repent hurting the divine in others, in myself. Mary, I repent.

"Then you shall see God."

Mary smiles, as I look about. I see trees, mountains, lakes, rivers, people. I see God as all existence. Of this Mary smiles, for it is true. God is everywhere . . . and nowhere. As the Son, he manifests in the concreteness of existence. As the Father, he is the invisible, unmanifested, forever manifesting spirit of heaven which comes from above as wind and fire. As Holy Spirit, he speaks in all tongues, all stories of the divine whether Christian or of all others. He comes ever anew to inspire me to see more, love more. And the Holy Spirit is that which moves between the Father and the Son, between the totally beyond and the totally present, between the ever-unmanifested and ever-manifesting, between the spirit and the flesh. And it moves in me, in all centers of my being. From the crown of my head, from the highest levels of understanding, spirit, and awareness, to the lowest. From the God above which is served, to the God below which bows to it. And this by bending of knees, by a poverty, chastity, and obedience, which makes one open, alive and attentive to the Holy Spirit, to the spirit of God as it moves upon the face of the waters, as it speaks in the holy tongues of myth and religion, as it fires us with a passion of love, of service. "Hail Mary, full of Grace, the Lord is with Thee." The Living Spirit of God moves in Thee. Let it move in me, as well!

Mother and Daughter II

That same Spirit spoke to me and said that my meditations, my celebrations, my prayers with the Rosary must now change from Mother and Son, to Mother and Daughter. For the last two Glorious Mysteries are a deeply feminine thing, between Mary and myself. I have submitted, and have been baptized, I have understood the Father and the Son. Now I will know the Holy Spirit in Mother and Daughter, in the moving of Mary's spirit over against, over upon, over into, my own.

Blessed Mary, continue to speak to me, and help me to realize what it is that the Holy Spirit wants to communicate.

Our Father . . . Hail Mary . . . Glory be, and I announce the fourth Glorious Mystery:

The Fourth Glorious Mystery: The Assumption

"Blessed art thou, O daughter, by the Lord the most high God, above all women upon earth. For he has so magnified thy name this day, that thy praise shall not depart out of the mouth of men. In every nation which shall hear thy name, the God of Israel shall be magnified on occasion of thee. Thou art the glory of Jerusalem, thou art the joy of Israel, thou art the honor of our people . . . Hear, O daughter, and see; turn your ear, for the king shall desire your beauty . . . And the temple of God in heaven was opened, and there came flashes of lightning and peals of thunder. And a great sign appeared in heaven: a woman clothed with the sun. And the moon was under her feet, and upon her head a crown of twelve stars . . . All glorious is the king's daughter as she enters; her raiment is threaded with spun gold. Sing to the Lord a new song, for he has done wondrous deeds."

Blessed is she, beyond all women upon earth. How blessed? For she was the first among us, the first woman to be so enobled, so honored, so magnified that she was taken up into heaven, into the new levels of existence, with a body. She was, in short, the first to have developed her consciousness and being so far as to have a new and everlasting personality, with a continuing etheric body, just like her son. The body, with all its desires, energies, structures, becomes so transformed by her selfless love of God, that it takes new shape. Oh, Mary, my words are poor. The poets sing of you, the prophets know you are the joy of Israel, as they say, and the glory of Jerusalem. Oh, Mother of mine, speak to me. Oh, Daughter of mine, renew me, for I am a woman like any other. I am a fallen woman like Eve, and a risen woman, like yourself, but, unlike you, I have not yet left this plane of existence, and I know, full well, that I shall be born again and again before I can be so transformed as to live at the levels of being where you now dwell. Speak to me, Mary, Queen of Heaven and Earth, speak to me and tell me what it is that the Holy Spirit wants of me!

"Pray" says Mary. "Pray. Fall on your knees and pray. For the stars that crown my head have their origin in the moon below, and in the earth below. Feel your feet and knees upon the earth, and pray."

I shall pray, Mary, I shall pray. I shall hold your Rosary close to my heart and pray. Hail, Mary, Mother of God. Hail Mary, Hail Mary.

"Hail Guinevere," says Mary. "And hail the Daughter of Guinevere. Guinevere loved. She loved two men, totally, fully. And hail Daughter of Guinevere, who has loved totally, fully!"

I was startled at these words from Mary. Could they really be from her, Mother of God? Or was I deceived by a Devil? But then, why not? Did not Mary love two, God the Father and the Son? And did she not, at last, become bride of the Paschal lamb? Was she not the bride of God the Father, and mystical bride, too, of God, the Son? It was true, a profound, spiritual-physical union. Why then, would she turn away from the love of my mother, Guinevere? Why then? Guinevere, my mother, also loved two men, and Mary respected it. She hails that love, rejected and blasphemed in the world, just as her own love was rejected and blasphemed.

"Love of God is all," says Mary, Mother of God. Love of God as he comes, as one and as many, as a Unity, or a divine Trinity of father-son-holy spirit. Thus does the assumption mean the raising of substance, of earth, of sensation, to the level of the divine. This is a forerunner of a new earth, a new body, spiritualized, sanctified, made holy by its devotion to God. The fall shall be over, and paradise regained. This Mary promises. And what does that Spirit want and say, Mary? What does it say?

"It has spoken, Daughter of Guinevere. It has spoken. It speaks through me and through you."

But what does it say?

"It speaks of a three, of a trinity, of a human-divine union. God, the Mother, God the Daughter, and God, the Holy Soul, uniting with the Trinity of Father-Son-Spirit. It has said that, Daughter of Guinevere. What more, Daughter, what more?"

Speak to me, Mary. Let your words come to me. Let your spirit mingle with my own. Let us unite, you and I, so that I know, indeed, what it means for Mother and Daughter to be One, just as Father and Son are. Let our word-prayers mingle and create a word which will rise up to heaven. Let the smokey, etheric, fire-watered earth rise up in the subtle-bodied spirit of the word which will reach the most high.

"It has so reached, Daughter of Guinevere. It has so reached. Speak not to me of union, but think of your mother, long since dead, risen up. Unite with her."

And now I see my mother, red-haired and beautiful, a Mary herself: both nun and lover, lover of two men and two God-men at that. Arthur, of the sword and Lancelot of the lance. Just as Jesus, the son, was pierced by a lance, and a sword went through the soul of Mary, just such a Mary was Guinevere, Queen. Guinevere, herself, pierced and lanced, like you, Mary.

I think of my mother and I love her, embrace her. And I see Mary embracing us both. For it is Mary, herself, who brings the Holy Spirit, through her Holy Soul, which unites Mother and Daughter, Guinevere and myself. It is that most pious, most high woman creature who first rose. She it was, that possessor of the feminine mysteries, energies, emotional-substantial-soul substances who rose up and joined with God. And my mother, a great woman not to be despised, was also a servant of that Grail, that mysterious container and vessel where spirit-soul-body are united. Hail Guinevere and Hail Mary!

After this vision of my mother, a day or two passed, and I was not satisfied with my conversation with Mary, the Queen. It had seemed insubstantial to me. And what a thing to feel, that a prayer, a dialogue, a meditation upon the glorious mystery of the Assumption should be "insubstantial!" What was worse, I felt a deep falling away into a pit of despair, for there came unto me a dark spirit of judgment. I experienced a sense of being blamed by others, of being attacked and judged, when they were not doing so. I felt terrible, but made matters much worse by brutally defending myself against this non-attack and thus attacked viciously in return. I thought of the "father-son" dream I had had some time before. I remembered the experience of seeing a father stand by as his son and other sons were in a circle with brutal, mechanical men who were systematically beating the children. And I wondered, was that brutal beating, that stupid attack, non-defense just what I was doing, or involved in? And I concluded it was so. And then, I thought, why do I have such a dark experience just now, when I am in the midst of the meditation upon the Blessed Virgin Mary's Assumption, and reflecting upon the flow of Holy Spirit between her and myself? Could it be that the Holy Spirit is itself so brutal, so inhuman and uncaring? Could it be?

Oh, Mary, I asked, can it be? Is it the Holy Spirit who is such a severe and implacable judge? It is the Holy Spirit which beats us so? Is the mechanical attack-defense merely an ancient tribal brutality, or is it from the Spirit itself? And why does this come just now? Oh, Mary, Mother of God! Mary, you who have seen terribly hard and hurtful judgments, from oneself to oneself as the worst, tell me, help me, I pray you!

"Pray" said Mary. "Pray for your immortal soul. It is the immortal soul who is tried, pushed, molded, judged. That is the one who is hardened, and made into a diamond. And yes, it is the spirit of God which comes in such a way. It is hard and penetrating and deep and, sometimes, even vicious. But it is vicious if we can only receive it mechanically, without love, without care. And oh, Daughter of Guinevere, the greatest sin is lack of love, and the greatest lack of love is lack of self-love. For God loves you, adores you, worships you, just as you do him. Are you not a mother who adores and worships her children? So is God. Are you not a daughter who adores and worships her mother, and even, me, her spiritual mother? So does God. So, love yourself, above all, for the divine is in you. Love yourself."

"But Mary," I said, "whence comes that hardness, that judgment, that blaming, is it from God?"

"I have already said yea to that, Daughter of Guinevere. I have said yea."

"But then you ask us to love ourselves when the spirit of God blames, is hard, is unloving, too."

"Yes."

"You ask us, then, to be more loving than God?"

"Yes. Are you not more loving to your children than they are to you? Do you not expect it? Are you not more loving to your parents than they are to you? Do you not expect it? That is the demand, the demand you make of yourself. Then, love yourself too. Even when God, as parent and child, does not."

"What a thought, Mary, to be more loving than God. That is blasphemy."

"Yes. But so I was, and was elevated."

So, Mary says that she was more loving than God, and was thus elevated. Is it true? Perhaps so. For she loved when God the Father abandoned His Son. She loved when God the Son abandoned the Father. She loved when both of them abandoned her. She loved, and did not cry out like the Son. She loved and made no wager with the Devil, like the Father. She loved more than either. It is true. And even more true is it that she did not become puffed up with this love.

She did not brag about it, proclaim it, even state it. It was simply so. So, Mary, the mere human, the very real girl from Israel, was elevated. Because she loved more, even, than God, she was elevated. Thus does she mediate in Heaven, thus does she stand between the Hard Spirit who judges and us. Yes, Mary, I see that you have loved more than any other mortal that has existed, and therefore, were elevated. Then, help me, Mary, help me to stand the friction between the great loving spirit of God, and the great judging spirit of God. Mediate for me, help me to love God more than myself, and love myself even when God does not! Help me, Mother of God!

"I shall help."

And with these words, I bowed before the Queen of Heaven who had passed beyond us all. I touched the hem of her skirt in pious appreciation and in sighing recognition of my need for her intercession. I now understand that even God-men-women and God-children need the help of Mary, and that the band of the faithful are right in asking for her intercession. Once again, Hail Mary! Mother of God. Intercede for us!

And now, the fifth glorious mystery.

Our Father . . . Hail Mary . . . Glory be.

The Fifth Glorious Mystery: The Coronation

"Who is this that comes forth like the dawn, as beautiful as the moon, as resplendent as the sun?. . . Like the rainbow appearing in the cloudy sky; like the blossoms on the branches in springtime . . . I am the mother of fair love, of fear, and of knowledge, and of holy hope . . . In me is all grace of the way and of truth, in me is all hope of life and of virtue. Come to me, all you that yearn for me, and be filled with my fruits. You will remember me as sweeter than honey, better to have than the honeycomb . . . So now, O Children, listen to me; instruction and wisdom do not reject! Happy are those who keep my ways, watching daily at my gates. For he who finds me finds life and wins favor from the Lord . . . Hail, O Queen of Mercy, protect us from the enemy, and receive us at the hour of death."

As I began meditating upon this final glorious mystery, there came into my hands—by chance or by the movement of the Holy Spirit I do not know—a little brochure by a lady who thought that the great image of your Coronation, Mary, the marvelous picture in Revelation of the woman clothed with the sun, the moon under her feet, and the twelve stars of a crown upon her head—all that represented a person totally awakened, totally enlightened. The twelve stars of the crown, she said, were representative of twelve important body-centers, all to be awakened in man. You, Mary, with all twelve centers awakened, were the perfect type-pattern of enlightened and "risen" woman, just as Jesus was the type-pattern for enlightened and "risen" man. An audacious idea, I thought, but one that ancients had known and believed, the lady said. She said that these centers were the true origin and mystery, even, Blessed Mary, of your Rosary. Each center is like a rose, just as the orientals think of the centers as lotus blossoms.

There is a center each in the feet, in the knees, and in the hands. These star-centers-blossoms have many meanings, but they open and bloom when the person "walks" in the way of God, when he spends much time "kneeling" in prayer and meditation, when his hands are at the service of others. The lady speaks next of a spine center, suffused with a red color, which aids in the purification and transmutation of the energies of the body. I wonder if she means by that the sexual energies. She then speaks of the solar plexus, green when awakened, which stimulates the life processes. For me, with my only-too-well-known experience of Sister of the Belly, I think that would mean what I experienced as Desire, desire for life and vitality, perhaps. The rose-center of the heart is golden and blooms, she says, when one truly loves others. That I understand very well.

The next center, at the throat, blue in radiation, is a center for speech, just as Grandson of the Knight discovered. But for him, of course, that was far more for creative speech, with his Muses. This lady speaks only of speaking no unkind and destructive words. Finally, she tells of the centers of the head, of one as image-building and the other wherein the power of the will is ever the servant of the spirit. These violet radiations, changing to gold, must be what I have known as Athene and Zeus, an image-center on the one hand, and the "servant of the spirit" must surely be your very own center, Mary, the highest one of all.

That is what the lady speaks of, Mary. She speaks of all these centers as stars in your crown of Coronation. She speaks of this rosary of flowers gradually being made alight in stages of initiation. From feet to knees, the centers initiated by Earth. From knees to generative organs is an initiation by Water. From generative organs to heart is an initiation by Fire, and from heart to the crown of the head, is an initiation by Air. When all twelve centers are alight, are awakened and informed, then the disciple is arrayed in the Golden Wedding Garment, just as Revelation proclaims, and the person is ready to meet the Bridegroom, God. Thus is the Marriage Feast celebrated, and the person then passes, she says, into the mystic rite of Immaculate Conception.

All this she says, Mary. And I am inclined to think that perhaps she is right. For is not that phrase that the woman is "clothed with the sun" a picture of a person fully illuminated, fully conscious and aware in every type of experience of sensation, feeling, thinking and intuition? And that must have been how you were, Mary. It also feels right that the Rosary, your meditation, should have such an origin. For is it not our prayer that we shall be enlightened, saved, transformed, and like you, ready to receive the spirit of God? I think so. Do you?

You nod. It is so. The woman understands you. Not in every detail, perhaps, for who knows how many centers there are, or blossoms? There may, indeed, be twelve, or seven or more. But of types and qualities of consciousness, of kinds of love and devotion, there are several, and they exist in us. And you, Virgin, are the highest. I see you, Blessed Mother, there with your feet upon the moon and bathed in sunlight, I see you. And I get a glimpse of what it all means, not only as the lady wrote, which seems true, but also as a sensing, a feeling, an intuition. You are the image of my Self, my higher Self, you show me the way. You are bathed in that marvelous sunlight of consciousness of God the Father, the Spirit which is above you and infuses you. That light from God comes in you, awakens you, fills you, so that you are made yourself, with your etheric flesh, into a heavenly garment, a wedding vehicle for the Most High. All your lights are opened. But you also stand upon your Sister, the Moon, that dark low center of magic of the feminine, too, of what I know as Witch, as Hecate. There, too, you stand; crowned with the sun of consciousness and light, standing upon the darkened light of the moon. Oh, Mary, greater Self, greatest one, I see that you are most intimately a part of me, my own uniqueness, but also more than me, the true Mary who has lived historically, is worshipped and adored and appealed to by others, and apart from me. You are, indeed, a mixture of me and not me. Mary, you are the living future of me, Daughter of Guinevere! The words escape me.

But let me listen to the song: You speak as "the mother of fair love, of fear and of knowledge, and of holy hope." Love, yes. Your love is so endless and boundless, we all know it. Fear, yes, you have taught me, in a secret way, to fear God, to fear the brutal power of the Holy Spirit when it comes in its uncaring way, yet caring, for it wants to make us shine like diamonds, like the sun, like you, Blessed Virgin. Knowledge, yes, for you, Mary, are like Sophia, you are Wisdom itself, for you look to and receive the most High. As the nun who loved you, worshipped you, adored you, served you, said: you embrace poverty: openness to the Spirit of God. You embrace chastity: aliveness to the love from God. You embrace obedience: attentiveness to God's Spirit. And this openness of poverty, aliveness of chastity, obedience of attentiveness you extend to God as he comes from within and from without, from yourself and from man. Oh, Mary, Hail, full of Grace!

Mary, I see you. The Spirit of God comes down, it comes to you, as showing us the way. "In me is all grace of the way and of truth, in me is all hope of life and of virtue." You are the way for the feminine, just as your son was the way for the masculine. Together, you fill the cross of our divinity-humanity, Mary, you and your son. I adore you.

As I looked at this great image of Mary, I realized Hope. I realized that hope is only for us mortals, not for Gods or angels, for they need it not. They, already fully saved, already fully on another level of existence, a heaven for us, do not need hope. But Mary, we need it, for we are mortal, and like you, have despaired, and yearned, and failed. Hope, too. I have hope, that I, too, shall have all my lights opened by God, that I shall have the kind of love and consciousness that will seem as "perfect"; as perfectly open, alive, and attentive, as whole in poverty, chastity, and obedience to the Sun, as I stand upon the moon. I hope that I, too, will be "enlightened" and will be ready thereby, for the Immaculate Conception, the transcending of this plane and the assumption into heaven, where new levels of being will be opened to me. I have hope, Mary, and I have trust. I trust that there will indeed be a time when there is a "new earth," where all mankind will be as "enlightened," when we will all be ready for the wedding garment, for the Immaculate Conception. I know that there will be a tent of all of us, our left arms held up in a collective unity, making us part of the whole where God and man dwell together, and where our right arms are for the connection with each other. I see this, Mary, I see this. I see that what for us, individually, is a realization of our totally highest personality, our total uniqueness, our own Mary, within, is, for God, an incarnation into woman.

I, Daughter of Guinevere, am one who suffered, has seen the coronation of Mary. I have seen, thereby, the divinization of the feminine. I have seen also the light coming from above, and have seen the divinization of man. Come, therefore, Grandson of the Knight, come to me and be with me, for I have seen that which you have seen. Come and be my amore, my spouse, my Jesus, and I shall be your Sophia, your wisdom, your love, your Mary. Let us mingle our spirit-souls and become as One!

I have seen your magical cones: the one below is the hat of the moon, of the dark-feminine-witch, facing down into depths. And the one above is the tent of God, where He dwells with man. Your abstraction, my concreteness; your maleness, my femaleness. Let us love!

VOLUME TWO

PART III
The Group

Grandson of Knight and Daughter of Guinevere

I have heard your story, Daughter of Guinevere, and I am here to offer you a proposal—not of marriage, I hasten to say, since, as you know, I am already married in the world. I offer, rather, a marriage within, a relationship of souls, in which we two could unite, could find our wholeness and happiness without violating any of our other unions and commitments. My proposal, in short, is that we pursue a joint quest. We have started from very different places, it is true, but we have found ourselves on similar paths. I began with the problem of lust and love, a conflict between the One and the Many. I was led, by the Magician, into history, into myth, into religion, and arrived at last, from One and Many, at Pairs, and pairs of centers within my own being. And you, Daughter of Guinevere, as a daughter of your mother (just as I was son and grandson of knights), began with the problem of the Pair. You tried to reconcile the failure of love, heal the lack of union, overcome the frustration of desire, the pain of duality. And you, too, came to the awareness of the centers of love and consciousness within yourself. So, in trying to understand and heal the problems of love and the passions of the soul, we have both come to the consciousness of the centers within the oneness of the human personality.

I think, therefore, that we might now be able to help each other find a way of union and understanding which would take us beyond our lonely quest, our private questionings and searchings. In short, I think that we two, together, could add a new dimension of consciousness, through a mutual process, a joint quest. I am eager to know what you think about it.

You smile and nod, warmly, shyly, yet openly. Yet you say nothing. That is all right, because I need to say something more to you. I am full of words: I need to say more because I am under pressure. You must know that what I offer is not just a generosity of spirit on my part, or even a recognition of the beauty and worth of a true equality and mutuality. In truth, I am in need. Despite ending my tale on the note of a vision of the Ascent of Man, the humanization of God and divinization of man, despite these "happy-ever-after" statements, I am despondent. Not that what I said was a lie or meant to deceive in any way; all that I said was true. It is, rather, that all my fine conclusions and lovely experiences are always "the last but one." Each realization, each fulfillment, does not seem to last very long. Each height of awareness, understanding, increase of love and consciousness is soon followed by despair, by a loss of vision, by a realization of failure. Somehow, all my fine reachings up into the heaven of the spirit result in a fall, a knowledge of my failure in the lower centers. I am, I suppose, a visionary, a dweller in the upper centers, but my realizations in the flesh, in the concreteness of life, in the fulfillment of my fine visions seem to be flawed with error, failure of nerve . . . Enough. Suffice it to say that I need human help from a person such as yourself. I am in the strange position of a man who can speak to Gods, address people in history and literature, can have ready access to both imagination and myth, roam freely and effectively in all those realms, yet cannot retain what he has learned. He forgets, loses, finds evanescent all that he has learned and achieved. He discovers himself, once again, in an abyss of doubt, sadness, self-recrimination and illusion. Such a one am I, such a Knight am I.

"Such a Knight," I say. Interesting. No Hero, I; I have already acknowledged that. But, to have lost that certain something, that "Chosenness," perhaps, that both my Father and Grandfather, Knights #1 and #2 experienced—that is sad. But then, Daughter of Guinevere, you, too, are not the great success as lover and attractor of Knights that your mother was!. . . Forgive me. In my own falling down from the heights of my fathers, I have also brought you down, and unjustly. Forgive me. Your quest, like mine, has been an inner one, and rather different from that of your mother, great woman that she was. It is certain that you, too, are great, fair lady. I hope that I have not fallen so low from the high point of my grandfather that I can no longer be considerate of women, find it necessary to waspishly snipe at them.

You nod your forgiveness. But still you say nothing. All right, then, Guinevere II. I take your non-answer as assent, which you have already given with your nod. We shall begin. Let me present where I am. In so doing, I continue in the tradition of my grandfather, but now I will present my need, not my experience with Gods and demons! I can do this best, I think, with a dream. You, too, have listened to and tried to understand your dreams, Guinevere II, so I hope that you will be of help to me in it. Hear my dream, coming, as it did, in the mood of despair that I was in:

I am seated in my "house," which is not my actual house. It is large and spacious, rather in an old Spanish style. Some others are with me in a dining hall and I am at the head of a large oak table which is very attractive and pleasant. I am aware that a number of people belonging to a group of which I was once a member are also present, but none is recognizable. This group was of people on a common spiritual quest, but the leaders thereof proved to be mean and despicable to me, so I resigned. In the dream I am uncomfortable in their presence but glad that one of the leaders, my old teacher—he who had been closest to me and a dear friend—is not there. No sooner do I feel this relief, than I see him there. He smiles at me and looks well and robust. He seems not to understand at all that he has hurt me very badly, despite all that I told him at the time, and that I do not wish to be in his presence. He shakes my hand, to which I feebly assent, because of passivity alone. I hastily beat a retreat into a neighboring room where I see a number of men at cards. I have no antipathy toward the game, but I am also unwilling to remain there, so I return. My old teacher is still there, but now others are dancing in the tile-floored living room. I see that at one place there is a break in the tile, the earth underneath showing at the center. A lone flower grows there. I am concerned lest the people trip or fall into the broken part and am about to say something about it when an aunt, a sister of my mother's, greets me warmly. I am pleased to see her—a fine, warm, modest woman, somewhat naive, but good natured. She tells me she has earth also in her living room, with flowers, but that she has it off to one side, protected by brick borders, and heavily cultivated. The soft, rich earth is only lit by the sun at a low, indirect angle, which does not dry it out. The dark richness of the earth is a very good thing. I agree, but am also concerned as to what to do about the old teacher. Should I ask him to leave, ignore him, or what? I awaken with this problem, in the sad mood which I have already described. I am aware that the old teacher was an unjust judge, a man who put presumed collective values above both his care for me, or his value of individuality, aware that this hurt was still haunting my consciousness, my living room. End of dream.

I understand some of the significance of this dream, Guinevere II. My own psyche is very much "Spanish" in that it comprises Spanish, European, North African, Moorish, Jewish, Christian, Arabic, Gypsy elements. Was this not apparent in my encounters with Don Juan and his compatriots, with Bluebeard, and the others? Sure enough, there is more to my psyche than that, but even Jacob and Jesus are represented in the Spanish foundation. So, then, my psyche is presented, and in a complimentary fashion at that, as solid, beautiful, and well built. I am in communion with others, at the head of my table. It is well. But the problem is then preserved of the persistence of my former friends and fellow searchers. I almost said "Knights," as were my father and grandfather. They lacked knightly virtue, in my experience, but they were, after all, fellow seekers for a long time. But our communion is long since over, and still they remain. Why? Is it because I am still hurt and annoyed? Is it because I am still possessed by anger, by desires for revenge, by jealousy, by frustration that my cause is not recognized? I think that all of these are true. I cannot seem to free myself from those dark feelings. Perhaps these feelings themselves sit with me at table, prevent my proper functioning at the lower belly centers, make me uncomfortable. But then, I am glad that the best and worst of them is not there. Best because he was the kindest and closest to me at one time, worst because as my friend he hurt me most deeply by presuming to judge me. But there he appears all the same: strong, robust, in better condition than ever. And he smiles, unconscious. Just as unconscious as he was when I tried to explain to him. I am helpless before him, I even allow my hand to be shaken. Very bad. And what is this, Guinevere II? Is this the outer experience that cannot be forgotten? Or is this an inner deceitful judge, unconscious, from whom I cannot escape? Both are true, of course. But I am rendered impotent thereby.

I run away to the room where men are merely collective in their game-playing. That must be the routine, unrelated competition among men: gain and loss, winner and loser. I do not mind it, but I really do not want to live that kind of masculine life either. So I am neither at home with the old teacher, nor with collective man. Sad for me. And even in my own house!

But now, my aunt comes. That fine lady, modest as the group and the old teacher had been arrogant, gentle and warm as some of them had been hard and stupidly cold, she comes. I am glad to see her. Feminine warmth is naturally preferable to the unhappiness of masculine collective struggle and judgment.

My aunt speaks to me about the other problem revealing itself, the crack in the floor with the earth showing, the flower growing. I realize that such a flaw, such an openness, can take away from the pleasure of those who share life and joys with me. Perhaps the flaw is my broken state itself, where my depression and unhappiness, my underneath failure show. But there, too, is revealed a flower, my gentleness, weakness, passivity, perhaps . . . You nod, Guinevere II, as if you understand and agree with my interpretation. And my aunt, too, is helpful, advises that I make a separate garden, and cultivate that dark soil, for flowers perhaps, and not have too much sun on it. "Indirect" light, she says. Now I laugh, for is she not like you, Daughter of Guinevere? Did you not learn about the "Indirect" from the Goddess Hecate, Queen of Witches? I think so. So, my kind and warm-hearted aunt instructs me in the "Indirect" also. Keep my earth in a corner, she says, not so exposed, but not hidden either. I understand that I must cultivate the earth of the lower centers. I must take good care to use earth and water, centers of Magician and Belly, and so, perhaps, make a garden bloom within my house. And that, after all, is very much in the Spanish tradition!

But Guinevere II, tell me, what do you think I can do about the old teacher? He is like the judging God of the Bible. He has a hard eye, which you have experienced as Hera. He, it seems to me, is an old image of authority, one that at one time combined the religious fervor of my grandfather with the loving warmth of my father, both Knights. He did have this, but he is, long since, no authority. How can I overcome that old authority? Shall I try to throw him out? Must I overcome "the fathers," the old representatives? Are they now just Pharisees, as you saw in your Rosary meditations? What do you think, Guinevere II?

"I think very little, Knight III. I feel. I feel sad for you. I feel just as despairing as you about that man. I feel just as warm and friendly toward your aunt. I would gladly take her place in your dream. I would gladly be your partner in this new quest for union. For union, of course, has always been my aim. Frustration has always been my fate, as well. Even I, I must say, have not been fully satisfied with my meditations, my path. For I, too, have been alone. I, also, have wanted a partner, a truly equal mate-of-the-quest who could help me on my path. True enough, I have had the help of Eros, and later on I have been in the land of Gods and Goddesses just as you have. I am deeply grateful for what I have learned and experienced, but I have always been aware of my need for ordinary human companionship. Indeed, perhaps you noticed that I felt myself with you many times. Even in my dream of the "amore" it was you that I thought of. Knight III, even though you have not known it, I have considered you my mystical brother, and I am only too happy to share a search with you."

"Agreed, Daughter of Guinevere! We are fully in concordance. Pardon my impetuousness, but I need to know from you, right now, what you think—or feel, if you prefer—about the old teacher? What shall I do? Try to get rid of him? Confront him? Inside or out?

"You are indeed impetuous, Knight III. Perhaps, as you say, your Belly regions are more assertive, less differentiated than my own. I know that you feel the Buddha therein. I know that you have been deeply aware of the negation of desire. But perhaps such a heavy negation has led to an equally strong but unaccepted affirmation. Thus your impetuousness . . . But what do I think, you ask. What do I think? That is hard for me. Let me wait a moment and reflect. All that you have said is correct, I think. At least, I should say, it makes sense to me. With such a judge as yours, with Hera, I confronted. I spoke to her and tried to understand. I finally did understand her nature as monogamous, as solitary, and in solitude. I accepted her, and she me, so I am not so troubled. But what you should do, I do not know. Hera is eternal after all, but your old teacher is very mortal, I think. You have long since outgrown him, I also think. If he were in your house and you did not want him there, would you not simply ask him to leave?"

"Yes, I have thought of that, too, Guinevere II. But I have been afraid if I ask him to leave, that he will simply come back again through another door."

"I see . . . Well, then. I think that we should experiment. Perhaps you can let me speak to him. I have no such strong animus against him as you do, nor as much attachment from old love. Indeed, I feel more like your aunt in this, more eager to cultivate a new garden! But, I can see that we cannot get on to the new garden until we settle an old question. Would he listen to me?"

"I think so, Guinevere II. I am willing for you to try. Come into my psyche and see me. That is, indeed, indirect, is it not?"

"How do you do, old teacher. I am Guinevere II, friend of Knight III. He has told me the story of his relationship with you and your group. He is quite uncomfortable at having you in his house. He cannot move, grow further, and is hounded by feelings of anger, hurt, injustice, desire for revenge and jealousy. He also feels impotent in the face of all these, and would be glad if you would stop hounding him, if you would even leave his house altogether and not bother him any more."

"I would be glad to do so. I do not remain here because I wish it. I, too, am constrained by this bondage. I, too, cannot move on. I, too, am rendered impotent by the unsettled questions."

"But in his dream, Old Teacher, you seem robust and happy."

"Yes, it seemed so in his dream. Just as he seems robust and happy to other people. Yet the crack in his floor is there, is it not? And, despite his great oak table, despite his fine house, despite all these things, the crack remains. Well, there is such a flaw within me, as well, but it does not show in his dream."

"And what is this flaw, Old Teacher?"

"I will not say, Daughter of Guinevere. I will not. I understand full well what his aunt told him, that one keeps the privacy of one's earth, that one grows one's own garden in a place of not too much light. I understand that and, therefore, will not reveal my flaws to others."

"But you judge the Knight badly, do you not? You hound him, and that is, indeed, unjust, don't you think?"

"I do. And I would make peace with him, if I could. Hence my offering of my hand. I would make peace so that I, too, could go on. I am old. Not so old that I expect to die at once, but old enough to know that new levels of life await me. My stay on this earth is already grown somewhat wearisome and I look more to a life in another place. And so, I would make peace."

"Do you hear, Knight III? He says that he would make peace. Do you want it?"

"I do, of course. But is that meant to be a peace within myself, within the psyche where I make peace with my own old authority, or is that outside?"

"Oh, Grandson of the Knight, you irk me! You make such distinctions when they are not necessary at all! You have not had access to your concrete old teacher for a long time. No wonder you have difficulty with the lower centers! You seem unable to distinguish between the inner and outer sometimes!. . . I am sorry. I am afraid, Sir Knight, that I, too, can lose the charm that my mother had. You can be impetuous, of course, but I can lose my temper! If you fail in the lower centers with impetuousness, I fail with temper in the upper centers. But, no matter. The old authority who combined the religious fervor of your grandfather with the warmth of your father, who carried the courage and devotion of grandfather, with the humor and versatility of father, that old teacher is no longer yours. He is ready to retire. But he feels trapped by you, too! Are you ready?"

"I am. But what is this flaw of which he speaks?"

"My flaw, of course, Knight III, is my judgment and my anger. Did you not guess it? You always saw me as modest, as warm, as forgiving and human. Only later did you see me as very judgmental and full of wrath. Now you know. My flaws are in poor judgment and too quick an anger. Now you know. I have exposed myself to you."

"Old Teacher, I know this. I knew this in you when you judged me so harshly and wrongly, and I know this, now, in myself. So, in truth, Old Teacher, I can see you both without, as that actual man I knew, and within, as those parts of myself which are the same. And so, Old Teacher, I accept you in myself as often showing poor judgment and being too quick to grow angry. I accept that in myself and now I can let you go, if you wish, to change. Or to remain if you wish, for I am free. But you are no longer my authority, that we can both see."

"Knight II, that is just what was needed. Let me go, now, and be like the plant that your aunt spoke of. Let me live in a quiet place.

Let me die and go into the earth. Let the harsh rage and the judgmental nature descend from the heights of the third eye. Let that jealous, angry, wrathful, judgmental streak come down from the heights of authority. Let it—and me—die a little and descend into the earth of the lower centers. Let it be without too much light, just as your dream suggests. Goodbye, Knight III, peace be with you. I shall descend. I shall go into the earth. I shall be born anew in a new form. Goodbye."

"And so, to my astonishment, I, Knight III, begin my new adventure, together with my partner and friend and mystical sister, Guinevere II, and find that that which has hindered, bothered, bedeviled me, wants to be free of me, too, wants to descend and lose its old authority, wants to be born anew in the lower centers, where I, too, will need to work. And so, aunt and sister, women of gentle love, they help me. Daughter of Guinevere, thank you. I love you. You have already shown me a Hecate way, a witch-way, the way of the indirect. You have already aided me in my quest and I embrace you. Let that Eye-judge descend. I pray that this descent will be a genuine one and that I shall not awaken tomorrow to be disappointed and dismayed once again."

"But no, Knight III. It is the old teacher who descends. He, it is, who will die and be reborn. You need not. Dwell here, with me, oh Knight, in our diaphragmatic center. For here you and I will look up and down, to heaven and to hell, and we shall grow whole and strong. Knight III, I love you. Knight III, you are as Eros to me, you are Amore!"

"More than I deserve, Daughter of Guinevere, more than I can claim. But I will be your mystical brother and friend. I will aid you, as you aid me. We will work together, enabling the cone above to become a tent, and the cone below to become a hat for the magical effect of love. Amor Brujo. Love: Magician and Witch; Love: Spirit and Flesh; Love: Friendship and Marriage.

Knight III and Guinevere II, II

"It is now five days later and I am, once again, fallen into an abyss of depression. Guinevere II, the same thing has happened as I complained about some days ago. From an understanding and belief in our joint quest, I have fallen away and down. I am not certain why this is so. Is it because once again I have received a hurt to my pride? Is it because I am continuing to be troubled with my resolution of the One and the Many, and finding that there is no resolution at all? Or is it because I have eaten nothing for two days and am weak and depressed merely because of lack of sustenance?

"You look startled, Guinevere II, probably because I have not eaten. Yes, it is so. Having understood the fall of the old authority, his descent into the earth, I have thought to let off from eating and, thus, to see how it feels to be really hungry, to know what the belly center has to say when it is not fed. For, as I have said, I have suffered much from a lack of control or fulfillment of the belly center, of desire and its negation. I want to know if that old guilt-maker, that old finger-pointer who has claimed to descend into the lower centers, truly resides there. What better way, I thought, than to fast and find out? Perhaps I would find a regulation of desire different than before. But, in truth, I am merely weak and depressed . . . perhaps only because I am hungry, I do not know."

"You seem ashamed, Knight III. You speak openly, but you look ashamed, as if you are leaving something out, or are . . ."

"Yes, Guinevere II, it is true. I am ashamed because I have to struggle with something so ordinary, so small as appetite! I am ashamed to admit that greed is also one of my failings! Not only sexuality and love in excess—which has a certain heroism about it, to be sure—but simple gluttony. Now that is no proper problem for a hero, is it? But, then, I denied being a hero, didn't I? And there I am. You are right, Guinevere II."

"What good is there in being right, Knight III? I feel your sadness. Once again, I do not think, nor do I enjoy being 'right.' Rather, I feel the despair. I feel your never-ending search after 'more,' whether food for the flesh or food for the soul. I feel your despair at 'no solution.' I am sad for you."

"I thank you for your empathy, Guinevere II, but I do not want to burden you. Come, rather, and help me with my quest, as we agreed. Come and see if there really is a change in that belly center. Once again, I shall begin with a prayer.

"Oh, Belly Center, place where Buddha the negator of desire dwells, and where Sister of the Belly lives for my comrade and sister, Guinevere II, center of passion and desire and their negation, of need and quest and their frustration, Belly Center, I, Knight III, descend to you. I have starved myself for two days, I have purged myself of all. I have weakened myself so that I could see you clearly. I have aimed at finding out, indeed, whether the old authority, whom I served and bent to, has come to your place and is now really undergoing a change. I am here with Guinevere II, my friend and sister. She comes with care, love, and devotion; she is here with her Sister of the Heart. Belly Center, I pray you. Show your state to me.

"I see a cave, Guinevere II. It is a murky place. In this cave is a small boy. He sits with great dark eyes in a corner. I am reminded of the story of my father, Son of the Knight. Did he not begin his life in a cave, without knowing who his mother or father were? Is this such a boy? Is this the state of my father, or a memory of some sort? Who is this lad? Guinevere II, can you help me with him?"

"I can. I am with you. I feel myself drawn into your vision, and can see the boy. Just as I was able to speak to your old authority, I now feel that I can see your little boy."

"Yes, you say he is my little boy. As you say it, I think that you are right. It is the little boy within me, not my father, the Son of the Knight. But is he, in truth, the childlike part of myself, or the old authority, already died and reborn?. . . No matter, it is the same, I can almost hear you saying. Just as it was with the old authority—it did not matter whether he was 'within' me or 'without.' Enough that one attends to this child. But how? Speak to him, I imagine.

"Little boy! This lady, Guinevere II, and I, Knight III, are here to visit you. Who are you and why do you sit in this cave?"

"He only sits and looks, Knight III. He only sits and stares. Let me speak with him. Are you hungry, little boy? Are you thirsty? Are you lonely? You nod. Like me, sometimes, you nod, but do not speak. Speak through me, then, little boy. Speak through me and I, Guinevere II, shall be your medium, whereby you can tell Knight III what he wishes to know. I shall be your medium and his. In this I can serve him with my heart, and reach you too. Will you permit this? You barely look at me. With those big and sorrowful eyes, you look at me. I must try and read your mind, divine your thoughts. But I will need some sort of sign from you that I am doing it correctly. Will you . . . ah, you just winked, closed one eye. That is my sign. There, Knight III, is that not an answer for the hard One-Eye of God? Is that not a splendid response from the belly from this child? One eye responds to a question, yes or no, whether I am getting his message! No judgment, no reproach, just a one-eyed wink of support or negation! How is that?"

"That, Guinevere II, would be splendid, indeed, if it works. Try him."

"All right . . . I hear him saying—without words, of course—that he has been sitting here in this cave for many, many years. Generations even. He is not, in truth, your father, Son of the Knight, or his image, nor is he anyone else, he is only himself. But he is also more than himself, for he is 'hunger.' He is 'hunger' for food, for sustenance of every kind. As such he is not only your child, Knight III, but also every child. He is that in every person that longs and does not find, that hungers and is not fed. He is all beginnings, and all frustrations, he is also endings. For endings occur when hungers remain unfed. They die a little and end in the cave of the earth, sending up clouds of pain, hurt, shame, thunderclouds of anger, revenge and frustration, rains of tears; in short, bad spirits. And it is that which you felt in your depression: bad spirits. These bad spirits come from this cave. All those frustrations send up their clouds."

"But what of the little boy himself, Guinevere II? He sits there, a living representative of unfulfilled hungers. What does he want?"

"He wants only to be recognized . . . He blinks an eye right now, as I was uncertain if that was what he wanted, but it is true . . . But now, Knight III, I see you falling again into despair. Oh, my amore, I see you sink into the abyss of depression. Have these fumes reached you and made you ill or faint? Ah, now I see you falling into the cave. I see you there with that little boy. No, I see you as blending with him, becoming him. I can hardly tell one from the other. You do not speak, you can not speak. You are this child of hunger, you are this child of frustration, you are this Child of the Belly. You have known Buddha in the belly, now you know the Child. Just as I have known the Sister, now you experience the Child . . . But I, too, grow faint. I, too, find myself weakening, failing. I, who have been with the Heart, with caring, find myself falling . . ."

"They are in the Belly Center. We, Knight III, Guinevere II and myself, the Child, are here. And now, when they are dissolved in my medium, I, too, can speak. But . . . slowly . . . Will you, now, who read this, will you wink your eye? Will you not acknowledge your place of hunger? Will you not descend into your own belly and find the Child therein? Then listen.

"A cave, plain. Hungers, plain. Sorrows, plain. Sleep therein. Take in a dream . . .

"They sleep, those two. And they dream. He dreams of food, for he is hungry. He dreams of potatoes, swimming in butter. Of lobster, swimming in butter. Of corn, swimming in butter. Of bread, swimming in butter. He hungers for butter, the fat, the denied part, that which is rich and luscious. He dreams, too, of the butter of life. Of the riches of fame, of fortune, of recognition.

"And she dreams. She dreams of love without pain. She dreams of a peaceful family. She dreams of loving connections and quiet joy. No pain to self or others. Thus they both dream.

"And I, the Child? I, the Child of Hunger? I no longer dream, for I can let them dream. I sit, and stare. I know the dreams, the pains, the longings. I sit and feel them, forever. Buddha sat here. He sat and denied the longings. He sat and denied the fulfillment. Not as a nay-saying, but as an acceptance of the lack. He, too, longed for the simple life, as Guinevere II, and for the fulfillment, as Knight III. But he said nothing, and denied the fulfillment. And I sit here, too. Will you join me?"

"But who is there to join? Who is there who is not Knight III, Guinevere II, or Child?. . . It is I, the Center itself. The Center speaks, endlessly. The Center speaks. A great Circle. With a hunger therein. Buddha beneath the Tree. The Child in the Cave. The Sister in pain of longing and frustration. All these in one circle: desire and negation; longing and frustration; beginnings and abortions. But there is fulfillment in the cave as well. Dream on, Knight III and Guinevere II, for there, too, is fulfillment. Let there be prayer for fulfillment, for that is what the Sister of the Belly could accept. Let there be meditation for fulfillment, for that is what Buddha could accept. Let there be hope for fulfillment, for that is what the Knight can accept. And let there be a waiting in prayer, in meditation, in hope, but also acceptance of lack of fulfillment, for that is what Buddha could accept, Sister could accept, and Child could accept. Let the Belly live for Being, which all can accept. So speaks the Center, itself."

"Now I, Knight III, will speak again. For I was awakened from my slumber, from my dreams. There came, from without, from places other than my own belly and my own desires, a statement of a nun, a letter to God from a religious lady which was so beautiful, so moving, that all my own cares and wants seemed trivial. There came, too, a statement from another lady, an alive, seeking, searching woman who was true to her life and, in her unfulfilled longings, she discovered that she wanted too much from others. She had to find some things in herself. And so, I, Knight III, in reflecting upon myself, upon my hungers and desires, have been fed in living communication from without: A loving Nun, full of heart, searching; a loving woman full of belly, searching. They search and feed me with their search. They want and give and I am fed thereby. Guinevere II, are you with me?"

"I, too, am fed thereby, though I am jealous. I want you alone, thus jealous. But when they can give when I cannot, why should I stay with jealousy? I, too, am happy."

"Let us, then, be joyful. This the nun's God and the lady's hunger showed me. Let us be glad of the hunger, and its fulfillment. The nun's God said that all frustrations and pains were preparations, that there was meaning. So rejoice!"

"I, too, Guinevere, Daughter of a suffering Queen, I, too, will accept and rejoice. In this acceptance, I will embrace the Buddha in you."

"And I will rejoice, I, the Child of the Belly. For a child must enjoy and rejoice, else he is not child, is it not so?"

And so the circle of the belly, filled with Knight and Guinevere, with Belly and Buddha, and above all with Child, rejoices!

"But the rejoicing is short-lived. I, Daughter of Guinevere, also feel a falling away, a loss, a pernicious destruction of self. Grandson of the Knight, like you, I felt a wholeness, a rejoicing, an acceptance of the Center of Belly, with Buddha, but rejoicing was short-lived. Like you, I fell again. This time it was only last evening. Last evening I slept hardly at all. Rather I was filled with jealousy, with fantasies of you with other women, and I was pained—in the belly. My heart understood. My heart with its feeling and compassion was neither jealous nor possessive, not hurt by your need for others, for the many. Indeed, my heart rejoiced that someone else, other than myself, came to you and could give you where I could not—whether nun or seeking lady. But I reckoned without my own Sister of Belly. She did not let me sleep. She was frustrated, in pain, did not rejoice. And so, I spent the night in my old conflict, my old awareness of the disparity between Belly and Heart. The two warring sisters, whom I had thought long ago to have made peace, continued to battle during the night.

"Oh, Grandson of the Knight, help me, please. I have gladly accompanied you in your despair and need. Can you help me with mine?"

"Yes, Guinevere II, I can, gladly. For I have secretly felt that your help was too one-sided, that the asymmetricality of our needs could not, should not, continue so long. And, I must say, I notice something new for me. Something is different: I am not guilty. In the past, when something I have done, something in my nature has caused pain to someone I love or care about, I have felt guilt. At those moments, I was unable to give care and love to them, since it was I who produced the pain. But now I feel differently. There is no guilt in me. It is true that my multiplicity, my receiving of love from others, has caused you pain. But you are my mystical sister and I love you. I have intended no pain, I feel no guilt. How, then, mystical sister, can I help you? How can I relieve, or make bearable, those painful clouds of jealousy, of possessiveness, of hurt?"

"It helps that you just listen, Knight III. It helps that you want to help. For I, too, am humiliated by my possessiveness, my narrowness, my smallness. But I must remember the bigness of Hera above, and I must remember the value of Sister of the Belly. And I must remember all of the Goddesses within me. Although my quest did not begin in such a way, I discovered these greatnesses—even the greatness of the greedy Sister of the Belly, and the jealous Hera. I can recover from my smallness, my fall into my own little child, who is weak, inadequate, insecure."

"You sound like me, Daughter of Guinevere, so quick to recover your larger self. For you, the larger self is in your heart, it seems, or in the Goddesses. But you also forget, I think, like me. You forget how small, how vulnerable, how destroyed you can become. Let me help you, if I can. Let me help you in such a way that you do not forget, that you can accept the smallness, not run away from the jealousy and possessiveness. Are these not the dark shadows of love? Just as my need for fame and superiority are the dark shadows of power? Are not love and power natural to men and women? It seems so to me. It depends, I suppose, on what one does with the love and power, that is what counts. It is there that we need to feel ashamed or worthwhile, not in our struggles with these. For, as the nun said to me, God has given us freedom, and that is the point of it!"

"You mention the nun, Knight III, and I am hurt. I know that my hurt is foolish. I know that . . . You see, I cannot even speak of these hurts."

"Guinevere II, I feel your pain once again. But now I feel a pain in my heart. My heart pains for your belly hurts. The tears well up within me. There is no rational answer, I know, else you would no longer feel those hurts and pains. Let me just stay here with you. Silently. Buddha sits and is free in the belly, to be sure. But he also has compassion, does he not? Let the Buddha in me, who knows all there is to know in both Belly and Heart, let him sit here in silence with you . . . I feel the pain in my belly now. I feel the shared pain. I feel myself in wordless union with you, Guinevere II. You and I, in joint painful quiet union. Accepting the pain, not running away."

"The pain lessens, Grandson of the Knight, it lessens and is gone. I know that there is a monogamy of each love, I know that there is a unique and perfect union at each level. I know these things. And I know that I will be slow to realize these things, make them real and concrete, manifest and true. And I accept my slowness.

"But Grandson of the Knight, there came to me, out of pain, a woman I had not known before. Unlike the nun who spoke to you, this lady came to me from within myself, or I think so. However, I do not think of her as a part of me. She could just as well be a ghost or previous incarnation of me. No matter. She came to me and said that her name was Maya. She is from India, though she had an English father. She was also a Yogini, in that she practiced Kundalini Yoga extensively. By quirk of fate, or the interpenetration of all events, she had heard about our struggle to understand and come to grips with the centers of love and consciousness within us, and she was very interested. Her own experience of gurus in India was such that it was difficult, almost impossible, for a woman to find a teacher who could help her on her spiritual quest without falling into old patterns of masculine domination. She had achieved a certain degree of enlightenment and serenity, however, by practicing meditation alone, and by trusting the lord Shiva, Himself, to guide her. Yet her loneliness in her spiritual state continued. She was happy enough in marriage, in family, in many departments of life, but she could not share her spiritual adventures. What attracted her to us was our joint quest, our mutual endeavor—for in that there would be no male domination—and particularly in an area which was her main interest as well—the centers of consciousness. She has come here to help us and share with us, if we so desire. She understands our stories, it seems, via something she calls the Akashic records. There is in the Etheric realm (which is a property of the Throat-Speech Center in our understanding), a record of what we have stated as our experience. And from our experience, she is most interested to gain information. Her way is Eastern and Oriental, although she has an English father and has been affected by the West very much. Because of this, she would like to know from us, share with us, if you are willing."

"I am willing, of course. I would, indeed, want to know more also. Will she join us here?"

"At the moment, she will stay by my side, as if she were a ghost being seen only by me. The reasons for that are not clear to me, but she prefers it that way. Perhaps she is still not fully trusting of men on spiritual quests, and must know you better. In any case, she is willing to speak to you, just as I spoke to your old teacher. But she reserves the direct connection just with me. Is that all right with you?"

"It is."

"Well, then, our pair is already becoming something of a group, is it not, Grandson of the Knight? As we discover the multiplicity of centers and the difficulties of reconciling them, then others seem to join us."

"Maybe so, Guinevere II. I am glad about the multiplicity, of course, though my wounds and disappointments from others make me doubt whether reconciliation or joint quests with more than two people really work out. Indeed, I am rather more friendly to the suspicion expressed by your friend, Maya, the Yogini. I do not blame her for not trusting me or any man. Indeed, I think that she is right. I am more inclined to trust women, myself. Let us be about the cultivation of our little garden, as it showed itself in my dream. Let us work on our own union, Guinevere II, and be grateful for the help of your friend, Maya. Let those who really want to join us do so, but I, for one, am satisfied right now, with our little pair. Well, that is something for me, is it not? To be satisfied with a pair, to be quite reconciled to a monogamy of a relationship! Perhaps the old teacher has truly descended into the belly! But, no matter, I am eager to hear what your friend Maya has to say."

Maya, the Yogini

"Oh, Knight, again I am attacked in the belly! Again I feel the pressure of pain and jealousy. Again I remember the pain of my love lost, my love gone off with another. It happened once, twice, thrice; it could happen again and again. And it is a living reality now. In truth, I do not have the stomach to be enlightened by Maya, the Yogini. Intellectual understanding does not sound good to me at this moment."

"Well, then, Daughter of Guinevere, perhaps your friend, Maya, can help you. If she knows so much of the centers, and of pain, of the destruction of jealousy and of possessiveness, perhaps she can aid you where I cannot."

"Yes. She says 'Do not weep, Daughter of Guinevere, do not weep. The tears of your eyes fall down on hard earth. The water of desire descends and softens the hard earth of everyday reality. It makes the structure of life muddy. I see that you must weep, it must soften. But do not weep so much, do not suffer. We are the playthings of the Gods, after all. They live in us, we suffer them, transform them, and are transformed by them. If you know this, if you know this in your belly, then the pain is less.' Thus does Maya speak."

"What she says seems right to me. But does she help your pain with her words, Daughter of Guinevere?"

"No, she does not. She sounds indeed like a female Buddha, accepting everything as it is. She is enlightened, no doubt, but her words do not help me. Maya, Maya, if you would be my friend, help me with your wisdom! Put your wisdom to use by reaching the marrow of my bones, the pain in belly, the reality of my life!"

"She says, 'Oh, Daughter of Guinevere, you ask much of me. You ask that I be magical, that I be like your own Hecate who can indirectly transform worlds. You ask that I be like Aphrodite Pandemos who can live all manner of loves in the world, in the one and many, with dark and light. You ask that I be like Sister of the Belly, who can be fully aware of all her needs and live in accordance with them. You ask that I be a Goddess. But I am no Goddess. I know only that a God and a Goddess dwell at each center, and that I continually watch the flow of the energy upward and downward. I am victim of these energies and also transform them. But I transform them by living them, by meditating upon them, by doing all those

things which you and Grandson of the Knight have also done. All I
can offer you is my comradeship. I can offer my care, what understanding I have, how these same energies, Gods and Goddesses, look to
an oriental psyche, but I can offer no more. The Goddess is very wild
in those lower centers, that we know very well. She softens only as
she reaches the heart."

"Tell me, then, Maya, tell me how you experience the Goddess at
those centers. Perhaps your knowledge can assuage my pain."

"Gladly, Daughter of Guinevere. At the Muladhara, the root support above the anus, where you have experienced Hecate-the-Witch
and Grandson of the Knight has experienced the Magician, we in
India know the Goddess as Dakini. Here the Shakti-Goddess, representative of the energy of the universe, is described as red and
red-eyed, striking terror into the unillumined. In her two right hands
she holds a spear and a staff surmounted with a human skull. In her
two left hands she holds a sacrificial sword and a drinking-cup filled
with wine. She is fierce of temper and shows fierce teeth. She crushes
her enemies. She is plump of body. Such a creature is our Goddess
in the Muladhara, Daughter of Guinevere! That center we know as
everyday reality, the taming of energies into the structures of life, of
family, of work, of institutions. This is the great Goddess energy that
we try to tame! But you know her in that center as magical, as a dark
creature, but of indirect effect. That is hinted at in our scriptures, but
I do not know that aspect of her very well, though I know what you
have discovered is true. But see how the energies of the Goddess look!
More like your Medusa, I think. And these energies: sex, hunger,
power, are red-eyed, are they not? They are wild and fierce. The
Goddess demands the sacrifice of man, that he mold his energies and
himself—thus her sacrificial spear. Also she shows us that we are
mortal and face death—the staff with skull. But she also shows her
spear—her fierce capacity to engage in competitive games and war,
in battle, as well as in her drinking-cup. For she can make us wild
with the spirit of nature, and also unconscious with it. Thus do we
need the taming of it in the battles of everyday life, the sacrifices to
her, and the endurance of a tamed elephant to survive. So, you see,
the Goddess is quite fierce in Muladhara.

"Nor is she much kinder in Svadhisthana, the 'proper place.' There,
in that watery place above the genitals, she is the Shakti-Goddess of
Rakini. She is described in that fierce and hungry belly-water region
as blue and of furious aspect. She has three red eyes and fierce teeth.
She holds in her hands a spear, a drum, a battle-axe and a lotus. From
one of her nostrils there flows a streak of blood. So, you see that here,
too, in the devouring, watery, fish-place, she is equally frightening.

She is still combative and furious: only a trace of change, the lotus and drum, appears.

"Finally, in Manipura, the 'plenitude of jewels' located in the navel, the Shakti-Goddess is Lakini. Now she is described as blue, having three faces with three eyes in each face, fierce and with protruding teeth. In her right hand she holds the thunderbolt and the weapon of fire, but in the left she makes gestures of dispelling fear and granting boons. She is fond of meat and her breast is ruddy with blood and fat which drop from her mouth. Perhaps in that fat and her enjoyment thereof, you recognize, Grandson of the Knight, your hunger after butter. In any case, you can see that she continues fierce, though now she holds weapons which are neutral (thunderbolt and fire), and is at least half-kindly.

"So, Daughter of Guinevere, the Shakti-Goddess energies of the lower centers, near anus, near sexual organs, and in the high belly, all of these are fierce and difficult. Only in meditation does one become free."

"I see, Maya, and I ruefully agree. I also see that perhaps I have been too narrow in my understanding of the energies: Magic at the anus, sexuality at the sex organs, hungers in the belly. The Goddess is hungry and passionate at all of these levels, is she not?"

"It is true. There are differences, but not so much as you think. She encompasses, after all, different aspects of one great Shakti, does she not? Do you not think of all the Goddesses as aspects of Love or Consciousness? So do we think of the Shaktis as all gathered together in one great Shakti, who unites at last, with the great God Shiva.

"And there, Daughter of Guinevere, we differ. For we know a God-Shiva is at each level, just as Grandson of the Knight found. Perhaps our experience may be helpful to you. For us, the God at Muladhara is the Child Brahma. I think that you experienced the Child in a cave, but at a belly level, did you not? For us it is at Muladhara. This Child-Brahma, the power-holder (in contrast to the Goddess, which is the power itself), is lovely. He has four hands, and holds the Vedas (our Bible), a staff, a gourd, and a rosary, and makes gestures dispelling fear. You can see that he is a symbol of family and culture, for he holds our holy books, the staff of support and order, the rosary which tells of our ritual prayers and ways of behaving, and finally, the gourd, the container and vessel of the energies. And this same Child-God is King of the Elephants, he is lord of those energies which are regularized, ritualized, and transformed into the energies of domesticated everyday life. If one breaks those rules and laws, Daughter of Guinevere, then the wild form of the Goddess breaks in. But he or she who would meditate, do Chakra Puja as we say, already transgresses those everyday rules, already calls upon the raw energies of the Gods and Goddesses, Shiva and Shakti. But at Muladhara, the God is a child, he is at the beginning; consciousness is only a child at the center of everyday life. But, perhaps, it is only a child, also, who can comprehend the wonder of magic, the energies as you two, Knight and Guinevere, have experienced in the Magician and the Witch!

"At Svadisthana, the water region, as contrasted with the earth of Muladhara, the God is Vishnu. He is a youth at this point, with four hands holding a conch shell, a discus, a mace, and a lotus. He wears garlands, gems, is handsomely youthful, and is lord of the Makara, the devouring fish. You can see the symbol there easily: the handsome youth filled with an interest in games and formal battle, in the shell from which he can call out to his friends, and the gems with which he attracts the feminine. In youth, are not the sexual energies in the service of refining the body, and in attraction? But he, too, has the lotus, just as has the Goddess. So, the deepest mysteries, the especially sacred flower, is also there.

"And, finally, at Manipura, the true navel center of the belly, the God is Rudra, the Old Destroyer. That ancient one, like your old teacher, perhaps, is red, smeared with white. He is the destroyer of creation, just as Brahma and Vishnu are creators. He is dark and fearsome, but his hands are in the attitude of granting boons and dispelling fear. Perhaps that is why, Grandson of the Knight, you experienced your own old teacher so ambivalently. For there is Rudra, the Destroyer, both frighteningly fierce and ready to dispel fear. Is that not so at the passionate center, where the fire dwells, where all the emotions are aroused? Those who can master the passion, ride the Ram of Fire, become masters of themselves, and of the fierce energies of the Goddess. Those who cannot do this are either victims in the crucible of fire, or are themselves the swastika-handles; they are burned or coldly and dispassionately destroy creation. As simple as that.

"And that, beloved pair, dear Knight and Guinevere, is how the Gods and Goddesses appear in the lower centers to us. There is much more, of course, of letters and numbers, of mandalas and tattvas, but that is enough for now, I think. Does it help you, Daughter of Guinevere? Does the ache in your belly become relieved to have this knowledge?"

"Knowledge helps, Maya, the Yogini. It is helpful to know. But the pain remains. Perhaps I shall stay with the pain and see if your knowledge really reaches me at my own belly center. And you, Grandson of the Knight, are you helped?"

"Yes. I would want to reconcile the differences, bring order to our different experiences of the Gods. Perhaps, I am like the child who seeks to bring order into the chaos prematurely. I will wait, Daughter of Guinevere. I shall wait and let you be the guide. For the reality of your pain is more important. That I have learned before . . .

"Daughter of Guinevere and Maya, I have waited patiently, wondering how next to proceed, how next to cope with our problem of the centers. I had thought that perhaps either of you would know the next step, since you, Maya, have the knowledge and experience and you, Guinevere II, have the pain. I only noticed, however, that Maya was now readily available, and apparent to me, that I did not have to experience her only through the intervention of you, Daughter of Guinevere. I could hear her myself. Even her outlines, her dark and luscious face and body gradually become apparent to me. But at the same time, while waiting for a next step from one of you, I had grown aware of a change in me. The old teacher had descended all right, and it made sense, indeed, from the words of Maya, that he more truly belonged in what she called the Manipura, the place of the emotions, the destruction which fires and scalds creation. His descent, however, has left a gaping hole in my center of the Third Eye. Before this judging and wrathful God-man occupied the center of that mind-consciousness place. Now that he has descended, it is empty. I am well aware, Daughter of Guinevere, that you have found not only Zeus and Athene as occupants of that center for you, but also Hera. In many ways, I think that my old teacher was a male version of your Hera. His judgmentalness, his demand of the single union, 'chosenness,' his rages and anxieties, all showed the darker features of the Great Goddess. But now he has lost his central authority, knows he must change, and has found a more rightful place in Manipura. Perhaps he has gone all the way to the child. I do not know. What remains, however, is this experience of an 'empty center.' My emptiness calls for another God, another leader and director. And I think that I have a clue as to what this new authority might be. But, before I go into that, before I attend to my own struggle with my centers, I see unrelieved pain in your eyes, and I am loathe to go on with my own experience and quest when I see you this way. As I have said before, your pain and its reality is more important than my need for order and understanding."

"Knight III, I appreciate your words and thoughtfulness. I wish that I could be more agreeable, or, at least, that I could let you and Maya know in what way you could help me. I only know that I am in pain, which comes in waves, and is related to my jealousy, my feelings of love lost, particularly that someone I love has sexual relations with another. And I am confused, too. For I had known only Sister of the Belly and Sister of the Heart. Now Maya has acquainted me with two belly centers: Svadhisthana, where desire and need reside, as I experience Sister of the Belly, but also Manipura, the abode of passions. I am wondering if I, too, do not suffer from a certain 'empty center,' Grandson of the Knight. But my empty center would be at Manipura, perhaps, that place of passions, of the destructiveness of action without reflection, of rages, and, perhaps, of the kind of pain which I experience. Hera is no help to me here, for it is not the loss of my spouse, or the betrayal thereby that I suffer. It is only the pain."

"Daughter of Guinevere, perhaps I, Maya, can help. Can you not consider what we know of the Goddess at the Manipura Center? Think of the Shakti-Goddess Lakini, as I have mentioned. She holds the thunderbolt and fire-weapon in one hand, but makes gestures of dispelling fear and granting boons with the other. Perhaps you are experiencing her just as the Grandson of the Knight experienced his old teacher, ambivalently. For I am rather sure that his old teacher is Rudra-like. Think now, does not your experience of pain have that same quality? In one hand you hold the thundering judgment of yourself or your loved one, along with the fire which burns you or him. On the other hand, you make gestures of understanding, are generous and kind. Is that not just the in-between place, between the desire of the Belly, and the generosity of the Heart? And is it not so that the passions at the level of Manipura are so destructive just because they are neither and both? The mixture of both can be felt as the most devilish of all, the most destructive of all, for it is betraying, deceiving, dishonest, yet true and loyal and faithful. Such a disordered and fragmented state was such a one as Buddha endured. He roamed up and down through those centers of Belly and Heart, from Svadhisthana to Manipura and on to Anahata, the 'unattackable' heart place. Just below, indeed, is a special little center, with the Kalpa tree and an awning, which is just right for Buddha. He roamed freely, and, therefore, was just such a one as you might need. Or, perhaps, you can speak to the Goddess Herself, the Lakini who is fond of the meat, and loves the fat. Sacrifice to her, Daughter of Guinevere, or call upon Buddha. For they can be your savior."

"All right, Maya, I believe you. I shall try. I shall pray to the Goddess and beg her help.

"Oh, Goddess of the Manipura region! Oh, Shakti Lakini, if that is your name as you come to me! I pray to you. I, Daughter of Guinevere, in the presence of my two friends, Grandson of the Knight and Maya the Yogini. I pray in their presence, but I pray only for myself. For Maya has known you in her way, and has found a certain solace. She has also been kind to me, giving me knowledge and care, but I am, all the same, alone with my pain, alone with the torments of my jealousy and hatred thereof. Goddess, help me, please. I would sacrifice the meat of my desire to you, I would give the butter of my indolent self-satisfaction over to you. I would give you what you want, if only that peculiar pain would be lessened, resolved, stopped. I would be neither possessive nor possessed, great Goddess, but I do not know how. Speak to me and tell me, I pray you!"

"I do not speak until full sacrifice is made! I do not grant boons until there is total submission!"

"But what is total submission, Goddess? What, blue-colored one, three-faced, three-eyed one, fierce, what is the total submission that you desire?"

"Come down, down; come up, up. Come to my center in your belly. Fix yourself there. Neither below nor above. Fix yourself really there."

"I try, Goddess, but I seem to find you above the belly, I find you at the diaphragmatic region. I find you at the place which I thought was the home of Eros and Aphrodite as humans, as the home of Knight III and myself. I am confused. Are you there, or below? Where am I to come? But you laugh, Goddess, why?"

"Because, Guinevere II, you are confused. But I shall help you. I shall grant you a boon, while I also laugh at you and have contempt for you. For I am so, it is my nature. Where I am is truly at the belly place, the navel place. I am there, and so is the God, whether you call him Rudra, or Old Teacher. Above me, and where I flow when Creation is right, is up, up to the Diaphragmatic Center, as you call it, for that is truly where the Buddha dwells. That, in truth, is a center of love and humanity, just as you thought. For is not Buddha a human being, no God? Does not Buddha have the kind of love which can endure the opposites of the Gods and not crack? He can go up to Anahata, the 'unattackable,' the heart place, and he can go down, to Svadhisthana and the place of Belly desires, and not be lost. But here, where I live in the Manipura, he can come only when I permit it, for I am mistress here. What you do not know, poor soul, poor Guinevere II, is that I always permit it! I always permit such a constant human being, such a strong, devoted creature as a Buddha to enter my place of passion as he wills. For he endured the total passion.

"He, the Buddha, is a great man because he survived the total passion, total emotion. He sat at his Bo Tree and achieved Enlightenment. This is known to all, it is known to your mystical brother, the Grandson of the Knight. The Buddha is dear to me."

"But, Shakti Lakini, Queen of Goddesses, how am I, a mere woman, no heroine, no enlightened one like Buddha, to survive the pains of such passions? Oh, Goddess, I am only a woman. You, Goddess, though a Shakti, are female. Is not our way with the passions different from that of a man, even if he is such a rounded man as the Buddha? Can you not help me?"

"Daughter of Guinevere, you are alone. You speak as if there is no help for you, no other person who cares for you. That is not true. Are you not upon a joint quest with your mystical brother, Grandson of the Knight? Does he not also suffer from the pains of Manipura? Was not his experience with the Old Teacher, with my spouse Rudra, just as painful, just as fragmenting, just as destructive as yours? Why do you not ask his help, also? Why do you not, together, make a chakra puja upon Manipura? My beautiful disciple, Maya, made her meditation alone. But you, Daughter of Guinevere, could have the help of a true friend and comrade, a man worthy of your care and devotion and love. Furthermore, I suggest that your friend Maya assist you, for has she not undergone her own experience? And is not Manipura the center which embellishes a Triangle? Cannot, then, three participate in it?"

"Shakti Lakini, you are right. I am sure that Knight III will assist me, for he, too, suffers from your Chakra, your center of passion and pain. Is that not so, Sir Knight?"

"It is surely so, Daughter of Guinevere. I am ready and most willing to share a meditation with you. Indeed, I hope very much to be freed thereby from my continuing guilt about my 'maniness,' which does leave me. Together, perhaps, we can arrive at an experience, an understanding, which will resolve our pain. Will Maya also meditate?"

"I, Maya, have meditated upon the Chakra of the Shakti Lakini and her consort, the Shiva Rudra, the Destroyer. I have had a most enlightening experience thereby. I would be ready to meditate once again upon this center, but I have been impressed, as you know, with how your western Gods also seem to reside in such centers. For example, what do you guess Sir Knight and Daughter of Guinevere, what God might reside in our Manipura?"

"I am quite certain that it would be Dionysos, Maya, for only such a one, among all our history of Gods and Goddesses in the west would have such an affinity for both passion and wildness, with the fire-water of wine, with the destructiveness of untamed furies, and yet with wonders to which we must all bow. Daughter of Guinevere nods, she agrees. It must needs be Dionysos then."

"Could you, then, Knight and Daughter, meditate upon the tale of Dionysos for me? Or, better yet, let me meditate with you upon that tale, and I, in turn, will be your helper with your Chakra Puja upon Lakini and Rudra."

"Agreed."

Stations of Dionysos

"A curious thing happens to me as I try to meditate upon the stations of Dionysos, ladies. I try to fix my attention upon his story, upon the many-faceted aspects of his life and service, and I grow faint. It is as if I smell fumes. I inhale an aroma of smoky substance which makes me grow sleepy and ill. I cannot fix upon anything and . . ."

"Oh, Grandson of the Knight, I, too, grow heavy-lidded and faint. I, too, cannot fix upon the story. Rather, I find myself sinking into . . ."

"You both are affected, I am sure, by the fumes of the God. I do not know very much about Dionysos, but I do know that Rudra, the Destroyer, has the fumes of hell about him. The tattva of the region of his center includes expansion and heat, but it also focuses on the anus. At Muladhara, the organ sensation is smell: the organ of action, the feet. And at Manipura, the organ of sensation is sight and color, the organ of action, the anus. Thus, the fumes from hell which you sense are, no doubt, like Rudra's. Did I not also learn that Dionysos, in one form, has both the Underworld Queen, Persephone, for a mother, and subterranean Zeus for a father?. . . They do not answer, the two. They are already quite overcome with the fumes. Pity, they do not know the yoga methods for holding of the breath, for concentration of the energies and consciousness. Still, Manipura, as the midway point, as the center for passions, surely tries to overcome consciousness, so perhaps it is best that these two lose their awareness and fall into deep sleep. But how can I contact them? How can I tell of their dreams? Before I was a shade to them, but now only I am conscious and they are shades!

"Shades in the underground state. Where are you? I will consciously, willingly, sink into that state, and let be what will be. Then, perhaps, will we know what it is that the Shiva-Shakti wants. Oh, Rudra, Destroyer, I beg of you, in your own form or that of Dionysos, grant us a boon. Grant us a vision and understanding, a means to cope with your energies anew which is right for all three. Oh, Shakti Lakini, Great Goddess, grant us a boon, a way to live the energies of your being, a way to emerge in the midst of no-consciousness. I, too, sink; I, too, fall away; I, too, succumb to fumes, to faints, to . . ."

They faint, they fall, they sway, they drop.
They mingle, comingle, they pray, they stop.

What does it matter that they sway?
What does it matter that they pray?

Gods cook men; in golden crucibles we bake them.
Men eat Gods; from blasphemous bellies we do stem.

No reason to it; no rhyme.
No answer for it; no time.

Fall away. Fall away. Fall away. Faint.
Maya away. Guin away. Knight away. Plaint.

"So speaks this voice. It seems like Rudra, though mild. I can hardly find my way into the crucible. I am in it. I swim in a blue-red sea. I am cooked in a purple stew which has as its other pieces of meat my companions Knight III and Guinevere II. But they are limp. We are small. They float face up, while I swim. The crucible falls away, into the bottom of the sea.

The crucibled pot, the swastika-handled vessel has a bottom which seems made of copper, the metal of the Goddess. But on that sea-bottom is nothingness. Here is a deadness, an emptiness which is a stillness of zero. This is not the splendid stillness of Buddha, the quietness and ecstatic peace of having overcome all the straying thoughts and demonic emotions. It is a deadness of . . . And I now know that what I believed before was wrong, that the Knight and Lady were separate from me. We are all three one, but dismembered. We are cut up into small pieces which float in the stew. The dismemberment is not like the holy brokenness of the Muses, however. It is a death-dismemberment. It is fragmentation and nothingness.

"Oh, Rudra-Dionysos! I, three-in-one, fractured into many, suddenly know what it means to be cut off from you in your emotion, your passion. It means nothing less than the nothingness of no life. No life, no emotion, no change, no heat nor expansion. No fire. I am cold. I am dead. To be deprived of you, oh God, is death. But to be overcome by you, oh God, is also death. Let us, then, die to ourselves, and awaken to you in the way that we can know Manipura anew, know Dionysos anew, know Rudra and Lakini anew."

"The three-in-one I, the dismembered union of Maya, Knight III, and Guinevere II, faints from the fumes and dreams. I dream: I am in a large room, a bedroom I think. In one corner there is a huge painting which attracts me. It is quite colorful, full of bright shades, with life-sized figures of a boy and an older man. Then, suddenly, the older man seems to step out from the painting, to come alive. A question occurs to me: was he truly in the painting all the time and miraculously came to life? Or was he merely standing in front of the painting and only looked as if he were in it? But there is no answer to my question. Instead, the man goes over to another corner and begins to use my things as if they were his. He writes in my notebook. I grow annoyed with him and start to remonstrate about this behavior, but again am disconcerted to see that he seems to shift identity. He is dark and Mediterranean-looking at one moment, then Oriental the next.

"As I awaken from the dream, I am aware that I am I, Knight III."

"And I am aware that I am I, Daughter of Guinevere!"

"And I, too, am aware of being Maya, the Yogini!"

"Yet, in our faint, in our unconsciousness, we three were as one. But I had the dream, I think."

"But I had the dream, too!"

"And I, also!"

"So, all three had the same dream when our identity was as one. Overcome by the fumes of the God, rendered unconscious by the smoke from his fire, we must have experienced him. It must mean that he was showing his nature to us: as child and older man; as Mediterranean and worshiper of Dionysos; as Oriental and follower of the Buddha. Strange thing that, of flowing identities, of loss of consciousness. Mixture even, among us, a blend of male and female. But was not Dionysos said to have strongly feminine characteristics? And is not Buddha, too, pictured as almost feminine in his compassion, and soft in his roundness? Perhaps this was a direct experience of the God."

"But the boy and the man in the dream were not Gods, I think. They seemed quite human to me. It is true, though, that if the man stepped out of the painting, then he is as magical as your Magician, Knight III!"

"True. Then let him speak. Since he is alive to all of us, let him tell us what he wishes. Look, he seems to be writing in the notebook, just as the Magician did. Let me see what he is writing."

"It is true that I am mortal and human. It is also true that I am magical. For I shift my being. Sometimes I can be a medium of the God of love. In that form, Daughter of Guinevere knew me as *amore*, though she thought this was you, Knight III. Sometimes I can be a medium for the Lord of Passion, Himself, Dionysos . . ."

"The written words stop and now I see the face of this man. I, Grandson of the Knight, see this man, but he does not seem friendly to me, Mediterranean or Oriental. Rather he seems fierce and cruel.

Rather, his seems more like the wicked face of the Old Teacher when he was fierce and cruel . . . I do not trust you, man. You say that you are a medium of the Gods, but you seem fierce and cruel and untrustworthy. Perhaps you are the God, Himself! Or perhaps you are possessed by the God, which would amount to the same thing!"

"You speak wisely, Knight, wisely indeed. For how else can man know the Gods except through the medium of his experience? His experience of trees, of stones, and, of course, of men? If I am fierce and cruel when I speak for Dionysos, then am I not the experience of passion itself? Is passion not fierce and cruel? Does passion not strike terror into one, unless he submits to it?

"It is true, say I, Daughter of Guinevere. I do not care what men say or think. I know, from my pain and jealousy, from my rage and passions, that what you say is true. You are a God! You speak the truth of the God!"

"He speaks like the Shakti Lakini, I think. But perhaps your Dionysos is like the Goddess, after all, as we have said. I do not see how he is like Buddha, however. Where is his calmness, where is his standing fast, his peace amidst the storm of passion?"

"Hah, you question me, Maya. Rightly. For what else is the Passionate One, the Possessed One, if he cannot also stay calm amidst the passion, stay unmoved amidst the swirl? So can I also be. Can you? Or you, Sir Knight? Guinevere II already admits to be possessed in speaking of the passion, but what about the middle place? The Buddha place, under the Kalpa tree? Beneath the Heart, as you say, Guinevere II, but above the Belly? Do you see?"

"I see, I think. In the midst of the cauldron of fire, in the midst of the dismemberment of passion, one must be both Mediterranean and Oriental. One must surrender to the God, worship him, submit; and one must stand firm in one's humanity, not move, not submit, hold fast until 'enlightenment' happens. Thus do I understand. Is my understanding correct, oh man of the picture? Do I apprehend what you wished us to know?"

"You comprehend very well, indeed, Sir Knight. Comprehension is easy for you. But can you live that? Can you both submit and resist? Can you be both possessed by the God and stand firm? If you can, you will be a medium just as I am. You will be both mortal and magical, as I am. For I submit to the God, and am his medium. And I stand firm and am, thus, human. So am I magical. I live in the point between creation and destruction. When the passions overwhelm, there is destruction, death. But also when the passions are lived, submitted to, contained, then do I fly upward, upward to Anahata, the unattackable heart, and to Vishudda, the purifying place of the creative words. And yet I remain, as Buddha remained, under the tree between Belly and Heart, between desire and love, between self and other, but very human all the same . . . But what of you, Daughter of Guinevere? You embraced my place of emotion very quickly, indeed. Now what do you have to say about the paradox, about the standing firm as well as surrendering?"

"I can stand, oh man of the picture. Like my mother, who withstood the agonies of loving two men, I can withstand the agony of losing a love. I can stand, also, the pain of jealousy, of grief, of guilt, of possessiveness. I can stand these things. I would wish, however, to overcome them. There, I think, I am no Buddha! I am not sufficient unto the paradox . . . But, perhaps Maya is."

"Yes, I think I am. For I have withstood. I am toughened by life and experience. But I treasure the openness of Guinevere II. I treasure that capacity, even to be possessed."

"Yes, you are right, Maya, the Yogini. If one cannot be possessed, cannot be overcome, then one is not human any more, and not even in the service of the God! For you, too, Daughter of Guinevere, are necessary to the God; yours, also, is the attitude which he needs. Now, then, look at the Stations of the God anew. Look at his life. I, as a fourth, will join you in your worship."

There are many tales of the God, Dionysos, and much ambiguity surrounds him. Even his parentage is questionable, for sometimes he is the son of Hades, the Underworld Magician, sometimes the son of Zeus, the Lord of Gods. And so, too, does his maternity seem in doubt. Is it Persephone, Queen of the Underworld, or the mortal woman Alkmene? All are true; all of the stories carry a truth of this great God. For he is magical, like the child Brahma, and a son-God to both the great Magician and the great Witch. When he is at Manipura, he is identical with his father Zeus, wild and authoritative. The ancient portraits show him as a mask, carried by men to the worshippers, or having a mask-face. And he holds in his hand the kantharos, a wine-jar with large handles. So does he appear.

Appear to us, oh God! Appear to us, and show us your mask, your kantharos-jar. Reveal to us your nature thereby, on this our first meditation upon your being and your nature!

There now appears the figure of a man, lithe and dark, like some Eros. He is Mediterranean, yet Oriental, just like the man of the picture, yet he is different, for he has an air about him, a numinous quality which makes us know that we are in the presence of a God. He speaks not, but chills run down our backs, cold and warm fevers roll around our spines as if a serpent is coiled about it. But he does not speak, this God. Instead he takes the mask and puts it over his face and then removes it. A child is revealed, a boy-God, belonging to Muladhara, to magic. Next, a youth is revealed, muscular and athletic, belonging to Svadhisthana. Now, the older man is revealed, the bearded one who dwells in Manipura. He is passionate at all three. He is, indeed, Zeus the ruler, but a second Zeus. He is a Zeus of women, whereas the true Zeus, above, is a Zeus of men. This three-fold God of the lower centers moves round about his cauldron of passion. He comes as a child, as a youth, as a bearded one, to ensnare, to entrap, to embroil and devour the feminine. For he is passion itself, whether magical-sexual, hunger-consuming, or emotional-authoritative. Speak to us, Lord, tell us, inform us!

No words come from him, no clarifying forms or shapes which would contain him. For he has his own forms, the forms of his being as a body, as a mask and as a jar.

The handles, the handles! The mystery is in the handles. Hold and be held, for the handles are serpents. And now the mask is cold. Each handle is a serpent, cold, and we each hold one. Holding, we are weighted down, entrapped. We are holding the God, and are held thereby. But, as we hold, the mask begins to move its lips. It speaks. Not the God himself, not the moving body-man, but the dark mask. And now we remember that Dionysos is Lord of the Theater. He is Master of the Play, of the tragic performances in which men and Gods appear, collide and have life. The mask lips speak:

"Words come, words go. Plays. Coldness remains. Death. A death's mask am I. Passion portrayed. Death. The coldness of portrayal. Death."

The mask stops speaking, and we are puzzled by its words. Why does the Lord of Emotion speak of coldness and death? Why does he say that his is only a death's mask, passion merely portrayed? Is he telling us his truth? Or is he telling us only what we are doing to him? None of us knows. Yet, you, man of the picture, you may know, better than we. For you were a medium, a magical man for him. Tell us.

"'I do not know, I do not care.' That is what he is saying. Can we comprehend that heat of passion and coldness? Can we comprehend not-knowing, not caring? Can we comprehend abandonment? Can we participate in the embroilment? This he says, as we hold the cold serpent handles of the cool wine jar. If we are embroiled in it, we will be hot and passionate, but dead to consciousness. And if we do not become embroiled in it, we are also dead: dead to emotion, dead to life. The play portrays death. Words form: All is death. Childhood magic, youthful body charm, aged authority: all death. This is what he says to me."

Your words are like his, Man of the Picture. For you, in and out of a picture, are life and death. You, too, in art, are like the coldness of drama, the coldness of art. You, too, say that art and drama are the coldness of passion remembered. Death.

And now we four are all suddenly gripped by the same emotion, the same image of a play, a dance, and we remember. We cover ourselves with our inner products, we paint ourselves with semen, with smegma, with feces and saliva. We cover ourselves and do a stately dance. We wear tails and we wear horns; we remember our Lord has horns, horns of the ram, no doubt. We dance and descend into the pot. We embroil ourselves in the liquid wine of the Kantharos. We are dissolved in the passions of the body, and we know that Dionysos is Lord of Vegetation. He is Lord of Life, and the Drama thereof: the life of the spirited body, as magical child, playing; as athletic youth, striving; as powerful old man, ruling.

Dionysos II

The first tale of Dionysos is not about his three states of being, but has to do with the fact that there are indeed, two beings called Dionysos. The first of these is the son of Demeter or Persephone, the second, of Semele. Not only does our Passion God have at least three centers, three states of being as child, youth, old man, but he also is two separate beings and has two mothers! What a multiplicity he is! What a manifold creature-God he is! That is a proper God to be considered by us, who must deal with the One and the Many, with the Passion and the Dispersion.

So, Zeus begat Dionysos upon the Daughter, with the sanction of the Mother, in a deep cave. The maiden worked in wool, weaving a great web, a robe for her parent, which was a picture of the world. And while she weaved this web, Zeus came upon her in the form of a serpent and begat that God who was to be the fifth ruler of the world. This great divine child was immediately blessed with toys, with divine gifts for the divine boy: dice, ball, top, golden apples, bull-roarer, and wool.

While the child God played with his toys, Titans came, instigated by jealous Hera, who always resented her husband's other matings. The Titans came, faces chalked like spirits from the Underworld where Zeus had banished them. But they came and tore the divine boy to bits, tore him into seven pieces and threw these into a cauldron standing on a tripod. They boiled the flesh and then roasted it upon seven spits. Zeus appeared, having smelled the flesh, and with his lightning hurled the Titans back into Tartaros. The child-god's limbs he gave to Apollo, who took them to his own prophetic place at Delphi. But the Titans, who were burned by the steam and fire of Zeus' lightning, formed an ash, and from this ash, the followers of Orpheus taught, men were made. Thus was the fate of the first Dionysos, son of Persephone.

But this same first Dionysos, as son of Demeter, went into the earth. The earth-born beings tore him and boiled him, but divine Demeter gathered the limbs together. From this gathering came the vine, Dionysos' last gift, for he, himself, was Oinos, 'Wine.'

Some say that one limb remained and this was known as head, or heart, or phallus. But all say that the God was horned, as if he himself were a goat or ram, to be sacrificed. Thus the tale of the first Dionysos, son of Persephone, son of Demeter.

"I, Grandson of the Knight, can understand and feel for the beginning of this tale, that Dionysos was born of uncertain mother, of two mothers, even, Mother and Daughter, and in a cave. For just such a fate belonged to my father, the Son of the Knight. My father, of blessed memory, was no God, but his fate was similar to that of the God. He, too, had two fathers, a God-father and a Father-God, and his fate was to find himself. He had to search, to go on a quest to find out who his mother was and who he himself was. This, too, must be the fate of the Passion-God, the Divine Child who is born in such a way. His task must be to inquire as to who he is. Was not one of the gifts to the child that of a mirror? It was also hinted that Persephone served Pallas Athene, the thinking one. Therefore is not reflection an aim, in the service of the Culture-Goddess? I think so. For passion requires that one become more aware. Emotion drives us to understand more.

"But what was Persephone doing when invaded by the Great Father? What was the Underworld Queen weaving, with her great web, the image of the world? Was this the magic place? Was this the same effort as the Magical Witch, Hecate, weaving that image of the world from the darkest depths? Was this the dark, negative, unconscious service of the world-image that she was making, in service of feminine consciousness, Athene? It seems so. It would seem right that the great Father, that Eye of Consciousness, would come to the dark Goddess of the Underworld, would unite with the magical, indirect way of world-making, of soul-making. This union of eye-consciousness-vision with the dark-underworld-vision, produces an amalgam which is none other than the Passion-God. The high ruling center unites with the low ruling center, and three God-faces appear: child, youth, and man. Passion appears. And passion, emotion, is the God who rules the world!"

"And I, Maya, understand the gifts for the God. For the Child-Brahma, the Youth Vishnu, and the Aged Rudra all hold such objects in their hands. And these objects are all symbols of the God's work, his play, his function. So, then, it is right that the divine boy have dice—square like the mandala at Muladhara, divinatory like the gift of Apollo. It is right that the God have a ball, and play like the youth Vishnu at Svadhisthana, that he have his roundness and fullness of being. It is right that he spin like a top, that he whirl with the creation, that he carry the cones of above and below, just as in your vision, Grandson of the Knight. For the top is a cone like yours, and spins on its point, just as the Gods play with our being, whirling us around a center. Just so are the golden apples, the wisdom-giving knowledge, the fruit that appeared at the wedding of Zeus with Hera. Just so is the Goddess jealous and offended; as if only she can bestow that emotion and knowledge; only she can have that union with the great God. But the bull-roarer, the thundering gift from the father, the emotion-laden initiator into the powers of nature, the powerful voice of creation is given Dionysos, too. But the wool I do not understand. Lambs' wool and rams' wool. Victim and victimizer. Cloth-maker, clothing maker: is this a gift for the child-God? For Dionysos?"

"I think that I might understand, Maya. I, Daughter of Guinevere, inheritor of a whole tradition, can feel the answer. Were not our first parents in the Garden of Eden? Did they not eat of the Golden Apples? They were driven by passion to do so. And their first act was to don clothing, to take leaves, skins of animals, wool of sheep, and make garments. The Bull-roarer and expulsion followed. Playful unconsciousness is followed by desire in the form of the snake. Consciousness and passion is followed by need for covering and for sacrifice. Our first parents, when they knew what they had done, made sacrifice. They sacrificed a unicorn, the tale goes. And this strange one-horned one, this ram-goat with a horn, is he not a Rudra, a Dionysos, a ram's horn announcing the at-one-ment of men with God once again? That is how it seems to me."

"But what of the following, say I, Man of the Picture? What of the torment, of the dismemberment? What of the Titans coming to seal the boy's fate, to cut him into pieces, by will of Queen Hera? What of that? What of that roasting of seven pieces? Do you see the Titans as giants of destructive emotion banished by the great consciousness of the Father? Do you see them as dismembering a union of dark and light, sent by the jealous Hera, who can tolerate no union besides her own? I can see it, and, no doubt, so can you. But can you feel it? Can you sense and endure a dismembering, burning, roasting state of yourself, of your own Passion-God? Let us do it! Sink with me, my friends. Sink with me into the cauldron. Let the swords of murderous rage cut us up; let the unjust rule of Hera send those vicious words and judgments; let us permit ourselves to be cut and boiled. It is said that mankind comes from the retributional burning of the Titans. Is it not true that from the taming of passions and from the cooking of oneself in them that humanness comes? I, a mortal and magician, have been so born. But let us sink once again. Let us be the voluntary ram, the scapegoat, the sacrifice. Let us join the child-God Dionysos as he is cooked in the vessel."

"I, Grandson of the Knight, am willing, for I discovered that the dismemberment of Bluebeard was nothing other than the torment of the soul in the birth of creation."

"And I, Guinevere II, am willing, for what else have I experienced besides burning torment, the conflict of dismembering emotions!"

"And I, Maya, have no fear at all of such events, for I have lived an experience of the transformation of Rudra and the Shakti Lakini, and I, as well, into gold."

"Let us, then, sink down. Let us permit the swords of negative judgment, of unjust criticism and abuse, come and cut up our dignity, our pride, our value of ourselves. We see the cold-hearted Goddess. Speak, Goddess, tell us those sword-words which cut us up and make us mad, render us impotent in our passion and rage.

"She laughs. She does not speak. She merely shows a cold eye and a hard smile. For why should she cooperate with us? Why should she help us in our voluntary submission to such a sacrifice? We are, indeed, stupid, for she sends the Titans only when they are not expected, not wanted. How foolish of us! Dionysos, son of Persephone is redeemed by an upward-moving motion: he goes up to Apollo and becomes a prophetic intuition. But Dionysos, son of Demeter, also goes down; he is re-membered by Demeter and becomes Lord of the Vine, God of the Grape, of the intoxicating spirit from which passion can descend into blessed unconsciousness or ascend into the Bluebeard-Muse state of words which sing.

"Come now, Hera, come now Bitch-Goddess! Can you not speak? We reject your principle! We welcome this union of Zeus in his maniness with Persephone of the depth, the magical realm of Hecate. We welcome this union of Zeus with Demeter, with the Mother-Goddess of the heart, who can love and seek and serve, and is forever repairing, re-membering, and healing! We welcome this union of the Great God, and we defy your monogamous Oneness. Hera, do you hear?"

"I hear. And I obey. I will send you the sword-words which you desire. I will send you the cut-pain you seek. I will rend you with them. But you will not stand firm. None can. Not men, not Gods. None can. Only solitariness can. Only silence can. So, you can only run from me to me. Run from the vicious words, cutting judgments, run from jealousy, rage, indignity, revenge. Run from these, where? To solitariness, to aloneness, to no words, no thoughts, no feelings, no life. Run there!"

"Great Goddess, we run. We run and we sink. And we know that it is only by surrender to the Gods, by submission of God to God, by the acceptance of the burning fire and thunder, that man is born, that humanity results, and that inspiration above and below occur.

Goddess, in your fierce eyes, we see you as Rudra's consort, too, as the Shakti Lakini, for you are fierce and bloody. You are descending from your high place, too.

"Still and Solitary. Totally self-abandoned. Only this can save, only this can turn dismemberment into creation, fragmentation into whole-ness. Persephone inspired; Demeter healed; Daughter rose and Mother sank. And the God was healed thereby."

A second tale is told of the birth of our God. This story has him as son of a most mortal mother, Semele. It is said that Great Zeus did not mate with the lovely woman directly, but rather came to her disguised as a mortal man and gave her a potion to drink. This potion, made from the heart of the divine but-yet-to-be-created Dionysos, made Semele pregnant, and thus she was destined to be a Virgin Mother. Hera, learning of the union of her ever-straying spouse with a mere mortal, was enraged once again. Disguising herself as Semele's nurse, she persuaded the mortal woman to make a wish that Zeus come to her in the way that he came to Hera, so that Semele could know what it is like to be embraced by a God. And so she did, and so did Zeus then appear as lightning, as a fiery barb which straightaway struck her and killed her, her soul descending into the Underworld.

Zeus, the Father God, rescued the child-God, the unripe fruit, from the womb of Semele and sheltered him in his own thigh, making a paternal womb covered with golden buckles. So did the father bear the son, from below, just as he had borne Pallas Athene, alone, but from his brow. Having borne him, Zeus gave over the child-God to the care of women, in a cave. Three or four women, nymphs, mortals, gods, all have claimed to have cared for the divine child. After this, it is into the hands of women that Dionysos, Lord and inspiration of women, is given. Zeus, father of men, lover of women, but Lord of Men, gives birth, alone, to his son, Lord of Women.

To finish this station of the story of Dionysos, one must not simply leave Semele thus. For it is said that she did not merely die when struck by Zeus' lightning. She is thought of as resembling Persephone, who sojourned in the Underworld and had to be redeemed. The tales say that brave Dionysos had to redeem his mortal mother. It is said that he journeyed to the Underworld in search of her, but he could not find her himself and needed a guide and pathfinder. As a price for this service, it was said that he was to promise total feminine surrender—only if he could do this would he reach his mother and bring her back. This he promised and this he fulfilled, partly by attitude, and partly with the help of a phallus made of figwood, which he erected there. This pathfinder and guide was the phallus itself, called Polyhymnos, "the much sung-of." And then Dionysos brought

Semele back, and made her immortal. She was named Thyone then, "the ecstatically raging," and so are named his priestesses. Thus did Dionysos redeem his mortal mother and bring her up to heaven.

"I, Daughter of Guinevere, can readily grasp this tale of the God. I can understand, just as my mother understood, how it is that the Great God Zeus with his thunder and lightning, his power of sound and light, of word-creation and vision-intensity, can come to a mere mortal woman in the form of a passion of the heart. His once-born-future-born son, Dionysos, passionate ruler of women, can so come. Has not every woman experienced love this way, when it is divine, as if God-inspired? Has not also every man, when attuned to God, felt his own soul to be so deluged, rent, invaded by the thunder-lightning-passion of him? And even when it comes in mortal disguise. I have known the God as he appeared in a most mortal love, and treasure it, whether in the form of Amore, Eros, or in the form of my own true friend and brother, Grandson of the Knight. I do, indeed, know how this feels. And I know, too, how the monogamous one, jealous and possessive Hera, enters in. Immediately that one is penetrated by the most-high-God, one is also jealous and special, one thinks of oneself as honored among beings. Even Mary, that lovely mortal woman who was destined to be divine, felt this. We all feel this. And, worst of all, we mortals, we mortal women especially, need to know what it is, really, to be embraced by the God, to feel his full and total presence. Semele, poor Semele, was so different. She, too, was vulnerable to this jealousy, this deception; she, too, was not content with her experience but wanted more. She received this 'more,' and was consumed. So are we all consumed by divine love, found wanting, unable to contain the fire, the holy electrical vibrations of tumultuous nature, which then explode us and send us to our death. But, Lord, you who can enter us and explode us, cause us to die, can cause us to be reborn and come anew into life or into heaven itself! Oh, Semele, I know you. I, Daughter of Guinevere, who have known my own mother's suffering, and even that of another God-bearer, Mary, understand what you felt. I, too, can bear witness. Though I have not born a God, I can bear witness to the births!"

"And I, Grandson of the Knight, can guess what it is like for Zeus, the great Father-God, who finds his light too much for his mortal love to bear, and must suffer the loss of her. He must redeem his son, his pride and his opposite, and bear him himself. He must guard this son in his own thigh, his own most vulnerable spot, and there take great care. Is it so, can the great Eye of Heaven, Lawmaker and ruler, omnipotent and grand, become like a mother of a son, as well as his father? Can the great one, in his own soft place, as feminine and womblike as any, bear a son who is his opposite? Who is passionate rather than wise, sensitive rather than strong, effeminate even, rather than masculine? Can such a proud father embrace and give birth to his opposite, Zagreus, who is hunter and hunted, broken up into fragments? Can mighty Zeus bear this? In so bearing, in so being womblike in his own soft thigh, he acknowledges his own soft, vulnerable and feminine nature, he gives assent to his own passion as well. Can mighty Zeus do this?

"Well, he did do it; the tale says that he did. Let the golden buckles of parental care keep the great child-God, Son of the most high, sealed when none is there to help him. Oh, Dionysos, God! I know you, for your fate and being are so much like that of my father, the Son of the Knight, just as your father was so much like his father, in turn, the Knight. As mortals, as father and son, they were like you, but they did not have the father-son protection for each other, that warmth of masculine care that you knew. Or did they? The Charioteer in the Cave, silent and far seeing, was a kind of Zeus-Hades himself. And my father's ladies were loving women. And his son a further representative of Dionysos, or of Zeus? I think not. For I am—my sister and friend, Daughter of Guinevere, tells me—an 'amore,' a human Eros, and that I believe. I am a product of a great father and grandfather. Does not a union of Zeus, the wise and fiery, with his son Dionysos, the passionate, result in a male love, in an Eros? This I believe and experience. But in so doing, mighty Dionysos, I do not abandon your worship, I do not deny your greatness, I do not deny your hegemony of the centers below, one-two-three."

"Then I, Man of the Picture, Medium of the God, can feel myself in his search. I can feel his search for his mother, as, perhaps, you, Grandson of the Knight, in sympathy with your own beloved father, can empathize with such a voyage. But imagine God doing this! Imagine! It is easy for us, as mortals, magical or not as may be, but still mortals, to realize our loss, our need for our mothers, or need to redeem the mother, but for a God? Remarkable! Such is the understanding that the god Dionysos is an incandescent emanation of the Quest, for he, deeply and movingly, seeks out his mortal mother. We know that the Gods need men, seek them out, use them, devour them, possess them; we know that men need Gods, are sought out, are used by men, devoured and possessed; we know this. But do we know of a God, of mortal woman born, who seeks her to redeem her in the Underworld? This we do not know. But Dionysos knows. He, Lord of Passion, worshipped by women, Lord of them, he knows; he seeks out his mortal mother, suffers and becomes effeminized in order to find his way to her. What immortal God and principle is this: in service of the mortal feminine, will become fragmented, like Zagreus, effeminized and broken into the million vulnerable parts that the worshipful Semele experienced with her Lightning-Lord, Zeus? The Son allows himself to undergo the experience of the mother— shattered, impregnated by the powerful male force—and thus redeems her. And he creates this force himself, both by attitude, allowing the masculine to overwhelm him, allowing himself to be feminine, and also in deed. For he carves a phallus from the tree, he lets it guide him. He lets it enter into him, as if it were some mere perversion. But perversion it is not when so done; travesty of nature is it not when so done, for the God knows what it is: that a male God can surrender, like a woman, and follow the phallus of his own creation outside of him. Deep thing this. It harkens to the Smithy God. This phallic creation is made from the Tree, from the Tree of the Centers of Life, which go up and down the spine, just like the Kundalini. The God submits to this creation of the spirit-in-the-flesh and thus finds and elevates the feminine, mortal soul to eternal life. Thus do we find our immortality, male and female, thus are we ascended into heaven: by submission to the God and by creation therefrom. And thus does our inner tree tell us that our souls are immortal."

"True, all true, but a very masculine way to perceive all that event, say I, Maya. You are, indeed, Man of the Picture, a magical man, but you belong, still, to the male world of longing for creation and effect, of the rising forever into the spirit realm. I, as a woman, earthy, know the other part of that picture. I can know what it means to be a priestess of the God. Can a man know what it means to submit to Polythymnos, 'the much sung of'? Can a man know what it means that the priestesses are named 'Thyone,' 'ecstatically raging'? Can men know that? Can men know the fierce furies and ecstatically raging screams and passions of a woman serving the God? I have known your Dionysos, as Child Brahma, as Youth-Vishnu and, above all, as Old Rudra: I have known them, and their consort, the Shakti, and have been wild, overwhelmed. I have known 'the much sung of' and have known the ecstasies. But can man take us this way? What mortal man can endure us this way, to love us when we are priestess-possessed? They run from us; can not unite with us as we unite with the God. Who can do that?. . . Forgive me. I have fallen back to my old view of doubt of men, doubtful of the existence of men who could truly be gurus, truly serve the great Shiva and Shakti. I know that there are such men. You, Grandson of the Knight, though modest for good reason, are such a one. Forgive my own raging. Forgive my own being Thyone, and my own speaking out of the maligned God, Himself!"

"You hear me, brave ones. You hear me in my tale. You hear me in the stories of me. You hear me in your meditations. You hear me in your statements from each other. For each has a truth of me. Each has a part of me. Child am I, new and magical. Youth am I, bold and unswerving. Aged am I, ruling and tyrannical. For I am the son of my father, and the father to his son. You know him, you know me. Dream your dream onward; tell my tale onward. Reflect your reflections onward, and thus will you worship me, and thus will I enter into you and speak."

Dionysos III

"And now, further will I speak. I, the God, Dionysos, will speak
further to you. You have accompanied me, thus far, as the child, as
the boy who was snatched from the womb of his dying mother and
contained by the father. You have also known me as the boy who was
cared for by women. Come now, with me, to my second phase, to
my youth. Come and see me in the place that you, Maya, the Yogini,
call Svadhisthana. Come and see me in the Belly place, as you call it,
Daughter of Guinevere. Come and see me in the place you once called
Buddhistic, Grandson of the Knight, and you now know as that of
Vishnu and myself as youth. Come to me there. Experience the
madness of it, all of you. You, Man of the Picture, already know, for
you are my medium, but you others, imagine now, if you can, the
madness, the raging and shrieking of the Maenads, my priestesses.
You . . . you women, share now that raging lust, that passion, ravenous love, roaring anger. Know it as madness and rage. For here is
desire—no sweet mothering caring, nor self-sacrificing mother love
of the centers to be found lower or higher. Here, women, you sacrifice
the child, you tear him apart. Here you become destructive if you do
not worship me, love me, desire me, fill me and yourselves with the
wildness of the wine-passion, the hunger for lust, for touch, for desire
itself. Come women, dance in my fashion, dance the tambourine,
dance to the flute and drums. And dance no stately dance for me,
no graceful turn. Dance with your head back. Throw your heads back
and scream. Scream the blood-curdling scream of lust, of desire, of
rage. Hold your long robes and open them, reveal your sex, your hairy
hungers, your lascivious movement of flesh. Engage yourselves and
enrage yourselves with the fleshy movements of desire. And carry the
thyrsus, hold that long staff and be proud of that pine-cone which it
honors. You, Knight, you know the cone, now know it as the fruit
of the pine, of a tree which serves me. And know, Knight, that you
are honored by meeting me here, for men do not see when women
worship me. They can not. The Yogini is right, the men cannot stand
it. But you can, Knight, for you can be feminine, be shattered, be
totally surrendering. Few men can do that. So serve me, and be served,
like a woman, like a God, like me. Now dance, and be mad. Know
that you sacrifice the child, your child, but also that child is I. That

child is the God at the beginning: needy, orderly, mother is there. But now mother is gone, only passion is there. Do it, do it, do it."

"But we cannot, Lord. I, Man of the Picture, can say this. We cannot follow you in this. We cannot, for who can summon passion, evoke passion, surrender to passion with just a word? And how is it surrendered when one summons and controls it? Your tales speak of the women, three in number, industrious and staid, who did not worship you, submit to you. You made them mad and they cut up their children in sacrifice. And there were others as well. We are willing to serve you, worship you, but how do we do that in ordered state, in measured motive, in foot-tapping dance?"

"Well said, Man of the Picture. You submit to me, worship me, but are not possessed. But do you not know? You have already worshipped me, sacrificed to me, followed me! Do you not remember, Grandson of the Knight, how you have run through the hills, suffering a madness of guilt and pain in your loving of two and more women? Do you not remember? Do you not feel in your bones the memory of the madness of the rage, the pain, the lusts and desires at the same time? Do you not recall that? You nod, you ruefully nod. Now, then, you can recall how you worshipped me, served me. And you also forget the vine, how you loved it, adored it, and, in so doing, in risking fame, reputation, profession, 'good manners' as spelled out by silly old women-men and men-women, how you served me.

"And you, Daughter of Guinevere, do you not recall how you suffered the agony of your love lost, your pain and hungers? How you have been mad with grief, with passion, with hunger and lust? How you suffered all these things and did not cower? In all this have you served me, worshipped me, sacrificed to me.

"And you, Maya, your whole way has been mine. You have gone off alone to the mountains, to the forests. You have surrendered yourself totally to the passion of the meditation, to the forces which rend. I need not tell you, you already know. For you have worshipped me as Lord Brahma, child, as Lord Vishnu, youth, you have worshipped me as Shiva, Himself! I need say nothing more to you.

"And you, Man of the Picture, you know. For you are me, in human form, and I, you. You know it, I know it. Let your friends know it. So, now, all three, know that you have already done my office, my service, my place.

"And now you must know that it was also I, in you, who suffered. I it was, in you, who was child broken up into small fragments. The childish, the weak, the immature, the inept is broken when there is initiation from child to youth, from the tenderness of childhood care and form, to the passion of youthful lusts. So it was I who suffered—

and, it was you. For you have suffered the sufferings of Dionysos, you have known the results of the sacrifice of the child-God: creation of the liquid spirit. The melting of your hardnesses (do you not know this, Maya), the growing of your softnesses (do you not know this, Daughter of Guinevere), the testing of your strength (do you not know this, Grandson of the Knight), your becoming an image of the God, and realizer of the God (do you not know this, Man of the Picture). In the creation of the wine, you create a transformation of the blood of the God, a refining of the flesh, an incandescence and incarnation of the spirit. For, along with bread, is not the experience of the God in wine? In bread and wine? You already know this, Knight III, and Guinevere II. Now, soon will come a new imagery, a new experience, listen, now, and wait . . ."

We have heard the God speak, and we wait. But we also continue his worship by the review of his story, his tale as given to us by the fathers, the grandfathers, those of the past, of the men and women who knew him as they cultivated the vine, as they partook of the grape.

The God appears as a youth, standing upon a promontory overlooking the wine-dark sea. He stands, long dark curls upon his head, royal purple robe about his strong shoulders. Pirates come and, spying the handsome youth, bound ashore from their many-oared ship, intent upon kidnap and ransom from what must be a king's son, they thought. But the royal youth only smiles. The cords and bonds with which they tie him fall away, and he merely smiles with dark eyes, and stands quietly at the mast. The helmsman sees this and calls out to his comrades that this is no king's son, but a God. "Let us set him free at once!" But the captain pays no heed, for he wants only wealth. And then the ship is gathered up by a great wind, and wine begins to pour through the ship, sweet to drink and sweet-smelling. Vines sprout from the sails and grapes hang down. The mast itself becomes like a tree-laden vine, and oarsmen grow frightened. But now the youth, no ordinary king's son, takes on the form of a lion, roaring mightily. And he makes a bear to appear, standing on hind legs and threatening. All grow mad with fear and wonder—all except the helmsman who keeps his right mind. The lion seizes the captain, as the rest of the crew, in mortal terror, leap into the sea and turn into dolphins. Only the helmsman is restrained by the God, who takes compassion upon him. To this same helmsman, the God reveals that he is Dionysos, son of Zeus and Semele.

"Thus the tale, and thus the image of the God in his sea appearance. That the God, as youth, should be among the waters is clear. For is not the water the element at Svadhisthana? Just as earth was at

Muladhara, and Fire at Anahata? And is not the handsome youth just such a wind-inspiring, water-changing God? But what is the meaning of this tale in the stations of the God? Why is it that he sometimes appears as the boy on a dolphin, and that only the helmsman, who recognizes him, is spared the excesses of madness, and receives compassion? Who among us can fathom it? Man of the Picture, you, the human medium of the God, speak to us, tell us."

"I will speak, but only if the God will reveal himself to me, use me as his medium. Thus will I speak. I listen and await. The God speaks. In slow speech he comes to me, and so I will speak and hear, hear and speak.

"He begins on the land, as a child, he says. He begins in the stage of earth, of order, of mother-love and care, beloved by women. As a youth, he is desired by men, but only for profit and wealth is it so, only for ransom and power. And thus is the God of passion, of emotion reacted to by men: no respect for the energies therein, no regard for the royal raiment of their own feelings, their own passions. They want only power and wealth. But the God only smiles: he knows that on the watery depths of he psyche, on the unknown, uncharted, wind-tossed waves of the wine-dark sea that the passion-God can only be worshipped, respected, cannot be tied to the mast-tree of the centers and kept in tow like some mere object. The helmsman sees this. That part of the soul which keeps an eye upon star and wave, upon fate and feeling, that part of the psyche which holds the round, spoked-wheel totality of balance, that respecter of passion, only he can glimpse the power. Captain, ruler of the bark which seeks only private gain, sees nothing. And the wind increases, the vines grow. The sweet-smelling, sweet-tasting senses of youth appear at first (are not these organs of sense at the first two centers?) and dumbfound our young spirits. But they proliferate and extend: the spirit that cannot recognize the passions becomes terrified. The God becomes lion, roaring and roaming, and man becomes a terrified victim to his own hungers and passions. The bear stands up and looks human: the mother-Goddess makes men into frightened little creatures (hail Shakti, devourer!). At last, the ruling principle is overthrown, and men become mere fish, transformed into servants of the God against their will, dolphins upon which the God can ride. Only the helmsman, he who recognized the God, steers the vessel, has a hand upon the totality. Only he receives compassion, receives blessing. This helmsman, this steady-handed one, is called Akoites, a 'husband' of the God. And he is also called Ikarios, the first man to give hospitality to the wine-God, but who was killed by his countrymen because they thought that the drunken ones were poisoned. Is this not the fate of one who is respectful of the God? He is wed to the God, but rejected by the mass of men. So, one is subject to the God in one form or another: as his clever steed, as his terrified and raging mad one, or as his spouse. Hail to the wine-God, who has a home on the wine-dark sea!

"Hail to the God! He will rule us, from the midriff; embrace us, from the belly; support us, from the root-support. We can salute, hail, and be like the helmsman, keeping our hand on wholeness, with an eye to the powers, and be blessed. Or we can arrogantly try to rob the powers for ourselves and be damned by our own concupiscence! Or we can merely be clever little playthings of the God, mere barks for those energies and powers to ride! For the child in us, it is natural to play. It is even permissible for the youth of our lives to be possessed by the God. But in the aged days, we need our Helmsman, or we are lost. Hail Dionysos, Hail God, we salute you. We salute you in the childhood of our days, the youth of our days and the age of our days, and we are all of these all of our lives. We salute and bow: played with like a child, embraced by you like handsome youths, and aware of you like wise helmsmen. Hail!

"And now to another station, a final tale, perhaps, in the life of the God. For now we come to the God triumphant. The word itself, the triumph, comes from the hymn to Dionysos, the great God, a *thriambos*. For in the final appearance of the God, after the times he is hunted and persecuted as a child, after he has driven the maenads mad and wild, there is the period of transformation, even of transfiguration. At that time, there is a great triumphal procession. In the maturity of the God, there comes an ordered dance in which the 'raging' women are converted into happy companions. The God is no longer a hunted child, or male-female hermaphroditic youth, but now a bearded man whose femininity resides in his great long robe. Now, his followers go through the world, and the animals are tamed. It is known that the wine, the spirit of Dionysos, can tame all animals, even leopards and panthers. Dionysiac women kept such tame ones even in their homes.

"And the one most connected with the God's triumph was none other than the mortal woman-cum-Goddess who was destined to marry him, Ariadne, the holy and pure. Ariadne it was who saved Theseus, the hero. Everyone knows how she used the thread, or the shining wreath, to guide him through the Labyrinth, the baffling maze where the hero had killed the Minotaur, his wildly raging brother-bull. Everyone knows, too, that poor Ariadne was left alone on the island Dia by the hero, not because he was wicked and ungrateful, but because the God had appeared to him in a dream and ordered him to do so. But Ariadne did not know this. She knew only that she was alone on the island, whimpering, in pain, and a sinner, for she had helped the hero to kill her own brother.

"Alone she remained on the island, until the God appeared to her, coming as her rescuer and bridegroom. And Dionysos it was who came. He came as husband and lover, in his maturity he came. And he brought the transfigured Ariadne to Heaven, as if she were some pure and noble Goddess like Persephone Herself. Or even like Aphrodite, for some say that at this point she is worshipped even as Aphrodite-Ariadne. This ascent began on the 'heavenly' island of Dia, from which Dionysos becomes the husband of the transfigured one, crowned with the golden wreath in the heavens. Thus the tale."

"Yes, thus the tale, and thus is our understanding enhanced. I, Grandson of the Knight, understand. At the maturity of the God, at the time when he is really understood, really related to by the spirit as helmsman, then he comes into his true rulership, his true place as tamer of the wild instincts, as informer of the soul who serves the hero. For Ariadne is, indeed, like the mother of Dionysos, in need of redemption. But now it is the mortal woman herself, the poor soul who guides and leads the hero. The God was shattered and reduced in being a woman and feminine, under the guide of the great phallus. But now he weds the feminine, the mortal woman who herself is the guide of the mortal man. Thus, too, is the soul, which aids the hero, which uses both the care of feminine thread, feminine patience in weaving a life, and the golden lamp of consciousness in freeing the heroic. And the maze is the confusing spiral of the belly center from which one must rise. It is the devouring, devastating, Svadhisthana place of potential madness and grief from which the energies rise, and the soul is wed at Manipura. The soul unites with the God and is transfigured right up into heaven."

"Words, words, Sir Knight, words! I would feel it, I would know it! I, Maya, would experience Manipura risen to the highest. I would know this!"

"And I, too, Maya. For is not the Daughter of Guinevere just such a woman in need of redemption? Am I not just such a one? And is not Dionysos the close consort of women especially?"

"All right then, ladies. Let me, then, be your Theseus, and let Dionysos be your love. Let it be so. Sing, then, a triumphal hymn to your great Lord. Sing, for I suddenly become aware that I, too, who have forsworn being a hero, have asserted that I am cut from a cloth different from my father and grandfather, now aver that I, too, would be heroic. But I would be heroic only in the way that Theseus was heroic, in the service of the Gods! And I would bow and bend and worship to the Ariadnes of this world as well. And I, like the Knights, my fathers, would serve you, Lady Guinevere and Lady Maya, for, though mortal women and full of failings, just like me, you are my Goddesses! And you, Daughter of Guinevere, you have cherished me as your *amore*, and I bow before you as an Ariadne, as a heroine who has accompanied me upon my way, who has given me a thread and a light."

"All right, then, Knight. But I, Guinevere, will proclaim that you are no Theseus for me, dear man, but a loving brother and friend, for you do not leave me alone on some island. Rather, Knight, you are for me a mortal Dionysos, and in such a way would I unite with you!"

"But not for me, Knight and Lady, not for me! I, Maya, am no Lady, I am of the east. I am of the place where Alexander conquered and spread his seed and his culture and where he returned with our wisdom. I am a lonely follower of the God, and have known him as Brahma, Vishnu and Rudra. Let me know him, now as your own Dionysos! Let Him enter into me, and transform me as I would be! Let me sing the hymn!"

> *Passion finds a home in my breast.*
> *It crawls from below and rises.*
> *Like a child it crawls, from the magical meridian,*
> > *from the nursing nexus*
> > *from the nestling cave.*
> *Passion finds a home in my breast.*
> *In my belly it boils and sizzles.*
> *Like a youth it struts, from the hungry haridan,*
> > *from the gonadal groin,*
> > *from the genital grave.*
> *Passion finds a home in my breast.*
> *In my midriff it settles triumphant.*
> *Like a man it rules, from the whole-spoked helm,*
> > *from the wine-filled woman,*
> > *from the mid-point stave.*

"That is a poor hymn, I think, Maya, a poor one, indeed! Try, rather, a prayer to the God and let him speak through you. That, perhaps, is what I would try."

"Do it, then! I am not piqued by what you say, Guinevere II, for it is only too true. But then, I have been no poet, after all. I have composed only one poem, to Kundalini, but I have no pretension along that line!"

"All right then, Maya, I shall try . . . Oh, God, you whom I have known in my own centers of root and belly and midriff, you whom I have experienced in my own friendship and love with the Grandson of the Knight, and in my love for others, my passion for others, I implore you to speak, to sing your own hymn in praise of yourself and use us, your poor instruments, to sing your own praises. For we can sing of you and for you. And we can speak and guide, but only if your forces, your shining face and your light, transform us. Help us to tame our animals and not be devoured by them. Help us to love them and respect them, but not turn them into clawless house-monsters. Help us steer through our passions as the helmsman did, with an eye upon your star; with respect, with verve, with care. Help us to keep whole!"

"All right, then, creatures, all right. I, Dionysos, will speak. I speak to your state and I speak to your time. I speak to that which is presented to me. You have meditated upon my nature and deeds, you have worried over the state of my being. You have pondered the energies and my toll. Well, then, the hymn is already sung, the deed already proclaimed. If you are not yet exalted, Maya, then I regret it. If you are not yet whole, then, Daughter of Guinevere, I regret it. If you are not yet a hero, Grandson of the Knight, I have compassion! Do you know then, what I say? That passion is elevated, is transformed, moves higher even than the midriff, and climbs even into the heart! For a heart without passion is mere soft sentiment and dull honeycomb. And a passion without heart is like a fire-destroyer of wine-intoxicated demons. So, you three, you see me changed. For you have changed. All three. And you, the fourth, the Man of the Picture, you are my man, for you are me, in them. You are my man, my mortal one, I salute you!"

"I, Man of the Picture, am sheepish, and dumbfounded. I melt, I am shattered by this honoring from the God! I am like him, and am softened. I am become gold. And now, look you, for I wear the golden wreath. I, image and man, wear the wreath of triumph of the God!

"And I proclaim that it is not the hymn which celebrates, it is not the heroic deed which proclaims, it is not the submission which the God desires, it is merely that one be Medium, one be child and youth and ruler, that one be helmsman and whole. Dionysos, my Lord, I am an Akoites, I am husband and helmsman, and so, Lord, are they."

Grandson of the Knight

"So, all is well with the Lord Dionysos, all is solved. That may be true for you ladies, with your joyful surrender to that great God, that passionate leader of the feminine, but I must say, ruefully, that all is not well with me. You may remember, a little time back, that I was suffering from a malady of the 'empty center.' I had known the experience of having the central place, the ruling eye, the locus of discriminating consciousness, occupied by my old teacher, who was himself emotional and judgmental. He came down, you recall, to the Dionysian centers, the places below the heart. The result was an 'empty center' in the ruling place of the head. I, like my fathers before me, had God, the Father, ruling with his angry and judging third eye, right in the middle of the forehead. But now, he has descended and there is an empty place. I can trust, indeed, the rulership of Dionysos as Rudra, as passion of the dark-sea. I can very much feel at one with the Man of the Picture, a kind of Akoites, who holds his hand on the helm of that vessel. I can even see that which was not spoken of before, that the wind which pushes those sails, which stirs the wine-dark sea of Dionysos of the Belly, is that wind of the Heart-center, Anahata. That smoky place, with its feeling and love, gently and firmly stirs the sea, and also calms it. So that the Helmsman, the man, must place his bark, the fragile nature of himself, fully upon the passionate sea of Dionysos, relate firmly to the winds of Anahata, where Jacob and Sister of the Heart dwell, but also look out to the starry heaven, or the sunny sky, for he needs to navigate his bark by them. And it is that center, the single hot-eyed center of the sun, or the manifold lights of the stars, which no longer serve me. Rudra ruled in the wrong place, now he has found his home. But the ruler-eye, the heaven eye is an 'empty center.' I know, Daughter of Guinevere, that you have found adequate rulers there: both the great Father Zeus, and his culture-building daughter Athene. I can even see that you recognize the Queen Hera. Indeed, Hera has been a female version, I believe, of the Rudra-Dionysos ruling me at that place. But I have no leader or ruler there anymore. I can fully accept yours, Daughter of Guinevere, but I am uneasy."

"What would you say to embracing mine, Grandson of the Knight? My Kundalini center at that third-eye place, between the eyebrows we call Ajna, 'Place of Command'? It is a most high place, second only to the most high, Sahasrara itself. At Ajna, there is no animal symbol at all; as if that center of the reality of the soul does not require a bodily reality. Our yogins, at that center, realize that they themselves are a dream of God, that we are all enacting the dream-drama of the great divine. But that is not merely such a mystical center, Knight, for we know it as the Tattva of Manas, of mental faculties. The mind, now, is at that center. Do you know what the Gods are like at that center? Shiva is called Shambu and he is Atman himself, lustrous like a flame, and he is, himself, sparks surrounding a golden light. Do you know what that means? It is as if the golden light of awareness of the Self shines brightly, and all the sparks of inspiration, of consciousness, radiate from this great center. So is Shiva, the Male God, at that point.

"And of the Goddess? Shakti? She is none other than Hakini, with six faces. She holds a rosary, a skull, a drum, a book, and is seated on a white lotus. She has the prayerful attitude like that experienced by Daughter of Guinevere in meditation upon Mary, but she also knows the reality of death, the noise of the drum summoning the Gods, the book which commemorates and proliferates these sum- monings and experiences. Finally, the Goddess knows and rests upon the pure white light of the lotus-center. Thus is our center of Ajna, thus is our center of consciousness. Would you know more?"

"I thank you, Maya, for your wisdom, for your words, and for your help. All that you say seems right to me and true. And, indeed, I would know more. And yet . . . Do not consider me, please, as chauvinistic, as either too much with the male or with the West, but I am a man, after all, and a westerner, too, and I feel the need to find my own mind-center, my own ruling place. Perhaps, indeed, Maya, that is the point. That I cultivate my own mind-center anew, and discover what it is that rules me, that thinks for me. I knew, indeed, that the Old Teacher was not only an emotional Judge. Mostly he was not really. He was only such a tyrant when another center, Eros or Dionysos, perhaps, would claim rulership, a center-ship; then he would send his arrows, thunderbolts, perhaps, like some Zeus. But I do not believe he was like Zeus, for he was more like Hera, as I say, or, more accurately, a Rudra-Dionysos. But now that I have the great image of the Helmsman on the sea, with the blessing of the God, now that I have become myself like the Man of the Picture, now I must look to the Sun or the Stars, to find my way of navigating.

"And now I wonder at my own images, of the sun and the stars. The eye of Heaven, as sun, as light, and the many eyes of heaven as night-lights: light is my symbol it seems, and once again I face the dilemma of One and Many, of one day-light, and many night-lights. Could it be that it is the Lord of Light that I seek? If so, that would be represented by Apollo, perhaps, for is he not the Lord of Light? Just as Dionysos is lord of luxuriant vegetation, of the vine, of wine and the passions, of the earthy and watery spirit of nature, just so is Apollo Lord of Light. For his light was not that of the sun alone, as for Helios, but for light in general. Perhaps I should meditate upon this God, do my worship of his stations, in order to understand my own dilemma of the empty center of light, of the eye or eyes of Heaven. What do you ladies think?"

"I think it would be well, Sir Knight. In my own meditations upon Athene, I have found a feminine way to wisdom, to culture-building, to consciousness. And I would welcome your own study also. Perhaps I, too, could help, for I am not so smugly satisfied with my consciousness that I would seek no other."

"And I, too, would welcome your meditations. As I have said, I have been attracted to your western ways of meditating, your western Gods, and I would be glad to learn, and should you wish it, to aid with my own Manas, my own understanding."

"Well, then, ladies, thank you. I do not know if I will succeed to find an experience that will fill my now 'empty-center' but I shall try. My meditations, in the past have helped very much, so once again, I will attempt it. And what better Lord to serve in this way than Apollo Himself, who is no less a great God than Zeus and Athene!

"So, then, Apollo, called also Phoebus, the Pure and Purifying, you who are Lord of Light, shall I see you? Will you come and participate with me in a discussion? Will you help me fill that eye-center, that mind-place which has been vacated by your opposite, the Lord Dionysos? Will you, with sweet reason, with your gift for moderation, help me grasp what the Lord of Light is all about? And how am I to grasp you? By means of the tales about you? Or from what the scholars have said? Or by dialogue with you? All of these, I suppose, but even more, I think. Yes . . . think. For how else is one going to find a new way of thinking, a new way of light? How, then? Are you there, great Lord?"

In answer I see only that famous statue, the Apollo Belvedere. I see the handsome and great God, but he does not move. He holds an object in his hand. Some say it is an aegis, some say it is a weapon in his battle against the Pythian Dragon. But, to me, it takes the form of a snake, a Python, itself! As I look at the image of the tall and handsome God, I see him firmly holding the snake, the wriggling thing. Only the snake moves, the God does not. But now the stone of the God softens slightly, and the lines around the mouth move and the lips shape themselves into a smile. Apollo looks at me quizzically, but benevolently, as if to say, 'Who is this mortal and why does he approach me? Does he not know that no one worships the Gods any more?' He laughs in my fantasy, and says, 'It is fashionable nowadays to believe that God is dead, is it not?'

Now, I ask myself, is this the God speaking to me? Or is this merely my own fantasy? This God sounds strangely clever, but also rather skeptical. Who is it, God or fantasy? The statue looks at me again and speaks:

"Ho, Knight III, I know you. I know your kind. You would encounter the God, you would embrace the God, you would capture the God, you would even serve the God. But you would keep your own hegemony. You would keep your own service. You would keep your own . . . you know what? Your own fantasy. For you would be master of the world, you would be ruler of your own mind! Well, then, would you be ruler of your mind, then I must perforce remain a fantasy. Is that not so?"

Well, I have to take in what this statue of the God is saying. He is challenging me, right to the core. He is saying that I will submit, I will serve, except that I will remain master of the mind! I will remain the distinguisher between fact and fancy, between image and reality, between the vagaries of the flow of soul, and the concreteness of the world of matter. All that would I do. So, then, I must, perforce, have been identified with my own mind! I must have thought that I and my Mind were One! Well, then, for one who has struggled and suffered the One and the Many, this revelation of his identification with the One, and the One Mind at that, is, indeed, surprising.

"All right, then, Apollo, Lord of Light, I recognize that I have been identified, been undifferentiated from what I chose to call my 'mind.' I admit that I have maintained rulership, the leading decision in what was fantasy and what not, what was light and what not, and, in so doing, have been the Lord of Light myself! In so doing, I have then inadvertently allowed the Lord of Passion to rule me as apart from me! I have unconsciously been Apollo, and, therefore, have struggled with the opposite ruler, Dionysos! All right, then, I abandon my claim to be the Lord Apollo. I abandon my hegemony, my rulership, my belief that I, myself, am God almighty, that I, myself, am ruler of the light of my mind. I abandon this in principle, Oh Lord of Light, I abandon this straightaway. I will assert, instead, that I am the home of the One and the Many, and that I am former and formed. But I will also bow to your wishes, Lord of Consciousness, of light, and will listen. I will be grateful of light, not owning it, and sharer of passion, not fighting it. In short, great one, I shall serve you by meditation, by dialogue, and as you wish!"

"It is good that you added, 'as you wish,' for once again you were setting up strictures, conditions, what you would do and not do. Well, then, Great Knight, Lord of Light, what then can a poor God have to do with such a great and clever mortal, what indeed!"

"Enough, Apollo, Lord! Though I am no great God Almighty, I can still wield a critical cut, I can run from you, serve another. Or, as you say, have you not heard that God is dead'? And is it not worthwhile that someone recognizes you and your power?"

"Well said, Sir Knight. You are almost Greek. Pity that you are not. But, then, the world moves on. Greeks and barbarians give way to new Greeks and new barbarians. And, if you will serve the Light, then you will serve me. Enough. Go, now to my stories, to my 'stations' as you Christianly are pleased to call them. Study them, reflect upon them, and then we will talk again."

The statue resumed its hard, material, non-alive, unmoving, non-fantastic quality, and was once again like any stone. Any stone at all, any stone at all. And yet the stone of the God. The Stone of the God which said that I had claimed his power, really, and had deceived myself. So, now, the speaking image of the God retreats, and is once again, as he said, 'dead.'

I mused: the living God dies and turns into stone. Thus do the people proclaim, "God is dead." The living God, when he no longer speaks, becomes only a dead God, and the miserable ego becomes identified with it. So, when one says, "God is dead," he is also saying, "I am God." Or, at least, that "I am taking over the God's function." Or, perhaps, that men take over the God's function. Or, we no longer worship that function, but use it. True. But, in the course of development, when the function fails, when it changes, when it dies and must be reconsidered, then, once again, does the function become a God. And, then, further, the God which one inadvertently worshipped, becomes relativized. So, have I said much? Or little? I have said my words as they have come. Have I thought? Or have I been thought? Oh, my! My mind is being turned in upon itself. I have abandoned the critical function, and have become lost in the questions. So then, let me follow the God, let me meditate upon his stations, his story, and then I shall find if I think, or am thought!

Apollo I

Apollo was born of Leto, the Goddess, granddaughter of Ouranos and Gaia, Heaven and Earth. But she was also daughter of the Titan Koios, whose name is the same as the sphere, "ball of Heaven" and "Heaven's pole," and of the mother, Phoibe the Moon Goddess, the Pure and Purifying. Thus the progenitors of the great God, he who is only third in rank behind Zeus and the heavenly Athene. It is said even, that when Apollo appeared among the Gods at Olympus to join them, drawing his splendid bow, all the Gods rose from their seats to honor him. Only Leto, his mother, remained peacefully seated beside her spouse, Zeus. Clothed in dark raiment, but sweet and mild as honey, she took bow and quiver from her son's shoulders, rejoicing in both the Light God, and his twin sister Artemis, the virgin.

So, then, light is born, the heir of heaven and earth. He is, further, the light of Heaven, day, and the light of night. But these are not Sun and Moon, as is known by our ordinary vision, but out of our deeper vision. He is the light of day, the lord of consciousness, which is like the father of Apollo Himself, the Great Zeus. He is also the night light, the purifying light of the feminine, the soft light of the other pole. Already I glimpse that the great Lord is a union of Lights, male and female. Already I glimpse it. But let me not proclaim the light as he enters the mountain of the Gods, let me first see to his birth, his appearance in the world.

"A day has passed, Apollo. A day between which I felt my eager anticipation to meditate upon your birth, your life and your meaning, and the day which is today, a time of despair, of listlessness, of a hopeless being downcast. And, in between, I have fallen victim, once again, to emotional orgies of anger and rage, to compulsive hungers, to states that I had not fallen victim to since before my encounter with Dionysos, since before my awareness of the coming down of the ruling center of the eye to the passion center of the diaphragm. All is lost—so it seems. I am back at the beginning, where it started. I began with the statement that all my changes, all my deepened understandings were mere intuitions, did not meet the reality of my hungers and my emotions, my desires and my affects. And here I am, once again. So, then, I am appalled, Apollo, I am dismayed, Dionysos, I am horrified, Hephaistos and Hermes, Hera and Hecate. I am chagrined, Gods. And devastated. So, I cannot, in good conscience, merely go on with my appreciation of you, Apollo. I need your help. Come, once again, enliven yourself in that statue, smile that smile, grasp that snake, and help me to overcome this state of possession-dispossession that grips me. I pray you."

"I come, Knight. It is an easy matter for me. Your words are right: possession and dispossession. You are alternately possessed by the desire and emotion, and you are dispossessed of your senses. You are possessed by your senses and dispossessed of your reason. Allow me to show you how to hold that snake, that wild python of your emotion and hunger. It is thusly: firmly, at a little distance from the body. You neither crush it, nor submit to it, you neither battle it, nor are overcome by it. You hold it, and, holding, make it speak, make it cough up its desire, its wisdom, its prophecy. Such is the way it is done. At some slight distance, and with an inquiring attitude."

"I will try, Apollo, I will try, Lord . . . All right, then. I address you python: Snake of my hungers, insatiable; snake of my emotion, unquenchable; snake of my coldness, unwarmable; snake of my demonism, unassailable, speak to me, tell me what it is that you desire, what it is that you believe in true wisdom, that you prophecy. My Lord Apollo has so commanded me, and him do I serve. My Lord, master of prophecy, of the Tripod, and of the Temple wherein you live and are worshipped, has so spoken. Speak, then, python, and tell me your words!"

"I have no words. I have only cunning. I crawl in every corner, every crevice, every open place. Where understanding is not, there I am. Where wisdom is not, there I am. Where light is not, there I am."

"I, Knight III, servant of Apollo, grip you. I hold you tightly. I feel your skin, cold and squirming. I feel the strength of your fibers, forceful and independent. You are like a phallus, though you are of hunger and emotion, of belly and midriff. I hold you, and command you to speak, beg you to speak . . . Ah, you laugh, for I both command and beg. It is true: as a servant of Apollo, I can command; as my miserable, unhappy and despairing self, I beg. And I can be both."

"As can I, Knight III. I, snake-son, known to your grandfather, can be both: commanding and wise, highest of the high; and lowest of the low. So can I."

"Speak, then, your wisdom, snake. I neither command nor beg, but I request."

"The mortal says 'please.' It is well. I will reply. What, then, is my wisdom? What, then, is my desire? What, then, is my prophecy? My wisdom is that I coil in the belly and below. Maya calls me Kundalini. My wisdom is that I know at the deepest levels, at wordless places, in witch-like wonder, in magical marvels and I rise. And, my desire, what is my desire? My desire is to rise, to rise from the lowest place, to belly, to navel, to heart and beyond. My desire is to rise and be fulfilled, to be like the smoke which rises from the burning branches, the transformed wood of the Tree of life. I would rise to where the highest fruits are, the most perfect round melons, the most lush apples. I would rise."

"Then rise, snake, say I, then rise! If your desire is to rise, and your wisdom is to know from the wordless places of magic and wonder, then rise. Why do you insist on fulfillment and not only rising? Why do you demand satiation and concreteness, rather than rising? You speak, python, of rising to the highest centers, but you demand fulfillment at the lower ones!"

"It is true. But my rising is not only rising up, as the tree rises from its roots deep in the earth and reaches toward heaven; my rising is also a rising downward, a reaching down from the roots of the same tree which grows in heaven and reaches down to the incarnation, the fleshification, the senses and their realization. I rise up, and I rise down. Thus my rise, and thus my wisdom, and thus my desire. And thus, poor mortal, your torment. And thus, poor mortal, your knowing neither up nor down, fulfillment or spiritualization, satiation or ascesis. Thus, poor mortal, you are 'mortified.' For the mortification is also to become mortal, human and whole."

"I cannot stand it, snake. Endlessly does this process go on, until I am worse than before, not better. I am no Jesus, I am no Buddha, I am only a poor Knight, and a not very heroic one at that . . . And what of you, python, undergoing these ascents and descents which are all 'risings'? What do you feel, what do you experience, what do you want for yourself?"

"It is good of you to ask, mortal Knight, few do. What I want, I, the great immortal embracer of the 'I' is to enhance the 'I.' I am that energy, I am that light-bringer, I am that darkness of the night-light, I am that brother to the Christ, I am that life force in the hands of the great light Apollo, I am the Dionysiac brother, I am that which is to be gripped. Some call me female, some call me male; some call me darkness, some call me light. I am only a partner . . . I feel now the grip of my Lord Apollo, my brother and my master, my enemy and my friend. I feel now his grip."

"I begin to feel it, as well, python. Perhaps this Lord of Moderation, of rational choice, of firm decision, can begin to grasp you in me, begin to hold you in me. I feel it in my back, in its pains at the base of the spine, where you begin. There, in the base are you coiled, oh snake! There from the base do you rise up and, as you say, 'rise down'! There, where my pain comes, do I need the grip of the Lord, both there and in that gaping center of the inner forehead, of the third eye. I feel the grip. And now I feel my two hands, the right one at my forehead, the left at my back. As if I must have a hand, a fist, a grip on each place: I must grip both you and Apollo, be gripped by you and Apollo. For, if strong, I can feel my strength of gripping, if weak, I can feel my weakness of being 'gripped.' No words, you say, snake, no words for your wisdom, but I doubt what you say. For the words lead to double words, to double meanings: possession—a big word; gripping—a big word, full of opposites. And now, I know you as my grandfather knew you, and my father, too, though in another form, as the Binarius, a devilish demon of opposites, held and being held. And as Kundalini, too, for you are both former and being formed, you are both the God Shiva and the Goddess Shakti. And yet, snake, you would be held, you would be gripped, by God and Man, by Apollo and myself. Grip, grip, I say to myself, grip and be gripped. Possess and be possessed. But my Lord Apollo, I so much need You, You Lord of moderation, to moderate, to help me grip rising above and below, spirit and flesh, not, my Lord, in some mere 'moderation' of pallid men, but, Lord, to help me moderate the battle, contain the conflict, survive the terrible toil, the mortifying melee, the horrible holocaust which is my soul-being, my spirit-flesh. Apollo, I grip the python. Help me moderate!"

"Those, indeed, are the proper words, Knight. That is the right attitude. I am glad that you ask me to 'moderate' and not be a mere symbol of pallid 'moderation.' As I said, and as you now begin to glimpse: hold the snake firmly in your grip, strongly in your hand, away from the body, but not outstretched. Hold the snake and moderate it, but ask of it, respect is, and it will soon speak its wisdom, give of its prophecy . . . Enough, now, you have felt some fingers of my grip, you have felt the bite of its tongue; meditate now, upon the tale as told of me."

"Pain, pain, Apollo! Sorrow, sorrow. I try to meditate upon your tale, upon your birth, with its gold and grandeur, but I suffer only pain. I cannot begin the meditation with the birth, as it should begin. Rather, I shall begin with you and your enemies. I shall begin with pain and battle, with giant and snake, because those are what I feel now. So, forgive me, Lord, I can not begin at the beginning, but shall begin with the tales of your enemies who appeared immediately after your birth. And perhaps, Lord, it is not so far from the plumb-line of proper devotion to you, proper observance of your rites, for as soon as you are born, there is already battle, there are enemies, there is war. For the great God, Apollo, adored and feared as one of the trinity of most high Gods, is a son to be reckoned with. So, then, the first battle, Tityos.

"Tityos, the giant, the tale says, was a phallic son of Zeus and Elara, who attacked poor Leto as she was approaching Delphi. This great giant grew so great in his own mother's womb that she perished of him, and he was born of Earth, in whom his father, Zeus, had hidden him. This same giant attacked the good and gentle Leto, and it was only Artemis who laid the giant low with her arrows, or in another tale, it was you, Apollo, who did this. But it is also said that Tityos was struck by Zeus' lightning himself for this. As his punishment, he lay in the Underworld at his full length of nine-hundred feet, while two vultures tore at his liver. Or else a serpent tore at him, and the liver grew again with the moon. Thus the tale.

"What does it signify? That the giant, phallic earth titan, who was too much for his poor mother, who killed her in his birth, is also your brother, great Apollo. For is not his father the same as yours? And was not your birth also a great travail for your mother, who suffered nine long days and nights? It is true, great Lord. Your brother, your evil other half is merely too much, too powerful to be contained by the good and gentle soul, by the feminine which must labor long and hard to contain the fruit of the Great God, the Father. And, as it attacks and hurts the poor Mother-soul, it must be killed. It is killed, then, by the Virgin Sister, Artemis; yes, that which is virginal in the soul gives no birth at all, it is enemy of the too primitive, too concrete, too masculine. But it is also killed by you, Apollo. You, Great Light Lord, you with your arrows, so different from Eros your other brother, your arrows destroy the phallic giant. Your arrows are sparks of light, of understanding, of consciousness, a penetrating vision which can peer through the darkness of passions, the rape-force which would destroy the soul. And so does Zeus, the great Father, destroy the titan with his lightning-sparks of intuitive understanding, his electric charge which sends the giant to Hell. It seems right.

"But I recall stories of my mother, who was like a Persephone. She, poor thing, had the task of going into the Underworld, after suffering her own rape, and freeing those horrible ones. She could listen to them and have compassion. My poor, suffering mother was a heroine of redemption. I wonder if I could also? I wonder, indeed, if Apollo would accompany me in this act?"

"I would, indeed, brave Knight. For I am known as a just God, a fair one, as my later tale demonstrates, when I did servitude for my murderousness, and like a mere mortal, also received punishment. I am, therefore, willing to descend with you into Tartaros and glimpse, once again, that vile giant who attacked my poor mother. You are right, however, in seeing that he is a brother of mine. Indeed, I, too, inadvertently, caused my mother great pain. I, too, almost killed her with the bigness of me, but I did not. Let us visit him."

"And so, Apollo and I, God and mortal, descend into Tartaros, just as my mother did, there to see the great giant, suffering the damnation of his vitals perpetually being torn. And the moon, the moon: it heals with the moon; with the night light of the God, and the true light of the Goddess.

"Oh, Tityos, giant and God, you are the misbegotten son of the great God, and I see you in your grief and horror. I, too, though mortal and son of no God, am repeatedly torn in the belly by rapacious hungers, by my vulturous and insatiable lusts and irrational desires. And these, too, are forever shot down and killed by my virginal pretensions, by my rational expectations, and by my visions of higher truths. In short, you-in-me are forever killed by Artemis, by Apollo, and by Zeus. Because you are too much, you burst the soul, you rape the good and gentle mother. Oh, giant, how to end the suffering you cause and the suffering you are caused! It is endless. With each day, you are devoured anew—just as you devour—and each night, with the light of the kind-not-kind Goddess, you are made whole again. Let us weep together, giant. Let us weep, Tityos. I, a mortal, understand you. I, a mortal, summon my Lord Apollo, my Lord, Zeus, and Artemis, the Mistress of Animals, I summon them all to witness and to share our weeping. Most of all, I summon Leto, who it was that you sinned against, indeed go on sinning against. For there is a forever hurt of the soul which tries to give birth to a new and great light. But come, Gods, are you not also guilty? Come Zeus, are you not Father to such a monster? Come, Apollo, have we not seen that Tityos is your brother? And come, Artemis, do you not merely flee from the male, virginally avoid the power? You nod, I think . . . I do not see you clearly, but I feel your nod of agreement. Apollo, my Lord, sit with me and see the pain. Help me with the vultures, help me with the giant. I beg of you!"

"Grip, grip, Knight. Grip."

"Grip, you say. All right, I hold the vultures in my hand, and they bite at me, gnaw at my hands. I take my hungers in hand and they bite at my effectiveness, my grasp, and my way of touching others. But now, Tityos arises and looks at me, kindly. He is huge, but he himself is gentle. He, now, holds the vultures; he, now, grips them. Power with power; hunger with hunger. What does it mean?"

"Grip, grip, Knight. Grip."

"I grip, and I hold. Tityos grips and holds. Apollo grips and holds. And now Apollo merges with Tityos, as if the statue, mere stone, takes on the flesh of the split-off Underworld brother. He becomes of human proportion. Indeed, he enters into me. And now I, Knight III, am part of the God. There is a union of Apollo, Tityos and myself. The God, united in an upper and a lower, a light and dark, a spirit and earth, joins in me and is mortal. And now I see the center of the inner eye, the third eye of the forehead take on a glow. It is as if the eye must take on the earth of the phallic giant, the purity of the virgin Goddess, and the electric inspiration of the Great God. All these, blended in the clear-sighted, balanced light of the Son-Sun-Light God, Apollo. Very beautiful, very right, but very hard to achieve.

"I will proceed further with your enemies, Apollo, for it is with your enemies that one can, by contrast, perceive and understand your light. So, it is told that your real enemy was the snake-dragon Python, who had previously pursued your mother, Leto, seeking to prevent her from giving birth. So, soon after your birth, great Lord, you visited Delphi, where the Python—also a son of Gaia, Mother Earth—had his lair. His lair was said to be a cave, or else he coiled around a laurel tree.

"But it also said, Apollo, that your enemy was not Python, but Typhon, the dragon who was conceived by Hera, without her lord and husband, Zeus. Typhon it was whom she conceived alone in anger, because of the ever-non-monogamous strayings of her spouse. Further, it is said that there were two dragons, not one, and that one was Python, or Typhon, a male dragon, but that the other was Delphyne, a female serpent. It is said that Hera gave the one evil thing into the charge of the other, dragon to dragoness. And often it is said that you, Apollo, killed not Hera's offspring, but that the Python lived in great amity with you. Indeed, pictures show him as guarding the Omphalos, the sacred navel-stone and center of the earth. He, Python, the great oracular seer who spoke to your priestesses at Delphi, the Pythia, peacefully and carefully surrounded that center stone.

"So, then, Apollo, was the Python your enemy, or was it Typhon, Hera's parthogenous son? Or was it the female serpent, Delphyne? Tales say that you were but a child, in your mother's arms, that you came with unshorn hair, your mother's son, bow and arrows in your hand. You shot arrow after arrow and slew it. The paeon rang out for you, your song, for you were born to be your mother's champion, and in your smallness slew the great female serpent. But it is also said that the great dragon, Python or Delphyne, was dissolved by the sacred power of the Sun, and after its putrefaction, the place itself was called Pytho.

"I believe that I can understand this confusion of the tales, great Lord Apollo. The confusion is one not of identity, but of sequence.

Surely it is that the dark threat to you and your mother, which came from Hera as the terrible dragon, as either her offspring Typhon, or her own nature, Python or Delphyne, is that powerful force of nature, that snake-like passion of dark desires, of black intuitions, of jealousy-possessiveness-greed, all those dark places which have belonged to the Navel-place of Dionysos, the belly region which is both labyrinthine and desperate. They begin as the dark dragon, Lord, and you conquer them. You, with your bright light, with your arrows of clarity and understanding, your 'grip' of your moon-shaped bow, you are the one who can grasp and overcome those dark forces. And they die, they putrefy, and under your command, your aegis, they transform into oracular statements, dark and light intuitions. You transform their destructive power into creative power: passion becomes creation. And you, Lord, can take on the name of Python, and Lord of Delphi, itself. Only then, Lord, does the snake wrap itself upon the navel as the center of the universe, only then does the Python, ennobled and enlightened by your arrows, become the guardian of the Center, that place from which oracles come. For oracles come not from the head, from the third eye. The wisdom of Apollo and the lightning ideas of Zeus come from there, but oracles? Unseen and dark, unknowing yet knowing anticipations? These, surely, come from an informed belly, a penetrated and light-giving source. Just as a true love comes from an informed heart, a heart hit and transformed by those other arrows, the arrows of Eros!

"All that is clear, Apollo, all that is transparent. What is not transparent is how that great event occurs, how you, in reality, bring yourself into being out of the horrors of your birth, how you, in fact, cope with the dragon of the great vengeful Goddess, how you transform the Python of your brother Dionysos, the place of emotion, into your true brother and co-God. How, great Lord, does this occur, and how can it occur in my own being?"

Apollo and Hera

"Knight III, you ask me how it is that I transform, that I battle and overcome, that I become Lord of prophecy, as well as light. You ask these questions and I will answer. But consider, first, the tale of my birth, for I feel as if I am not properly existing in your world, until you reflect upon that."

"I will, great Lord.

"It is written that all lands were terrified of the birth of the great Lord, he who was to be third of all the great gods, after only his father Zeus and Athene. Poor Leto went from place to place, but, since it was said that Leto might give birth only in a place on which the sun had never shown, this was difficult, even for a goddess. Jealous Hera had willed this, and with her I shall have to deal myself, just as my sister Daughter of Guinevere did.

"But the tale continues that Delos, that island which only rose as the Goddess came to it, that island which was shrouded in darkness because it was not created until she came, that pitiable and miserable crab was shrouded in gloom, and there it was that the Goddess came. Nine days and nights did she suffer in utter anguish of childbirth. Nine days and nights did she labor in pain. And why? Because Hera the Jealous had so willed it. All the Goddesses were there, excepting only Hera, and at Hera's bidding, the Goddess Eileithyia, who assisted at divine child-bearing. Thus was there pain.

"But, finally, the Goddesses sent the messenger Iris to fetch the mid-wife, Eileithyia, promising a golden necklet nine ells long. With this promise, both Goddesses relented and came, like two turtle-doves. And then, just as the mid-wife appeared on the scene, Leto gave birth. She gripped the palm trees which grew there and kneaded the land. The soil laughed beneath her and the God sprang forth. As he appeared, the light of day began. What was wolf-light, twilight, day-break, became golden with the sun. Gold, gold. The foundations of Delos turned to gold, swans circled singing, the leaves of the olive tree goldened, as did the river Inopus itself. Even the cock which was present at the birth of the God, gave witness to the sun-rise gold.

"Apollo came forth swaddled with gold. Nor was he suckled, this God-child. Themis gave him nectar and ambrosia, and he sprang forward saying to the Goddesses: 'Dear to me shall be lyre and bow, and in my oracles I shall reveal to men the inexorable will of Zeus.'

"This is the story of your birth, great Apollo, and some of it I can understand and fathom. I can see that the Lord of light is born only after great travail. I can see that you bring forth and proclaim your great gifts of lyre and bow, of music, of the seven-stringed instrument and the vehicle of the archer. I can see that your hand rules both the centers in evocation, and the centers in action, in lyre and bow. I know that like Ajna, you are born to come from the 'place of command.' And, like the Hindus, you are fed with nectar and ambrosia from the center above, and that you serve the will of God the Father. All this is clear. Even clear is that all urns light in your presence, all that was dark turns to the light of the sun, and that the cock, who proclaims his joy at the emergence of light, his ecstasy and dancing in moonrise and his proud witness of sunrise, should be your bird. Just as the palm is your tree, and the laurel, too, the wreaths of hero and victor. All this I understand, great Apollo. But of Hera, I do not understand. I do not understand with my bones how she hounds your mother and yourself, how jealousy, possessiveness, greed, all the dark emotions continually have their sway. You battle the dragon, but in your own God's name, why do you not battle Hera?

"Why do you not battle her, yourself, Knight III?"

"All right, great Apollo, I shall. Daughter of Guinevere was able to do this, and I shall try, also. But I have felt this great Goddess less from within myself than from outside. From women have I experienced this dark place and, like you, Apollo, I would rather be a young lord in service of the Goddess against the Goddess. I would rather be a servant of the Mother, Leto, gentle and loving, and against the Queen Mother, Hera, demanding and treacherous, vengeful and jealous."

"Do you not know, Knight III, that the one is the shadow of the other? That the Great Mother Herself, origin of them all, is genetrix of loving gentility and hating violence? Do you not know that I fought the one in the service of the other?"

"I know, great Lord, but I cannot do it. I fail. I am not up to such a task. I am a mere mortal, a failing man, a poor fellow who cannot even choose what he wants, let alone fight the great dragons of the feminine destruction. I need your help."

"You have it, use it. Think. Speak yourself to the great Goddess, and think."

"All right, great God . . . Hera, mighty Goddess, enemy of Apollo, enemy of the many loves, many relationships, enemy of man, really, I address you. Hera, mighty Queen, I am a mere mortal man, victim of the pythons which you send routinely, those dark passions spawned by you in your aloneness, and I, unlike the God Apollo, am killed by them. I implore you to desist, to cease, to make me less your enemy, and more your friend."

"You speak of death, Knight III, but you seem quite alive to me. You, mighty hypocrite, speak of pain, of death, but you survive rather well, I see! Better yet, think of the deaths, emotional and spiritual, of the women who have loved you! Better yet, think of them, and not so much of yourself! Then, perhaps will I give some thought to your poor and bedraggled state. You have been loved to excess, loved more than most. You have been loved by mother and daughter, by wife and mistress, you have been loved and you make claims! I find that disgusting! Better should you be grateful for the loves, bend to the loves, acknowledge the loves, than that you should ask for more love. And from me, he wants it! From mighty Hera, who loves only Zeus, my great Lord, from me he wishes love as well! Oh, Apollo, mighty son of my great Lord, how can you support such a foolish mongrel? How can you bear it? And you, Daughter of Guinevere, how can you claim as brother and lover such a silly, greedy one?"

"Hera, mighty Queen, you speak the truth. I, a poor Knight, have been loved to excess. I have been loved more deeply by a wife than any man has a right to ask. I have been blessed with as loving a daughter as any father has the presumption to hope for. I have been loved by as loyal a mistress as any lover can claim. I have been loved by female friends, and even foes, greater than those that I know. And, with all these gifts, I am still greedy. I am still greedy of greater love. Just like you, Hera, I want more! More, more, more! And are you not thus, great Hera, Goddess who is never satisfied? Are you not ever clamoring for more, more, and only, only, from your Lordly Spouse? And how am I different? I ask for more, from more people, but I also give, I think. Or so they say. They say, indeed, that I have given much. And I know, from my encounter with Don Juan and his friends, with Magician and Eros, that I am capable of love. So, then, Goddess, I acknowledge my great gifts from women and Goddesses, just as you say, but proclaim that I also have loved."

"It is true, Knight III. I must smile after my angry outburst. For I am often angry, as you know. And, as the tales say, my anger is unbounded. But you forget that the tale of Apollo's birth says that I finally accompanied Eileithyia, the mid-wife, that I, too, was a turtle-dove, that I, too, relented in my anger."

"It is true. But am I ungentlemanly in reminding you that the tale says that it was Zeus who took anger from you? Do I do you an injustice when I say that you did not give up your anger of your own accord?"

"It is true, Knight III. . . . But tell me, Knight III, could you endure the spectacle of a spouse, or any loved woman, cavorting with the

Many? Could you endure your own jealousy, possessiveness and greed in silence? Could you?"

"I could not, and have not. I acknowledge it. What more can I do? How can I overcome? How can I obtain your good will rather than your venom?. . . Silence comes from you, Goddess. No sound. Have you already retreated into your Solitariness, your Aloneness? Have you already abandoned me to an aloneness which I do not want?. . . No answer. Apollo, great Lord, what say you? No answer. No answer.

"All right then. You, great Gods, you do not answer. Let me then sigh and submit. Let me then state that I, too, have no answer. I, too, can retreat. I implore you both to a dialogue; I beg you both to take up your claims. I wish that you would resolve your differences with yourselves and leave me, poor mortal that I am, to bear whatever decision you make . . . Ah, do I hear you?"

"He is right, you know, Hera, the mortal is right. You are, indeed, too single-minded and vengeful and wrathful for this new breed of man, this breed of a new era. He is also right about himself, is he not?"

"Him I despise, Apollo. Him I do not value. I wonder why you spend your time with him. He is nothing. It is only that poor girl, Daughter of Guinevere, and all those women around him that I worry about, care about. Foolish things, they should abandon him. Then he would feel the value of the single union! Then he would know the aloneness!"

"Your quarrel is with your spouse, I think, not this mere man. Your pain is with your Lord, my Father, I think, not this poor Knight. What do we Gods want of mortals, I sometimes think? Why do we bother them so? Why can we not merely have our way with them and not require them to engage with us, serve us, and even help us transform ourselves. I think that we are far too demanding of them, as if they, too, are Gods! Which, of course, they are! And, I think, that poor mortal of a Knight, like his ancestors, knows it! Perhaps that is why you despise him so, Hera. Perhaps that is why those women take after him so, for they know it, through him, and you know it!"

"Quiet, Apollo, quiet! Even though you are the great son of your great father, my spouse Zeus, quiet! You do not treat me with enough respect. You do not realize that I am Queen of Heaven . . ."

"No, my great lady and Goddess, not Queen of Heaven, I think, you are Mistress and Wife of My Lord, Father Zeus, and his consort, but Queen of All? I think not!"

"Yes, yes, yes, You are right. I know it. I rue it, as well. And it is well known. But how do you think it feels to be so dark and dreary? So angry and possessive? It feels not at all well. Do you not forget my other sides? That I gave birth to two daughters, Eileithyia, the helper in child-birth, and Hebe, 'flower of youth'? That I was mother to Hephaistos, the creative one, as well? Why do all only remember my pain, my grief, my anger and possessiveness? Who can help me with those?"

"Perhaps I can, Hera. For, do we not dwell together in Olympos? And is it not the wish of the mortals that we live in peace? And are you not also, like me, a natural resident of the center of the Place of Command? Are you not also, like Zeus, your spouse, Athene and myself, part of that ruling place? Can you, then, live with that multiplicity?"

"I cannot. I can tolerate it, indeed, must tolerate it. But I cannot accept it."

"So be it, then, the mortal is right. None can dissuade you. Neither mortal nor God. And, surely, not I. But I it will be who will forever kill your dragon. I it will be who will forever send arrows against your darkness and subdue it. I will forever take from your kingdom and make it my own!"

"For that I have no fear, great Apollo, for that I have no hatred! Did I not relent with your mother? Did I not give up anger at your birth? I do not fight wisdom or light; I do not banish joy or fulfillment. But I do not grant it, either. One must fight for it, one must transform for it!"

"I hear you, Hera. I, poor Knight, have listened here to your words with my lord Apollo. I listen and am appalled. I rue the day, for myself, for men. You are heartless, though you claim not. Apollo used arrows to transform the darkness and become its master. But what is to become of your heartlessness? What is to become of your merciless way? What is to become of men? Athene's war-like ways are transformed in protection. Dionysos is transformed as guardian of the helmsman. Even Hecate is wearer of the cone-hat and transformer-of-the-indirect-effect. And where are you, then? What positive thing do you do? You speak of Hebe and Eileithyia, your daughters, you speak of Hephaistos the creative, your son. They, indeed, are wedded to man. But what of you, Hera, what do you want of us? What will you give to us?"

"A model, Knight. A model. Will you love your spouse as I love mine? Will you give such devotion to the great spirit as do I? Will you give birth to the flower of youth, the assistance to creation, and creation itself, as do I? Will you be jealous of the creation? Will you?"

"I try, Hera. I love my spouse, within and without. I love my creativity, within and without. I love the spirit, within and without. I do, I do, I do."

"Then do. And feel my blessing when it comes. Feel my warmth in the loving union. Feel my care, as well."

These final words of the Goddess, these brief and poignant words of she-who-will-be-obeyed, she who will ever serve the spirit, ever serve creation, ever serve the flower of youth, these words silenced me. I felt only a touch of her loving care in them, but I felt the power of her devotion, the power of her commitment. These are very great forces in the universe, indeed, I thought. Very great. And yet, I was puzzled. Hera surely serves these things, as she claims, but she is seemingly very selfish. She serves creativity, it is true, by giving birth alone to the creative God, Hephaistos, but she is often his enemy and shows him no love. She serves the great spirit, Zeus, it is true, by her total devotional monogamy, but she shows not love for him personally, only for the spirit which he represents. And, in truth, she gives birth to the "flower of youth" Hebe, and to the helper in childbirth, but she withholds these from others. In other words, she has all this power of devotion, of creation, of the beauty of youth, of the service to the spirit, but she is, as I have said, 'selfish.' So, now, Apollo, my Lord, this have I learned about the nature of the powerful feminine principle, she is selfish in all these things. Is it possible that she is the prototype of us poor selfish mortals? Is it possible that she claims the service of all these lovely things, but is really representative of our little egos, our selfish selves? It seems like that, rather. But are not all the Gods selfish? Are they not like man himself, out after their own needs, their own desires, their own peculiar principles? It seems so. What say you, Apollo, God of understanding and light? What say you to what I have concluded?"

"I say, Knight III, that you conclude too quickly. You are like my Father Zeus, having an intuitive lightning flash and thereby deciding that that is the whole truth. It is too quick, too little, too insubstantial. Hera, it is true, is wedded to herself, and is, thereby, seen as narrow, as self-centered. But, as you say, are we not all this way? Are we not all focused in upon our own way, our own center, our own principle? It is quite true. It is meet, therefore, that the ruler, the place of command, be occupied by such a one as myself, who sees the light, but a light and dark light, who sees the reason, but sees the music, too. And it is also right that I am not the only ruler of the center, but in that same place of command there lives my father Zeus, the great creative, multiple, ruling, intuitive spirit who goes to and fro in the universe, here and there, up and down, in heaven and hell. It is, as I say, right that he also be ruler, for he cannot, will not, be contained, will ever seek above and beyond, below and back, here and there. My God, my father, is my equal and my Lord, and I gladly join in his rulership. And so, too, can we share this rulership with Athene, daughter of the great Father. For is she not the servant of civilization? Is she not mistress of the greatest city-state of all? Does she not serve and adore, worship and embellish all those traits in God and men which will lead to the communal enrichment of spirit and soul, of beauty and understanding? Enough, for it is obvious that she shares rulership of this great center. As I have said, the power of the spirit of the Father, and the power of the soul of the Daughter, is combined with me, the power of the mind of the Son, who can link reason with art, mind with feeling, I belong here, too. For am I not known as leader of the Muses? As player of the lyre? Of the gentle rulership of all the seven strings of centers, high and low? Clear. But think, now, is our threesome of Spirit, Soul, and Mind insufficient? Do we not need, in our rulership, that engendress of the concrete, of flesh? And who else than Hera, herself, Mistress of my Lord who is ever-searching and ever-moving? For Hera serves all these things and is narrow and spiteful and difficult, dear Knight, because realization in the flesh is always difficult. The vision is always greater than the fulfillment, both for Gods and Men. So then, in Hera, Zeus meets his Kronos, Jupiter meets his Saturn, but in feminine flesh. The opposite of limitless possibility meets the need for concrete realization in space and time, in the flesh, in the hardness and narrowness of time, of space, of one love at a time, one child at a time, one creation at a time. Thus is my mistress and Queen Hera! Thus is the wife of my great father, represented in the most high places of command, for she is your own representative here, Oh Man! Great Hera, in her selfishness, narrowness, egoness, is that representative of the vessel of man's poor mortal frame himself, of the Many become One, of the Multiplicity become Singular, of the Possibility become Actual! This, Oh Knight, is Hera. This, Oh Knight, is Hera Maligned. Hera, to be adored, to be loved, for she needs your love, she needs all this, as she has said."

"Oh, my Lord Apollo, your words astonish and delight me, they humble and elevate me, for I understand. I hear you and I understand. I feel now for the great Queen, the mighty Hera, who is a vessel like me, and ego like me, a needy, difficult, spiteful being, like me, for the flesh is like that—complaining, matter is like that—resistant, reality is like that—narrowing. I shall try and treasure her as do you, great Son of the Great Father. I shall hold, in my heart and head, in my mind and body, the Quaternity of Leadership of which you speak: God the Father, God the Daughter, God the Son, and God the Mother, a foursome of leadership of spirit and soul, mind and flesh, and to these will I bow, to these will I give over the place of command.

"For this alone, great Apollo, for this glimpse of the depths and necessity of Hera, the Queen, I am forever grateful to you, forever beholden to you."

"Be thou beholden to Hera, Knight, for she needs your love. I need not your love, but your attention and devotion to my tale, my story."

"And thus will I proceed, my lord Apollo. But in deference to your words, and the mighty Queen Hera, let me say my poor words to her.

"Oh, Hera, mighty Queen of Heaven, forgive me for not understanding you. Forgive me for holding you in insufficient respect. Forgive me for not loving you. For I have not loved enough and cared enough for my own poor limits, my own mortal frame which is forever hounded by all the possibilities of the spirit, all the needs of the soul, all the pressures for creation and order. I see you better now, thanks to Apollo who really appreciates you. And I shall try to see you as best I can. And please, Goddess, accept that if I love you insufficiently, it is also because I love my own limits in the same way. That, too, is a limit which I would burst. And, in bursting, accepting; in acceptance, bursting; in loving you, Oh Monogamous One, loving myself; in accepting You, accepting myself, becoming 'Self-ish.' Goddess, I bow."

"You speak well, Oh Knight. Rise, and continue your devotions to Apollo, mighty Lord."

Apollo II

A story is told, that after Apollo captured the rocky place of Delphi, he sought his first priests. Some men from Crete were on a ship bound for Greece when Apollo leapt into it in the shape of a dolphin, sprawled upon it, and steered it straight to Delphi. Then he sprang, as a gleaming star, straight from ship to temple, from which he appeared as a long-haired youth before the frightened Cretans, making them his priests.

"Apollo, this tale shows you much like your brother, Dionysos. You capture the seafarers and bring them to your service. You come, too, as a dolphin, the most human of fishes, but also as a star. I think I understand: the Cretans, those inheritors of the tradition of the Great Mother, the primordial religion of the Mediterranean, will be your men. You overcome their bark and lead them. But, whereas Dionysos, with his mighty passion and wind, frightened the sailors-pirates and turned them into fish, you, yourself, Lord, are the fish! You, yourself, transform yourself, you are like the Lord God of a later age, the great fish, Christ, who transforms himself into the leader and the food of men. I think it is true, it is more like the Son of an upper level that you are; brother to Christ above, as well as brother to Dionysos below. For you, Apollo, are the leading one, the reasoning one, the link between the powers of the great spirit below. Without you, Jesus and Dionysos would war forever, and you, great Apollo, link to both. You are a star to be followed, a leader to gaze upon, just as the Helmsman, in service of Dionysos, steers his vessel, and looks upon the stars, among which you are a bright one. You are also a star like that which announced your greater brother, the star of the East. I understand. And, as youth, you are the handsome, virile, athletic god, a god of flesh as well as spirit, and in this form do you mediate for us.

"There are many stories, Apollo, of how you built your famous temple at Delphi, and the forms it took. Some say it was built by bees, of wax and feathers. Yes, the diligence of the Queen Goddess is yours, just as Leto adored you, and even Hera modified her sting. Wax congealing and feathers flying, religious adhesion and spirit soaring, these, too, are yours. But it is also said that you came every year in a chariot drawn by swans, just as did your mother. For you are, indeed, the son of your mother, her defender. How could it be otherwise?

How could the great Lord of the Center of Command not defend and protect the feminine, from itself, even to itself? The son of the great father, and brother to great brothers above and below, must also be son to a great mother, and, yea, even two mothers, else how could he command?

"And now I must tell you of my further thoughts, great Apollo. I have thought that the center which you occupy, along with God the father, God the mother, and God the daughter, must also be the center of God the Husband and God the Wife, for are not Zeus and Hera primordially thus? And it must also be the center of God the brother, which is you and, because you are not only brother to the brothers above and below, but to your sister, the Virgin Artemis, that she, too, is implied or hinted at. Further, great God, and without malice, or presumption, I would aver that the highest center of all, the Sahasrara, the place above even yours, where Jesus and Mary live, is the center of God the Man, and God the Woman! These my thoughts, great Lord, infused by you, informed by you, enlightened by you."

"It is so, good Knight, it is so. Go on with my tale."

"So, great Lord, it is said that some men also set your temple afire, led by the sacrilegious Phlegyas, himself father to the woman who was to be mother to your great son, Asklepios. You struck him with your arrows and he had to make his atonement in the Underworld. Some say that he suffered eternal punishment, but others that he only made his penance and was spared. It must be the latter, great Lord, for you are not vindictive, you are not the vengeful one. And, was it not true that poor Phlegyas was not, indeed, sacreligious toward you, he was merely enraged that his daughter was so badly treated by you? Do we not all know the tale?

"Poor Koronis, the 'crow-maiden,' having your pure semen inside her, was attracted to another, Ischis, the strong 'pine-man.' And so, in her mortal way, with limits and desires, she lay with him, unfaithful to you, great Apollo, but also in secret. Do you demand such utter devotion to yourself, great Lord? Poor Koronis did wed her mortal lover, while you merely came to her, impregnated her with that great healing god who was to come. Why did you grow so furious, why did you so harshly treat the poor father Phlegyas, who was merely angered that you and Artemis were so cruel to his daughter? For Artemis sent her arrows to Phlegyas and there was much fire and pestilence.

"I know, great Lord, that at the last moment, when Koronis was burning in her own funeral pyre, that you snatched your son from her, the great healer Asklepios, and spared him, bringing him to the Centaur Chiron to be taught the art of healing. I know that you spared the son, but what of the mother? And why so harsh with the father? Ah, great Lord Apollo, I had hoped that you would be a God with less vengeance, less pride of a foolish nature, less demanding of total devotion to you alone by the poor feminine. In this harsh act you were more like Hera, herself. And, indeed, it is said that when news of Koronis' unfaithfulness came to you from the white raven, that you, just like your angry sibling Athene, turned the raven black. Your anger cursed the bringer of the tidings, just as irrationally, just as cruelly as any lesser God. What say you, great Apollo? What say you to my charge? I charge you with irrationality, with cruelty, with lack of compassion, with vengeance, with being less moderate than you claim. What say you?

"Knight, I accept the charge. I accept the blame. But go on with my tale, go on with my stations, go on with what the stories say of me, and see if I, indeed, remain such a one-eyed, forceful, vengeful, cruel God. I think you speak of early stages of my life, my stations, my devotions. Though a God, I grew. Even Gods can grow and change, good Knight, or have you not learned this?"

"I have, of course, great Lord, and for this reason do I continue my devotions, my meditations, my work at transformation. As you say, Apollo, I shall continue."

"It is said that another enemy of yours, good Apollo, was Herakles, himself, the hero-son of Zeus and Alkmene, who is, thus, your half-brother. It was said the poor Herakles, bloody and ill, came to your temple in Delphi and asked for healing, but received no answer. He thereupon stole your sacred tripod from the oracular Pythia. It is said that you fought with the hero, Apollo, and that Zeus settled the dispute: Herakles returned the tripod and was given help by the oracle. Another time you fought, I think it was over a stag, an animal sacred to you and your sister. Is the hero your enemy, Lord?"

"Only he who will steal my tripod. My triangular basis, my trinitarian nature, as you already know, is my own cone, just as you have yours. I will not have it stolen. By neither man nor God."

"It is true, Apollo. Zeus, himself, required that you desist from destroying the mortal, Herakles, for your father knew that his mortal son was destined to be among the Gods, that man, product of mortal and immortal is meant to be deified one day. Your father knew it. And thus did he, indeed, entrust and return your oracular prerogative to you, but thus, too, did he see to it that Herakles fulfilled his need. I am struck by this, great Lord. It is nothing less than that man has a right to his healings and oracles-prophecies from the God, just as God has the right to be master of them. Man tries to wrest his healing and knowledge of the future, and this fails. But God, too, has the requirement to give these things to us. Is this not so, great Apollo, moderator and law-giver? Are not these the obligations of God to man, and man to God?"

"It is so, Oh Knight, it is so. And it is just this that I learned from my father, Zeus, the great lightning one. I, too, learned of justice and balance, did I not? Go on, and see how it was that I learned, and suffered. For I, after all, with my fish nature, and light nature, suffered just as did that other Son, who came after me."

"All right then, I shall continue. Perhaps, I, too, shall learn, just as the God, in his modesty, has claimed that he learned in his life. Now that I reflect upon it, that in itself is remarkable: that God recognizes that he himself learns, undergoes changes. I do not recall many experiences of God when he has so admitted it. Very well, then, Apollo, great Lord, I am not disappointed in you, I am continuing to learn of your mystery, your wisdom.

"It is said that in order to atone for the killing of the serpent, Delphyne, the female dragon which he slew immediately after his birth, that the great lord Apollo had to serve an ordinary mortal, a king named Admetos, 'the untamable.' This atonement lasted for a 'great year'—that is to say, a nine-year period. Only after this could the great Lord return to Delphi and his temple, as 'the Undefiled,' the Phoibos and clear light, with a wreath and a branch of the sacred laurel tree. Yes, great Lord, I can see what you were referring to: you cleansed yourself of your vicious murder, which itself needed to be done, by performing the service of an ordinary mortal. Just as you had no compassion for the mortal Koronis, your mistress, just as you failed to give Herakles what he needed, you needed to come and serve man, to see how it is that man suffers. Your lack of care was followed by the justice that you serve man, caring or not. And in so doing, you regain your light, your undefiled purity of the rounded orb. You regain your laurels, your victory, and, in truth, your merited leadership of men, your rulership of the centers. In this, great Lord, I admire you; for to be a leader one must be a follower first; to be a victor, one must have failed; to be served by man, one must have been his servant. And this is true for God or man, I see.

"It is also said that during your 'great year,' the pastoral time of your service to Admetos, the 'untamable' man, that you yoked a lion and boar together for the King's chariot, thus helping him win Alkestis to wife. You thus, great Apollo, helped mortal man to tame the opposites in himself, the great leading lion of Zeus, the father, grand and glorious and mighty, but with a powerful roar of spirit, together with the boar of Dionysos, the Son of the lower centers, of the ravenous belly and passionate midriff. These centers, wild and unruly, yoked together, carrying the vessel of mortal man, helped him to wed his own soul, his feminine soft nature which could make him truly whole. And this did you help man do. And thus do you help me, too, great Apollo, to unite the wild and ruling fiery Lion-lightning of your father Zeus, with the wild and ruling watery passion of Dionysos, the Boar. And you do this. You, Dolphin, you Swan, you Stag, you Star, you do this.

"And you also saved Admetos from death by making the Morai, the hard fates, drunk. In this you knew the winey nature of your brother, you served the passion of the brother below, just as you had served your own passion for order and balance by yoking the animals before. And you saved a man from death! Oh, great Lord, this is not vengeance! This is not eye for an eye, grievance! This is eye for an eye, life for a life, repentance! For you saved a life where you had let one go. You healed a soul, where you had denied it! I comprehend, great Lord, how you learned.

"And when it came a second time for Admetos to die, his wife went in his place, and was brought back by Herakles. In this, great Lord, that which you gave was given back: man saved man—and woman—from death, and that which you denied to man was achieved by man. By the same man who was to become God. This is very deep and heavy, and larger than my own poor mind can grasp in its entirety. But I see it, I see it: it is the pattern of justice to man, and justice to God, the balance of back and forth, of one leading the other and back again. And this, in your form, Oh Apollo, is the ruler, the Karma, the heavenly interplay over which you cast your pure, undefiled, victorious eye, the phoibos of light.

"But, Apollo, it is also said that the reason for your servitude to Admetos was that you had slain the Kyklopes, or their sons, and that you did this because you wished to take vengeance upon your own father, Zeus. Zeus it was who had smitten your son, Asklepios. It was said that Asklepios, saved by you and brought up by the Centaur Chiron, grew great in healing. Brought from the brink of death by his father, the God, suckled by both a dog and a goat (the Underworld companion of Hecate and the animal of Dionysos, too), he became so great a healer that he even resurrected heroes among the dead. So great a healing, so much an intrusion into the prerogatives of the great Zeus, himself, brought on the wrath of the God, and he demolished the healer with his lightning. You, then, Apollo, in vengeance upon your father, thereupon killed a number of the Kyklopes, those Titans who gave your father his thunder and lightning, those one-eyed creatures who sport their vision on their forehead!

"What does all that signify? That the son of Apollo become healer, transgresses. In his mortal nature, he not only heals men, but defies the great rule of Divine life. Only the God can be allowed to sever the thread of life and re-weave it. Zeus kills, he sends back to the Underworld that which was saved and redeemed by Apollo. Translation: the gift of healing, even to the re-creation of the dead, put into the hands of man, with his arts and sciences, brings on the wrath of the hegemonic intuitive divine, when too presumptuous. Just so have civilizations and ways of healing and knowing risen high, to the point of new creation, even, and were then torn down by the wrath of the divine itself. In vengeance, the moderate god then takes away the one-eyed thunder and lightning sources of the father. Intuition as leader; thinking as leader: both draw their power from below: from the power of the titanic lower centers, and from the efforts of man. The war continues, in heaven and on earth. Was it the Prologue in Heaven where God wagered with Satan? Was it not also in heaven that God struck God? The battle continues, until there comes a sweet peace, a union which makes it brotherly.

An alchemist has said that the yoking of the opposites, the achieving of union brings not a sweet peace but a warring peace, not a bitter wound, but a sweet wound, not a permanent healing, but a permanent healing-wounding. The wounded physician heals others and himself. That is the truth. And that is the truth of the tale: of Apollo and Asklepios, of Zeus and Apollo, of Father and Son.

Apollo III

"Apollo the just, Apollo the healer, Apollo the light-bringer, with all your names and epithets, great God, you are also a lover. Not a lover, of course, like Eros is a lover—for he, like Aphrodite, is love itself—but you are, all the same, a God who has loved much. At this 'station' of my reflections upon you and your tale, I will try to understand the nature of your love.

"It is said, great Apollo, that you had many loves, and that many of these were tragic. Furthermore, it is said that you loved youths of both sexes. I do not understand this, neither the tragedy nor the bisexuality. One wise man explained the reason why boys were included among your loves is because you are often represented at just the age at which a boy would leave his mother's nest and live together with other lads. This is not so convincing to me, I think. So, then, let me meditate upon a tale or two of your love for these boys.

"The most famous of these was Hyakinthos, son of the incestuous union of the Muse, Kleio, and her father, Pieros. Aphrodite brought this about because Kleio had scolded the great Goddess for her love of Adonis. Scold incest, she demonstrated, and you will engage in it. So she did. And the divinely handsome Hyakinthos resulted, mothered by Kleio, whom I know very well as Muse of History and 'bringer of fame.' It is further said of this same Hyakinthos that he was sought after by the singer Thamyris and Erato, 'Awakener of Desire,' as well. But the truth is that Hyakinthos resembled the great god Apollo, himself, not only in appearance, but in having a virginal sister very close to him, Polyboia, by name. Sometimes, even, there are images of him as a being with four ears and arms. In any case, the God loved him and played with him. They played athletic games, particularly throwing the discus. One noon, the God accidentally hit Hyakinthos with the stone. From the blood of the handsome one, there arose the hyacinth, brilliant wildflower with the dark blue blossom.

"What is the meaning of this love, great Apollo? I can see that you love the fruit of the incestuous union, father and daughter. Are you not known as the leader of the Muses, yourself, Lord of Music? And is not the union of the Father Spirit with the Creative Soul one of the main things I learned as I studied the tale of Bluebeard? And is not your center, the Place of Command, directly above that of the

Muses, where speech and poetry reign? And that you, together with your own father, are the leader? Yes, all clear. Besides which, your own center is shared with a Father-Daughter union itself, Zeus and Athene, is it not so? Yes, I see it. But why should this offspring be a male, and beautiful. Why should you long for him? Why should you accidentally 'kill' him, though we know that such Gods do not die. Why, indeed, should there by the 'accident' at all? I do not understand.

"Perhaps, great Lord, your love of the youths is symbolic of your attachment to the divine and youthful spirit in a young man as he, in fact, does leave his nest. Are not such young men beautiful, usually? And inspired, and optimistic? Are they not deeply attractive in the youth and promise of their spirit? Perhaps you love all beginnings of the spirit, great Apollo. Perhaps you wish to educate, inform, and play with all those new outcroppings of beauty and grace which can lead to even greater spirits in the future. It seems likely. I can even see that you hint at another kind of love than that which Eros or Aphrodite embrace, a love of man for youth, of father for son, of men for each other. Do not the Christians call it Agape? A friendship love, a warm love, a love of male for male? Yes, it seems likely, perhaps even certain. But then, why is there destruction, why pain? Why does the symbol of wholeness, a round stone, crush the head of the youth, and why does there bloom a hyacinth? And why is noon emphasized?

"Oh, perhaps I can understand that, as well. The new spirit is always crushed by life, isn't it? Did not I, in my youth, and my father and grandfather before me, like all men, have oh so many ideas and plans, ambitions and goals, inspirations and ideals? And, are not these ideals and goals, plans and inspirations, often crushed by life, by the hard and bitter coldness of the facts which intrude upon them? And, does not Reason itself, unwillingly, 'accidentally,' crush so many of these blossoming flowers of expectation? I think so. And the passion and warmth and blood of these lovely mental inspirations are returned to the earth, returned from the animal to the plant level, from upper regions to lower, from upper centers to lower, from consciousness back to the unconsciousness of nature, there to re-blossom as the mystical blue centers, the grails of the gentle hope. The hot 'noonness' of light crushes these youthful things and they fall back, fall away. Yes, many of my ideas and ambitions have so fallen, despite the love of the God. Is this so, Apollo? Do I reason rightly? You nod, but do not speak, so I will consider a second male love of yours.

"Among the boys you loved, Apollo, there is Kyparissos, 'Cypress.' Kyparissos seems to have been a double of yourself, as, perhaps, all these beautiful boys are copies of yourself. And, therein may lie the meaning. Are these lads human and semi-divine copies of your own archetypal self? Are they, on the human level, living the fate that awaits the youthfulness and growing of the divine reason, wedded to musical feeling, merciful justice, a wholeness which is crushed in the noon of life where everyone learns that reason crushes, that it is separated from feeling, that justice is rare? Yes, Apollo, I see that is some of your message. But let me continue the tale of Kyparissos, your twin. This lad also unintentionally killed a creature he loved, in this case a stag, animal sacred to you and your sister, Artemis. This stag had golden antlers and wore silver ornaments upon its brow. It was a tame and willing mount for the beautiful Kyparissos. One hot noon, Kyparissos mistook this stag for an ordinary one and sent his spear through its head, killing his beloved. He wanted, then, either to die or mourn eternally. And you, great Apollo, in your wisdom, turned him into the Cypress, the sorrowing tree which is evergreen, and sacred in the regions where Persephone dwells.

"How, then, Apollo? Do all men kill the thing they love, as it is said? It seems so, for even God kills his own beloved. And, he kills his own image. Every new incarnation is loved and dies, from God to man, from man to animal. And all reside eternally in the plant, whether blue mystical hyacinth, or green cypress of eternal death and birth. What is said? That the Gods of above, and the humanity of above is more evanescent than the centers below; that immortality is at the level of the plant. That I vaguely understand, Apollo, but not enough. Will you speak to me, answer me, guide me in understanding this, your tale of love?"

"I will speak, Knight. But you must listen carefully, and with ears like the stags, sharp, and with eyes like the Hyacinth, blue and open, spirited and deep. Can you so listen with eyes and ears?"

"With ears I can listen, of course, but like the stag? With my animal mind? Yes, I think so. And with blue eyes? Eyes of heaven and eyes of the sea? Can I look-hear? Yes, I think so."

"Well, then, Knight, if you can so see and hear, then you have learned already, you have learned already. You have learned that the young God always dies. You have learned that before, as you said. But now you can see that what dies is the merely beautiful, merely potential, merely youth-God of great promise, but no achievement. It is not only by accident, as you have guessed, that such great beauty-children are destroyed. It is by an even deeper power, the hard stone of the round earth, as you have said, and the harsh light of middle day—these do destroy. But not forever; they bring new forms. And if one can, like you claim, learn to think these thoughts with the ears of the stag with the golden antlers, all the better. For one then has the penetration (by spear) of his golden male animal wisdom, ornamented by the female silver of adornment. And thus is the stag sacred to both my sister and myself, female and male. For, is not my wisdom the gold of light, but is it not adorned by the flowering silver of the Muses? Soul penetrated by spirit, I think you said. Look now, it is animated by animal, is it not?

"And think, too, of listening with hyacinth eyes: blue of heaven, and blue of sea. Inflow of the divine waters which come from beyond me, from the center above, from Sahasrara as Maya called it, and beyond, from the ever un-manifested, ever manifesting spirit of new creation. And from below, from the region of my Lord Poseidon, the Magician, from the waters of Hades, and from the deep mystical and transient spirit of the tender flower.

"So, then, listen with the animal ear and the flower eye. Listen and the Godly wisdom will be transformed from a mere playful beauty to a depth and height which is eternal. And this I love even more: eternality of creation. Suffice."

"I hear your words, Apollo. I hear and I assent. I take in and digest, and know that wisdom informed with nature, is the answer. The animal wisdom, speared by man, penetrated by his effort, brings sadness but eternity of devotion and love. And the youthful wonder, penetrated by the stone of totality, brings, from bloody passions, a gentle mystical joy, a loving spirit of high-low wisdom which is forever. I see and hear; I hear and I see: I understand."

"But you were also a lover of girls, great Apollo. Agape and wisdom, knowledge and comradeship were not your only aims, you loved the maidens as well.

"In your love for maidens, great Lord, you were not Lord and Master, One and Unique, but great Homer tells us that you often had a rival for your love, and that love with you was a dangerous thing, not only for the youths, about which I have already wondered, but for these maidens as well. I shall speak of your first love, Daphne, she whose name is the same as that of the laurel tree, sacred to you. Divine Daphne was a child of the God of Rivers and the Goddess of Earth. She was a wild virgin, much like your sister Artemis, herself, who also had her own sacred laurel trees. Now Daphne was not only a wild virgin and in the forests, hence distant from men, but she was also loved by another man, the handsome youth Leukippos, 'the white stallion.' Leukippos disguised himself as a girl in order to be near his beloved, but was discovered by her girl companions whilst bathing. The result was either his death or disappearance. Daphne, pursued by you, great Apollo, begged Mother Earth to save her, and was turned

into the laurel tree. Thereafter was the laurel your favorite tree, a
branch of which you wore as a wreath, the round victory symbol which
you bequeath to male and female, youth and age.

"Thus the tale of your first love, great Apollo. In a way, like my first
love, great Lord: frustration, desire, love . . . and loss. I wonder how
you felt; so great, so handsome, so gifted with everything, and yet
reduced to having a mere mortal as your rival. And poor Leukippos,
handsome and like the pure young animal thing that he was, he could
not accompany the daughter of river and earth, he was discovered.
The other fiercely feminine, wildly virginal sides found him, and he
died or vanished. And, of course, it is so. When we mortals peer at
the divinely virginal, whether your sister Artemis, or even Athene,
and surely of Daphne beloved by the God, we cannot bear it. We
succumb. We lose ourselves and our lives. That which is naturally
pure and virginal, untouched and divine, is too much for us. Did not
the biblical tale, told my fathers before me, speak of the pristine
paradise, pure and undefiled, intolerable to man? We long for it, try
to stay within it, but die, just as did Adam and Eve. We come from
the vision of immortality to the clear experience of mortality. We
die. But you, even you, great Apollo, are not wanted by this creature,
this divine offspring of river and earth. She calls upon her mother to
save her from you. That must hurt you, indeed, even though you are
a God. Or are not Gods hurt? Do they not suffer from feelings of love
frustrated, rejection, lack of fulfillment? I know that some are so, for
that has been my experience, too. I have learned, at great cost, that
the Gods undergo pain and transformation just as do we mortals, and
the change in the one brings the change in the other. I have
discovered that we are a twosome, a marriage of God and man,
unbroken union. For there is union even when there is breakage, there
is separation and apartness and evil, but God and man are together,
like peas in a pod, I think, as the Yogini once said. So, then, if it is
true that the Gods suffer, then surely do you, great Apollo, suffer the
sadness of the loss of your first love.

"Is she, then, lost to you because she is like your sister, an ever-
present taboo of incest? You still desired her, I think, just as you were
attracted to the beautiful Hyakinthos, himself a product of the incestuous union of the Muse, Kleio, with her father. But the Gods are
permitted incestuous unions, I think, just as royalty are, so, I do not
understand . . . I must think more, great Apollo, for that would be
your message. Let me think with stag antlers and blue hyacinth eyes,
as you told me to do. You long for union, with the son of the Muse
of fame and history—incestuous—and the daughter of the union of
river and earth. And the union is denied in you, just as it is denied

mortal man. Instead the flower results, or the tree.

"Ah, great Apollo, the tree! The tree, the tree, the tree! Was this not the great vision of my Grandfather the Knight, and all of his friends? And have I, too, not had this vision of the tree growing down deep into earth and up into heaven? Is not the cone, above, below, merely an abstraction of such a tree? And have I not learned that all the Centers themselves, of which you are a ruler, make up a tree? All the centers are themselves like the Tree of Man, or the Tree of the nervous system, with all its branches, or the Tree of the blood system, and finally, the Tree of the Kundalini, the tree about which the serpent, your friend, coils itself. Thus, then, the plant and the tree are those vegetative, natural, autonomic, earthy centers within us that you rejoice in, great Apollo. It is said in the tale that you rejoiced in the tree of Daphne, the Laurel, she was your favorite! Now, I see, now I can see with spear antlers and hyacinth eyes, with the gold of mind and the vision of heaven-growing-from earth: what you long for, great Lord, is union itself. You long and worship that Tree of Life that my Grandfather also worshipped, you adore its bisexual nature, for trees, like men, are male and female in one. You adore your sister, the twin of your soul, whether she is within you or outside you, you adore and treasure. You long to unite with her, but accept her in the Tree, in the great, marvelous Tree of Life, where you come to life in mankind. Great Apollo, I understand. And I understand, too, that you wear the wreath of this tree upon your brow, and you bestow it to me when victorious: for you are the leader, the victorious, the place of command is yours, and that which you give is the mastery, the realization, the recognition that the tree of life is garland for the mind, that the realization and union of all the centers is an achievement, a great honor. For you voluntarily give up your incestuous union—in the flesh—for a greater union. But that greater union is not just 'spiritual' as some claim; no; it is a union of above with below, of spirit with flesh, of blue eye and earth, of water-earth like Daphne, with air-fire, like you. And so, the Laurel, tree of Apollo, sacred sister-lover to him who would love and unite and adore the Tree of Life. In this, great God, I understand you. In this, I see you as leader of Muses, as united with the tree and, above all, as seeker of union, as server of union, as he who treasures the light above and below.

"You smile, Apollo. Your reward for my realization is the smile. Like some Mona Lisa, like he who would know and lead, but rejoices quietly in being understood. I rejoice in you, great Lord.

"There are many tales, Apollo, of your love affairs with girls. There are stories wherein you transform yourself into a tortoise to win your fair one, only to change again into a serpent and terrify her. Thus you were with Dryope, daughter of Dryops, 'the Oak-Man.' This playful nymph, friend of the other oak-nymphs, the Hamadryades, was impregnated by you and secretly wed another, bearing your child.

"Is this how you are, great Lord, with women or men's souls? Daphne, daughter of water and earth, escaped your love and was turned into your favorite tree, the Laurel. Now Dryope, daughter of the spirit herself, can become yours, but only in secret. You come to her gently, as the kind tortoise, to win her love. What nymph, what soul cannot be enchanted by God coming as a safe and slow creature, covered above and below by a protective round shell of wholeness? Did not the God of Israel also come as the turtle, with the voice thereof? And sing sweetly and joyfully? And, great Lord, when you so come to that soul which is already begotten by the tree spirit, by the realization of the many centers, then you are cordially greeted. But you transform into a serpent, into your own wily and prophetic and cold nature, phallic and self-seeking, not gentle, and the feminine soul is terrified. Of course. But then she gives birth to your offspring in secret. Though wed to another, she secretly bears your seed.

"I think I see, great Apollo. This is a second stage of your worship, your realization. The first stage is that of Daphne, who must first become the tree. The soul, product of the union of water and earth, the lowest two levels, must first realize that it is the vessel, the tree of the whole soul of man. Only then does the second stage occur. Now the soul, daughter of the tree-spirit itself, is able to receive you, first playfully and then in your serpent-like prophetic nature. But it must carry your seed secretly.

"And now I must speak of a later stage, the story of your union with Kyrene. But first, to complete the tale of Dryope, it is said that the Hamadryades captured her, after her wedding and made her one of themselves. The soul was not yet strong enough to be free, to contain your seed and be wed as well. No, she fell back and was captured by the soul of nature.

"But, Kyrene, Lord, was not such a one. She was a great virgin huntress, much resembling your sister, Artemis. She was the daughter of the mortal King Hypseus, which refers to the heavenly heights, and a water-nymph. Thus, Kyrene was the union of air and water, a higher level, just as your first love, Lord, was the product of the union of earth and water. And this Kyrene is more your match. For Artemis gave her two hunting dogs, with which the virgin huntress protected her father's herds against beasts of prey. With spear and sword she stood guarding them, and she could even wrestle a lion, unarmed.

"You were astonished, great Lord, you were deeply impressed by this daughter of mortal and nymph, of air and water. For she can battle the lion heats, the passions of midsummer of which you are too well aware. Lord, did you think of your own dog-star, Sirius, which comes in the heat of summer? Did you think of your own too-hot nature, too much light, too much heat, perhaps, for the mere mortal soul? Were you impressed by this figment of creation of the union of mortal with nature, with human spirit and soul of nature. I think so, Apollo, for God, I know, is always seeking union with man, always longing that man be strong enough to unite with him. And now, at the level of Kyrene, at the third stage, beyond Daphne who becomes the tree, beyond Dryope who cannot sustain the secret, and is captured again by nature, beyond these two comes Kyrene. 'Kyrene,' you are thinking, great Lord Apollo, 'this mortal soul will not collapse and fall back into nature, into unconsciousness; she will sustain my spirit, for she is strong like my sister, Artemis, and can wrestle lions, can take on the heat. And she serves her father, man, and protects his herds. She I must unite with.' So you thought, Apollo, I am sure.

"But the tale goes on that you summoned the wise Centaur Chiron from his cave, close by. This same Chiron, healer and father of healers, advised you to take Kyrene secretly to wife. So, great Lord, you inquired of the product of the union of horse and man, of that which had appeared before in the form of your rival Leukippos, but is now your friend and confidant; now you ask your own wise and healing animal nature for aid. You bend down to unite with the animal-human soul and consult your own. And so you did. You carried off Kyrene, the wild virgin, in your golden chariot drawn by swans. Oh, Apollo, in your chariot you must have been like the great Charioteer, glimpsed by my father, Son of the Knight. You must have been great and beautiful with your bride, drawn by swans. My father saw you in that form, I think. And it made him a poet, touched by Muses. You took your bride to the north of Africa, and consummated your marriage with her, your union with her, upon the golden couch.

"And Chiron prophesied that Kyrene would bear a divine son. This same son would be taken by Hermes and brought to the Horai, those Goddesses-three who are of 'the correct moment,' who tell the truth, do not deceive or betray, and bring the glorious fruits of the earth. So Hermes, messenger of Gods, communicator, brings the fruit of your union with the mortal soul to the Horai, and also Gaia, mother earth. And they, marveling, drop nectar and ambrosia between his lips, making him immortal.

"Is this tale not like that of Maya and her Gods? Is this not the tale of the falling from above of the great nectar and ambrosia which soften the divine, makes it soft and fruitful? And is this not also a Christian tale, where a divine-human child is born to a mortal woman, a virgin who is capable of sustaining such an enormous event as receiving the great God? So it seems to me, Apollo, and so it must also seem to you, you who see so much, know so much.

"And of this son of yours, Apollo, this second Apollo, what is he called? Why he is called nothing less than Aristaios, 'the best god of all.' Is that not a confession of all that I have said? Is that not a portent, a foretelling of that birth of the Christ child, that divine-human being who would also be the best god of all? And is it not hinted that the union of you at your third-eye place, the place of command, with the soul-tree-human-place of Kyrene would result in a center higher even than your own? That Sahasrara place, that place up in the skull where Christ and Mary dwell, ever open to the nectar and ambrosia of the ever-transcending God. And thus, Apollo, your own Aristaios is none other than the divine child, the Jesus child, the Christ-child, he-who-has-come-will-come and is 'the best God of all.'

"So you took your second Apollo, second Zeus, Aristaios, to the cave of Chiron, where he was brought up by the Centaurs. Healing, he learned from them, but also was he taught by the Muses, who gave him other arts of healing and soothsaying, as well. So, Aristaios, the chosen one, became the darling of Muses and Centaurs, of the Horai and Gaia, and he guarded the cattle, the herds. Aristaios it was who protected the people from the plagues, from the hot days of summer, for the winds blow for him in summer's heat. He invented the beehive and bee-keeping, did this God-man, and the oilpress, and the making of cheese. These things did he do.

"Perhaps he found the way of community, the bee-hive, just as the God-man who followed him told us of the community of men and women, of brothers and sisters, through love. Perhaps he shows us the oilpress, the way to get the goodness out of the pressure of opposites, and hard good matter out of the milk of the great-Goddess. I do not know, Apollo, these are not clear to me. But I do know that he was the first to lay snares for wolves and bears, and to have freed Sardinia from wild birds. He thus could cope with the wild nature of you, great Apollo, you who carry still the nature of your mother as wolf, and of your sister, Artemis, called bear. This mortal found a way to snare, to capture and make less dangerous these wild, capricious, devouring, characters of the brother-sister gods themselves, you Apollo and Artemis.

"Strange it is, Apollo, that such a God-man, such a significant figure should not be more famous. He is so much like a Jesus, really. I think of my Grandfather, the Knight, who knew of such things. For he knew that such Gods were anticipations, forerunners. And I, too, know that your son, Aristaois, was a reality, and an anticipation of the later child-God Jesus, just as Kyrene was an anticipation of mortal Mary. I think I understand, great Apollo, great God, that you continually look to find mortal man and woman receptive to your spirit, open to you so that conjointly an even greater God, an even greater and higher center can be born. And I can see that the stations of your life, the successive loves show you as ever eager for this union, ever serving the Tree of Life, wanting to unite with the soul, and eagerly waiting and serving this event. Until Spirit, which is you, unites with Soul, which is psyche, in the flesh, which is Matter, by means of the Tree of Life, those centers in man. Thus your tale, Apollo, thus your stations."

Apollo IV

I have completed the stations of your life, Apollo. I have circumambulated your nature and your loves and I think that I have understood you. I have understood as best I could: eye of reason and judgment, passion of light and justice, service of man, need for union, master of the Tree of Life, teacher of youth, instructor of the spirit, lover of men, lover of the soul, raising of the soul to the Tree, and further, uniting at last with the Virgin and producing the God-man, the child who is yet to come. All these and more; all these I have understood, taken in, yet something is lacking. Oh, Apollo, I understand too quickly. With my quick Hermetic eye, my Gemini nature perhaps, ruled by your Brother Hermes, I am myself like quicksilver, quick to understand, quick to flow, but quick to forget, quick to lose. Do I really know you? Do I know you as you are?

Do I know that God who was described as coming into Delphi with drawn bow, fragrant robe, with the lyre in his hand? Do I know that same Apollo appearing on Olympus among the Gods, making them all seized with longing for music and song? Can I visualize it? When you appear among them, great Apollo, the Muses sing in antiphony of the immortal gifts of the Gods and the sorrows of poor, ignorant, feeble men. The Charites, the Horai, Harmonia, Hebe and Aphrodite, all these nine Goddesses, dance in a circle, each holding her neighbor's wrist, as you play. Artemis, too, enters into the dance, while Ares and Hermes sport with the dancers. And you, great Apollo, leader of all, leader of the Muses, of the Charites, Horai, Harmonia, Artemis, Hebe and Aphrodite, you play and they dance. They dance as you show them, for you, great Lord, are *Musagetes*, "leader of the Muses" and *kitharodos*, "Singer to the Lyre." Beautiful and tall are you, and the poet says that you brought Nature into Harmony. Yes, that is you, great Apollo, for this I did learn as I meditated upon your liaisons with the nymphs of the tree. You, indeed, bring Nature into Harmony as the poet said: you bring the warring nature of the soul, its uneasy mixture of earth, water, fire and air into harmony with your own higher spirit and thus is there a union in the great Tree. Your serpent coils around it in healing like your son Aesculapius, in wisdom, like your prophesying oracles, and like a new child-God, your son Aristaios, "best God of all."

The poet also says that you are the splendid Apollo of Zeus, that you "unite beginning and end, and the plectrum of his lyre is the bright ray of the sun." Such is the hymn to you, great Lord, the poets know you. For you stand there in that center, the Ajna, place of command. You command all below you, Muses following, and you look up to your present and future son, he who will be open to the ever transcendent, ever renewing God above.

I would also sing a hymn to you, great Apollo, but that is too much hybris for me. I must reflect further upon you, great God, for it is not enough that I do your stations. I must really understand, with my mind, what you are about, lest you, too, fade away from me, and I, in my ignorance and feebleness—as the Muses say of men—lose all sense of having contacted you and your tale.

"Tell me, great Lord, tell me, great Apollo—for you have spoken to me before—tell me what you would of me, what you desire of me!"

These I will do, great Apollo, these I will do. But how should I tend the Tree of Life, the host of centers? How should I hold the light?

"That you tend the tree, hold the light." "You know my way, have your say."

"All right then, I shall 'have my say.' I shall speak of each of all your names, your epithets, and your attributes. I shall speak of them, comment. And then I shall ask your boon. I shall ask you to sing with me, for me, I shall ask you to lead me and the Muses in a song commemorating your being, your service, your virtue. This I shall ask. But first to 'my say.' "

"Apollo, you are foremost a God of light, for you are called Phoebus and Lycius. Indeed, you are the light bringer, the pure and holy light of Phoebus, not the sun, Helios, that natural orb, but the higher light of God and man, the light of consciousness. You are the light which seeks the maximum consciousness, the maximum union of man with his own nature, as the poet says. And, your light is great, in spring when it overcomes the powers of winter, as you did when you slew the dragon Python, or in summer, when the great power of your light is both good and evil, helpful and mischievous. For you are also wolf, great Lord, a hungry rapacious creature who hurts men with a devouring hunger for consciousness!

"And the people worship you and give sacrifice in the festivals of spring and summer, in the Delphinia, when you calmed the wintry sea. You brought peace to the tormented waters of the soul in its ever-changing moods. You brought—and bring—harmony. The light of your consciousness can give us peace. The people honor you in the Thargelia, in the midst of summer, that the crops might ripen, that the parching heat of your power is not destructive. For your light is destructive, too, even though you avert the vermin and pestilence, the dark and destructive, negative thoughts and suicidal, self-damaging effects of that same nature. For you tame nature and raise it to a higher level. Great Apollo, I salute you.

"But you promote the health of man himself. With your son, you do this. You serve the manliness of youth, the body-temple. You serve this, I know, so that the Tree of Life, the centers of the soul and its energies, can have a fit receptacle in which to live and work, so that the human personality, abiding there in the flesh, can serve and bring fruits from that same Tree. For this you are equal with Hermes and Heracles in the gymnasia.

"You are Agyieus, God of streets and highways, with a conical post to honor you. That I understand, great Lord, I know that cone-shaped post! I know that you are commander of the highways and byways of life, of men's exits and entrances, of their good and evil, and to discriminate them. Just as Aphrodite is in all their experience of love, and your opposite Hecate, also of the cone, is mistress of streets, of involvement, you, too, are master of the judgment of life, of the assessment of good and evil and their effects. And you have earned this by your own suffering, your own service of man. You are not a mere jealous Hera, or a vindictive, vengeful God, but a judge who has suffered and judges with light, not with selfish cruelty! So, while you are judge, you are also Alexacacus, averter of ills. You send the dreaded epidemics, but heal us from them as well.

"So, then, great Apollo, you are healer and savior. You are the God of mental and moral purity, of justice in the highest sense. As such did you not spare Tityos, the over-weening Niobe, and the Greeks before Troy? But you are also a helper to the guilt-laden soul, for you also committed the worst of crimes, a murder. You did your penance, and found your atonement, and thus did you purify yourself in the sacred grove and not return to Delphi until you could truly be a prophet for your revered father, Zeus. Thus, great Lord, you fly in the face of the God of vengeance, of eye for an eye, of blood guilt, which can only breed new murders, new guilt. You are great, supreme Apollo!

"Your light inspires, great God. Not only to the divination of the thoughts of your father Zeus, or through the ecstatic utterances of the soul while serving you, but also in the elevation and inspiring strains of Music. For not only are Atonement and Prophecy your realm, but Music, yet more, for you lead the Muses, you play your lyre. All these have you.

"What have you not, great Apollo? What is not yours? You calm the sea, bring the light, you are ruler of Atonement, Prophecy, and

Music. You give reason and the soul a harmony through the union of Nature and Spirit. What more can there be? Along with your sister, Athene, ruler of civilization, and your father Zeus, who rules all, unites with all, what more can there be?. . . Yes, I know, what all the rest of the Gods have: Aphrodite and Eros, Dionysos and Demeter, Hades and Hecate, all of them. Each has a remarkable, total place. It is as if, great Lord, that each manifestation of the Divine is everything. Perhaps in the end each spark of God is all God. And all the names, all the attributes are merely our way to apprehend, to take in, to give name and hence, limitation, to all that is greater than we ourselves.

"But I will not desist, for I would speak further of your attributes. You are lord of song, with your lyre and its strings. But deeper; each string is a center, a place of consciousness and energy, played upon by you, led by you in a great harmony which can make all energies, all Gods and Goddesses join in the dance of life and death, the dance of the union of man and God.

"You are the far-hitting archer. Your bow reaches out and touches man and beast, human and instinctual, you touch us all. For consciousness has its bow, just as Eros has: all life, all existence must be touched and penetrated by consciousness and love. It is so.

"You are the Pythian Apollo, the holder of the Tripod. The threefold chair, the conical post, are yours, just as the conical hat belongs to Hecate, your sister of the Underworld. There is a prophecy of the heights, as well as the depths. There is an understanding and prediction from consciousness at your place, as well as that of the irrational Goddess of the depths. Both are true. And they need not battle. Science serves you, and art: openly, clearly, rationally, but with feeling, with order, with justice. I salute you, great Apollo, but you, too, must salute your sister, Hecate, who rules similarly, in the deep.

"You are master of the bay-leaf, planted round your temples, for it is the bay, healing plant, and helpful for expiation that you are served. You are master of the palm tree, for under it were you born. You are lord of the Tree, great Apollo, for, as I have said, it is the Tree of Life, starting with Daphne, that you are leader.

"And among animals, the wolf is sacred to you. The wolf, that ravenous, dark and hungry nature, eager for man's crops, that wolf was your blessed mother and—you. For you are also the help against your own darkness. We know, Lord, that God helps us against him, that the Lord of Light also has a darkness and helps us against this darkness. And he needs us for this, too.

"But the dolphin is also yours, great Apollo. That playful creature, who shows us that the water is navigable, that the seas of our unconsciousness, though vast, can be played with, swum in and enjoyed, just as you enjoy the dolphin, the friend. And so, also, is the swan sacred to you, for it is musical and white. And so, too, are hawk, raven, crow and snake, all connected with your prophecy.

"Apollo, you of Belvedere, you are all of these things. You are handsome and strong, defender of man, seeker of atonement, harmonizer of nature and spirit, all of this. Will you now sing to me, lead the Muses and sing?

"I will not sing, Grandson of the Knight. For you have sung. You have sung my praises, told of my attributes, celebrated my being and nature. You have sung a hymn to me, after all. Your tale itself is a hymn. And, if it is not to your liking, then change it. You have done your best, what more can be asked? You are touched by me, speak of me, speak to me. I am well satisfied."

"But I am not satisfied, great Apollo. I do not 'have you,' I do not claim you as my own."

"Who can claim me, Knight III, who can own me?

Who can own the Lord?

Can the Light, when He creates it?

Can Justice, when He makes it?

Can Music, when He sings it?"

"Thus you sing, great Apollo, thus you play.

You say, no poem—and you sing.

You say, no need—and you play. I accept it, I treasure it. I bow. I draw myself into an arch, and I send myself up to you. I fly to the center of my brow and look into my own third eye, and there are you. I fly in and see you, great ruler."

"Wait, then, and look, and perhaps a hymn will come to you. You need not be Homer to sing. You need not be a Rhapsodist, even, to play the paean. You need only sing from the soul, look from the eye, unite your own nature with your own spirit. Only that . . . ha . . . only that. But peer, Knight, peer into the new eye which guides you. Peer and see that no longer is anger and vengeance there, no longer is blood-jealousy there. There is light and dark, to be sure, wolf as well as lamb, but there is . . . harmony, reason, sweet order . . . but I will not speak for you. Look and then sing."

"I cannot sing, Apollo, for I have already sung. I have said my prayers to you. I have performed my worship. I have meditated, reflected. I have tussled, struggled. I am satisfied."

"So, then, good Knight. You are satisfied. It is ended. Follow me, observe me, peer into me. Make me yours, as I will make you mine. Let our eyes meet and, in meeting, unite. And, in uniting, penetrate.

And, in penetration, become one. Be thou my son, be thou my Aristaios, as I am son to the father. And we shall be son to father, and father to son, and, in so being, creating. And, in creating, becoming; in becoming, divining; in divining, knowing the wishes of that other Zeus, that father of us all, ever unmanifested, ever coming to us like the ambrosia and nectar of my childhood, ever creating anew."

And now great Apollo put upon me a laurel wreath, a round halo for my good head, which will touch nature, the Tree of Life and my good Lord all at once. I am knighted once again, but by a Greek God, a Lord of Harmony, of blend of spirit and nature, and my soul will be ruled thereby. And the crown is sweet upon my head. Let healing and Musing, divining and atoning, be my way. Let me lead and be led. Let my poem be a paean, let my rhapsody be a celebration of my great Lord, Apollo, Light-bringer. And let him dwell in my head, like the laurel which rests upon it, lightly, with grace, with harmony, with light and joy. Let him find pleasure and sanctuary as a dweller in the center, the place of command.

PART IV
Union

Guinevere II

"Grandson of the Knight, you have been spending an unconscionably long time in your meditations upon the great God, Apollo. I know full well that this reflection has been very important to you. I am aware that this embracing of a new consciousness, a new 'place of command', is central to you, as far-reaching as was the dream in which your old teacher lost his hegemony. I also feel that what is important for you is important for me, because our union is the central thing, is it not? Or is it? In your pursuit of understanding and transformation, you seem to have forgotten all about me, abandoned our joint quest. In fact, you have been so absorbed in your meditation that you have failed to realize that Maya is no longer here with us at all! Are you aware of that? And you have had the temerity to suggest that it is women who are self-involved! Well, perhaps we are, but we usually concern ourselves with our loved ones, our relationships, and, being involved with them, we are involved with ourselves. My self does not exist apart from you, though you, I fear, would not say the same for me! So, then, Grandson of the Knight, please awaken to the fact that I am here! Have you forgotten that your initial problem and difficulty was in the area of passion and love, for one and many, in spirit and flesh? Have you forgotten?"

"So many questions and statements, Daughter of Guinevere! So many barbs and pushes. You begin to sound like Hera! But, then, you may be right. I suppose you are right, after all. In my absorption with the problem of Apollo and the rational mind, the light of consciousness, the new "place of command", I really did forget about you and about our joint quest. Forgive me. I am here. At your service!"

"Good and well. But you needn't be about 'my service'. I am not like those Ladies of old, whom the knights served in that way. Even my mother, indeed, who was a great lady served by Knights, outgrew that kind of formal relationship. She became a complex and subtle woman in her own right, with husband, children, lover. She served her own spirit, and was not just some white-gloved, delicate maiden who had to be protected. So, then Grandson of the Knight, you would serve me best by serving our joint cause. You would serve me best by both serving your own spirit and our mutual aim, which, after all, is love and union."

"Enough, now, Daughter of Guinevere, of chastenings and admonitions! I have agreed to your reprimands. I have agreed that I am to blame. I have apologized and presented myself. I am fully agreeable to our joint quest. Enough, now, of your complaining! Have you not overcome the limitations given you by the struggle between Sisters of Belly and Heart? Have you not, yourself, confronted and related to the Goddesses of all the centers?"

"I have, Sir Knight, and Gods as well. I will leave off now from reprimands, and tell you what has happened during the time you have concentrated upon your task. Much has happened, indeed. First of all, as I said, Maya has gone away, returned to her own realm where the Hindu spirit dwells. She left us the outline of her knowledge of the centers. She was satisfied, for the moment, with what we were doing, but she also went away because she was attracted in another direction. Another man—a priest of sorts, I think—spoke to her of Kaballah, of Tarot, and such things, and she was intrigued by that. She said that I was to send you her greetings, to explain that she had to be about the enhancement of her own search, as you, Sir Knight, would fully understand and that she would return to us if we needed her."

"I understand and appreciate. My father had an interest in Tarot, and my Grandfather a very important relationship with a lady Kabbalist, about which I have read. I regret only not being able to say goodbye to the Yogini, and give thanks for her help."

"I believe that she knew that. But there is another matter, as well. Not only has Maya, the Yogini, left, but during the period of your meditation, another lady, a priestess of the occult, came to me and gave me some hints about our work."

"Some hints?"

"Yes. She said that she, too, had been attracted by our efforts, for such work makes itself known in the Cosmos, attracting those who are on similar searches, similar quests. She said that she feared that we might suffer from either of two great dangers: of proliferating our investigations endlessly and ending in a chaos of 'everything being everything', where all Gods could be found at all centers, and there would be no union at all of us or Gods, or alternatively, that we would be limited merely to the potential, merely to possibilities of things and that our work would be as thin air."

"That seems right to me. In my struggles of One and Many, I have often felt just like that, to be dissipated in the Many, or narrowed to a thin and unfulfilling One."

"And I, too, with the pairs. Ever new pairs, always transforming, always changing, or tepid union, unsurviving, unfruitful. But then, this priestess of the occult said that the essential problem was not to get too lost in either the potential or the actual, the ever-possible and the concrete realization. She said that the true dilemma was between the manifold vision of Jupiter or Zeus, as he dwells in the Place of Command, and the narrowness, earthbound concreteness of Saturn of Kronos, who dwells in the Earth, at the sexual centers, or, at the "root support." She said that what we had experienced as a cone, or two cones, meeting at a common circle, could also be visualized as a funnel. The upper end is receptive to the ever-unmanifest; all-seeing Zeus open to spirit which comes in from above in ever-multiple potentials. These fires funnel down through the throat, heart, diaphragm, belly, all the way to the earthy center itself, where concretization and matter lives most totally. The problem, so to speak, is between God the Father and God the Son, between the Eye of God and the Phallus of God, between God as spirit and God as matter. Fundamentally, the conflict is between the many possibilities and the few concrete chances of realization. Here is where people fail, where pain and suffering arise. Here is where we should focus our attention. We should, in fact, attempt to reconcile these two warring centers in such a way that they truly unite. Only then can we attend to our personal union, as well."

"That is remarkable, Daughter of Guinevere, and very much along the lines of my own thinking and my own situation. My horoscope shows a similar conflict. As you know, my sun is in Gemini and my mind, therefore, is ruled by a mercurial intuition which fits very well with the rulership of Zeus and Apollo, just as yours is suited to Athene. Moreover, a powerful planet of mine is Saturn, which lies painfully and structurally imprisoned in Scorpio, a most intense and passionate sign. So, then, my nature has been a battleground between a most intense spirit and a most intense flesh, a many-sided and volatile intuitive mind-spirit has struggled with a depth-seeking, monomaniacal earth-spirit. So, your priestess' observations sit well with me."

"The priestess also told me some other things. For example, the center of the Son, wherein you encountered Jesus, and I, Mary, is also the realm of Mercurius, or Hermes, that winged messenger of the Gods who travels between the ever-unmanifested and the ever-manifesting. That trickster and wise one, is a son unto his own and is just as much a resident of the highest center as the Christ-consciousness and the Mary-consciousness. So, then, when you speak of your mind being ruled in Gemini by a Mercury, a Hermes, a Mercurius, you are more right than you realize.

"She also told me that the Lord of the Belly region, with his watery plane, was as much Poseidon as Sister of the Belly, just as Hades dwelt, along with Kronos, in the nether regions and in the earth. Demeter was Goddess of the Heart, and even old Ouranos, the great Sky-God, dwells in the throat, in the place where you experienced Bluebeard and the Muses. In short, the priestess said to me, there are One and Many at each center, and that it is only convenience that allows us to choose now one aspect, now another. She said that Maya, who knew of the ancient Hindu Kundalini magic of Yoga was mostly right in thinking of each center as having a God and Goddess, a Shiva and Shakti, and that all the pairs—here was she speaking in my language, my star-chart and nature—were aspects of the One Pair. Energies transformed in spiritualization, they moved upward; in concretization, they moved downward, came into being. Thus the central problem is that of above and below, of Jupiter and Saturn, of Zeus and Kronos."

"Understood and agreed. But how should we go about understanding and reconciling this pair of opposites? How can we proceed with this strange father and son? Should we continue our meditations upon them, upon the nature of Kronos, upon the nature of Zeus?"

"I think not. And so thought, too, this priestess of the occult. She thought that we could together—and I emphasize the word 'together,' trying not to be nasty or bitter as you accused me before—meditate upon their joint myth, meditate upon how they came into the world, how they came into being, and what their struggle was. If we could understand and cope with that, then we could take up our own problem of union from center to center."

"Again, I am in agreement, Daughter of Guinevere. Let us begin."

"Now you seem to be very eager to begin, anxious to take up our joint effort. But I am not so ready. First of all, I think that we should re-dedicate ourselves, offer up a prayer and a resolve to work together, as if we were two alchemists, a seeker and his mystical sister. I feel, sometimes, that you have lost this sense of the mutual prayer aspect of our work. But, I, too, am to blame. I am aware that this bitterness creeps back into my conversation with you. I become carping and nasty even when I am not feeling that way. I am afraid that this darkness in me, this bitterness will interfere with our work. Just at the last moment, perhaps, just at the time when our total devotion will be required, this autonomous anger in me, this pain of the sister of the belly, may reintrude itself and ruin our labors. Can you help me with it? Can you relieve this harsh and bitter place?"

"Daughter of Guinevere, I am most ready and eager to pray once again, to re-dedicate myself to the task, together with you. I am equally eager to reconnect with our feelings as alchemists of the soul, as transformers of ourselves and the Gods. I am exalted and pleased by the idea of a joint prayer once again, as well as a serious effort at joint understanding of the myth of the great Gods, Father and Son. For all this, I am grateful and ready to join you. But, with your bitterness, I feel at a loss. I suspect that whatever I would say would only temporarily calm your ire. I think that it is so because you are, indeed, like the Goddess, Hera. I am of the opinion that your bitterness is just as big a problem and pain for you as my One and Maniness has been for me. The pairs have been no problem for you, for you have embraced this duality, enjoyed it, found it correct. Your bitterness is the pain of the frustrated pairing. You bitterness is your cross, if I may use that expression, just as the One and Many has been mine. I can only suggest that you accept this cross of bitterness as your own dilemma, just as I have had to accept the One and Maniness as my own. I think, indeed hope, that just as the problem of One and Many, of Father and Son, of Eye and Phallus can be resolved, just so can your bitterness be resolved. But not by me. I cannot resolve it for you. I am not your redeemer. That lies, I think, within you. I can search for redemption together with you, but I cannot provide it for you. Agreed?"

"Grandson of the Knight, you have used true words. I bless you for it. You have shown me, more clearly than ever before, how I seek for the union in the pair as an escape from my own inner union. I can see it now, even if it may fall away from me again. I will go with you, I will share with you this dilemma of the opposites, knowing that my bitterness is my own problem of the opposites, of the frustration of the union, just as your frustration of union is One and Maniness. Enough. I shall try and carry my own spirit and frustration, just as you carry yours . . . Let us pray.

"Oh, Gods of Fathers and Sons, Mothers and Daughters, Sisters and Brothers; Oh, Gods of Centers within and without, we, a pair, come and seek your aid. We seek to continue our quest, to resolve our crosses of pain and lack of union. I come in my bitterness, in my frustration of lack of union, but I also come in love for my fraternal companion, my mystical brother, my treasured lover, the Grandson of the Knight. We come together and hope to come to a deeper understanding, a truer love, a fuller union. Aid us and bless our efforts at transforming ourselves, just as we aim to provide better vessels for your transformation. We kneel and stand, we fold our hands, and raise them in supplication. We beseech and cry out, but we also stand in dignity and value, for you have made us and created us, and we go on creating you. We come together, male and female, man and woman."

"And we come alone, great Gods. We come alone. We come

together in a joint quest, and we come alone, knowing that every man, every woman, is somewhere always alone with God, always alone with his/her Maker, whom he/she makes. We come in both ways, and we expect and know you in both ways, Oh Gods. For you are alone, totally unmindful of humans and our ways, totally apart and uncaring of us, and also very mindful, very caring of us. For you need us, love us, just as we do you. My friend, my companion, my lover, my sister, Daughter of Guinevere, has spoken true words for me, we come as a pair. But we also come alone. Bless our aloneness and our togetherness. Bless us, and permit us to bless you. Enlighten us in our darkness, and participate with us in our attempt at the increase of love and understanding, together and alone, one and many."

"And now, our prayers completed, let us begin. You, Grandson of the Knight, tell the tale first, for you are a speaker and teller of tales."

Ouranos, Gaia and Kronos

We already know that in the very beginning of things, before there were any Gods at all, that there was Night, or there was Chaos. We know that out of those primordial, undifferentiated beginnings, before there was any consciousness at all, before there was any order at all, before, indeed, there were any Gods at all, there was a nothingness, a void, a "yawningness" of chaos in which there was a thirst for air, for spirit, for order, for light. And, out of the Night, out of the Chaos, there came first the Egg. This World Egg of wholeness was the very first form. Out of it came the God with the golden wings, Eros, God of Love, the firstborn. That we know, for upon the beginnings of the great God of Love, we have meditated and suffered. Some say it was Eros himself who caused the sky and the earth, who were also in the Egg, to join and mingle. But others say that Sky and Earth came from Chaos directly.

Now we are concerned with the beginnings of Kronos, latterly called Saturn, and how it was that this deep and tortuous thinker came into rulership and fell. It was said that the Earth, broad-breasted Gaia, gave birth from herself to the God of Sky, Ouranos, so that he would be her equal and would cover her, as starry sky, completely, and be an everlasting abode for the great Gods. This she did. Great Gaia, of the Earth, bore and mated with Ouranos, of the starry sky, and she gave birth to the three Kyklopes with the round eye in the middle of the forehead, with their thunder and lightning. She also gave birth to Titans and Giants, to say nothing of the six brothers and six sisters of creation, the youngest of which—and here, at last, is the beginning of our troublesome God—was Kronos.

Ouranos came every night to his mating with Gaia, but from the beginning he hated the children whom she bore. As soon as they were born, the mighty God of the sky hid them in the hollows of Mother Earth and would not let them come to the light. Not only did he do this deed, which made gigantic Gaia groan and swoon under the affliction, but he took pleasure in the deed.

"Now, Daughter of Guinevere, before we proceed with the tale, let us understand what it signifies thus far. What does it mean that Mother Earth creates the Starry Heaven? What does it mean that she creates him as a co-equal partner and then creates with him? Is this

like you and me, a pair? But, if so, it is as if matter or flesh precedes
the forming spirit, the reality precedes the potential! Is this how it is?
Is it similar to the awareness, even, that mortal man creates the Gods?
Just as poor Earth can create the starry sky, so much more vast and
great than she, to cover her? Is that what is meant?"

"I do not know, Grandson of the Knight. Your even posing of the
question seems vast and deep to me. I am honored that you see the
flesh, the woman, the feminine in such an originating light, such a
creating place, but I am inclined to think that here Gaia is to be seen
as simply the Creative principle in itself, as much male as female, as
much neuter as gendered, as much spirit as flesh. Creativity simply
longs to be creative. Creativity longs for the union from which it
springs. She can do no other. I know this from my obsession with the
pairs. And you know this, Grandson of the Knight, from your hunger
for creativity. Was not your experience of the Muses, with Bluebeard,
just such an insight? And, I have even been told by that same priestess
of the occult, that some say that Ouranos, Himself, as a sky God,
dwells in the center of Creation, the place of Muses and Bluebeard.
He, the origin and container of the starry sky, beyond all the earth,
water, fire and air of the lower centers, is in the ether-place of
"Purification" where creation occurs, devoid of the flesh. So, then, can
not Gaia, who herself created the God of the Sky, couple with him?
Can not creativity herself couple with the forms of creation which are
both her partner and her son? It seems feasible to me."

"Daughter of Guinevere, you astonish me. Your words are convincing and your clarity is greater than mine, even after all my meditation
upon the clear Lord, Apollo. Your light is like Athene, I see, fully
cognizant of the need for creation, for mental-birthing as the nexus
of civilization. But how do you understand that the great Ouranos,
the originating and forming principle, hates and rejects the created
ones? What does it mean that he hides them back in the troubled
body of Mother Earth? That he keeps them from the light? I should
think that the starry sky, with its primordial concern for the round
of eternity, for the need of coupling alone, hates change, hates
consciousness. He longs only for the continuing union, for an eternity
of union. In that sense, he would then agree and, perhaps, mirror
your need for union, Daughter of Guinevere."

"You attribute too much to me, Grandson of the Knight. Just as you
rightly made me face my bitterness and not lay it at your door, oh
Knight, permit me to tell you that you are throwing upon me your
own need for union. I long for union, it is true, but I think that you,
too, have this need, but do not accept it as readily in the pairing way
as do I, hence your perception of the mote in my eye. Understand,

then, how I see it. I think you are right that great Ouranos despises
the fruits of his creativity, his spiritual semen which results in concrete
union. He prizes more the pairing union itself. Perhaps he is threatened by the products of this union, which could, even, unseat him.
Perhaps he had an intuition that the development of the Gods would
dethrone him, would find him less of an authority, and would demote
him from his place."

"But one has to explain the God's enjoyment of his wicked work,
Daughter of Guinevere, and the groaning of Gaia under the oppression. The pleasure Ouranos takes, I think, is in the secret creation
itself. Not only does he enjoy union and the creation, but he also, as
we have surmised, treasures eternity and no change. The story,
therefore, shows how he can both create and not have change, can
both couple and not have consciousness, need not become aware,
even of himself. It is in this that he takes pleasure. Furthermore, the
Goddess, Creation herself, must carry the whole burden, and it is she
who groans for freedom, for bringing the new children of her union
into light. It is like the experience of the need for fame, for the Muse
Kleio. One needs the fame to verify oneself, to be recognized, to have
one's children come into light. And this is because the children
oppress if not allowed to be born, and because there is a need for light
itself. The starry sky has no need of light, after all, it is the dark earth
herself who needs light! That is the crux of the matter: earth needs
light, and sky needs darkness. As if each of the principles longs and
requires its opposite and it is in this that the two principles are in
travail, are in opposition, are in loving hatred of each other."

"Splendid, Grandson of the Knight! You have answered even better
than I. You have found the secret, I think, for you have come to the
deepest place of the principles themselves, of the Light principles of
Ouranos, and the Dark, creative principle of Gaia. Splendid. Your
words are better than mine, and I will say no more. You know, having
struggled with the Muses, and with the Ouranos who dwells at the
center where Muses and Bluebeard live, at the place of 'Purification.' "

"Thank you, Daughter of Guinevere. But, before I accept your
congratulations too quickly, let us continue the tale and see if we
really understand. The great Goddess Gaia, groaning under her burden, brought forth iron and made a mighty sickle. She then took
counsel with her sons, complaining of their father and asking them
to punish him for his wicked ill-doing. Ouranos was the first, she said,
to ever do a shameful deed. All the children were fearful, and none
spoke. None, that is, except Kronos, the tortuous thinker. Kronos it
was who spoke and gave his promise to his mother to rectify the great
injustice. Kronos spoke and said that he cared nothing for his father,

who was the first to perform a shameful deed. So, Gaia, rejoicing, gave Kronos the sickle and arranged her plot.

"Ouranos, coming at nightfall to his beloved, inflamed with desire, covered the earth and lay all across it. Kronos seized his father with his left hand, took the sickle in his right hand and cut off his father's manhood, casting it behind him into the sea. Gaia received the blood of her spouse and gave birth to the pursuing, witchlike Erinyes, Giants, and Ash Nymphs. From the manhood of Ouranos, we know, there emerged from the sea the great Goddess Aphrodite. Foam-born she was: a union of water and air; flesh of the phallic member of the great Starry God of Heaven. Thus was the great God dethroned. And thus, a story teller states, that since that bloody deed of Kronos, since that castration of the Father by the Son, the Sky no longer approaches the Earth for nightly mating. The original begetting came to an end and was followed by the rule of Kronos. Thus the tale, thus the story that tells us of the beginnings of mighty Saturn, known as Kronos by the Greeks.

"And that tale, Daughter of Guinevere, makes me mindful of the bitterness of women, the suffering of the feminine. The Creative suffers in her need for light, need to bring forth, and grows bitter and resentful at the oppression of the Sky principle itself which is satisfied with darkness. But the plots, the plots! That is how the witch begins, it seems. Oh, Hecate, more I learn about you; now I see that even the fierce Erinyes are born of blood and pain!. . . But I do not understand, really, I do not grasp what it is that Gaia is about. Is it that she wants her oppressive lover and husband overthrown? Does she become hard and crafty through the oppression? Does the feminine invent such cutting tools because of the pain of oppression? It could be. But it could also be that the sickle, a symbol of the harvest, is invented because man and creation want to see and experience the fruits of their labor, their effort, else they die. Man and the Goddess must invent hard, discriminating, reasoning things, even against the primordial formless form of the God, himself. And the story says that the God, Ouranos, is like a devil, for he is the performer of the initial shameless deed. Oh, God, are you the origin of evil? Are you the first darkness? Is light and order the origin of no more light? It seems so. And this profound hunger for darkness on your part, oh Ouranos, this deep need of your nature to not serve your own nature but its opposite, results in the first evil. It seems so. And so it has seemed to me. When I have gone against my own nature, when I have, in my need for union with an opposite, gone against my own principle, I have appeared most evil. Others have seen it so. For, in so doing, I judge myself harshly, identify with the negative part of myself. But, what is seen in the face is the feeling of evil itself, of the wrongdoing itself, not the punishment thereof! And so, Ouranos, do I understand your devilishness, thus do I have compassion for your first evil deed."

"So do I, Grandson of the Knight. Your understanding of him, his principle, makes the compassion well-founded. But I also have compassion for the Goddess, she who must be harsh. The sickle, created by her, is a death principle within the life principle. She, poor Goddess, must create the method whereby her loved one is defeated, her lord is shorn of his creativity. So the tale tells us of the end of the primordial creation, the time of the natural union of the opposites. The story says nothing of their suffering, but I can sense it, I can feel it. Ouranos and Gaia, Heavenly Sky and Creative Earth, must have suffered enormously, for their primordial nightly union was at an end. Natural creation ceased, and now, as in the tale telling of the expulsion of men from paradise, creation can come only in travail, even among Gods. A new principle of creation needed to appear. Out of the natural needs of the first Gods, those creatures born of Night and Chaos, of Eros and the Egg, came pain and new creation."

"But what of Kronos, Daughter of Guinevere? What of the deed and nature of this God, who has been the center of our enquiry, what of him? How do you understand his dastardly, yet necessary, depotentiation of the Father? Is he not like a righteous judge himself? Does he not despise his own father, judge him harshly, and in the service of his mother's plots, rob the sky of his own creative manhood? There is something rotten in it, even—or perhaps because—it is done in the name of righteousness, in the name of the punishment of the wicked father. I do not like it, I think."

"What man can tolerate a vision of such an act, Grandson of the Knight? What man is so safe and secure in his manhood, his creativity, and his own nature, that he can easily visualize castration of God or man and not become queasy, uneasy. It seems to me that this is the parallel of the suffering of Gaia, the horror at not being able to bring forth one's young. Is this not the same suffering, in the feminine, as castration in the male? Is it not the worst thing to imagine, for a woman, to endure endless childbearing without relief, endless pregnancy without birth, endless containment within oneself of all the potential, and no actualization—is not all this horror a parallel to the suffering of Ouranos, the castration of the male?"

"Of course, Daughter of Guinevere! You have hit upon it again, you have struck pure gold! You are absolutely right! The punishment of the spirit for rejecting the creations of the Earth is the taking away of the creative principle of the Heavens! It is just so. And now, Daughter of Guinevere, I can say back to you what you said to me:

you express it far better than I. Perhaps this same Ouranos has gone to your own voice-box, center 'of Purification,' your own etheric place where creation is no longer the concreteness of the flesh but in the spirit . . . Yes, I think so."

"But the positive effect of this act is the birth of Aphrodite, the new Goddess of Love. With that we have both, just as with Eros, dealt fully. We understand, I suppose. We have experienced Aphrodite Ourania, daughter of Heaven, know of the exalted status of the voice-box, of love spiritual and potential, just as we have experienced Aphrodite Pandemos, earthly, concrete, creative love in the flesh. Of all that we have already spoken. That a new love is born of that horrible deed, we understand. But what of Kronos, the one who is central to our interest? Again he escapes our understanding.

"Can we grasp this dark and tortuous God? Can we know him from his deed? Can we have insight into him? Even before we knew him in relation to his own son, Zeus? I do not know. He seems dark and dreary to me, vindictive and cruel. Is limitation always so? Is it by chance, or is it a truth that the name of this God is equivalent with Time, and that time is a limitation just as he is? Kronos, the Limitator; Kronos, the end of the funnel from which all the possibilities must realize; Kronos, the castrator of the spirit of heaven, the sky; Kronos, he who will depotentiate all the potential power of the spirit. But also Kronos, the server of the Mother; Kronos the courageous one who takes vengeance against the darkness of the primordial spirit; Kronos the powerful; Kronos, whose dark deed results in a new development of Love. Yes, all these things are Kronos, all these things. And yet I feel that we do not understand him. Perhaps he will speak to us, perhaps he will speak for himself.

"Oh, Kronos, master of the dark world, will you speak to us? Will you tell us if we understand you, if we correctly appreciate your nature and your deeds? I see you now, sitting there, baleful and dark, in a round, inward-turning reflection upon yourself. The dark mantle is upon you and you are old and dreary."

"I am dreary in this form, young Knight, that is true. I cut and slice, am baleful and tortuous, rigid and cruel. But only in the face of initial evil. I can be no son to such a father, no server of such a one."

"Yes, I see that. But now your face lightens, you seem to grow younger, or, if not younger, then at least lighter. And I remember that you are God of the Harvest, that there was much to your celebration, as well . . . But as I look, you go back into your mantle, into your ancient shell. And I know that not even Daughter of Guinevere can bring you out. We must continue with your tale, reflect and meditate upon your nature and deeds. Only then, perhaps, will you stay with us, inform us."

"Grandson of the Knight, do not turn away so quickly from the great Kronos. Please do not say that not even I, Daughter of Guinevere, can bring the God out from his mantle. I fear that you fear too much; you evade the consideration of the act of castration, the act of depotentiation of manhood. If I can bear the thought of the suffering womb of Gaia, the perennial restriction of her birth-giving, then you can face Kronos' deed, can you not?"

"Daughter of Guinevere, I can only try. I did not realize that I was evading. I can visualize the raising of the sickle, that crescent-shaped bow, and the severing of the genitals of the sky. If I am the sky, if I am Heaven itself, I cannot imagine it, but as a man I can. I can feel myself bloodied and impotent. I can feel my secrets and powers cut down, being impotent, bereft of power, having no creativity, no movement. I can see the baleful God doing this to me. I have more difficulty being this God, doing the act of Kronos. Yes, now I can see it. I can see myself severing the genitals of my enemies, and those who have hurt me, not recognized my value, my humanity. I can visualize myself doing this with glee and with righteousness, just as did Kronos . . . But, having done so, having imagined the deed from both ways, from the side of the Father and the Son, from the castrated to the castrator, what have I learned, what achieved?"

"Do you not know what it is like then, Grandson of the Knight? Are you not, then, a pure spirit dethroned, a powerful and cruel matter dethroning? Does not flesh conquer spirit, does not the power of time, of reality, of earth conquer potential? Is not reality King over potential?"

"Yes, Daughter of Guinevere, yes. You are right. I feel it, and I weep. I feel that struggle in my being now, thanks to you, and I know the failure of spirit to subdue flesh, the failure of ether to be ruler of matter, the failure of ideals to suppress instincts, the failure of conscience to rule desire. I feel it. But of my enemies, of my experience that the more limited ones, the narrower ones, the less visionary ones win the victory, is that the same? I see that it is: limitation and smallness defeats potential and bigness; inside and outside it happens, now and in eternity . . . But I will not weep, Daughter of Guinevere, I will not weep. For my vision will triumph again. The vision, the consciousness, the spirit, though defeated, renews itself and comes again in another form. Consider: does not Aphrodite emerge out of such a deed? Does not love and a new form of the feminine emerge out of such a bloody encounter between Father and Son, Spirit and Flesh? So, let my own vision be enhanced, let my own understanding take precedence, for I see that the Center of Ouranos, the etheric place of Purification where later the Muses dwell, battled the Kronos of the earth center and that what was produced was another center, a center of Love. And I see that this love can dwell in Heart and Diaphragm, in Belly and Phallus. So, then, the depotentiation can show me how the centers develop after all, how the ultimate union of Spirit and Flesh can change, transform, and effect each other anew. Just as Ouranos and Gaia, in their original love, covered each other in joy each night. I can see my vision come again, grow new phalli, achieve a potent power to expand, to reach into the cornucopia of new ideas, new understanding, and new possibilities of realization in the flesh. So it is. Can this be so for you, Daughter of Guinevere, when you consider the pain of Gaia, poor Mother Earth who could not bring forth her young?"

"That was easy for me, Grandson of the Knight. I can do that and, one day, may need to experience that more directly, just as you have. But I am content. For my need now was that you should not run away from the experience, for, in so doing, you would evade your own realization of how the spirit renews itself. In that, my own need is met, my own child is brought to light, for your realization is a child of my flesh, a concretization of my desire! Let us go on with our story of the Gods, and our meditation upon their nature."

Kronos, Rhea and Zeus

"Kronos, now become first King of the Gods, wedded his sister and fellow Titaness, Rhea. From this Titaness, Daughter of Sky and Earth, who gave birth to six male and six female Titans, there were now produced three daughters and three sons: the Goddesses Hestia of the Hearth, Demeter, and Hera, future wife of Zeus; the great Gods, Hades, Poseidon and Zeus.

"Daughter of Guinevere, I already perceive the meaning. I already have glimpses of understanding of what that conception and birth means: from the initial battle of only two centers of Spirit and Flesh, of primordial Titans who are not yet Gods, there emerge many Gods and Goddesses, to rule and encompass each center. Is not Hades a God of the occult earth center, just as Hecate becomes its Goddess? Does not Poseidon, according to your occult priestess, live in the water center of Svadhisthana, just above the Muladhara of Hades? And does not Zeus ultimately rule at the place of command, Ajna? Ruling over, even, the next lower center where Ouranos dwells in the ether of Visshuddha? It is so. And consider further: Hera dwells with Zeus, as we know. Demeter, the Great Mother and caring, feeling Goddess, is surely a dweller in Anahata, the 'unattackable' heart center, as one can guess, with Hestia holding sway, as hearth Goddess, in the Belly. So, then one can already see the development and differentiation, just as I surmised!"

"Grandson of the Knight, you jump and leap! No sooner has some insight of the spirit been released for you, from your sharing in the suffering of the Gods, than you become possessed with it! No wonder you constantly complain of not 'realizing' anything for very long, not being able to 'really' transform. You are always possessed and caught up with the spirit, with the potential. No wonder Kronos looks at you balefully! Please continue the meditation upon the tale, and save your awareness and insight for a time when I, with my own feeling and sense, can join the quickness of your mind and intuition."

"Agreed, Daughter of Guinevere. Well said. Let us continue. But now, perhaps, it is time for you to take the lead, for you to tell the tale."

"All right, I shall."

"The story of Kronos tells us that the great Titan-God devoured all his children as soon as each of them had left the mother's womb. This hungry king of the sons of Ouranos was told by his mother, Gaia, and his father, the starry sky, that he was fated to be overthrown by a powerful son, and, therefore, in order to protect his hegemony, he devoured all his children."

"Daughter of Guinevere, please stop at that point. One must be able to understand and cope with this darkness. Is not this son just as dark and miserable as was his father? Is not the swallowing of one's offspring just as dreary and dismal as the hiding of them in the womb of the great Mother Earth, Gaia?"

"No, Grandson of the Knight. You fail to see that some development has taken place. It is gruesome, to be sure, and not, from our present perspective, the kind of situation or consciousness which we would treasure, but still, we have to see this as a step in the growth of consciousness and love. My goodness, Grandson of the Knight, I think that I learned this lesson from you! Must I teach you, remind you of that which I learned from you?"

"Yes, Daughter of Guinevere, I think that you must. I have told you that I often forget what I have already learned; it vanishes from me. I apparently need to be given back that which I have given, in order to truly make it my own. I can see that perhaps what I gave was inspiration or intuition, given me by the Gods themselves and not an integral part of my own understanding, my own being. So, then, I welcome your giving me back my gifts.

"Yes, I can see that what you say is true—there is a development in the tale. Great Ouranos, of the starry sky and pure spirit merely hid the offspring in the folds of Mother Earth. He longed for darkness and no change. But now Kronos, his son, who punished his father for hiding his young and for resisting change, does the same but from a different vantage point. Kronos is afraid of being dethroned; he knows from his own parents that he is destined to be relativized, just as was his father, and he fights it. But he swallows his young himself, he does not push them back into the mother. What does that mean? That he, himself, integrates the creations, he merely keeps them in himself. Ouranos tried to keep all in the dark, Kronos tries to keep things to himself. Ouranos' deed was merely selfish, Kronos acts out of fear. But his previous righteousness against his own father's darkness now stands out for what it was, mere personal gain and desire. Both Father Ouranos and Son Kronos, by their very selfishness and lack of perspective show themselves to be incapable of leadership. So, then, they are doomed to be overthrown, no matter what they do. It is only a matter of time. Would that political life were also so governed! Unfortunately, the least able to govern often continue to govern.

But, I suppose, that ultimately they, too, are overthrown. In any case, it is clear that the pure etheric spirit of Ouranos is depotentiated from rulership because it hides creativity and the new back into Mother Earth, the lower centers, and its power can only be like Bluebeard, to train the Muses, to refine the soul so that it can speak all the better.

"Kronos is no improvement. For he devours the new and keeps it to himself. He is like the greedy power king who also belongs to the lower centers, for he, too, is against light, not for itself, but because he wishes to maintain hegemony."

"Enough, Grandson of the Knight. Enough of interpretation, let us go on with the tale. I can see that you really do not see this as a development, that Kronos is even darker than Ouranos in his deed, but let us wait and see how it is.

"Rhea, the wife of Kronos, just like the mother Gaia, was terribly grieved by this devouring of her children. When she was about to give birth to Zeus, she turned to her parents, Earth-Gaia and Sky-Ouranos, for help. The parents heard their daughter's prayer and helped her to see and participate in bringing into being the already-decided-upon future. As it is with fate, it is also fated that the one who must take action does so! And so it was with Rhea; she, with guile, hid her newborn child from the terrible Kronos and gave him, in its stead, a great stone wrapped in swaddling clothes. Mighty Kronos did not realize the deception and swallowed it.

"Years went by in which the young Zeus grew and finally was strong enough to conquer Kronos by both force and deceitful cunning, even compelling him to yield up from within himself all his swallowed children. Thus Zeus liberated not only his own brothers, but also those of his father, whom Ouranos still held captive. Among these were the Kyklopes who, in gratitude, gave Zeus their own thunder and lightning."

"All right, Daughter of Guinevere, we can see the triumph of Zeus. Let us pause before considering the final act in the drama of Zeus and Kronos. Let us try to understand the Gods and their deeds to this point.

"I see the change as a shift of the use of guile, a shift of clever consciousness, from Father God to Mother God, from masculine to feminine. The guile of Rhea, deceiving the power-devil of Kronos, reconnects with the parents and truly anticipates the newer value, the development of Zeus. And is not Zeus, the great one, possessed of both force and cunning? He is more clever and more powerful than the older principle, and, I think, he is more benevolent. He not only is after the power of leadership itself, he also frees old powers, those of his father and grandfather, his brothers and uncles. And he does not 'castrate,' he does not vengefully destroy or maim. Indeed, if I remember the tale aright, he merely banishes Kronos to the edge of the earth, but that edge is truly the Isles of Blest, a most pleasing and joyful place!"

"It is true, Grandson of the Knight, but let us wait to consider where Kronos goes after his defeat, and try to grasp more clearly what it is that is happening. What you say of guile and force, of power of consciousness and strength, and of benevolence, too, makes sense to me. It is also shown in the freeing of the powers of lightning and thunder, belonging to the one-eyed Kyklopes, which Zeus then takes on. Great Zeus indeed becomes the ruler of Ajna, the place of command, for he is all-seeing, with intuitive flashes and powerful sounds. His Oneness of vision, coupled with the Maniness of his creativity should please you mightily, Grandson of the Knight! And Zeus merits this place of command, along with Athene, of civilization, and Apollo of reason and grace of spirit. All of that has been established, we know. But it took a long time for all the sons and daughters of Zeus, all the differentiation and integration of Olympus to take place. Do you know of that part of the tale, Grandson of the Knight?"

"I do, indeed, Guinevere II. The myth contains numerous stories of the battles of Zeus with the Titans. Zeus, who had thrown his own father into captivity was himself threatened with the same fate. Just as Ouranos and Kronos were both dethroned, Zeus was also faced with this eventuality. Not only did his sister, Hera, try to bind him, as well as Poseidon, his brother, but even his daughter, Pallas Athene, was said to have attempted such a thing.

"It is as if the Water-region, like Svadhisthana, the Poseidon place, tries to usurp leadership, to make desire primary rather than consciousness; it is as if the monogamous Hera tries to do the same, as if the judging-vision of unity tries to conquer and bind up the maniness of consciousness and creation; it is as if the use of consciousness for civilization, the feminine wisdom of Athene, also wishes to overcome the power of both vision and creation; it is as if all of these want to take the lead and command, but they fail.

"Oh, Great Zeus, I see your greatness to defeat these encroachers! I see your greatness even more in being able to share your power with the Heras, the Athenes and the Poseidons! And yet the stories tell us that you did not do this alone. Thetis, that great Goddess of the sea, brought you, from the depths, the 'Hundred-armed' one, Briareos. He it was who came as your guardian, and all your rivals were sore afraid. Oh, Zeus, from the depths of the sea, from the most profound reaches of the places where Poseidon comes from, you receive your support as well, and you are certain to win. For you unite the above with the below, the vision with the desire. No wonder Hera cannot contain you! No wonder none can overcome you! You unite spirit and flesh even in yourself; you unite wisdom and desire, intuition and sensation, air and earth.

"The tale says that the Titans battled you even after Briareos aided you against your fellow Gods. The tale says that you won over the sons of Ouranos, the sons of Heaven, only after many years of war, whereas your battle with the Gods was brief. The old Titans fought from their summit, you and your brothers and sisters from Mount Olympus. That was a terrible battle. But Gaia showed you the way. On her advice, you and your siblings fetched the two other 'hundred-armed ones' and, strengthened by nectar and ambrosia, the food of the Gods, they helped you. These primordial powers, fed with the new tastes of the upper centers, now join together and end the dominion from below.

"And so, a union of above and below, of consciousness and power, of spirit and flesh, of cunning and force. These bring about true leadership, these bring victory. That is the secret of Zeus. Mighty Zeus won, and then enchained the Titans in Tartaros, as far below Earth as earth is below the sky. An iron wall encompasses them and Poseidon keeps them behind it. And the three hundred-armed-ones are trusty guardians.

"Zeus, the ruler of consciousness, keeps suppressed the more primitive and negative forces, with the help of that which he has civilized, contained, transformed. His powers are greater, and he achieves a leadership in which much can be included: Hera, Poseidon, Pallas Athene, his erstwhile opponents who become his co-rulers, and even the Titans Briareos, who serve him because Mother Earth herself desired it.

"Oh, Zeus, you are like the favored sons of the Bible, who are aided by their mother in overcoming the less progressive brother. You are like a Jacob, favored over Esau by his mother, like him who sees the way into the future. Mother nature is like that, it seems, wanting the development of something better, wanting the products of earth to expand, grow, evolve, and find new being. Nature wants consciousness, new light, and will ultimately support that which will bring both light and depth, spirit and flesh.

"Zeus, my hymn to you seems wrong, or ill-timed, for I and my mystical sister have been attempting to understand your father, Kronos, he whom you banished to the outermost edge of the earth. But now we can look at what you did with him. The tale says that you banished Kronos to the outermost edge of the earth, to the place called

Isles of the Blest. And there did Kronos have dominion, there did he take the Golden Age, which was said to have existed when he was ruler of things. There, also, does Kronos reign with Rhea, in his own huge Tower, bathed by the breezes of Ocean. And there, great Zeus, it is also said that you visit and are brother to your powerful father, the old God, Kronos.

"Daughter of Guinevere, I see the dilemma, or part of it. There is Zeus, the all-seeing, the great leader and promoter of creativity with the spirit; but his rule is not identical with mankind's happiness. And there is Kronos, the baleful, the concrete, realizing one, the one of earth, banished to his dark tower among the Paradise Isles; his rule is connected with mankind's joy. What a paradox, what a horror! We shall have to understand what that means.

"Does this mean, Daughter of Guinevere, that as long as consciousness— that potential to see and know more, to unite with more, that openness to the evolutionary process of the divine—involves itself with men, then are men never content, never fully happy? And, does it mean that the limitation of matter, the narrowness of the concrete, the funneled tube through which the great cone of Zeus enters, will always be dark and structured, like Saturn, always produce limits, but is, because of its very concreteness, allied with the pleasure of man, his Paradise? It seems so . . . And so, I suppose, is Kronos banished to a place outside of the system altogether, to the Isles of the Blest. This paradise is at no center, no place in the tree. It is away and far, always 'elsewhere.' And thus, poor man always is in search of it. Does not the tale say that Zeus and Kronos, Son and Father, are truly happy together on those Isles of the Blest? That there Zeus visits his father and both are joyful? Perhaps what is meant is that the spirit and flesh are happy when together in Paradise. And, perhaps, it is true, indeed, that those who live a union of Spirit and Flesh, of Zeus and Kronos, are blessed, live a life of Paradise, on Isles of joy. But, when they are in conflict, then there is banishment, then there is pain, and battle. The original Paradise, the original state of man's joy was only under the rule of Kronos, the rule of the Concrete. But Kronos cared nothing for humanity, for creation. With the inception of Consciousness, with the rule of Zeus, all this changed, and now there is toil and pain, creation and conflict, expansion and evolution. This is just like the Biblical tale, is it not?. . . Guinevere II, are you there?"

"I hear your ruminations, Knight III. I hear them, and I think that you are right. But it is not enough to simply know this paradox, to simply be aware of the union of the joy-of-man with the dark God, Kronos, and the pain-of-man with the light God, Zeus, to know of the parallel with our own Bible, all that is not enough. For it is only a help in consciousness, a help in Zeus, no fulfillment of Kronos, no realization of the concrete, the flesh, the life. Were we not convinced of the necessity of Paradise on Earth, realized visions?"

"Yes, Guinevere II, but we cannot bring them about. There are powers, Gods, greater than we. We can work, transform ourselves and Gods, but at last, does not the funnel reach up, does not the cone go beyond Zeus, even? Is there not the Christ, even, above him? Is there not the love-consciousness which is also a Son, which opens out to the ever-new, ever-manifesting, ever-unmanifested? You have already known that, I think."

Kronos and Zeus

"Days have passed, Grandson of the Knight. Days and nights have passed and it is the winter Solstice of the year. It is the time of sadness, the time when one senses chaos, darkness, 'no room at the inn.' There is longing for a savior, a redeemer, a new day, and a light which will bring peace and joy. I have reflected about what you have said. I have thought about our limitations, and about Kronos. It is true that we can only transform ourselves a little, can only affect the Gods a mite. We are human and mortal. We die, just as the sun dies, the year dies, and even God dies. But the sun and God are reborn, we know that too. Something else has saddened me, Grandson of the Knight. Not the Solstice, nor the sadness of limitation, nor year's end, nor the waiting for the savior, but something else. What saddens me is the struggle for power between men, and even between Gods. I say 'even,' but do not men realize that their struggles for power, for hegemony, come from the Gods? How sad it is: Kronos against his father Ouranos, Zeus against his father Kronos, the battle goes on and on."

"But it ended, Daughter of Guinevere. Did not the tale say that Zeus triumphed and that there were no more battles between father and son? That the Titans were banished, and that Zeus did not destroy his brothers or his father? That Zeus and Kronos even live in joy and contentment at the place of the old God, the Isles of the Blest? So, there was an end to the father and son battle, there was a beginning of something new."

"True. But the image goes on for eternity, and the power struggle between men continues, does it not? And always at the cost of delicacy, sensitivity, all the gentle values."

"The struggle continues, Guinevere, it is true. But I am awed by the picture of the battle ended, by the image of all the Gods ruling their own 'centers' in the various parts of soul and spirit and flesh. I am enchanted by that. I am even delighted that the story tells us that Kronos and Zeus are eternally happy together at the Isles of the Blest. Can you understand what that means?"

"No."

"Well, then, let me explain how I understand it. Olympus, where Zeus lives, is the realm of the Gods, the spirit, the link with the airy region. The Underworld, where Hades and the Magician live, is the deeply material place which is both matter and non-matter, where there is both the earth of everyday life as we know it, and the inner workings of that earth which is the web of magic. And, of course, there is the water of Poseidon, the collective waters from which new life comes, that ever-unconscious place which brings forth new images, not new spirit like the air, nor earth. We know, also, of the fire region, and the air of the heart, the ether voice region of the Muses and grandfather Ouranos. And Zeus, with Apollo rules from an even higher place, beyond earth and water, fire, air, and ether.

"But Kronos, what of him? He is at that place where only heroes go. It is nothing less than the place of paradisiacal union, the place where spirit and flesh become one; the place beyond all the centers within the spirit, soul and body, it is beyond the person himself. Kronos is not only limitation and concreteness, he also stands for concrete reality as fulfillment. When visions unite with the concrete, in the phallic tower of wholeness, which is just like the cone, there is heaven on earth. When one has such an experience, one exists on the islands of the blessed, one is included among the heroes of all time. At that moment, one is raised to the level of those great ones. Such is the blessed place and time! It can happen to us, once, twice, many times. It can be a Nirvana, an Enlightenment, but not like the Buddha place of the Kalpa Tree, the in-between chakra, nor even the highest place of Sahasrara, but that very earthy, very human place of Paradise on Earth. Such blessedness can happen, Guinevere II. I have known of it, and so have you, I think. And so have our parents and grandparents. Even though we are mortal and limited, failing and full of fault, we are made of great stuff. We have had that taste of the heroes, have dwelt for moments on the Isles of the Blest!"

"True, Grandson of the Knight, or we would not be on such an eternal joint quest. One longs for what one has tasted, I think. You are right . . ."

"Further days have passed, Daughter of Guinevere, and I, too, have experienced the problems of the season. You spoke, some days ago, of the Solstice and waiting for the redeemer, he who will come to repair chaos and darkness, who will bring peace and joy. We talked and realized the paradox of Kronos and Zeus, the dark God of limitation being associated with joy and pleasure and the light God of extension being associated with pain and ever-expanding evolution. We also realized that Zeus and Kronos, like lion and lamb, can lie down together at the Isles of the Blest, the place-state of heroes, where potential and actual become one, where vision and realization, father and son, are one. And we realized the similarity that Greek union has with the Biblical quest, where father and son become united at 'the end of days.' But, Guinevere II, since our chatting, I have come upon a man who is sore put, who is ailing and fractured by a judging, hard conscience which does not let him have any sway. I have had further glimpses of the Kronos hardness as judge, as he presents himself to another, not to me. And I am silenced thereby. In my day, as you know, I have been hounded and harassed by the great Eye of God judging me, criticizing me, demanding of me. That wicked old teacher, who ruled the roost, as you recall, came down from his perch, and, with your help, I was able to find a new eye, a new judge, a new vision, warmer and clearer. It consisted of the wisdom of Apollo, the vision of Zeus, and the culture-building of Athene, as well as the need for total union of Hera. So, I was helped. But here, now, is a man who is not helped and has asked for mine. I can give it to a certain extent, but only in part. The Kronos in him must be softened, must allow the children to live, the child in him is enjoined from play, joy, and pleasure. But I am a limited observer: participator and actor to be sure, but limited. Now I want to achieve a view of that Kronos and Zeus, that Eye-Father, Eye-Son combination which is larger than myself, larger even than that of this man who is harassed unjustly by the judge. How, Guinevere II, can we address ourselves to this vaster Judge and soften him, and not be limited by the belief that we are only in ourselves?"

"Grandson of the Knight, you startle me. You have never before been so concerned by your subjectivity. You have assumed that you were dealing with the Gods themselves, with the heroes themselves. You have not troubled yourself too much with that doubt, have you?"

"Not exactly, Guinevere II. But you do not understand. I have always paid close attention to the facts and character of the 'evidence,' of the 'stories' as passed down. In each 'station' I have been careful not to violate the revealed information. I have immersed myself in it and then asked for the God or Goddess, Hero or Heroine, to speak to me, to reveal himself-herself to me. And they have done so, usually. That they have done so has led me to believe in the 'objectivity,' in the 'transpersonal' character of what they have had to say. Not just in me, but how it really is."

"Your grandfather, the Knight, was not so sure, was he? He reported his visions, his experiences of God and demon and then asked that others tell their experiences."

"That is true. But he did not try and link his personal vision to revealed systems, as some of his friends did, and as I have tried to do. I do not claim that mine is better, far from it. My grandfather's vision and experience were, in a way, purer, more forthright and direct. But he has been he, and I have been me. It is so. Passion, love and pain have pushed me to this point. But, Guinevere, why do you labor this? Have you not been with me? Have you not felt the same need as myself?"

"No, I have not. I have been more at home with the personal, either subjective or objective, but in a more contained way, as you know; I have not worried about the state of the world, or systems of thought or religion. My pain is what drove me. You know that. I wonder though why this problem should affect you so now?"

"Because I truly want to transcend, to have an effect on the God which will be . . . I don't know what word to use. Helpful? Effective? A kind of Abraxas, I suppose, or Hecate effect which will change the universe, and not only myself, or only my own image of the universe. In some ways, I know, the only effect can be from myself, from my own example of my being. I can effect this suffering man, I suppose, only with that. But I would like to address this Judge and soften him, not just for me, but for mankind . . . My, that is a presumption, isn't it, Daughter of Guinevere?"

"Yes, it is. But do try it. And let me participate, as well. When you spoke to Jesus or Mary you were not falsely modest about speaking to such figures. Why, then, cavil at your addressing God the Father who judges?"

"All right, Daughter of Guinevere, I shall try. I shall speak my prayer as it comes:

"God the Father, whether you come as Zeus the all-seeing, as Kronos the limiting, or as zealous Hera, God the Judge, I beseech you, hear me. I have tried to comprehend you, to soften you, to do your bidding as best I could, to save the childish and small and helpless in me from your wrath, to save you, even, from yourself. I have done all these things and I am gradually more at home with you. I feel greater ease with your judgments of men and deeds. I am more supportive of your views and also ready to keep my peace about them, not force them upon others. But now, Judge, union of Kronos and Zeus, listen to me, not as you present yourself to me alone, as an inner voice, nor even as a combination of inner voice and voice of history and revealed wisdom, but present yourself as You, as transcending the mere personal. Is that possible, great Judge?"

"It is, of course. But even as I say it, Knight, you will now think that I come only from inside you. What has happened to you to lose your awareness, your certainty of the powers of the Gods which transcend you, which live in their vastness both within and without? You had it, have you lost it? Your grandfather was never so foolish as to doubt it, neither your father."

"But, great Judge, both of them were chosen, were certain of their specialness and task, whether of quest or service."

"And are you not chosen?"

"Yes, and no. Which means, I am not so sure. If I am no longer chosen, perhaps I chose. Perhaps that sense of power is now more in the me who reflects, chooses, decides. You know, that very man of whom I spoke, even though great in his field and in his life, became aware that he had never truly listened to himself, to his inner voices, and did not have his own views on all the variety of 'sins,' the 'transgressions' which society judges. I have listened, surely, and have had my views, molded by you, of course, but now I am not sure . . . But what has happened? God, the Judge, I was going to beseech you to be kind to this man, to soften your hardness not just with me, but toward others, for mankind surely needs your gentle firmness, not your condemnation. And now it devolves back upon me! This is truly confusing."

"Grandson of the Knight, let the Judge be for a moment, and listen to me, your mystical sister. Your confusion is because you are losing the sense of differentness in yourself. Father and Son are becoming one. You are becoming yourself a whole and, therefore, it is difficult to know who is judge and judged, who is father and who is son. As you become a whole man, old identities blur."

"True, Daughter of Guinevere, but again what of the transpersonal, what of the God himself, apart from me and my changes, my developing or not? Can I not effect that, in that suffering man, for example?"

"You keep asking the same question, Knight. You do not listen to me, your judge, it seems. You were once chosen, you were once a son to your father, a grandson to your grandfather, a son of Gods, too. You still are. You can do nothing else than what you can do. It is given. You have lived the given and the possible. They are one in you. And, in you, this blend shows a change in the Gods. It is true. It is objective. Can you not see it in me, hear it in me? And, as proof, you who have known Apollo and can no longer abide intuition alone, will find that your 'effect' will be felt, too. Your 'effect' will be that of the transformed God in you. For it is changed. As you have worked, just as your father and grandfather and all the seekers before them, you have changed a measure of the Judge and each aspect of the divine to which you have addressed yourself. And the proof is in the experience. One must sense it, experience it. For the effect of Zeus is in Kronos. Zeus' vision is not realized apart from reality, apart from man and men, nor, indeed, from his father and grandfather. Do you not see it? There is a trend from Ouranos to Kronos to Zeus, a succession of rulers, just as there is a succession from Knight I to

Knight II to Knight II. All are needed, all continue in the germ, in the seed, in the tableaux of eternity, in the records of man. Just as you spoke with Don Juan, just so does permanence continue: in the hard records of Kronos, but also in the Etheric records of the place of Ouranos, the creative place where all is known and continues. But my words fade, Knight III. My words and I, too. For you and I become one, and as I fade, I come into you and . . ."

"Guinevere II, did you see it? The Judge has vanished from sight, come into me, become me. There is a union, a softened but firmed union. The male wholeness will show, have an effect. It will change or be changed, I know. Words fail. I am at peace."

"It is good, Grandson of the Knight. Peace comes. At the end of a union, peace. No great bells which ring out, no hymns, but a quiet acceptance, recognition. He who sought recognition, Muse of Fame, recognizes himself; he who was chosen, chooses. Peace."

Witch and Judge; Devil and Soul

"Grandson of the Knight, you have found peace, a union of Father and Son, Kronos and Zeus, potential and actual, possible and given, vision and limitation, all those male unions which have made you feel whole as a man. I have felt them with you, known them, and recognized their fading away as a pair of warring opposites. But now something has happened to me, something which has made me gloomy and despairing, just as I used to be. My experience, like yours with the poor man being judged, came from an encounter with another. Mine was with a woman. Here, too, was a great woman, one who achieved much, risen high, and become downtrodden, beaten, trammeled by an experience of a man she loves but whom she thinks is mad, and drives her mad. She is distracted, ruined by this experience, and I am compassionate with her, feel as you did with your male friend. But I, too, at moments, think that she is mad with herself, perhaps, that she misperceives the situation, or, at least, that there is the Witch in it, or the Devil, which causes each to accuse the other of badness or madness, wickedness or unconsciousness. And I, too, have been caught in it. I, even I, who know my own madness at times, know how I can be swayed and lose perspective, even I become caught and can no longer care for her and myself at the same time. Oh, it is a painful place, and one that you also know, Grandson of the Knight!"

"Yes, Daughter of Guinevere, I know it well. I, too, am inarticulate in it, can hardly describe it. In a way, this is similar to my Grandfather's experience of the Gods, when he was condemned whatever he did. I know it myself. And I am as impotent in it as I was before. All that has changed for me is that the Judge, in his rage, no longer rules as he did, but now there is the vision of Zeus, the reason of Apollo, the service of culture of Athene, and the emotion of Hera, all in the place where only Dionysos ruled before. But what of you, what of your rulership?"

"I do not know. I have accepted yours, I think, with the addition that I felt that Hermes, the Messenger and Trickster was in the place of Jesus, higher, even, than your multiplicity at the Third-Eye. I had also felt that the deeper rulership came from below, from great Hecate, herself! She, of the indirect effect, of the dark vision, has been my ruler, as you call it . . . But now I am aware of a further battle than the one of which you have spoken. Not of Father and Son, and all the vagaries thereof, but of Witch and Judge, of Soul and Devil, of magic and reason, of dark and light . . . in short, of female and male, of Goddess and God. That perennial battle—on the human plane, on the divine plane, in the soul of man, and in the relationship of man and man, woman and woman, man and woman—is what bends my head and crushes me. I am as puzzled by it as ever."

"Daughter of Guinevere, I think you are experiencing the crushing of that same pair of opposites in your soul. Can I suggest that you deal with your confusion as I did mine? By addressing these opposites and trying to get them to unite, to merge their warring differences, so that both can live in your soul? Just as I had to do with Zeus and Kronos?"

"I shall try, Knight III, just as you did. Perhaps you can help me. Perhaps you can do for me what I did for you, give you that objective,' outside support . . ."

"Well, Daughter of Guinevere, that is where you are already lost. Oh, my lamb, listen to your Witch-Goddess, listen to me, Hecate, and be assured that as soon as you succumb to male 'objectivity' you are lost. All males believe in this, including, especially, the males who reside in a woman's soul. As soon as a woman believes this, she has lost only inter-subjectivity, and indirect effect. The rest is illusion."

"But Hecate . . . and I am surprised that you are here so quickly, without being summoned or implored . . . Hecate, I cannot be sure who is right: you, with your wisdom, or your opposite number, a male Judge who can give the rules, the 'evidence,' the collective or objective truth. You may both be right. It is a devil for me to have to choose which is right. For then I, too, am trapped into being the 'Judge' or higher authority, thus hurting one side or the other! Just as it is when I am in such a dilemma with a person. Take, for example, what I experienced today with that lady. Was I the witch? Was she? Was her husband? Or were the witch and devil there all the time? Oh, Hecate, I am small, I cannot cope with such a thing! I would prefer for you and the Judge, or Devil, or whatever it is, to resolve this difference."

"I am willing, Guinevere II, but the males are touchy about this. They prefer to 'rule,' to believe themselves in possession of 'truth,' and are not willing to share hegemony, share power, to realize that all centers have an authority, all Gods and Goddesses have a certain style and potency, wisdom and compassion. The top male Judge does not like that!"

"I shall help, Daughter of Guinevere. I, Knight III, shall help. I shall summon the Gods of the Ruling Center and demand that they cooperate!"

"I am grateful, Knight III, because already I am aware that I fall asleep, am attracted to other things. I think that this may be the witch herself, desirous that I not be conscious, that I remain in that state of sleepy unknowingness, for only in that way does she retain her total power, her secret leadership. Ah, that is it, the witch retains power only when indirect, when the ruling conscious side is lulled to sleep. Oh, how to reconcile, how to bring about her cooperation, too!"

"Only, Daughter of Guinevere, if you renounce judgment, if you renounce statements of opinion, if you renounce categories of pseudo-reason."

"Was that you, Hecate?"

"It was I."

"But the Judge exists, reason exists, opinions exist. If I renounce them, I renounce the Lord of Consciousness, I renounce perception, I renounce another God!"

"I asked you to renounce their hegemony, Guinevere II, but not their existence. I know they exist."

"But to what should they submit, then? To you, to a world of apparent fact which is not fact, to uncertainty, to others' opinions, to others' perceptions, consciousness?"

"I do not know, Guinevere, I only know that the hegemony of the 'Light' God must end, else you will forever be subject to the battle."

"And now I truly grow weak, I truly lose consciousness, I truly feel unable to cope . . ."

"Guinevere II, she is wrong. I, the Judge, I, a voice of reason, say she is wrong. Hecate is wrong. I, Apollo, am no enemy of hers, but she is wrong."

"How do I know you are Apollo? The Devil uses all sorts of names; who can I trust? I am now, myself, in the grip of madness, I think, I do not know whether to trust what I hear, what I see, even what I feel!"

"Oh, Guinevere, let me hold you! You can trust your mystical brother, Knight III, for you know I would not willingly hurt you. It is true I might do so unconsciously, but not willingly. Perhaps that is all that is meant here."

"Your holding me helps, Knight III. Indeed, only the human touch, the warmth of a human hand and heart is all that helps in the middle of such madness, uncertainty, loss of reality, loss of judgment, loss of . . . I almost said 'soul.' Only a human touch. You help. But that is not enough. I must find a way to unite these two warring pairs, lest they destroy me. I know I have been in such a battle before; I know that you have, also, that everyone has. Many times. But now, I must resolve it or we, Knight III, you and I, will not be able to have our own union. Just as you had to resolve the problem of Father and Son, Male and Male, I must resolve the problem of Male and Female, in their destructive union. I must do so before we, you and I, can unite and proceed as we wish, to unite ourselves in a mystical union, and unite all the centers in that way. Believe me, Knight III, my wish, like yours, is to achieve this union, but first Witch and Judge, Soul and Devil must unite.

"And do you know, I can see it, grasp it. The Witch is the soul, really, very personal and subjective and inside. And the Judge is a Devil, really, very impersonal and objective and outside. And each becomes destructive when its value is not recognized, or when it affects the other . . . but I cannot go on . . . For my words already show my impotence in being able to reconcile them!

"Oh, Goddess Hecate, I beseech you! Oh, God, Zeus or Apollo, or Judge, whoever you are, standing in Father Judgment, I beseech you!

"As I said it, as I besought their aid, I again caught a glimpse of the pair. It is Father and Daughter, Mother and Son, is it not? It is male and female as destructive parenting, too. Again I know, and again I lose my way. I again become unconvincing to myself and the words are hollow, the consciousness is mere labeling, the understanding is tawdry. I will acknowledge my impotence to the two and let them speak to each other. Let them, did I say? What presumption! No wonder they are both annoyed with me, as if I had the power! I will implore them to dialogue together. Again I beseech you, Witch, again beseech you, Judge, again I beseech you, Soul, again I beseech you, Devil! Speak to each other. Live in some semblance of union in me!"

"Knight III? Knight III? Are you there? You nod. My plea had no effect. Rightly, perhaps. Because there seems to be an additional polarity of struggle here, between inner and outer: the reality of the inner life with its visions, 'objectivity,' and the reality of the outer life, with its demands and 'objectivity.' I seem to be unable to find my orientation in such a power struggle. I lose both 'objectivity' and a sense of direction. Another woman said to me that when confronted with a discrepancy between feeling and reason—or as so judged by an outer male—that she would take an 'inner' voyage to see if it 'felt right' or 'made sense,' either one! Which is to say that if something 'felt right' it did not need to make sense' or if it 'made sense' it did not need to 'feel right.' I think that was beautiful. For she accepted the total authority of both her 'feeling-intuition' or 'her reality-thinking.' Either one was sufficient authority. Beautiful. But what if they are in conflict? Or what if someone outside says there is a discrepancy that cannot be explained. That is where I am right now, Knight III. I am struggling with this and sense an aloneness in it, though I would welcome company."

"You have my company and support, Guinevere II, just as I had yours in the conflict of Zeus and Kronos, and even in my long struggle with Apollo. But I cannot solve it for you. I would welcome your solution. I suppose that you must think this through for yourself, and, thereby, come to your own inner authority and union, just as I have had to struggle with the descent of the Dionysian Judge-Teacher. I am there with you, but only with emotional support, just as you were with me and the Judge. You are sorting things out and I like it. I particularly like what your lady friend said about 'feeling right' and 'making sense.' A beautiful way for the soul-witch and the judge-devil to each have an authority! But what, indeed, does one do with confusion? Just wait? I suppose so."

Witch and Judge; Devil and Soul: II

Time passes. Days pass. But I do not learn, I do not understand. I do not resolve the confusing, hurting dilemma of the madness of the authorities, of witch and judge; devil and soul. I sit like a poor creature in the web of the great spider. On the one hand the web is gossamer, soft and jewel-like, so delicate and sensitive that every movement of mine seems gross. If I move, if I make any kind of motion, then my own action can affect all dimensions of life, all vulnerable areas of loved ones. My movement can hurt another who, even unknowingly, is touched by this underground web of human connections, human relationships. Even objects can be affected. At the next moment, this same web can feel like a rough and fibrous rope, or a heavy and rusty iron chain which keeps me totally immobile, paralyzed and unable to move. This web makes me furious and oppressed, and I flail out to release myself. Such is the web of the Witch. Thus is the realm of the great Goddess Hecate who works her indirect effect. Is this, too, the realm of the Goddess Hera, who works her own brand of power? No, I think not. Hera is experienced as witch-like when Zeus or a mortal male feels limited in the natural expression of his own power, his own principle, but she is not indirect. She is direct . . . But no matter, the web is the same. For there is the feminine with no love in it, only power.

The Judge, I suppose, is the masculine with no love in it, only power. And I experience only a negative power, like the Devil. But what is the Devil? Assertion of ego power? Attention to nothing but one's own need? Yes, but not only that. For it is also an attribution, is it not? That one blames another for one's own darkness, that one is oneself mad and blames another for it! Thus, the Devil is like the Witch. Thus are they both . . . But I do not free myself, I do not accomplish the task that Knight III said that I should, to resolve witch and devil, soul and judge, just as he resolved Kronos and Zeus, Father and Son, possibility and limitation. I do not resolve the struggle of inner and outer, of reality and fantasy, of power with power, I do not accomplish this . . . So, then, trusting in the intuition of my mystical brother, Knight III, I shall, once again, ask the pair to come together, to . . . And now I sink, just as I did before . . . into . . . sleep, sadness . . . unconsciousness. There is a scene.

The scene is a woman in chains. She is being judged. There is nothing for her to say, she has no defense. The judge is a dark, austere, intense-eyed, triangularly bearded man. One, of course, could visualize him as the Devil, but to me he seems to be merely an aristocratic Spaniard, like one that my mystical brother, Knight III, has known so well. Well, then, Judge and Devil are One! But the woman, what of her? She is full-bodied and equally intense, but her eyes are closed. This is a dungeon where she is being tried and her eyes are more suited to the outer world, whereas those of the Judge can peer like an owl in the darkness of night. So it is Judge-Devil facing the human soul.

Could it not also be the dark-witch, peering and intense? Could it not also be Hecate, at home with the dogs of night, looking sharply and carefully at the soul in the shape of a man, as a frightened and agonized creature tied to a post or to a cross, and cannot move? Yes, of course.

Well, then, what then, what then? What am I to face, to understand? That the spirit is on trial? That the soul is on trial? That when the feminine is on trial, the male spirit is tyrant, and vice versa? It seems a small awareness. Oh, the hell of the paralysis, I cannot move in either direction. I beseech you, powers, help me!

The words come: "You must go deeper." From what source, I do not know. All right, then, I shall go deeper. I go down into the earth, into caves and holes, and come upon the opposite side of the globe of the earth and am descending-ascending into the air, into the atmosphere and cosmos. I rise higher and higher, and look down from a great height indeed. I see the whole earth itself from a vast distance, and only outlines show themselves. I go higher and higher, and now I enter a room which shows me meditating upon myself in a central place. I see myself. I am passive, and totally absorbed, apart; and I am way down below, involved and busy in that world of earth. I am here and there, there and here. I am far removed, objective observer. But I am also participant, active worker, and liver of life. And what is down deepest in the earth, even beneath the web of relations, is the vast view of the heavens, the dream of the dreamer. It is as if inside is out, and outside is in. And that thought, itself, is madness-making. I crawl into this meditating self and grow calm. Now I no longer feel so strange, so confused. It is as if I can retreat and be utterly alone and far removed. I accept the paralysis of the witch and the enchainment of the judge: non-moving. I do not move, I do not speak, and I am very peaceful. I now know, as did my mystical brother, Knight III, the Buddha center, the chakra of peace, the place between judge and heart, between male and female, which is neither inner nor outer, but is peaceful; which is neither active nor passive, but is still; which is neither reality nor fantasy but is silent.

Yes, this is the resolution of Witch and Soul, Devil and Judge: the no-mind of non-action. And what is it? To abandon the power-struggle altogether. To neither fight nor retreat; neither argue nor defend; neither assert nor deny. This silence is no abnegation, it is merely a recognition of the lack of power to change anything. Thus no devil, thus no witch. So, I am silent.

"Knight III, I think that I have found it. Like you, I shall be silent . . . But silence is not enough. Now I can enter into the woman on trial, who stands enchained. Now, too, I can enter into the woman who is enmeshed in the web of the spider. I enter in and am not paralyzed. I attend. The words speak, the Prosecutor calls out:

"This is the woman on trial. This is the creature who cannot speak. This is the perpetrator of crimes too horrible to speak of. This is she."

" 'And what are these horrible crimes?' asks the Judge, who sits austerely and intently upon a thronelike chair, as if he were God Himself. 'What are these crimes?'

" 'They are too horrible to speak of; therefore I will not speak,' says the Prosecutor. And all present nod wisely.

"And I, Guinevere II, wrapped in the chains of the criminal, can smile, can even giggle. For now these horrible judges begin to lose their power over me. As I giggle, they look at me in horror, but also in puzzlement.

" 'Why do you laugh,' they say, astonished at me.

"Because you are so foolish,' say I, and I laugh out loud. 'She who was judged, judges, but she judges not in anger, she judges in laughter.' And I laugh aloud. I stand up from my chains, and they fall away. I stand up and embrace the prosecutor, and the judge and laugh. They have no choice but to laugh, too. They are startled, but they laugh. And I am free. Do not ask how. Just accept, just retreat, just know . . . and laugh.

"But what of the other side, the woman embroiled in the web, who cannot move? She who cannot speak lest she hurt another? What of her? I enter also into her. I am crucified-embedded in this web and cannot move, but I am peacefully silent. I go into myself, into the far place below the earth and above the heavens which is peaceful. And now I know that this place is like the Isles of the Blest where Knight III went with Zeus and Kronos, Son and Father. For this is a place outside of above and below, spirit or flesh, even outside of space and time. I understand that Kronos is in this place of no center at all, for it is the Buddhist chakra of the Kalpa Tree. It is the place-below-the-earth-above-heaven which is no-mind, no power. And there it is that one can go when in the midst of the mad-making, mind-breaking, power-dealing struggle of male and female, of Witch and Judge; Devil and Soul. For there power falls away; there one is fully human and fully in Buddha-hood, one is free. Remember Guinevere II, I say to myself, remember your own lesson to yourself, which is, for you, just like that learned by Knight III . . . Knight III, are you there? I have learned that which you knew."

"I know, Guinevere II. I have stayed and supported and waited, just as you did for me. And you have learned that which I learned. Welcome to the chakra of peace. Welcome to the wisdom of the in-between place. Welcome to the Isles of the Blest."

And so we embrace, do Knight III and I. We embrace at the place where he is at the Isles of the Blest and I am at that beneath-earth-above-heaven place of blessedness. Where peace is.

"Now, Knight III, I think that we are ready. Now that the conflict has been resolved, of Father and Son, Eye above and below, for you, and of Witch and Judge, Devil and Soul, for me, we can proceed about the task of which you spoke: of our union. Let us proceed through the centers, let us unite in the circles, and therefore, be free."

Knight III—Guinevere II

"Some days have passed since I have seen you, Knight III, and things have changed with me. I have had a dream."

"Things have changed with me, also, Guinevere II, and I, too, have had a dream. It seems as if all my good intentions are thrown over by dreams and I think it is much the same with you."

"That is true, but I am not so pessimistic, nor 'thrown over' as you always are by these events. You are ever surprised and chagrined that perfection is not reached. I understand that perfection is never reached as long as we are mortal and alive. I look forward to the next step, the next 'working out' of things. Knight III, I am content if you are with me, if we are only together in our quest. But I also know that, as a woman, that is my way and nature, and that for you, as a man, you must always seek perfection, the ultimate union, the higher place, immortality . . . You nod, ruefully, but I also see that you accept me, my place, our work. Let me tell you my dream, and let me have your help with it. And then I shall hear yours and give you my help if I can. For do we not aim for a more perfect union between us? In that aim, my desire for union and yours for perfection, we can meet. Before trying to take our union through all the centers, we can try to cope with that which emerges within us directly. But, enough of words, listen to my dream. All right? You nod, so I shall proceed.

"In my dream, there is a known-yet-unknown lover of mine who comes to visit me. At the same time there is now visiting me a former lover, one who saved me, in a way, from the pains of unfulfilled love with this one who now comes, but he also proved to be not right for me. Now, both men are there and I am embarrassed. The one who comes knows that I love him more, but I can see that he is jealous of the other. And the other, famous in his own right and having all that he desires, is jealous of the one who comes because he has me. As for me, my feelings are mixed. I wish no pain, yet I am naturally pleased that two men desire me. And yet I am embarrassed. What to do? End of dream."

"I know your dream, Daughter of Guinevere, I know your state. Are you not, indeed, daughter of your mother, who had two loves? Have you not loved me and another, as well? I know that you have spoken of your monogamous nature, but you have been confronted with the two, I can see it. In a deeper sense, I know that you are confronted not only with two men, two rivals, two warring brothers. You are confronted with two principles in opposition, two great spirits which are attracted to you and you to them. Oh, Daughter of Guinevere, you are like the soul, the human mortality which tries to contain a Zeus and Kronos, a Christ and Hades, or, for that matter, the brothers Zeus, Poseidon and Hades! And these are sometimes at war."

"You are right, Knight III, and I love you for that, for being right. Indeed, in my dream, you are like the known-unknown lover. I feel him to be a spirit of the inner world, a wanderer among the Gods and Heroes, Goddesses and Heroines of myth and legend, of story and fantasy. He is my inner spirit, he is like you. And the other is also like someone known to me, a man of fame and wit, of power and success in the world. I know him, too. It is true that one has been the substitute for the other. To go with the spirit of the inner world, who does not want me alone, or to go with the spirit of the outer world, which I find not adequate. Thus my fate. And thus, too, do I see my resemblance to my mother, the great Guinevere, who loved two men. But her two men were different, they lived and existed in an outer reality. Her struggle was between romantic love and conjugal love; mine is between the within and the without."

"Yes, Guinevere II. I am glad that you see that. But can you not also perceive it as I have suggested? As a need to reconcile warring brothers, warring principles? A way of loving both so that neither is hurt nor offended, both satisfied?"

"Yes, but impossible! I know that. Hence my continuing monogamy. But, I also know that monogamy is not monotheism, there can be many Gods, of course. And yes, I can serve and love different principles, both within and without. But each at a time, each a monogamy, each a relationship alone. Have we not already learned that, Knight III? Have we not accepted it? Have we not realized that each center, for example, has at least one pair, and each pair has its own monogamy, own union? The One of the center, the Many of the Pairs—or so I thought."

"Yes, Guinevere II. I have thought so, too. But now your dream presents this conflict, and it must be resolved. You need to resolve the problem faced by your mother, but in a new way. Listen, now, to my dream, and let us see if it is related to yours."

"Dream away, Knight, and speak away. I am with you."

"In my dream, I am at a kind of gathering, worldly, at the home of a couple whom I know. This couple is successful in the outer world, but also has an appreciation of my inner world. At this gathering, I

see a woman with wild and disheveled hair. Her face is very puffy, as
if she has had a birthmark covering it with raised flesh, or as if she
has been seriously burned in a fire and the scars remain. In addition,
there are many places on the skin which seemed to have opened, and
some blood shows. The wounds have been re-opened. Next to her,
and holding her hand, is a young girl, her daughter. The girl's face
has only a little of the birthmark-burn appearance around the mouth,
but it, too, has openings in it. It is as if the wounds of the mother are
now being repeated in the daughter.

"The woman, with intense eyes, begins to shout at me. She both
implores me and chastises me for some unknown crime or lack. I
retreat a bit, not knowing why she does this. I can only say to her,
as the words come out of me, 'I am not the Judge.' And, as I say so,
I am aware that the spoken word 'judge' is also written, with the
initial letter capitalized. The judge is 'The Judge' to whom she should
address herself, I think. As I say these words, my hostess comes by
and tries to calm the woman. She says, as I did, 'He is not the Judge.'
I awaken in pain and sorrow. End of dream."

"Knight III, your dream is as deep as you are. And I see that you
are as marked as I. You, indeed, must continue the task begun by
your father, the Son of the Knight. He had to cope with the problem
of the rape of Mother and Daughter, of having no mother and needing
to find her. And now you must struggle with your father's problem
just as I must cope with my mother's problem of the two lovers. Even
though we are quite different from our parents, it seems that we must
take on these tasks. In so doing, perhaps we are worthy children of
our parents, after all. For what more can a child do than try to solve
the unsolved problems of the parent? Is not all history just such a task?"

"Yes, of course. But what do you say to my dream, Guinevere II?"

"I say that the women represent your own soul, marked by 'birth'
to be special, to be burned by the fire of the spirit. Your own soul cries
out and rages, for it is continually scorched by the spirit, fired by it.
The wounds are re-opened all the time. It is as if the fires come from
above, from beyond the Christ center, from the Pentecostal descent
of the flames of the spirit of God, as well as from the sexual-passionate-
desirous fires of Muladhara and Svadhisthana below, and from the
passion-center of Manipura, too. All combine to scald the soul. I think
that I see the mother of this dream as a kind of Demeter, a heart-soul,
where you are generous and loving and giving out. That Anahata
center of yours, full of love, cries out in rage, for she is burned by the
continuous invasion of fires from above and below. And the daughter
is her renewal, her own being seen afresh, perhaps. Or, again, perhaps
it is a new Persephone, a new Goddess from the Hades center, destined

to be raped and brought into the Underworld afresh and then rise up once again. Of that I am less sure. But she, this soul, seems to place blame wrongly. She makes you her judge, and against you she cries out. And you—rightly, I think—say that she should cry out to God."

"Your words are like a balm for my wounded soul, Guinevere II. Your words speak the healing wisdom of truth. You are right, indeed. Mother and Daughter in my soul, of my soul; Mother and Daughter, problem of my father. Mother and Daughter, the rape and wounding of the feminine within me by the passionate and fiery spirit as it comes from above and below. What shall we do, Guinevere II, with our dreams? What shall we do with our struggles? You to reconcile opposite spirits, me to help heal a ravaged soul?"

"What can we do? What can we possibly do without God's help? I think that we should kneel and pray, like the alchemical brother and sister that we are. I think that we should pray, like the mystical pair that we are. Let us pray for help and guidance."

"Agreed, Guinevere II. Let us pray . . . Let the God beyond all Gods aid us. Let the spirit beyond all spirits come to us and assist us in our efforts to heal and understand, to love and be understood. Oh, Lord, each of us is now with a pair; Guinevere II and I, each with a pair. My loving sister faces two warring brothers, and I face a wounded mother and daughter. We are now six. Just as my grandfather was with the six of creation, and my father was with the six and redeemed by the Charioteer, now Guinevere II and I are with six. And we await that which will heal us."

"And I pray, too, Knight III. But I do not pray for guidance, nor even healing. I pray for love. I pray that the same God beyond Gods to which you pray, that same fire beyond fires, spirit beyond spirits which you beseech, will love us and find its own way to reach us, despite our seeking, asking, searching. For He-She-It needs us as well; let us not forget what we have learned. I, too, pray."

"So, we sit and pray. We sit and meditate . . . But the others should come in as well, the Mother and Daughter, the warring Brothers . . . Now, here they are. Mother and Daughter, pained; warring men, inner versus outer power, pained. Let us sit, silently, as if Quakers or Buddhists."

"It is strange as we sit, like shadows of our parents. You, Knight, with Mother and Daughter, both wounded, both screaming, as it was with your father. And I, with two warring men, like my mother. And yet, you are like one of the men, and, I suppose, I am like one of the women. But, no matter. Let each speak. Just as your father and my mother sat together and let the voices speak, let us, who have begun from very different places and assumptions, let our quarreling voices speak."

"I will speak, I will speak! I must be heard! I must be heard! I do not care if I am One or Many, like someone's mother or not. I do not care if I am Mother of Mother and Daughter. I do not care if I am Goddess or mortal. For none of these things do I care. I care, finally, about pain. Pain, pain, pain! An end to it, a pause in it. Please. Let someone judge. Let someone say. Let someone speak out against this pain! It is true that the fires of the spirits above and below have scalded me, just as you have said. It is true that I have borne the mark of the Gods, as you have said. It is true that I screech and complain and cry out for justice, just as your dream hostess implied. It is true that I cut a sorry figure in the world. All this is true. But who will speak against pain? Who will cry out that the feminine is continually hurt? Who will say that the loving, tender, mother-daughter union, devoid of aggressive anger, devoid of hatred, devoid of rivalry or competition, should not be broken? Who will say these things? Will you, Grandson of the Knight?"

"I will speak for you, Mother, I will speak. I will speak for the feminine, for relationship, for the flesh, for the suffering of the soul. I have spoken out before and been thwarted. I have committed myself to the feminine, to the Goddess and have gotten misunderstood for my pains, have gotten rejected for my pains, have gotten sneers and contempt for my pains. But I have spoken out, do not rail against me, please. But I must also speak out against you, dear soul. For you maintain your innocence and you are not. The feminine is not devoid of guile, of rivalry with other females, nor of all those violent things that are only attributed to the male. Feminine violence is with the tongue and the trick, that I know. For I have learned much from the Witch and know her trade! Still, dear lady, I will speak out for you. I will continue to serve the feminine, the Goddess, but would that I could do it without screaming or screeching. But I will speak in any case."

"Then I will silent be. I will be still. And my daughter will heal. We will be healed, thereby, when you are our friend. Speak as you will, when you will. Speak for us."

"I will speak. But you must contain. Let the spirit come from above and below. Let the fires burn inside you. I know your pain. I know your suffering. I will protect you, but let the fires come."

"It is enough. I would have cried out to heaven, but you, mortal, man, Knight III, speak words enough. You do not retreat, run away. You know, and in knowing, serve, and in serving, find, and in finding will make us well."

"And I, too, will speak, Knight. I am, perhaps, still a whimpering child, though I grow very fast. I will grow and know. I have tasted the fires of pain as had my mother, but I know. I know as you do. And I will grow and know, just as she has. You will find me not an innocent, not a guileless one, not pretending, but one who will . . .but no more words from me. I, too, will be silent."

"Ladies, do I know? Are you like the women whom my father encountered? He found Mother and Daughter, and both were Mother to him. But you? Very mortal, like my own soul. Are you, Mother, mistress of the heart, giving out and caring? I think so. And are you, Daughter, mistress of the belly, taking in and devouring? I think so. For you are new incarnations of the Goddess-Mortals known by my father and I embrace you. And I embrace you not as my own Mothers, but as my friends, my sisters and equals, just as my mystical sister Guinevere II is my equal. In this, perhaps, have I grown a centimeter beyond my father; though, of course, none can surpass him in his knowing of the cave, of the Jewish Mother and Daughter who became Sisters of the Church, having witnessed the crucifixion. But mortal though I am, I can know you, Mother and Daughter, as within me: as the human pair of my centers of Heart and Belly. Guinevere has known this in her own right. Now so do I."

"I, Guinevere II, will also speak. I understand the women, I understand you, Sir Knight, but I am perplexed in my encounter with these men. One man who serves the 'within,' the other who serves the 'without.' How can I love them both, serve them both? Yes, I can see that I must serve the masculine, just as you serve the feminine, Knight III. I can see it. But seeing is not fulfilling. Understanding is not success."

"I think it enough if you are willing to serve the masculine, Guinevere II. I think that, in itself, is an advance beyond what your mother discovered, though, of course, like my father she was a very great lady, greater by far than we are. Yet, it can be an advance for you to know that you are serving your own spirit, your own maleness, and that you can serve it both within yourself and in the world. That would be a step forward."

"Yes, but let the men speak. Your women spoke and you responded. Let them speak."

"I will speak, for I am offended. You loved me once, when you had enough of this other, with his mystical vision and unwillingness to love you in the world. You loved me then. You loved my dash and gaiety. You loved my success and power in the world. You loved me. But you grew tired and let me go. And now you love the other once again. You love this would-be genius who has no fame. You love this conceited one, poor one, failed one and I wither with my fame, I wither with my success, I wither with it all for I have no love."

"And I, too, will speak to this man. I am not offended by him, I envy him. I would have the fame that he has, the success, but I cannot. I am loved, yes, and treasure it, but I want still more. And, above all, I would not hurt, I would not cause pain, if I could. Can you love us both, Guinevere II? Can you love and support two, without hurt to each? Can you?"

"I do not know if I can. I do not know. For I have loved the one and have suffered thereby. To love and contain two spirits, I do not know. I do not know if I am big enough."

"But Guinevere, listen to me, your mystical brother. It is not that you must contain both, I think, but that you must serve both! Can you serve the masculine, with its need for power, success, fame, as well as the mystical vision, the passionate love, the inner search? Can you support both of these? Can you serve them?"

"I can, Knight III, I can! And I can serve them both in you!"

"Guinevere, you embarrass me! You make me into a God who can do all those things!"

"You are not a God, Knight II, yet you are! You are my mystical brother! You are the one with the mystical vision, the passionate love, the inner search. And you are the one with a need for power, a need for success, a need for fame. I can serve both, in you! And thus is your need for the Many served, as well as my need for the One!"

"Yes, I can see that this is so for you, Guinevere II. I can see that, and I can treasure it. You make me thoughtful. If you can serve the masculine, and the God, through me, then it is both impersonal and personal. But, can I do so with you? Are you, indeed, like the Mother and Daughter of my dream? I do not know.

"Yes, I can see glimpses of it. You have been burned by the passions, just as had the Mother. You have been torn by the fiery spirit of God and Man! You have been shrieking, complaining shrew and beautiful, passionate woman. And you have been child as well. Hungry child, seeking; abandoned child, hurting. Yes, you can be mother and daughter. And now I see it, ever more clearly. For have you not also struggled with your own inner sisters of Heart and Belly? Have you not been a loving, generous, outgoing, warm mother and serving? And have you not also loved and devoured as daughter? I see it! Guinevere, you are the woman and girl! Mother and Daughter of my father have become Woman and Girl and inner for me, and they manifest in you. You are Queen to my King, my mystical sister, my equal, my bride. You are my love outgoing and my passion of need. And I shall serve you, as incarnation of the Goddess, just as you serve me, incarnation of the God!"

"Now I see a blend, Knight III. The warring brothers come to rest within you and I love you."

"And I see a blend, Guinevere II. Mother and Daughter come to rest within you, and I love you. Let us be about our task and unite ourselves in the circles of the centers. Let us be whole!"

Circles of the Centers

TOP

"Daughter of Guinevere, let us begin with a prayer. We should begin at the top, at the place where the great unmanifested spirit of God enters into us as human beings. Let us begin there with our prayer, and hope that an incarnation will take place, the spirit will descend, enter into us and unite with us from center to center, until it reaches the depths of our being, the nethermost place of manifestation. Then, perhaps, the cycle can continue and those self-same energies can rise up, spiritualize, until they again reach that great unmanifested God which we love and serve, and whose consciousness we both treasure and enhance. In coming down we shall be western, Greek, and without struggles of materializing. In going up we shall be eastern, Hindu, and shall reach for those places beyond the stars of the many-leafed lotus which encircles our skulls. So, Guinevere, pray with me.

"Ah, great Father spirit, unmanifested, come to us. Descend, if you will, to our highest place, the topmost source of being, just as you did with Jesus, that excellent type of God-man who achieved an enlightened Christ-consciousness and served you fully. Descend, if you will, just as you did with Mary, that excellent type of God-woman, who was your spouse and knew you in poverty, chastity, and in obedience to your great spirit. Let the great unknown Father embrace his wife, the soul; let the great union of husband and wife produce the God-man, the spirit who serves and is served. Let the Pentecostal flame descend upon us.

"Oh, Mary, I feel you first. I feel your love envelop me, I feel the great compassion, the mystical encompassing of care which covers my loneliness, enhances my separation from God and men. For were you not so, also? Were you not also set apart and lonely? And was this not both a trial and a blessing? So, too, do I feel it. I feel that center alive with the fire of you, the warmth of you. I feel my skull tingle with that blessed spark of aloneness which reaches out to other alonenesses. I glow with that utter individuality and separation which reaches out for total union. I, the Knight, feel it, and you."

"And I feel you, Jesus. I, Guinevere, feel the suffering man of spirit, I feel the way and goal. I sense you being about your father's business, serving the spirit of love and of wisdom in the great white light which is at once heat and searing truth. Be about God's service, you say, and I follow you."

"But be about your own service, says Jesus to me! He says imitate me by serving the God within you. I grasp the legs of that God-man. I, Knight III, proud and free, heir of proud and free men, embrace the legs of that God-man and will not let him be off, independent, in the service only of God, the Father. Stay and be with us, I say. Stay and help us in our aloneness. Stay and show us how it is to be God and man, independent and apart, stay. This do I pray.

"And he says, 'Nay' . . . Thus does this God-man speak to me, Guinevere. He says 'nay.' He says nay to staying, nay to remaining, nay to uniting with us. But he says 'yea,' does this God-man. He also says 'yea.' He says yea to uniting with each other. He says yea to the union of spirit with spirit, flesh with flesh. He says blessed are those who unite, blessed are those who come together in the union with God.

"But who is this spirit incarnating, this God-man, Jesus? Who is he in me? I have done his Stations, I have meditated upon his life, I have spoken to him and of him, but who is he, in me? Who is this spirit incarnating, who?"

"And who is she, this woman, this wife of God, Mary, who was both wife of God and father to him? Who is she, in me? I have meditated upon her rosary, I have spoken with her, embraced her, but who is she, in me? Who is this love-soul, receptive to the God above and outflowing in compassionate, universal, forgiving love to man? Who is she in me?"

"The highest of the high, Grandson of the Knight, the highest of the high, Daughter of Guinevere. The highest are they, the highest, for they reach up and out and beseechingly to God beyond image, beyond being, beyond sound, and they pour down the sweet flow of that self-same fire-water-milk-spark of sweet-tasting spirit-love as it comes to them. They are they, sweet pair of lovers, pair of mystical sister-brother, they are they, and they are they in you. A mystical happening that, a truth beyond mind and eye, third or fourth."

"And who is this that speaks, who is this that can speak of God the Son and God the Mother-Wife? Who is this who can authoritatively say who is the Jesus-within and the Jesus-without? Who is this who knows the Mary concrete and the Mary of image-sense? Who is this?"

"I know, Grandson of the Knight. I, Guinevere II, Daughter of a great woman, daughter of she who knew God in both Christian and pagan ways, I know. For he-she who speaks is none other than the Holy Spirit itself, and that Holy Spirit is none other than Hermes, Messenger of the Gods. He comes with winged feet, with bursting cap, and he speeds between God and man, with the messages of each. This Hermes, this mighty Mercurius of God, is both malely male, as spirit, and femalely female, as flesh, just as every alchemist knew. And I know, great brother Knight, I know. I know this winsome, wild, weatherbeaten, watery, wily, willful creature who goes to and fro, more than any angel, more than bird, more than creature in heaven and earth. For his realm is both heaven and earth; his realm is between God beyond and God incarnate between God and man. And he is she, of course, as I know, I, daughter of a great woman who knew. Hermes, the great, wed to the love which produced the union of God and Man, Aphrodite, is reproduced as Hermaphrodite, say some, but we know Mercurius, himself, the strange one who conveys up and down."

"You know, Guinevere II, and you sing. The Messenger speaks in you as if he were not only Hermes, he and she, but Pegasus as well, a winged poet horse which I knew only with the Muses, only as the upward-soaring creation of Poseidon, himself. But you know, Guinevere. Do you also know that Trinity of God, the Father as unincarnated spirit, God, the Son, as spirit incarnate, with that unincarnate-incarnate Hermes moving between them, a Holy Spirit both insubstantial and substantial? Do you know that trinity?"

"I know it, Knight III. And I know that self-same God the Father, wedded to the human soul, Mary, and producing the son both God and man, the Son, both flesh and spirit, the son, both consciousness and love. I know that trinity also."

"Yes, Guinevere II, you know. And you know, as woman, as soul, better than I, the trinity of God, the Father, God the Woman, with the Holy Spirit of Hermes moving in between to produce that son. That wind-whisper has moved in your ear just as it did in Mary's. It moved and created. That new consciousness resides in you. Unite with me, Guinevere II, unite with me. Live with me the trinities, Father-Mother-Son, Father-Holy-Spirit-Son, Father-Spirit-Woman, and finally as we know it, spirit-soul-flesh, consciousness-love-incarnation. Oh, Guinevere II, let our duality embrace these trinities, let the threes join our two and make us One!"

"They unite, they unite. I, Hermes, Messenger, known by God and man, can speak. They unite and I observe. I observe and unite at once. For one eye is always awake and roams back and forth. One eye never sleeps. One eye, not the third-eye of Zeus, wise and creative, but the wakeful eye between God and man, which resides at the lotus place of union as a great open flow of fire. I ascend and descend, and neither is better, neither is worse. I bring back and take forward, I am I. What better angel of God to be? What better servant of man to be? I, known as Hermes, known as Mercurius, known as Holy Spirit, I know. And Jesus and Mary knew. And these two know, for the Jesus-sense and Mary-love are in them. I see them unite and become one: three into two, become One. The mystery. Spirit is descending from above the top of the triangle; spirit is falling from above, apex of the cone. In falling, there is rising, for from rising, is falling. God knows this, men do: intuition to God, rising-falling; love from God falling-rising."

"But sink, now, Holy Spirit, fall further into matter, fall further into creation, fall further into the depths of man, so that God can know himself, find himself, love himself. Sink now."

"And who is this who speaks? Who is this who speaks when even spirit is still?"

"It is I. It is the I Am who speaks, who leaves when even the Messenger stays, but stays when the Messenger leaves. For I AM is the statement and the being which is awake, which is."

"Stillness, and the spirit descends once more. Knight III and Guinevere II, united in Jesus and Mary, united in the trinity of God, united in the duality of man, come lower in their worship, incarnate God.

THIRD-EYE

"The spirit-flame of love-light descends, Guinevere II, and dwells now in that Third-Eye, the place of Zeus, all-seeing, intuitive in his vision of the Many, the many possibilities for consciousness and love. Great Zeus is a father God, thus a leader, for he is father to Gods and heroes and men. He is a son, for he is son of Kronos, God of limits, and therefore not the transcendent God of all. He is a brother to the Gods Hades and Poseidon. Thus he is a democratic leader. Great Zeus at the Third-Eye, with his lightning intuition, thundering emotion, visionary union, is the producer of the creative. Him do we serve, Guinevere II, magnificent Zeus.

"But also Apollo do we serve, Guinevere II, beautiful Apollo, of reason and order and harmony, a son and a brother, and leader of the Muses. Prophecy is his, he is the player of the instrument of the soul, the many centers of consciousness and love touched by him in harmony and beauty. Apollo is here. Zeus is here, Guinevere II, with his possibilities, but Apollo, too, with his order and wisdom."

"Yes, Knight III, light of my life, the Gods are here, but the Goddesses, too. Have you forgotten the daughter, Athene? The consciousness of the culture-builder? The vision of civilization? The leader of the greatest hero of all? The darling Athene, who is the consciousness of society, and yet, the consciousness of the feminine realizing itself? Have you forgotten what I, too, have learned?

"And Knight III, love of my life, have you also so easily forgotten the great wife of God, the solitude and solitary in the love of the One? Mighty Hera? I know that her love is of the one union, the one God, not the love of Mary, nor Aphrodite, but she is of love, too, is she not? Impersonal, love of God, not men, alone, deep, searching. This is the love of the feminine in its total devotion and total isolation. Not to be forgotten, eh, Knight?"

"I do not forget, Guinevere II. Here, in our place of command, in our place of consciousness as rulership, there is surely a quaternity, a balance of forces above and below, male and female. I know that love in this center is more for creation, for order, for reason, for consciousness, but it is here. The quaternio of God as husband-wife, as father-daughter, as mother-son, as brother-sister, but, above all, of God-alone as man and as woman, all here. Let us pray to our Gods of the Third-Eye, Guinevere II, and let them come to us, enlighten us."

"We pray, great Gods, we pray and we wait."

"Great Zeus appears to me, Daughter of Guinevere. He appears like a vigorous man in the prime of life. I see him, but I see the divine Athena being born from his head. She comes right out of his forehead, just at the place of the Third Eye. I see the Goddess emerge with a golden glow that is breathtaking. I am bathed by her glow, immersed in her aura, charmed by her smiling beauty. I feel her envelop me as I am haunted by every memory of the beauty of culture experienced. I am transported to her great city, to Athens and the top of the hill on which are magically, monumentally, the most beautiful buildings in the whole world. I am there with her, and the sun sets as she dazzles me with her temple, overwhelms me with her statues, enchants with her wisdom and charm. From the wisdom of Zeus she comes, but she comes as herself. I am enveloped."

"And I am charmed by Apollo, Knight III. I see him, so overwhelmingly handsome that I cannot bear it. I hear his lyre and I faint with pleasure, I smell his breath and I can sniff hints of the spirit above which have never come down to me before. I hear his voice and I know that the measure of his sweet words of love and wisdom could make me happy for the rest of my life. I am enveloped."

"Now Hera smiles upon me, Daughter of Guinevere! Hera smiles. She of the jealous and angry visage, she who is interested in no man but God himself, she who respects only the monogamous union, she looks upon me and smiles. She smiles upon me, the sinner; she smiles upon me, supporter of the many loves; she smiles upon me who would serve creation, consciousness, would even be her enemy. She smiles upon me. For she is aware that I have known such solitariness as has she; I have known betrayal, as has she; I have known the longing for union, as has she; above all, I have been as devoted as she. So, she smiles upon me. And a dark light, deep violet in color, covers me. I am enveloped by the light which goes out from Hera, goes out from Zeus, and plays itself out from the lyre of Apollo, the sunset-crown of Athena."

"And Zeus speaks to me, Grandson of the Knight. Zeus, the magnificent, speaks to me. He enters me like a snake, like a swan, like a word, and he speaks in sounds which are the voices of mountains and clouds, lightning and thunder. He speaks to me. But just as my spirit begins below, is below, I feel him there, and here. What is below for you is above for me, sweet Knight, or so it seems when the God comes to me. Was it so for Mary? Was it so for . . . But no more speculation, Zeus is in me. And I, too, will conceive from the father, who is also the son, who is also the husband, who is also the lover, who is also the brother, from him will I conceive. And, in conceiving, find the God also in thee, my brother Knight, who is husband, lover, son, brother and father."

"We are overwhelmed and covered, Daughter of Guinevere! Unite with me, here in the center of the diamond-light, the violet-light of Zeus and Hera, and the golden light of Athena and Apollo. Do you see them around us upon that diamond? Zeus and Hera above and below us, Athena and Apollo at our sides. And we will shine like that same diamond which is of the Gods, is that self-same shining star. I see it now, feel it, know it. That diamond shines at our forehead, it is the Third-Eye, and we are blessed."

"We are blessed, Knight III, we are blessed and loved."

THROAT

"The spirit descends, Daughter of Guinevere, from the 'Top,' from that indigo light, down through the Third-Eye, the violet diamond of light, down to the Throat. Now we are in a blue-gray place where the word takes on flesh, and the flesh becomes word. Oh, Guinevere, here is the magic of that circle, the many radii of Muses, the strands of the soul becoming creative in love. Here is the home of Bluebeard, and of Ouranos, the power God whose dark spirit tests and tries the soul, just as the sky God did to Mother Nature. The soul moans and complains, trying to bring forth its creations, and ultimately does so. And, in so doing, a man like me becomes Hephaistos, the smith of creation, and a woman like you, Daughter of Guinevere, becomes a poet of the soul."

"I know, Knight III. Through you, my love, I know. For here relationship becomes sacred, holy, in the word. For this is the place of spirit become matter, matter become spirit, and, hence, the circular place of the soul. The expression of that circle is of the union of the one great dark spirit at the center and the maniness of the soul's creative potentialities like spokes of the wheel. Love is the wholeness of the expression, many Muses in one Aphrodite."

"And the blue-gray light of the word is creation. Consciousness, fierce and artistic, forces creation; the drama of life is realized as art."

"Enough of words, Knight III, let the words become Word, let the dance of the soul around the circle of the Muses fill your mouth with praise, with joy, with acclaim to God who has made this possible."

"In the beginning did He create. In the beginning was the Word. In the beginning was Love made manifest in sound of creation. The lightning flash of Zeus and the thunder thereof came down and was spoken in the words of the poet, the sighs of the broken-happy soul who became a vessel for God's creation. I weep, Guinevere II, I weep because my words stutter, my heart overflows and the sad-sweet songs of that dark God who loves me burns and scalds me, makes me express . . ."

"Do not weep, Knight III. The tongue cannot contain all, any more than the heart. Each center must do its own task, but cannot do it all. Do not weep, Knight, for you have wept enough. It is enough to know that you have spoken. It is enough that you are child of a poet father, grandchild of a spirited father, and creative child of God."

"Daughter of Guinevere, my love, I see a vision. I see us in that same blue circle, I see us as the same poles, the same radii, the same spokes. Together we make a diameter, together we go around that circle of the Muses of the soul, together we join that love center where the totality of the Muses, Aphrodite herself, dwells. We then are spirit and Muse, consciousness of creation and love. We are crushed and crushing, creating and created. We are word and flesh, matter and spirit. We make it, find it, use it, become it, express it."

"I am with you, Grandson of the Knight, and my throat is parched for you, longs for you, is embraced by you, for you are my beloved Bluebeard, Ouranos, Eros."

"And you my Muse, my Aphrodite of the soul, my Mother Earth whom I both embrace and oppress, cherish and battle."

"We whirl in our circle, our wheel of creation, and blue becomes gray, gray becomes blue. Heaven descends and ascends in the word-vision of . . . 'In the Beginning, God.' "

HEART

"And the spirit descends even more. From Top and Third-Eye and Throat, from Triangles touching in a Cross, Indigo, to the Violet Diamond, to the Blue Circle, we descend, in the process of the incarnation of God, to the Heart.

"The heart. I know this place, for this was the home for my Grandfather, the Knight, this his castle. He was a Jacob, struggling with God, serving God with passion and love. He was a grasper of the forces of the spirit, the divine spark, and would not let go. And he loved God, as an Eros with a fierce vision, an intensity of love and consciousness which ever has its eye on the God above. That was my Grandfather."

"But remember Demeter is here, too, and Aphrodite Urania, the outflowing of love as well. Do you not know the Ruth which is the rival of Jacob in devotion? Do you not know that flowing of love to God and man which is not just universal, like Mary, nor in the passion of the soul as with the Muses? For here is the love of man, devoted and accepting, the love of God, passionate and reaching. Here is love in time. Feeling."

"Heart, heart. I have said it, Daughter of Guinevere. What more is to be said. For the heart is the center, the place of the pure air, the lungs guarded by the blood of life. I know that outflowing and that up-flowing. And so do you. Let us unite, Daughter of Guinevere, in interlocking triangles, in a Star of David, hexagon of heavenly passion! Let us be like Jacob, like Ruth, like Demeter and the Urania, and let our love flow toward each other and toward God."

"I love you, my Knight."

"I love you, my queen, my sister, my friend."

"The orange leaves of flame flicker about us. The warm color of feeling envelops us. We are contained in it."

"And the orange leaves of flame flicker from within us, Knight. The warm color of feeling goes out from us. We envelop others in it."

"Be enveloped, Guinevere II."

"Be enveloping, Knight III."

"Orange flame, heart blood, love-light flows."

DIAPHRAGM

"And now we descend lower yet and come to the diaphragm which is no 'center' at all, but an idea, a thought, a place. It is like the Tree of Life, or the Tree at which the Buddha sat, the Bo of Being. Here, sweet Guinevere, we are we, you and I. Here, I know that I am just a man, a mere mortal, and limited. The Gods are above me in the centers and below me in the centers, but here I am just me, in-between. There is spirit above and matter below, but here I am, a man of some spirit, perhaps."

"And I am just a woman. I am an ego, a person who can sit and meditate and act and love. I can know you as an 'amore' sweet Knight, and I can be merely 'aware.' "

"And that is what we are, male and female, man and woman. I embrace you, Daughter of Guinevere."

"And I embrace you, Grandson of the Knight."

NAVEL

"Come, Daughter of Guinevere. I see you wandering with your mind all over creation. We have passed the Diaphragmatic place where we just are we. Now we must descend from those upper spiritual centers and come down to the matter centers, the places where word and image and idea are flesh and emotion and sensation. Come, Daughter of Guinevere, come to this next place below, the Navel. Meditate with me upon the triangle here and its yellowness.

"Do you remember the significance of this place, the place where the teacher descended, where Dionysos dwells, and also where Ares-Mars finds his being?. . . You shake your head, as if you do not remember. Well, it is right that you do. For here Knowing, itself, is sacrificed to Being. Emotion is more important, here, than knowing. There is a 'now' of movement, of change. Dionysos is here, a place where union becomes disunion, where that which is old and withered dies. Death is here and violence—Ares-Mars dwells here—but also the heat of emotion and passion which transforms the mere desire of the center lower than this, the Belly. All these things of disunion, emotion, Being more than Knowing, all this is here, Daughter of Guinevere."

"But what of love, Grandson of the Knight? You speak of consciousness, and an end to the kind of consciousness which is knowing or intuiting or feeling, an end to becoming and finding, a surrender to Being. All this you speak of, but what of love? Did we not learn of it before? Did not we find Dionysos anew? And is there not love in it? I think so, Knight III. The love here is called Ecstasy. Here are the manifold experiences, of orgiastic unions—of disunions too—in passion. There is violence, but there is ecstasy. And ecstasy is love. The Goddess here, Persephone, the divine Daughter of Demeter, was just like your grandmother. And she is daughter to the Heart, as Persephone was daughter to Demeter, who was just like her mother. Persephone lives here in the cave below the Heart, at the Navel. She crawls inside and is transmogrified by passion, while her dear mother, full of feeling, goes out to mankind from the Heart. Persephone, the initial innocent turned wild, is abducted from the depths below, from the deep magical place of Hades, below even, the earth. The passion of emotion is united with the magic of darkest depths . . . But I will not speak more. To speak is to rise up, and here we must stay with the emotion, with the heat of the fire which burns and transforms."

"But stay, Daughter of Guinevere. You are right. I see it. And I can see that Ares, the War God, is also here. For is not battle also a form of passion? Have not the ancient warriors always spoken of the ecstasy of their strife? Do not the followers of the Wotan find paradise, Valhalla, a place where they fight all day, drink all night, have their wounds healed to fight again? Yes, I see it: Mars-Ares all day, battle; Dionysos-Persephone at night, drink. The center of ecstasy. And is it not so? That battle, aggression can be lived to the full, but no destruction occurs, healing takes place? Would that it were so!"

"Perhaps it is so, Knight II. Does not passion, when transformed, renew life, not take it? Passion renews love, when transformed. Ares and Dionysos both have a place among Gods, and we must adore them and treasure them, here, in this center, just as we can Persephone. Even I, a woman who abhors fighting, killing, aggression, can adore the great God Ares, for he loved Aphrodite, after all. I can love the great God Dionysos, for who can reject him and stay sane? Ecstasy comes, passion comes: it comes in love and battle. Let them unite, then no destruction, then no dismemberment which cannot be re-membered, and re-membered, healed, and, healed, made whole."

"Well said, Guinevere II. Now embrace me and love me, with a passion. Let us battle and fight and make love. For you can take in all my violence, all my power when I love you. Your passionate, receptive heart and belly and vagina can take me in. For the violence is of love and of passion."

"I can, good Knight. Ecstasy. Passion transforming the aggression of combat, the desire of sexuality, into the spiritual fire of Dionysos, the ecstasy of the union-disunion, of love. Just as Aphrodite loved the War God and produced the union, Hephaistos, the mighty creator, could catch them both in his web."

"I can see it, Guinevere II. I can visualize the union of Ares with Aphrodite, raised up by Hephaistos and his web of creative spirit. I can see a battler like my Grandfather, the great Knight. He battled hard and long, but always in the service of God. With his golden lions upon his chest, he was a server of the passionate ones of the yellow center."

"And I can see Dionysos, striding above the wine-filled sea. The women all follow him and are wild with joy and pleasure, drunk with passion. And I, too, for I will not fight and withdraw from him, thus become mad and insane with passion, I will worship."

"Let us worship these Gods, Guinevere II. And let us show our piety by uniting in passion."

"We do, Knight III."

"Thrust and counter-thrust, scream and counter-scream. Madness of love, madness of battle, ecstasy of disunion, apart in many pieces, fragmented by passion. Healed by love, made whole by acceptance, renewed by worship. Thus speak I, the God of the center of passion. Navel. Place of birth and death, rebirth. Thus speak I, Knight and God."

"Yes, Knight III, you are the God, and I am the Goddess. I am Persephone, raped from below, redeemed from above. I am a woman, like another, but a Goddess. And I am a soul torn by battle and by passion. But I contain them, keep them in. And I contain you, my God, my Knight, my man. I am torn thereby, broken thereby, but healed thereby, made whole."

BELLY

"Daughter of Guinevere, I fear I have lost you. Again, we descend, when we are required to concentrate on another center, you wander, you are gone. But now it is not your mind which wandered, as it did at the Navel, at the Omphallos of the World, you are distracted by the ten-thousand things, by all the desiring and not desiring. Come, Guinevere, come!"

"Oh, Knight III, oh, foolish Knight! You speak of my coming with you to the next center, the Belly center, and my not being with you. It is true that I am not with you, but only because I am already there at the Belly center! I have been there, distracted with desire and non-desire, I have been there, waiting for you. And now you complain that I am not there. For shame, good Knight, for shame! Listen now and recall, for I know more of this center than you. I have known sister of the Belly very well. I have known Aphrodite Pandemos, the Goddess of love who lives here, full of desire in the flesh, love in space. Sex, sex, sex is here. Sex as sensation, and sensation as energies of matter transforming. Love is here, Love as desire, need. Yes, I know it. I know love as desire—consciousness. To know, at this place, is only to devour, to take in and feed. To know is to know that one is alone, but there is a difference between self and others, that one is in need. But it is also to know the opposite, the negation of desire. Buddha was here and raised himself up, up beyond Belly, beyond desire, and beyond Navel, beyond passion, all the way up to the Diaphragmatic place of no-mind, of peace. But I am here, and live here with my Belly-sister. I am already here and I know it. So, if you think me distracted, it is because I desire and do not desire, I want and do not know what I want. I am a raging lion, a wandering animal, a hungry fish, a whale not to be denied."

"Forgive me, Guinevere II. I realize that you are right, and I have been too stupid. I, too, have known desire, known the hunger and wrath of the fish, the wild whale, the lecherous Leviathan. I know, too, that God is in that form here, but is he not also mighty Poseidon, the Earth-shaker? Does he not also own the sea, and shake the land? Does he not stir his trident, and cause life to grow, water to run, horses to be born? He does all of this. And I know Aphrodite Pandemos as well. How else could I have encountered Don Juan, how else coped with Hera, the great Goddess herself? But you know more, Guinevere II, it is true. You are more aware, more knowing, more loving in the Belly place than I am. So instruct me, lead me, show me, how we can unite, how we can celebrate, worship and come together in this place."

"Dance with me, Knight. Dance with me as the Son of the Knight, your father, watched Belly herself, the great Baubo, do the raucous dance of the Belly. She wiggled her belly and swayed it, thrust forward her womanhood and displayed it. And she held the phallus in hand, in hand, she held the phallus in hand. Dance and sing, flow with the source of desire."

"I will dance, Guinevere, I will dance and sing with you. I will flow. And I shall be your phallus, I shall be your Eros Pandemos, and I shall sing and stamp my foot, I shall stamp and be Poseidon, I shall shake the earth and make the waters flow."

"We dance, and sing, and flow. And rivers flow through us. We weep, and in weeping, cause a stream. We flow with the stream, and sleep. We flow down to the sea, to the place of Poseidon, and Leviathan. We are devoured by sea and fish. We are within. We accept the devouring. We are together, in the cave of the Belly. We are together."

"I love you, Guinevere II, I love you."

"I love you, Knight III, I love you."

Peace.

ANUS

"Lower we go, Guinevere II. Lower yet we go, beyond the green crescent of the Belly place, down to the brown square place of Anus, the deep, dark center where Hades lives. Here is not earth, it is as far beneath the earth as earth is beneath heaven. Here is the home of Hades, the Magician. Here is the home of the Lord of Transformation, the changer and shaper. The Magician shows himself far above, way up in the throat place, but here he begins, here he starts afresh in image, in literature, in history, here is Hades, spiritual changer and transformer, but in the magical way."

"And here, too, Knight III, is Hecate, the Witch, mistress of magic. Here is the mistress and queen of the indirect effect, the mover of occult forces. Dark changes, concrete; heavy matter, the web of relationships in the spider region, from the plumbing of below. Hers is love and darkness of the witch, below, unseen."

"Yes, Guinevere, all in darkness, unseen. Forces unseen, indirect. Magic unseen, indirect. Lord of Transformation, of flow into new shapes and forms: Mistress of Magic, the indirect effect. Here we are. We both know, but how unite, my lady? How unite in transformation and indirection?"

"Come with me, flow with me. Let us continue the journey from the sea, from the Belly place, from the Cave where dwelt the God and Goddess. Let us continue below the land, below the sea, down, down. Can you see us? We are transformed, dissolved into images. We are fragments and molecules and atoms. We are neutrons and protons and positrons. We are mere electrons. We are. We. And the non-visible forces effect, we are there. We still exist, for we are soul, and we are image, and we are God. We are."

"We, Guinevere, we are."

"We, Knight, we are."

"And now we are at the bottom of the cone, at the bottom of the Tree of Life which dwells within. We are in it, and it is in us. We are in it, and are it. Upper cone and lower cone come together. We have descended into the depths of matter, into the bottommost place of the concrete and have discovered that, at the end, matter is spirit, and forces are indirect. Electrons exist, images exist, soul exists, forever. And, at the end, matter is spirit. Some have said, 'There is no truth in matter,' but they are wrong, for the truth is that matter is spirit. But perhaps they are right, for they say only spirit exists, which is also true. But they do not know that matter is spirit, too."

"Matter is spirit, too."

"And now we are ready to ascend, ready to ascend. We have descended from the heights at the top, we have incarnated and grown more and more into flesh, into matter, and have discovered that at the bottom of matter is spirit. We have come down and now we are ready to ascend. So, now, let us ascend, Knight III."

"Guinevere II, just as we descended in the western way, let us ascend in the eastern way, in the Kundalini way, which has a history, knows a truth, follows a form. Let us use it."

"Then lead, Knight III, lead and I shall follow."

Kundalini Way

MULADHARA

"In the square, Daughter of Guinevere, we begin at the beginning, at the root support of being. We begin where there is family and structure, where the earth of life is solid and square. Here, the elephant, peaceful and sturdy, carries the load of life, family, society. We begin where Shiva is a Brahma, a child with staff and gourd, with a rosary, in peace. For God is a child here and we care for him. God is a child when one is safe in the family. God is a child, for all is order, all is peaceful, all is safe. All opinion, all belief, is given. And the Shakti, dear Guinevere? The Shakti is a many-armed hell-witch, she is Dakini, red and furious, spear and sword in two hands, drinking a cup of blood in another, holding a skull staff in a fourth. Family and structure and order are child-like, when the forces of nature are wild and ravenous and battling.

"Come with me, Daughter of Guinevere. Come and feel the cohesion of family. Come and sniff the smells of earthy tent, of family sweat, come and touch your feet upon the reality which is illusion. And why illusion? Because we know: all structure is childlike, all structure only keeps the wild Dakini at bay. So huddle with me, Daughter of Guinevere, huddle and be close. Huddle and cling as we shield ourselves from the wild Goddess, whose energy and desire will devour us."

"I shall huddle, Knight III, and I shall weep, for I know, like you, that all order is but a thatched roof against the lightning, all belief is but an earthen house against flood, all containment is but a poor vessel against the powers of the Goddess. But we—you and I—shall protect the child, shall cover him. We shall build a house of earth, but it shall be brick. This earth, shaped into the squares of our baked sand, shall come from all that we have suffered together, shared together, faced together. Our earthen house shall be us, safe from the floods of Belly and the lightning of Eye, because connected to it, aligned with them. This we shall do."

"We, Guinevere, shall come close. Let us pray for our union in Muladhara, the root support, where order and chaos are side by side, where sweet child and wild witch are King and Queen, where safety and destruction share a nest, were the Snake herself is awakened."

"We pray and we wait. We ourselves become a snake, curved into One. We are lost, oh Knight, we are lost in the order and chaos, in the energy of life. We are lost and we are One."

"Who, then, speaks, Daughter of Guinevere? Who speaks? If we are lost, and, when lost, united, when united, gone, who, then, speaks?"

"The Charioteer, oh Knight, the Charioteer. The God-man of your father and my mother, the same who was All in One, One in All. The Charioteer. The driver of the vehicle, the One who is there when all else is gone. He speaks."

"Let him speak, then, let us vanish, and let him speak."

"Words of union, words of love. Words of order. All these I speak. But . . . words of chaos, words of hate. Words of strife. Can you combine in these? Can you unite in these?"

"I can, Charioteer. I can love despite hate, unite despite chaos. I can."

"But I need, Charioteer, I need."

"Then love her, Knight, give her . . ."

"I embrace, I give . . . I am embraced, I receive."

"I love, I cherish . . . I am loved, I am cherished."

The Charioteer.

SVADHISTHANA

"We rise to Svadhisthana, the 'proper place' of water, where crescent moon shines on the devouring fish-monster of our desires. Oh Rakini, Goddess of ravenous hunger, blood runs from your nose, you stuff palm rice into your fang-covered mouth, while you bluster and threaten with your three-eyed, four-handed terror. You have a trident, just like Poseidon, your counterpart, with a drum-rattle, too, just like the roar of the earth-shaker, and a battle axe, fierce. Oh, fierce energies of the water-world, full of desire and passion, your consort is Vishnu, the handsome youth, garlanded and athletic. Consciousness now is a youth and fair, proud, more than the child of the earth. But the waters are fiercer yet, for they are even darker when we see them."

"I know, Knight III, for I know the moon, and I know the fish. And I know the contraction of the fear, the narrowing of vision when one knows that he does not know. I know the taste of urine and feces, of brine water and refuse. But I know, too, how we have conquered, you and I, how we have won and transformed belly-woman and hunger-man. We have won—and lost. For who can claim victory over Rakini in her fierceness? Who can be more beautiful than Vishnu, in his handsomeness?"

"How, then, can we unite, Daughter of Guinevere? How can we unite in this awful place, this tragic place, this holy place?"

"Come and kiss me, Knight. Come and devour me. I will take you in and devour you as well. We shall be the Kundalini once again, but like the snake biting its own tail. The fish-monster, snake-monster, will devour itself and be whole. Come."

"I become tail of the snake, fin of the fish. I come."

"I become head of the snake, head of the fish. I come."

"I am devoured by you, devoured."

"I devour you, devour."

"I am like the insect who copulates with his love in air and loses his head."

"I am like the queen bee who devours her lover and is alone."

"But I am there, I."

"And who is I? Who is I?"

"I, the snake. I, uroboros. I, insect-lover, I, bee-queen, bee-drone. I, the Charioteer."

"We dissolve in thee, unite in thee, are lost, are found."

"I, the Charioteer."

MANIPURA

"In 'Plenitude of Jewels' we rise and find the navel lotus, the passion place, the triangular crucible of heat and fire. Passion, now, Guinevere II, and color. Now we see and act, like the ram. Sight and color have we, but no thought. Emotion is great, passions wild, triangular battle, and mighty Rudra is old, red, destructive. Lakini, now, dispels fear. She is fierce and bloody, but a balance begins; passion moves us."

"Fire, heat, I see it, Knight, and feel it. I see the Kundalini, a serpent still, but now a dragon, spitting fire. Will you kill it, Knight? Or will you let it burn us? Knight, are you hero still, or but a man?"

"No hero any more, Guinevere, my woman. No longer will I smite the dragon, no longer pretend the conquest of the fire. Instead, let us warm our bones in him, the great fire-demon. Let us warm ourselves in the passion and know that we are human and alive. Come, Guinevere, embrace me, toe to toe, knee to knee, genital to genital, belly to belly, and, navel to navel. For we shall unite, bathed in the fire of the dragon, bathed in the color-heat of the Kundalini snake. And we shall be dissolved."

"I am dissolved, oh Knight. I am dissolved and melted in the crucible of God, and am decomposed into molecules and atoms. I am flesh becoming spirit, I am woman becoming whole."

"And I am man transforming in the heat of passion. I dissolve."

"And they dissolve into me, the Charioteer. For I am the snake. I am that clear mercurial fluid which is now earth, now water, now fire. I drive that chariot drawn by that mercurial snake. They dissolve in me, and I am they. Driver and driven are one, Knight and lady are one. Chariot and Charioteer; animal and man. Flesh and spirit; vessel of God."

KALPA TREE

"And now we rise once more, to the little chakra, which is no chakra. We rise to the diaphragmatic center where Buddha sits under the Kalpa Tree. We meditate, and come to the place of sheer human union. No more hero am I, no longer Knight. I come as ordinary man, with ordinary woman, and we sit with Buddha and meditate under the Kalpa Tree. We rise above the passions and reflect. We are free, no mind. We are free, no aim. We are free, no image. Free."

"And we are free because Buddha is here. Free because we know our mortality."

"And free because we laugh. For who is Buddha? Buddha is the Charioteer! He rides, and knows it. We ride, and know it. We are the snake, and we wrap ourselves about the tree. We are the snake and couple with the tree of chakras, the spinal cord of centers, we are the snake."

ANAHATA

"To Anahata we come, to the place of air. Our hearts are touched and we, in turn, touch the Goddess, Kakini, who is golden, who dispels fear. 'Her heart is softened by nectar,' say the sages, and we, too, are softened; we, too, can rise above the Kalpa Tree of the Buddha and enjoy the sweet touch, the warm feel, the gazelle movement of the Anahata, she of the hexagonic Seal of Solomon, great prince. We can enjoy. For here we are in our castle of the 'unattackable,' the lung-protected place where the small flame of heart-consciousness holds us. Here we are, Daughter of Guinevere, in the favorite home of my Grandfather, the Knight."

"Yes, we are here, Knight III. I move, I touch, I feel, and I can sense, I can see. I can see Jacob wrestling with his angel of God here, the passionate embrace of it. And I can see warm-hearted Demeter living here, searching for her daughter, loving men. Best of all, I can see the Sister of the Heart, who is the same as she and me, loving, caring, warming, holding."

"But look now, Daughter of Guinevere, look at the rod of Moses, look at the snake itself. It moves, it speaks, it points to that burning bush, that Tree of Life which burns without being consumed."

"I wrap myself about that tree. I entwine myself in gentle motion, I am both rigid rod and agile antelope. I am a dweller in the middle place of the Tree of Life, for I serve the Lord, embrace the Lord, and am contained in the Lord."

"And I, snake, feel myself in you. I, Grandson of the great Knight who knew you, as Moses did, served you, I, too, salute you, embrace you, find myself in you."

"And I, snake, Daughter of Guinevere, flow into you, am sinuous with you, feel my heart gracefully touched and divinely bitten by you. I, daughter of she who loved two men, I, too, am encompassed by you."

"Come then, and be in me. Come then, and live in the castle of air surrounded by fire. Come and be unattackable. Come and be rigid rod and supple flesh. Come and be a spiritual phallus, in the service of God."

"We embrace, Knight, and I flow like a snake. With you."

"We embrace, Guinevere, and I stand like a snake. With you."

VISHUDDA

"Ascend, Guinevere II, ascend princess. Come with me to Vishudda, the place of purification. Come to the circle, the Akashic-place which gives space and hearing and words of the mouth. Come to the library of the soul, the records of lives past, caught up in the ether, dwelling in the throat. Come to the beginning, come to the Word."

"In the beginning, God . . . and the word. We are the serpent, Knight, and we speak the word. Look at it, look at us. The word comes from his tongue of fire. The word plays from his cool-hot flame."

"True, Guinevere, but see Sada-shiva, seated on his great lion-seat. Look at the power of the spirit, here. Look at his five faces, his trident, battle axe, thunderbolt, sword, great snake, bell, goad, and noose. Look at him! The great spirit, a child at Muladhara, a youth at Svadhisthana, an old man at Manipura, rises and rises, and is at last so great that he is a King, a speaker and a snake-holder, a thunderer and bell-sound ringer."

"And the Goddess is white, she is purified."

"Let the snake speak, let the dragon proclaim."

"I have no need to proclaim, no words of fire to burn you with. My word is peace. My word is circular. In the beginning was the dragon. In the beginning was the fire. In the beginning was the tormentor of the soul. Now peace, now word of warmth. Now words of love."

"Only love, snake? And only in gentle ways, in peace?"

"Laughter, laughter. 'Warring peace,' remember, and healing of wounds re-opened. Passion does not die in peace."

"United, Knight, united. I, Guinevere II, take your tongue in mine. We kiss and unite, in tongue-kiss, in word-union. Snake."

AJNA

"We rise. Above the word, above the idea, even, to the place where ideas begin, where words are beyond air, beyond fire, beyond ether, even, and there is no element at all, no animal at all. We rise to Ajna, the place of command, to the Manas of mind which governs and sees and unites. We rise. And what is the God here? No longer a child or youth or man or even a great king. No. Now he is Shambhu the Atma, lustrous like a flame. Now he is sparks around a golden light. He is the spark, the lightning, the vision itself. Such is the God."

"We rise, Knight. Between the eyebrows we come, to that blessed third-eye, that visionary place where you found Zeus and Apollo, and I found Hera and Athene. There we are. And I see the great Goddess as we rise, the great Shakti-Hakini with her six faces of creativity. Rosary in her hands, and skull, for she is now full of prayer and cultural service like Athene, and aware of the loneliness and solitariness of life and death, like Hera. But the Goddess holds the drum, as well, for the thunderous knowledge of Zeus, and a book, for the polished wisdom of Apollo. All these she holds, because she is whole, and sits serene upon her white lotus. This is the place of command."

"And what happens to our snake here, Daughter of Guinevere? What results for Kundalini, the source of us?"

"We know, we know. For the snake is . . . look and see! The snake wears a golden crown, the snake curves upon itself in a graceful S and sees itself crowned in glory, for it commands. And we know, Knight III. We know that the Gods speak through us and command us. We know that the luster of the flame and its sparks soar and swim about us. The snake is crowned. Speak, snake, speak and command us!"

"I am the snake. Wisdom am I, wise. Life am I, living. Come and be wisdom, come and be life. Come and be crowned."

"We come, and, in coming, knowing. And in knowing, living. What do we know, what do we live? That God lives in us, and we in Him. We are crowned in the realization, exalted in the knowledge and experience that God is us."

"Then be chariot for the Charioteer, be realizer of the snake, be Knight and Lady."

"We dissolve and form, are spirit and flesh. End."

SAHASRARA

"But there is no end, not yet. For we rise still more. We rise to Sahasrara, to the thousand-leaved lotus itself, where our guru is Shiva Himself. We rise to where Shakti is the effulgence of ten milion suns, beyond mind, beyond speech, beyond life even. For we rise to the Void, to the shunyata where being is no longer being and there is Nirvana. We rise, Guinevere. No more snake, no more light, no more Knight and Lady, for we are dissolved. We are lost in the effulgence of God, in the ever-manifesting, ever-unmanifested at whose feet we dance in joy. But who is it that dances? It is the God. Dissolved, no longer an Eye, nor an I, but the man who is the son of God, his vessel, and the woman who is the wife and mother of God, his vessel. We are the Chariot of God."

"And I am the Charioteer. I am the beginning and the End. And it is Ended."

PART V
An East-West Tree of Life and Hymns

Seventh Center

Situation: Top of Head
Form: Diamond in Lotus
Color: Indigo
Gland: Pineal
Plexus: None
Animal: Lamb
Element: None
Function: Intuition (introverted-Jesus) and Feeling (introverted and extraverted-Mary)
Psychophysical quality: None
Organ of sense: None
Organ of action: None
Consciousness:

> *Jesus:* the Christ. Man aware that he is a "son of God," a God-man, an incarnation of the spirit. Consciousness serves the ever-unmanifested-ever-manifesting spirit above, while this self-same spirit ever-unfolds-ever-evolves-ever-manifests.
>
> *Hermes-Mercurius:* Dark spirit of consciousness, which is the Holy Spirit, transforming and transformed. Man aware of his own dark side and his paradoxical nature.

Love:

> *Mary:* A God-woman. Love is compassionate, universal, forgiving. The soul is committed to poverty, chastity, obedience, to that self-same unincarnated spirit above; which is to say: receptive, open, attentive to it. The soul is wed to God, mother to God. The love is a union, producing ever-new consciousness and goes out to mankind, merciful.

Characteristic: Upper Trinity

> (1) God-Father (unincarnated spirit) and God-Son (incarnated spirit) with the Holy Spirit (Hermes-Mercurius) as messenger and angel between God and man. (2) God-Father (spirit) wedded to Mary (soul), producing God-Son (consciousness).
>
> (3) Holy Spirit (messenger-angel) between God-Father (unincar-

nated spirit) and God-woman (Mary). A type of union producing intuition-consciousness and faith, love from God, and thence to mankind.

JESUS

Jesus, Jesus, Son of Man!
Consciousness are you? Knowing are you.
Then know, be aware! Tell me!
Tell me, in my humanity. Tell me.
How it is that God is a fire and a wind?
That God is a woman and a man?
That God is a circle and a square?
Tell me.

"I'll tell thee. I'll tell thee.
God is all one can see . . .
And not see.
What is not God?
Only that which is not blessed:
Out of sight of haloed light, holy fire;
Out of range of rugged wind, spirit's sire;
Not contained in human frame;
Not a form in geo'd game.
That is not God."

Then say, Sweet Jesus, say!
Say, man-light and man-wind!
Is irregular curve unblessed?
Is chaos not God?

"Yes and no.
For curve and chaos, unblessed,
Become God, blessed."

And man's task, Jesus?
Man's task?

"To give and receive:
Order and chaos
Curve and corruption
Form and be formed."

Blessing? "Redemption."

God-man? "Man-God."

MARY

Mary poor, Mary real
Mary compassionate, Mary heal
Mary mother, Mary wife
Mary soul, Mary life

Open, Mary, open
Open belly, heart and mind
To God-father, God-spouse, God-wind

Chaste fire-tongues scald you, transform you
Wild wind-hands caress you, possess you

Hermes dances on your soul
Angels cry, demons shriek

And God becomes a man.

God has crushed our human soul
Children cry, old ones shriek

Hell-blaze consumes us, torments us
Whirlwind embroils us, dements us

Close, Mary close
Close your robe and us entwine
From God-demon, God-villain, God-blind

Mary, my soul, my life
Mary, my mother, my wife
You are God-woman, heal
You bear God-men, real.

HERMES

Fly, great trickster, fly!
Fly to heaven, God's unseen eye
Fly to earth, man's unheard ear
Fly winged angel, fly near!

I know your darkness, Hermes, I know your light
I know your earthy jokes, your watery laugh
I know the fire of your alcheme bath

I will catch you in my vessel

In subtle body you will nestle
Moist-dry spirit flow through me
Solid-air ghost transform me

Foot, wing; man and God
Spirit, flesh; peas in pod
Top, bottom; you and me
Life, death; birds in tree

A pair, Binarius, I can see
A pair, Mercurius, you and me.
A third, most curious, rise from the sea
God-men created, for us to be.

LAMB

Lamb of God, what is it?
A weak, bleating thing? A sacrifice?
Yes, these.

But more:
Shorn of wool, vulnerable
Giving warmth, comfortable
Creature, created
Sensitive, soul-mated.

And more:
Hermes-Shepherd, Jesus-lamb
God is both, He said, "I AM"
Lamb of God is Son of God
Spirit of God is Shepherd
Hermes-Jesus, God and Man,
Gentle lamb and leopard!

And more:
The between. Mary.
And what is Mary?
The eye. You.
Soul as sheep, ewe. You.
Trinity: Shepherd, ewe, lamb
Such an animal! Such a God! Such a Man!

Sixth Center

Situation: Between eyebrows ("Third-eye")
Form: Eye in diamond
Color: Violet
Gland: Pituitary
Plexus: None
Animal: Eagle (Zeus); Swan, Hawk, Crow, Raven, Wolf, Dolphin, Snake (all of Apollo); Owl (Athene); Cuckoo (Hera).
Element: None
Function: Thinking (introverted-Apollo, extraverted Athene) Intuition (extraverted-Zeus, introverted-Hera)
Psychophysical quality: Mental faculties
Organ of sense: None
Organ of action: None
Consciousness:

Zeus: All seeing, intuitive vision of the Many, the many possibilities for both consciousness and love. Is Father and, thus, leader (of Apollo and Athene); is also Son (to Kronos, the concrete): is born out of and overcomes the material state to finally unite with it; and Brother (to Poseidon and Hades), thus a democratic leader among equals. Lightning intuition, thundering emotion, visionary union. Producer of the creative.

Apollo: Thinking, reason, ordering, harmony. A son, and primarily a Brother, friend of man, but introverted, thus apart. Leader of the Muses (creativity), master of the python (prophecy), player of the lyre (controller of the seven centers). Reason, therefore, is the leader, moderator, and regulator of life, but is second to Zeus, the producer. Where Zeus is possibility, Apollo is structure and order.

Athene: Consciousness is for culture-building, civilization. Born of the mind, devoted to the creation of better worlds. The feminine realizing its individuality, consciously. The masculine serving the architecture of the more perfect society.

Hera: Consciousness of the single union, oneness. Solitary, solitude. When no union of consciousness, total darkness, negation of consciousness. Creative in spite of itself.

Love:

Is Zeus-like (love of many), is Apollo-like (love of structure and order, harmony), is Athene-like (love of realized culture), is Hera-like (impersonal to men, personal to God). Love is of consciousness, order, creativity, understanding.

Characteristic:

Upper quaternity

Paradox of the One (Hera, Athene) and the Many, (Zeus, Apollo).

Mind.

ZEUS

Zeus, All-seeing, Lord of Many, Lord of One
Speak to me!
Tell of lightning-light and thunder-word
Tell of thee!

"In stone and stream I speak; in word and gleam.
I sound from high, the bell; but flow from low as well.
Does not the water whisper, just as thunder thrills?
Does not the rock shed light, just as lightning chills?"

A rock? Shed light?

"Yes, rocks shed light.
Look at dark mountain
When going down sun shines bright
In narrow valley's slant
On glacier's snowy coldness. Look.
Does not the rock reflect the light?
When tree is dark?"

It does.

"Then think. Think."

I'll think. I'll think.
Nature shows the light of God. Even the rocks do it.
Nature's stone—the self—speechless, changeless, hard . . .

Shows the light of God.
Look at rocks, unchanging. See God.
Look at stream of life, changing. See God.

I see, oh Zeus, I see.
Zeus is Lord of Rocks, Lord of Streams.
For there, in rocks and streams, He speaks
As well as lightning fire and thunder sound.
In earth and water, fire and air, He speaks.
And I shall listen.

And see, my Lord, and see.
For does not the light shine bright in narrow valley's darkness?
Does not the ray persist as cold wind shivers skin?
Does not the Lord return the joy when deep depression's past?
And make me laugh with warm sun's blaze, creation's eye, at last?

APOLLO

Lord Apollo! A hymn to you!
A hymn.
I see you, Lord
I see.

Dark curls, muscled flesh: Greek God.
Handsome face, open look: potent man.
Sleek snake in left hand, shaped lyre in right
Aura's gold about your head.
I see you, Lord.
I see.

But speak to me, Lord, speak!
Speak of creation, Muses
Of prophecy, snake
Of wisdom, light.

"All in the snake, all.
From snake to lyre to light.
I pray, you pray.
Hold.

"Would you create, serve Muse?
Then listen, hold.
Would you predict, be wise?
Then listen, hold.

"Hold and listen, then sing.
And singing, think.
And thinking, pray.

And praying, feel.
And feeling, know.
This the wisdom, this the light."

I hold, Lord, I hold.
The snake coils in my belly and rises, rises.
She rises, I hold.
And holding, know.

Python's flame breathes air to sacred lyre
Muse's strings sound mood to golden fire
Apollo's sun, Halo's glow.

"Never let go. Never let go."

HERA

Hera, Dark Goddess, Witch of the Eye,
I salute you!
Hail, fierce Goddess, jealous of the God,
I fear you.

I kneel to your aloneness, solitary
I bow to your withdrawal, darkness
I bow, I kneel, I fear, salute
But I weep.

No love, Goddess? No care?
Only jealousy, demands?
Only pain, no thought of Man?
Only You?

"Only me . . .
And you . . .
And God.
Only."

Bind my tongue . . . stillness
Cover my eye . . . darkness
Love my Lord . . . fierceness
Like you.

Alone, Hera-sola
One, Hera-mona
Devoted, fierce
Whole or null.

I bow, Goddess,
I know, Goddess,
I love, Goddess.
Like you.

ATHENE

Athene, fierce maid, city's wisdom, speak to me!
Tell of building's beauty, civic joy
Weave the dreams of pattern, thoughts of order
Show the Hero's way.

"The way is winding, you know.
The light is slanting, you know.
From winding build the straight
From slanting form the round.
Circle and square, you know.
The Eye, you know."

If I know, Goddess,
Why do I ask?
If I know, Goddess,
Why implore?

"You know, man, you know.
To speak, inform,
To mold, be 'informed,'
You know."

We know, Goddess, we know.
Born of the God, we.
Born of the head, we.

A thought, 'in-formed'
God thinks man, and man thinks God,
In-formed.
Man makes the world, the world makes man,
Re-formed.

Help us think, Maiden, help us when you can
Help us know the form, help us shape the plan.
Show us the straight, bare the winding
Reveal the slant, show the binding.

EAGLE

Eagle-bird, lofty!
Soul of Zeus, crafty!
So proud you are, aloof
Winged hateur, beaked tooth.
I see your height, your matchless vision
I know your might, your intuition
Spirit soars, nests on mountain
Thunder roars, heaven's fountain
Eagle-bird, far seer!
Soul of God, man's leader!

ANIMALS OF APOLLO

Apollo! Moderator! Leader of Muses! Player of Seven-Stringed Lyre!
Seven Centers lead You! Seven animals, too! Separate, together,
    entire!
Snake: galling Goddess, time transformer, love of life
Dolphin: want of waters, hungry hoarder, wishes' wife
Wolf: mighty mover, fiery fighter, passioned power
Raven: heart of hunger, spirit seeker, torment's tower
Crow: calling crier, speaking sagely, telling tales
Hawk: sharp-eyed seer, clear-eyed creature, vanquishing veils
Swan: land, air and water; bird-fish transformer, God-man-
    transcender, triad uniter.

CUCKOO

Cuckoo. Hera's bird.
Sings in Spring,
Time when Marriage Mistress is at peace,
    with her Lord.
  no jealousy, no rages
  no tantrums, no cages.
Cuckoo. Bird of Goddess.
Faithful Singer.
Time when she's no more in solitude,
    in blessed union
  no pain, no resentment
  full reign, full contentment.

OWL

Owl. Oo Oo Oo
All know your voice. Your eyes.
    Athene's bird, wise.
But do they know your wit?
      Your song is but a laugh?
      Your wisdom is but half?
Inner smile, by moon is lit.

Owl. Oo Oo Oo
All know your voice. Your eyes.
    Athene's bird, wise.
But do they know your passion?
      For beauty's form, a glowing face?
      For culture's norm, a golden grace?
Aesthetic maid, intense inaction!

Fifth Center

Situation: Throat
Form: Circle; Wheel with nine spokes
Color: Blue-gray
Gland: Thyroid
Plexus: Pharyngeal
Animal: Turtle, Dove (Aphrodite Urania); Winged Horse, Pegasus (Muses)
Element: Ether
Function: Expression and Communication
Psychophysical quality: "Akashic": space-giving
Organ of sense: Hearing
Organ of action: Mouth
Consciousness:

> A power God of the passions dwells here; a dark spirit who tests and tries the soul—like Bluebeard—and pushes all the creative products of the soul back into itself—like Ouranos. The type of consciousness is fierce and artistic, in which creation is compelled to express itself in a spiritual way. Central is expression and communication, in which man realizes himself as a God-man in terms of his creative work. The paradigm is Hephaistos, the creator. The drama of life is expressed as art and creation; man knows that God dreams life creatively and so—at this level—does man.

Love:

> The Muses, representing the multiplicity of the soul's creative gifts of expression. This expression comes into being from the union of the One great dark spirit with the Many of the soul's creative potentialities. Love is in the form of Aphrodite Urania, a great spiritual love which is a oneness from which all the maniness of the Muses emerge and to which they return. Love is a creative passion and a passion for creation.

Characteristic:

> Upper Unity
> > Dynamic (One spirit, many potentials)
> > Creativity

OURANOS–BLUEBEARD

Speak dark spirit, speak Heavenly Father,
   speak Ouranos, express!
Speak brutal lover, speak Devilish Brother,
   speak Bluebeard, confess!
Speak to such a one as I!

Conniving creature, crippled, cuckold, like Hephaistos am I.
Lacerated lover, limited, lupold, like Hera's son am I.
Speak to such a one as I!

"I speak; I speak:
Heavy, heavy, do I lean
From Heaven's height to earth's sore spleen.
Each night I come and sleep, weep.
Each night create, fecundate.
Each day I turn away
From Gaia's heart to sky-light's sheen.

Have you known such pain, such sorrow?
Have you known this strain, dread of morrow?
Daily change, endless round of God.
'Create, create' she says; 'An end, an end,' say I.
'I grown, I groan!' says she; 'No more new,' I cry.
Thus brutal, rough am I, not mild
Thus my glee at smothered child.

But son deposed me from my power
Do not fret it, do not glower
Castrate God does love create
Muse's soul takes shape from weight.
Heaven's earth travails no more
Creatured art is man at core.
Love fulfills the earth's creation
In spirit's growth, emancipation.

Dream on the tale, evolve the myth
Weave the light in bones and pith.
The web's dark tangle is the ground
With rain-drop jewels of speech, the sound.
Creative light heals endless round
Let words and joy and life abound!
The 'endless round' is God's own form, at last
And man's blind state of circled grief is past."

KLEIO

Kleio, Giver of Fame, Enfolder of History
Sing to me, embrace me!

"I embrace Hephaistos, serve God
But tongue-tied poet, mere sod?
No history, no fame,
Naught inspire, nothing claim."

You speak, oh Muse, all the same
You come when called your name
You respond when I implore
You never close the door.

Doors ajar shed some light
Little men claim some sight
Mortal men spark God
Creatures come from sod.

"I smile, 'tis true
I'll smile, for you."

OURANIA

Ourania, Heavenly Muse, star-gazer
Sing to me, embrace me!

"I embrace all men, need no song
Stars abound, sing sphere's music
Speak Fate.

Not Nemesis, nor Aidos, but Time
And Psyche's form stretched taut
Show pattern, show web."

I know Muse, I know.
At night, as I gaze
In quiet, as I muse
I know.

Patterned Fate.
Destiny from Character, they say

And they are right.
But character is chosen, is it not?
In Ourania's realm?
Before the birth?
Karma's choice?

" 'Tis true. 'Tis true."

MELPOMENE

Melpomene, Singer, Tragedy's face
Sing to me, embrace me!

"Would be enclosed by me?
Not likely.
Would you sing my song?"

Your song I'd sing, your clutch evade
Who seeks pain's claw, illusion's shade?
Not I.

"It comes all the same."
It comes.
"And, coming sometimes teaches."
"Sometimes not.
Sometimes not."

Dark face, sad face.
Always there.
"Always there."

Accept? Transform?
"Try."

Why?

"Sigh."

THALEIA

Thaleia, Comic Muse, Festive One, are you there?
Sing to me, embrace me!

"Comic song is easy:
Laugh at self.
Easy, but hardest.
Who can do it?"

Too much pain, too much conceit.

"But that's the one who laughs, man
He who knows
Too much pain and vanity.
In knowing, laughing;
To him, I sing.

TERPSICHORE

Terpsichore, You Who Enjoy Dancing, Mistress of the Lyre,
Sing to me, embrace me!

"No word, man, move!
Move to heart's desire.
Move to the dance,
Move to the lyre!

God's word is a line
Snake felt on the spine.
Move!"

KALLIOPE

Kalliope, Of the Beautiful Voice, Muse of Heroic Song,
Sing to me, embrace me!

"Hero's song is a sad tune
Have you known it?

To labor mightily, Heracles
To seek endlessly, Odysseus
Wander confusedly, Perseus
Suffer painfully, Prometheus
That's the Hero's song.

And for what to labor and wander?
For what to seek and suffer?
For fame? For art? For love? For mankind?
None of these."

Not even for God?

"Not even for God."

For the song.
For the singing.

Even in silence.
Even when none can hear.
Thus does the true hero sing.

"And thus is his voice made mellow by my own.
Heroe's song: Kalliope. For itself."

ERATO

Erato, Awakener of Desire, Muse of the Dance
Sing to me, embrace me!

No word from you, like Terpsichore,
But I see you, feel you.

Dark passion rising from within, awakened.
Limbs curl, flesh fulls, sex stirs
The flow.
Life awakened, the body moves to God's music.
Who can listen to the sound?
Who can flow and form?

Not I, Muse, not I!

Yes I, Muse, Yes I.

I can, can not; will, will not.

In this, embraced, in this, awakened.

For thus, the Dance.

EUTERPE

Euterpe, Giver of Joy, Flute Muse,
Sing to me, embrace me!

"I do not sing, I play!
In playing, joy!"

Play: How can a grown man play?
Tell me, pray.

"In playing, a flute.
In playing, an act.
In playing, a love.

"Thus making music, feeling

Thus making drama, being
Thus making love, living."

Thus Joy, Muse Mistress,
Thus Joy, Euterpe!

""Thus Joy."

POLYMNIA

Polymnia, Of Many Hymns, Muse of Story-Telling
Sing to me, embrace me!

"That I have done, and that I do.
And that you know already.
No poet you, nor your fathers, too,
But teller of tales, heady."

Like you, Muse, like you.
Do I speak, Muse, or is it you?

"No matter, we speak.
In speaking, knowing
In knowing, serving

"Story-teller of God, Him.
Muse of God, hymn
Fool of God, hmm."

APHRODITE

Aphrodite, Mistress of Muses
Sing to me, embrace me!

"You, Man, sing to me.
You, Man, embrace me!"

I will, Goddess, I will.
You it is I love, adore.
You will I serve, evermore.

As nine-faced Muse
In action and strife
In word and in image
As love in my life.

TURTLE AND DOVE OF APHRODITE URANIA

All see the turtle and the dove!
All glimpse the animals of love!
The one: to sing in spring, renewal bring.
The other: join together, pair forever.

Yet turtle, alone: two shells, slow. Speaks not at all.
   Yet speaks, alone: in time's flow. At God's call.
And dove, together: white song, coo. Sings long, sings new.
   Yet silent, when alone: lonely view. Sorrow's strong, full of rue.

So, the soul, in love's expression, God's discretion.
Silent, pain. Flowing, rain.
Turtle crawls and slowly speaks: stammer, stutter
Dove flies high and spirit seeks: clamor, flutter.

Turtle shells are two, in one
Dove's love union, same.
One and many, rays of sun
Love's expression, name.

Name? Aphrodite, Urania love!
Fame? Soul united, turtle-dove!

PEGASUS

Pegasus, winged horse, mighty mare of Muses!
Pegasus, fearful force, in you flesh-spirit fuses.

Medusa's blood, the witch defeated, flows in you
Poseidon's sod, earthquake trod, horse fleshes you

Yet wings have you, the mark
Soul's flight have you, the spark.
Blood and earth, transformed
Creation's task, performed.

A flight, of ages
A soar, of sages
The spirit's task in stages
A poet's passion rages

Pegasus, spirit's steed
Muses' heart, spirit's need
Pegasus, spirit's seed
Flesh made word, spirit's deed!

FOURTH CENTER

Situation: Heart
Form: Star of David, Seal of Solomon
Color: Orange
Gland: Thymus
Plexus: None
Animal: Lion (Jacob), Gazelle (Ruth), Cow (Demeter).
Element: Air
Function: Feeling (Extraverted-Demeter and Ruth; Introverted-Jacob)
Psychophysical quality: Movement
Organ of Sense: Touch, feel
Organ of action: Penis
Consciousness:

> *Jacob.* Struggling with God, serving God with passion and sense of chosenness, becoming Israel. Personal in relation to the transpersonal. Consciousness is intense, and the vision is fierce and commanding. The impersonal becomes personal, individual.

Love:

> *Demeter*, or another form of *Aphrodite Urania*, maternal, but outflowing to men in the world, personal. Is also *Ruth*, love as devoted, accepting. Love is expressed in *relationship* and not as a universal and primarily transpersonal love as in the type of Mary. Love is in time and place. Like the God of the Hebrews, the divine is realized in history, in time, in the human condition on earth. Feeling is intense and focused on values, the worth of man in the sight of God.

Characteristic:

> Upper Duality.
> Relationship is central: Man to god and men with each other.

JACOB

Jacob, Jacob, wrestler with God
As brother and heir, I call you!
Wounded, strong, thigh-marked, proud
Like Zeus himself, I see you!

"No foreign Gods will I know!
Nor kneel before stone pagan Baal!
To only the Lord do I bow,
For each of the others, gall!"

Jacob, Jacob, with angel blessedness,
Chosen son of the Lord!
Is not Elohim a Maniness?
Is Esau just part of the horde?

God speaks to men in many tongues
Not alone in Hebrew, nor only to the Jew.
In Sanskrit, Greek, his voice is sung
He chooses mankind, too.

" 'Tis true, my heir, 'tis true.

"Struggler with God is server of God
Whether chosen or not, you're His son.
The many-faced Lord gives men but one nod
The many names are but One.

"Unspoken, unknown, He chooses us all
No escape from His eye or His heart
Whether chosen or choosing, Mankind must stand tall
For God's love is the way and the art.

"With wrestle or wrath, we flow to the Lord
To men we pour out our passion,
Flame's feeling like leaves, chest's castle our sword
Heart's justice for all is our Reason."

Jacob, Jacob, your chest on my own
Our hearts, in unison, chosen
Our thigh-wounds, too, from angel-tear sewn
Our strength in our feeling, risen.

DEMETER, RUTH, APHRODITE
SISTERS OF THE HEART

Demeter, Sorrowing Mother: Keep faith
Ruth, Devoted Sister: Hold fast
Aphrodite, Passioned Lover: Flow out

All names are but one name: All loves are but one
Caring, loyal, passioned: Mother, Maiden, Mistress
Goddess One or Goddess Three: Flowing Love of the heart

Will You speak, Goddess, Dweller in the Heart?

"I will speak. I will speak"

Speak soft, words of love, speak low
The murmuring heart sounds a gentle beat
The passionate flame not a blaze
The fire of love sheds a delicate glow
The rhythm not measured in days.

The love of the heart is a loyal devotion
Commitment and caring its names
The love of the heart rises deep from the ocean
Connection and warmth are its aims.

Gentle leaves, warm delicate pulse
Are not heart's only mark
Love's personal, passionate, profound
The love of the heart is no lark.
Gentle and glowing: power and passionate
Goddess: Personal

Relationship

LION

King proud
Roaring loud
Chest-breath chosen,
Passionate.
Bellows air flows in
Heart's word flows out
Who can dare ration it?

The Lord, of course, the lion's master

Chooses and forms, commanding
Lion power, tamed by God
Jacob power, lamed by God
To serve and be served, demanding
Lion love, love of Lord
For this does heart beat faster

GAZELLE

Gentle gazelle
Airy antelope
Delicate deer

Your name is Ruth, graceful
Your name is Ruth, admirable
Your name is Ruth, devotional

Ruth love: loyal to tell
Ruth love: royal gazelle

COW

Carful cow, caring
Chewing cud, reflecting
Nurturing cud, nestling

Demeter, searchingly serving
Demeter, devotedly living
Demeter, generously giving

Demeter love: mother milk
Cow-eyed One: soft as silk

MID-POINT

Situation: Between heart and solar plexus
Form: Tree with Man
Color: Yellow
Gland: None
Plexus: None
Animal: Not animal, but plant, the tree.
Element: None
Function: Meditation (intuition and sensation)
Psychophysical quality: None
Organ of Sense: None
Organ of action: None
Consciousness:

> Meditative. A place of *Buddha*, under the Bo Tree. Man in his full humanness and connection with nature. An ego center in relation to Self. Detachment from possession by "demons" (lower centers) and "inflation" (upper center). Man and woman exist humanly between spirit (centers above) and matter (centers below). Consciousness is "awareness"; there is sensitivity and involvement in life, but separation also. Enlightenment. No-mind.

Love:

> Self-love is the seed of the tree of all-embracing love. The greater Self is the expression of the oneness of all things. Buddha is the realization of four kinds of love-compassion (as below), and is at work all the time.

> *Meta:* All embracing love; oneness of life (people, animals, plants)

> *Karuna:* Compassion, pity, pain in another's pain.

> *Mudita:* Sympathetic joy, pleasure in another's pleasure, friendliness.

> *Upeksha:* Impartiality, objective state, understanding of the fact that everything in its origin is conditional.

Characteristic:

> Lower Dynamic Unity

Enlightenment through meditation; detachment, stillness.

BUDDHA

Meditating man
Silent, empty, nature, whole
Fishing with no pole

Compassionate man
Smiling, sharing, showing, stand
Feeling with no hand

. . .

Meta-love oneness
Life teeming, embracing can
Buddha tree, fly, man

Karuna-love care
Compassion, pity, suffer
Buddha man Mother

. . .

Detaching woman
Separate, stable, seeing flaw
Caring with no claw

Enlightened woman
Lamplight, lovelight, lifelight, laugh
Wholing with no half

. . .

Upeksha-love know
To see, detach, enlighten
Buddha egg, hatch hen

Mudita-love joy
Laughter is enlightenment
Buddha friendly lent

TREE

Reflect, please, on trees
A tree is an animal
Which moves not at all

THIRD CENTER

Situation: Diaphragm
Form: Triangle with dot
Color: Red
Gland: Adrenal
Plexus: Solar
Animal: Goat (Dionysos), Cock (Persephone)
Element: Fire
Function: Emotion
Psychophysical quality: Expansion, heat
Organ of Sense: Sight and color
Organ of action: Anus
Consciousness:

Knowing sacrifices itself to Being. Emotion is more important than knowing; Being is more important than becoming. A "now" of movement. *Dionysos*: the center where union becomes disunion, where that which is old dies, where heat of passion transforms desire from below; leading up to the no-mind center above it. Consciousness is awareness through emotion: *Dionysos*. But there is also the experience of conflict, strife, power. Consciousness is awareness through conflict of opposites: *Ares*.

Love:

Love is of the many experiences, many emotions. Love is ecstatic, abandonment. *Persephone*.

Characteristic:

Lower Duality
Transformation through movement, e-motion.
Power.

ARES

Ares, Lord of Strife
Speak to me, inform me!

"Life is conflict, battle
Fight with me, wage war
Know the struggle's core.

"Swarm in rage, serve God
Contain the heat, grow strong
Power's use, our song.

"A man fights well who serves a cause
Battle's cry is tempered
The soul's a field of war which gnaws
With conflict's pain it's embered.

"A man's transformed by Ares strife
Aggression's sting is softened
Who holds the struggle, reveres the life
For God, his soul is strengthened.

"Serve the Lord, take Strife
Accept the conflict of soul
How else can a man serve God in his life?
How else bring the parts to a whole?"

DIONYSOS

Dionysos, Lord of Passion,
Speak to me, inform me!

"Life is emotion, passion
Come with me, be wild
Know abandon's child.

"Drink sea-wine, taste God
Shed the forms, grow free
Passion's pull, our plea.

"A man's alive who feels intense
Dry meaning's words are whetted
The soul's a sea of passion which rends
All change in emotion embedded.

"A man's transformed in passion's season

Dionysos wine dismembers
Who suffers a madness regains his reason
When for God, his soul remembers

"Serve the Lord, take emotion
Accept the passion of soul
How else can a man find change, transformation?
How else sense that God is a whole?"

PERSEPHONE

Persephone, Ecstatic One, Inward One!
Come out of Hades, come out of the depths!
Rejoin us in the world of your Mother, Demeter.
Rejoin us in the place where words can be heard,
And tell us of the Love in a central place,
Tell us of the Dionysiac place of ecstasy.
Tell us of the realm between Hell and Heaven, between Hades
    and Heart.
Tell us!

"You tell me.
Sing to me your hymn.
Sing and I shall reply."

Persephone, Goddess, we have known the love ecstatic.
We have felt the orgastic explosions of passion, kept up and nourished.

We have known the daylong love, the nightlong love.
We have known the pocket-kept desires, passions both held and let go.
We have known control and abandon, surrender and battle,
    until at last
We have thrown ourselves into Your hands.

"Not my hands, man, but those of Lord Dionysos, Lord Hades,
    Lord Poseidon.
Not my hands, man.
Mine is a dark deep ecstasy of innerness, and aloneness.
Mine is raped by another.

"Mine is an aloneness of a flower, a purple.
Mine is an ecstasy out of mind, out of heart, out of all but self.
Mine is not a Hera solitude, turning away in pain.
Mine is a Persephone solitude, turning away in pleasure, intensity.

"The soul adores itself, devours itself.

The soul takes in itself alone.

"And then, and then. . . .
Should two souls thus devour themselves, be alone, in solitude,
Then can they meet in that bridge of flow, of passion, ecstasy shared."

Thus, Goddess, you are she who can live in Hades, in Belly,
and in Heart.

Thus, Goddess, you are she who can bridge the realms!

"Most at home alone, man, most at home alone.
At the place where passion dwells.
Passion, ecstasis, Alone."

A mystery, the mystery of self, out of self.

COCK

Strutting cock, bird of power world
Why so proud, a fowl who cannot fly?
You do not fly, but die each night and go to Underworld
Each day you're born and crow the dawn when morning sun you spy.

You call and claim that death's not true
That there's a resurrection
Persephone bird, proud day for you
Rebirth, the Two's connection.

GOAT

Goat-God, wild, you stubborn power!
Who can stay you, not just cower?
And why should goat be goaty power?
Stubborn, strong, semen sour?

Does not the goat bleat?
Is not his flesh meat?
Does he not suffer heat?
Are hooves not also feet?
Dionysos God, this animal
Scape-goat, victim, killable
Sacrifice, torn apart, dissolved anew in carnival
Sacred vice, shorn at start, and born anew, not stillable.

Goat, goaty, fine
Powered, weak, sublime
The Now, in passing time
God's goat is in His sign.

SECOND CENTER

Situation: Belly
Form: Crescent
Color: Green
Gland: Lyden
Plexus: Hypogastric
Animal: Horse, Bull, Fish (Poseidon) Sparrow, Ram, Hare (Aphrodite Pandemos)
Element: Water
Function: Sensation (introverted and extraverted)
Psychophysical quality: Contraction
Organ of Sense: Taste
Organ of action: Hand
Consciousness:

Desire and its opposite, negation of desire; hunger to take in, consume. To know is to devour. Experience of difference between self and others. *Poseidon* with the trident: the thunder of desire moving in sea (unconscious), on land (in consciousness), brings activity and change into life. Consciousness is awareness of lack, of want.

Love:

Love in space, in the flesh. Sex as transformer of energies experienced in sensations. Sensation is central. Is love as *Hestia*: the hearth and nest needs. Is love as *Baubo*: the belly moving, dancing and laughing in its own sensations and hunger. Is love as *Aphrodite Pandemos*: love in the world, love concrete, sex in all its forms as desire and union in the flesh.

Characteristic:

Lower Trinity
Hunger: search for inclusion, extension, expansion
Need and Desire.

HESTIA, BAUBO, APHRODITE

Hestia! hearth!
Warm nest, cosy fire.
Baubo! belly!
Hungry maw, hot desire.

What powers through your blood!
What claims!
What channels in your flood?
What tames?

Nor are two of you enough,
It seems.
Aphrodite speaks, love rough,
In dreams.

In Belly place, Pandemos
The human race, you claim us.
What trinity! what power!
What energy! Life's tower!

Nest and hunger, sensuality.
Are these your love? Reality?
Hard to perceive, without grief.
Hard to conceive, compel belief.

For your passions overwhelm me, possess me.
Your drives overcome me, transgress me.
All limits—foreign to your eyes.
Restraint—illusion in the skies.

Can love a belly labyrinth be?
Can want, desire, be the key?
Buddha thought so, Jesus, too.
The one overcame, the other, too.

But you are females, Goddesses!
No male corset ties, no bodices! . . .
Save when you wish . . .
Save when you wish.

You bow to no male
To man or God, not for sale.
Save when you wish . . .
Save when you wish.

For Desire's your name

And it will have claim
From Goddess and man
From woman and Pan.

Together we'll worship
In cave's labyrinth, adore.
Our vessel, a hearth ship
Our course, toward the "more."

Inclusion, our aim
Sensation, our game
Life in the flesh, replete
Love in the world, concrete.

Hestia! dancing!
Baubo! prancing . . .
'Dite! romancing.
Man! enhancing.

POSEIDON

Mighty Poseidon, fierce God, thunderer!
Horse-maker, water king, plunderer!
You move our selves to hunger and to know.
Your trident stings and life begins to flow.

Awareness?
Desire!
Activity?
Aspire!

To love is to consume
To rest is but a tomb
To know is to devour
Each instant like an hour.

Take in, take in,
Unite!
Extend, advance,
More light!

But Pegasus, you fly
Restless quest soars high.
Poet-horse stamps fountain
Seas depths produce the mountain.

So, God, you give and take

Desire and negate
Life's flow is yours to start
You appear and then depart.

Your realm is land-sea stronghold
Your mystery is threefold
With brothers Zeus and Hades
With Goddesses, three ladies.

They are three, and you are three
Restless, moving, changing
Swimming deep, shaking free
Our stable earth endngering.

Wise men fight and then submit
Knowing belly madness
Hero's quest is roasting spit
Labyrinth's realm a sadness

But I can know, fell your staff
Sense the pull of power
There is joy in Nature's laugh
Even Buddha held the flower.

Sense, want, hunger, know
All these convey your meaning
Trident's sting is made to glow
When there are mixed with feeling.

Bellied heart? How?
Heartened belly!
Wanting light? Now!
Lighting want, not sully.

Desert's darkness opens clear
To green oasis, standing near
Water-desire, Poseidon-wet
Trident-love, Poseidon-net

You, God, will have your way
Who, my Lord, will say you nay?
With Goddesses-three and grace and bloom
Three and One, magnificent plume!

Mighty Poseidon, fierce God, thunderer,
Horse-maker, water King, plunderer
You move our selves to hunger and to know
Your trident stings and life begins to flow.

SPARROW, RAM, AND HARE
OF APHRODITE PANDEMOS

Sensual sparrow, rutting ram, hare in heat!
Lascivious creatures of Aphrodite!
    Sparrow shrieking
    Ram reeking
    Hare hunting

Do you covet and lust?
Or can you love and take care?
Is instinct just a force and a must?
Or can instinct show love and be fair?
    All yearning, squabbling, taking
    All burning, gabbling, mating.
Does Goddess speak Pandemos?
Is yours the love that claims us?

Such is love and lust for union
Such is love in belly life
Such is love in deep commonion
Even love for man and wife!

Without the belly love there are no children
Without the belly love there is no growth
Sparrow songs to nature hearken
Goddess speaks to us in both

Is ram not father of the lamb?
And sparrow sister to the dove?
The hare's no hurt to beast or man
All three belong to Goddess Love!

HORSE, BULL, FISH
ANIMALS OF POSEIDON

Poseidon's horse is earthquake formed
He stamped and horse resulted
The God's demand, the earth transformed
His want, in life exulted

Is bull no less than sacred horse?
Is he not cornucopia?

Taurus sign is vital force
Taurine time, Utopia.

And fish, the dolphin, West's "makara"
Swims the depths and knows
Of life's creation, strife, "samsara"
Laughs at pretense, pose

All three, the fish, the bull, the horse
Are tynes in sacred fork
Poseidon rides his three-fold course
His trident tries all talk

Until the horse has Pegasus wings
Until the bull is transformed
Until the fish in dolphin-speech sings
Until nature in words is informed

But trident's dynamic, man's life and his being
Depend on their animals three
The flow of there presence in body and feeling
Is to sense vital joy and be free!

FIRST CENTER

Situation: Anus (Between anus and genitals)
Form: Square
Color: Brown
Gland: Gonads
Plexus: Perineum
Animal: Dog and Cat
Element: Earth
Function: Sensation as Reality (seen and not-seen)
Psychophysical quality: Cohesion
Organ of Sense: Smell
Organ of action: Feet
Consciousness:

Kronos: Consciousness is concrete, everyday life, the structure of society, family, etc. as "given." Limitation of space and time. Awareness of matter, limits. Reality as the concrete.

Hades: At a deeper level is Hades, the Magician; Lord of transformation; changing, and shaping itself ever anew in images in the spiritual sense, but with concrete effect. Reality as evanescent.

Love:

Rhea: Daughter of Earth and Sky, wife of Kronos, she is the Great Mother. Her love is of the "given," in family, society, structure. She is mother of all changes and futures (of the Gods), though content with what "is."

Hecate: At a deeper level is Hecate, the Witch, Mistress of Magic. Her effect is indirect, she is mover of occult forces. As such, there are dark changes, there is a material web of relationships and love, but it is "below," is not apparent like Aphrodite's web, it is unseen. Love of Magic, of effecting changes in matter indirectly; and Magic of Love, of coming together in occult, non-rational ways.

Characteristic:

Lower Quaternity
Concretization; Transformation, Indirect Effect

KRONOS

Kronos, God of Structure, Lord of Time!
Kronos, God of "Givens," most sublime
You who scythed the heaven, bled the sky
You who make the leaven, tell me why!

Speak to me of limits, tell of stricture
Speak to me of matter, show a picture.
Are you narrow, cruel, or calm?
Are you small, or nature's balm?

"Form is given, that you know
Hard to transcend, hard to let go.
It is not only I who worship forms,
Man builds square houses, fearing storms.

"Did I not cut oppression? 'Make' love?
Am I for possession, freedom shove?
Paradise is my aim and was my father's claim.
Hold what is, say I, until the stars draw nigh.

"My son and I, we make a pair
In Isles of Blest, we find our lair.
Possibility is endless, reality contains
Ambition's soar is boundless, modesty restrains.

"You need us both to live, you know
None succeed so let us go.
Reality's a God, do accept it
Touch the sod, don't reject it.

"Draw it over like a blanket, feel no rupture
Taste the peace of order, sense the structure
There's your picture, most sublime
Reality's a blanket, not a crime!"

Kronos, God of Structure, Lord of Time
Kronos, God of "givens," most sublime
Tell me how, in your dominion
Structure's clamp is not a pinion?

"Narrowness is in mind's eye found
When it feels frustration
Peace of limits, freely bound
Brings cruel pain's cessation.

Let limits be lived, yea, limits be loved!
For 'possibilities' fulfillment.
The hand of potential in Reality is gloved
The union of both in the moment!"

HADES

Hades, Hades, Magician!
Lord of Transformation!
Speak to me.

"Change, change, change, no words
Image, moving matter
Change in Hades realm, dark birds
Then fly, they make no clatter.

"Ionic dot, atomic spot
Movement, transformation
Historic rot, artistic plot
All change, imagination

"All that is, is all that was
Motion, myth, mutation
Sacred thought is fertile fuzz
New gods, the soul's elation

"What is time but earth's rotation?
What is space but measure?
Permanence is permutation
Numbers form a treasure.

"Circle to dot, dot to space
Space to square and repeat
This is the story of the human race
This is the magical feat.

"But do not despair of the changes
No fault, no reproach and no blame
Soul's growth through the cosmos ranges
God's means and God's ends are the same.

"Change is true, but do not brood
The bread of life is 'illusion'
Fantasy is psyche food
The blood of life's transfusion.

"So come with me to my true place

And glimpse the magic station
'Transform' say I, at dizzy pace
Rebirth, soul's destination.

"My realm, 'as far beneath the earth', they say,
'As earth beneath the sky.'
Which is to say, another way,
I am, indeed, nearby.

"So play with me, change with me
Follow soul's transformation
And register, see, all the flow greet with glee
Fear no dark consternation.

"Dark sun sheds its light
Hell's moon casts no veil, nor derision
To feel its full might, one must see its full sight
Should one wish to partake of its vision.

"Divination's the key, awareness of me
The clue to magic's reality.
Soul's state not a fee, soul's death not to be
Mind's mold is spirituality."

RHEA

Rhea, Great Mother, Daughter of Earth, Daughter of Sky
Rhea, Wife of Kronos, Mother of Giants, will You draw nigh?
Tell how love is "given" and contains
Tell how love is present and can change.

"Pain I know, to pain respond.
Baby's cry, man's despond.
For birth is my lot, to bear and rebear
Child's loss is love's clot, earth's failure, despair.

"I feel all pains and sorrows
I know all future morrows
Yet knowing and being
Makes no change in feeling

"My husband and I love that which 'is'
Life's flow is mine, square's order is his.
My Kronos and I love all the 'given'
Yet change is my nature, toward change am I driven.

"Through permanence is mine, I am earth and the sea

Evolution and future flow out from me
To be and behold is man's lot in the world
To see and take hold, not falter, be whirled

"Zeus and Kronos, Father and Son
Potential and Actual, struggle's done
Union of change and permanence
Wisdom of sky, earth's residence

"A state, a time, a moment known
Permanent cretion, earth's wind blown
Moment felt, instant tasted,
Paradise on earth, nothing wasted.

"Do you see? Can you rise?
Come with me to Paradise!
Do you feel? can you tell?
Paradise is next to Hell!"

HECATE

Hecate, Hecate, Mistress of the Magic
Hecate, Hecate, Goddess of the Tragic
How much I have suffered you, hated you!
How much I have ruffled you, slayed you!

Though I would not be thwarted by you, ruled by you
I cannot be parted from you, fooled by you
So speak, Great Goddess, speak and tell!
Speak to me the sounds from Hell!

"Sounds words, space flight
Two things joining matter's plight.
Between the poles, magnetic measure
Indirect, effect I treasure.

"Broom and cat, my ornament
Sweep and Eye, my nightly bent
Do I see clearly, darkly?
Do I fight fiercely, smartly?

"Effect I would produce, magic
Reason to seduce, tragic
Hades realm, light and dark
Hecate realm, spite and spark."

Goddess, spider, weaver of webs!

Hecate, Rider, leader
I fear you, I hate you
I love you, create you!

Hecate, spider, weaver of webs!
No shield from you have I
From bare projections, I fair die!

Vulnerable am I, bleeding
Creature am I, needing
Paralysis from you, wrapped
Anger toward you, trapped!

"Man, do not mourn the web of spiders!
Love transcends the dark broom riders!
World-Tree spreads to reach all corners
Its fruit and flowers lift gloom from mourners!

"Two faces have I, malevolent . . . benevolent
World-spider and web, World-tree and love's bent
So smile at the moon, play broom and cat's tune
Sing in the dark, love fierce, know the Ark!"

Mold of Metal
Ark of Gretel
Gold of Goddess
Ink of Blackness
Crown of Creature
Hecate Nature

Times of tears
Rhymes for fears
Aims for effect
Games of direct
Instance of pain
Constance for gain

DOG

Friend of man, his fame
Civilized, loyal, tame
Fenced-in, "heel," must not tarry!
Guard-gate, child-play, fetch and carry

Yes, dog . . .
But, dog . . .

Cerberus hound, baying of hell
Boatman's sound, barking death's knell
Hands fingers in maw, feeling tooth's claw
Dark bite like a saw, scream catching in craw

Light dog . . .
Dark dog . . .
Yet . . . dog

Loving dog, fierce dog, true friend and true foe
His function with man: to be and to know
Together they face the way of the world
Together they brace the dark Underworld.

Dog . . .
D-O-G . . .
G-O-D . . .
God.

Is God not in dog?
Servant and Master, clear bright and blurred fog
Is dog not in God?
Instinct, Taskmaster, unite in the rod

Dog . . .
God . . .
Man.

Together: soul nature, spirit and flesh
Together: dog-man, two beings enmesh
Hecate, Hades, Hell and gnome
Kronos, Rhea, Heaven and home

CAT

All know the feline form,
Independent
Green witch eyes staring
Hearth's cold ice baring

All know cat-o'-nine-norm,
Condescendent
Mouse-kiss, tease-trick, cruel-reeking
Narciss', paw-lick, self-seeking

We know

But do all know the other side?
Introversion
That cats will come when one meditates?
That cats give love in man's darkened state?

But do all know the witch's ride?
Transformation
That night-roam and inner work are soul-food?
That fight-gloom and spinner-irk are toll-mood?

We know.

L'ENVOI

And what, at last do the Gods select?
And what, at last do centers effect?
Why Psyche, of course, in her butterfly state
Yes, Psyche, of course, love's soul and love's mate

It is Psyche and Eros who go through the changes
It is Psyche and Eros who flew through the ranges
Of center to center, straight up and straight down
Of center to center, each glows with a crown

The Lord speaks in Gods and in animals, too
The Lord, most of all, speaks in me and in you
For we are the vessel of God's transformation
Yes, we are the vessel, no group and no nation

The soul and the spirit unite in the flesh
The soul and the spirit delight and enmesh
In man and in woman, alone and together
In man and in woman, God's stone and God's feather

For God is both matter and spirit, at end
For God is both changing and permanent
In centers is He, for soul and for wife
In centers is She, behold Tree of Life

This the end of the work, Him
This the end of the work, Hymn
This the end of the work, Her
This the end of the work, Sir
This the end of the work, It
This the end of the work, Writ